Man Is by Nature a Political Animal

Man Is by Nature a Political Animal

EVOLUTION, BIOLOGY, AND POLITICS

Peter K. Hatemi and Rose McDermott

THE UNIVERSITY OF CHICAGO PRESS · CHICAGO AND LONDON

PETER K. HATEMI is associate professor of political
science, microbiology, and biochemistry at Pennsylvania State
University and a research fellow at the United States Studies
Centre at the University of Sydney. ROSE MCDERMOTT is
professor of political science at Brown University. She is the
author of numerous books, including *Presidential Leadership,
Illness, and Decision Making.*

The University of Chicago Press, Chicago 60637
The University of Chicago Press, Ltd., London
© 2011 by The University of Chicago
All rights reserved. Published 2011.
Printed in the United States of America
20 19 18 17 16 15 14 13 12 11   1 2 3 4 5

ISBN-13: 978-0-226-31909-4   (cloth)
ISBN-13: 978-0-226-31910-0   (paper)
ISBN-10: 0-226-31909-1   (cloth)
ISBN-10: 0-226-31910-5   (paper)

Library of Congress Cataloging-in-Publication Data

Hatemi, Peter K.
    Man is by nature a political animal : evolution, biology,
and politics / Edited by Peter K. Hatemi and Rose
McDermott.
        p. cm.
    Includes bibliographical references and index.
    ISBN-13: 978-0-226-31909-4 (cloth : alk. paper)
    ISBN-10: 0-226-31909-1 (cloth : alk. paper)
    ISBN-13: 978-0-226-31910-0 (pbk. : alk. paper)
    ISBN-10: 0-226-31910-5 (pbk. : alk. paper)
    1. Biopolitics. 2. Political sociology. 3. Evolution (Biology)
and the social sciences. 4. Sociobiology. I. McDermott, Rose,
1962– II. Title.
JA80.H38 2011
306.2—dc22

                                        2010048791

Deep friendship is universal and universally important. For a book devoted to the study of individual variance in the context of human universals, we would like to dedicate our efforts to those very few individuals whose true friendship have blessed us with universal sustenance and comfort, even in the worst of times. We treasure their place in our lives, close to our hearts.

Contents

Foreword   ix
James Druckman

Acknowledgments   xv

Introduction   1
Peter K. Hatemi and Rose McDermott

1   Evolution as a Theory for Political Behavior   13
    Peter K. Hatemi and Rose McDermott

2   Political Primates: What Other Primates Can Tell Us about the
    Evolutionary Roots of Our Own Political Behavior   47
    Darby Proctor and Sarah Brosnan

3   Formal Evolutionary Modeling for Political Scientists   72
    Oleg Smirnov and Tim Johnson

4   Modeling the Cultural and Biological Inheritance of Social and Political
    Behavior in Twins and Nuclear Families   101
    Lindon J. Eaves, Peter K. Hatemi, Andrew C. Heath, and Nicholas G. Martin

5   Gene-Environment Interplay for the Study of Political Behaviors   185
    Jason D. Boardman

6   Genes, Games, and Political Participation   207
    James H. Fowler, Peter J. Loewen, Jaime Settle, and Christopher T. Dawes

7   The Mind-Body Connection: Psychophysiology as an Approach to
    Studying Political Attitudes and Behaviors   224
    Kevin B. Smith and John R. Hibbing

8   Hormones and Politics   247
    Rose McDermott

9   Testosterone and the Biology of Politics: Experimental Evidence from the
    2008 Presidential Election   261
    Coren L. Apicella and David A. Cesarini

10 From SCAN to Neuropolitics   273
    Darren Schreiber

11 Conclusion   300
    Peter K. Hatemi and Rose McDermott

    Index   305

Foreword

James Druckman

There were few aspects of my childhood as predictable as the subject of our dinner conversations. The discussion invariably gravitated to the topic of nature versus nurture, with the point being that all one is springs from his or her environment. As a product of my upbringing, I came to share this belief. Another fundamental lesson from my social psychologist father concerned the importance of rigorous demonstration of evidence that satisfied the highest of scientific standards. For much of my career as a social scientist, these two values rarely, if ever, generated dissonance. But that has changed. The last several years have seen a dramatic rise, across the social sciences, in approaches that ground themselves in the fundamentals of human biology, including physiology and genetics. No social science discipline has been untouched; indeed, one might have imagined that the most resistant would be sociology, yet a 2008 special issue of the *American Journal of Sociology* entitled *Exploring Genetics and Social Structure* suggests otherwise. In some ways, political science has lagged behind. The present volume is an attempt to make up ground and move political science forward in the consideration of these approaches to explain important political phenomena.

The scholars at the forefront of this movement, including all the authors in this book, are careful, thoughtful, and rigorous scientists. It is for this reason that I find myself in a state of conflict: the substance of the argument counters my inclinations but the evidence, while like all research subject to critique, appears beyond reproach when it comes to serious, honest efforts to reveal social and political dynamics. While I am not yet sure where this leaves my thinking (other than uncomfortably conflicted), I am certain that reading this volume would behoove the entire discipline: critics need to assess what the approach offers at this point, supporters will learn of the latest findings and trends, and agnostics will want to know of a movement making its presence felt throughout academia and beyond (e.g., Lynch with Laursen 2009).

When I contemplate the larger research agenda on biology and politics, a number of considerations—some of which I am sure are more thoughtful than others—come to mind. In what follows, I discuss these considerations. These points are not meant as a checklist to be addressed in an individual study or even an entire volume of studies. Rather, they constitute a nonexhaustive and nonexclusive set of parameters with which one can assess the collective research endeavor. The points discussed also could apply to any emergent approach; for example, they map quite nicely onto the concerns that permeate debates about rational choice. My motivation for presenting them here is to provide a rudimentary framework for readers as they make their way through the volume.

My first point involves the basic questions being addressed: are they *politically interesting*? To many, the question of whether biological processes (e.g., genetics) impact political attitudes and behaviors is of tangential interest. It is akin to asking a question about a possible independent variable, and probabilistically, if one searches long enough, he or she will find significant correlations. A more compelling approach is to identify a topic of interest and develop a theory on why there may be a biological link. While extant work—some of which is discussed in this volume—has done this (e.g., work on the genetics of cooperation), it is critical to clarify the contribution to a general understanding of the phenomenon under study. Is adding a biological component akin to identifying an omitted variable? Is it isolating a more fundamental causal force that is mediated by other, nonbiologically measured variables? Is it reorienting the entire theory by replacing existing explanations? In short, there must be a substantive rationale to stimulate scholars interested in the political variable under study (e.g., cooperation, an attitude) to care about biology. If that involves more than adding another variable to the explanation (without altering what we already know), even better.

Second, virtually all scholars working on biology and politics recognize that interactive relationships between biology and the environment ultimately determine behavior. Exactly how this works lies at the heart of the research program. As prominent sociologist Jeremy Freese (2008, S28–S29) explains, "The years ahead will yield increased understanding of the biological mechanisms of genomic causation, and sociology needs to complement this by articulating the social mechanisms that cause genetic differences to be more or less relevant." Political scientists have begun to do this (e.g., McDermott et al. 2009), but what is incumbent on political scientists is to isolate not the social mechanisms but rather the *political levers*. Political context unifies the discipline, and incorporating unique political situations—which often involve the distribution of scarce resources—is critical. For example, social scientists have built the field of *social* neuroscience; what political scientists must do is construct *political* neuroscience.

Third, this volume brings together a host of perspectives including evolutionary biology/psychology, genetics, physiology, and neuroscience. The authors surely understand the relationships between these approaches. It is essential, however, that they clearly communicate how the different biological approaches relate to one another—how do the perspectives cohere with one another in terms of implications and assumptions? Does taking an evolutionary approach necessarily imply genetically driven individual differences? Does using physiological measures entail making assumptions about heredity? It is exactly for this reason—the need to compare and contrast distinct, but related, perspectives—that edited volumes (such as this one) that include multiple views are so essential.

Fourth, I have observed a commonplace phenomenon where individuals in their everyday lives assume that any *unexplained variance implies a biological (genetic) link*. For example, many believe one is born a genius or sports star, yet research suggests both result from fortuitous circumstances and, most important, deliberate practice (e.g., Feltovich, Prietula, and Ericsson 2006, Coyle 2009). The existence of wide variance in an attitude or behavior does not mean that the extremes of the distribution stem from innate skills.

The authors in this volume generally do not fall prey to this logical fallacy. I encourage others to follow suit by being extremely clear as to what can and cannot be explained. Environmental forces are not easily observed and thus failure to pinpoint a situational factor does not mean biology (which is unobservable to most) is at work. Just as scholars demand clear documentation of an exact environmental variable, they should also require identification of precise biological processes (and how the environmental and biological interact). This volume offers a number of examples of how this can be achieved.

My fifth point is a sensitive one, concerning consideration of the *policy implications*. Many perceive a connection between biological approaches and conservative ideologies (e.g., since biological approaches often privilege individual actions and responsibility rather than social situations). It turns out that relationship is more complex and domain specific (e.g., conservatives invoke genetic explanations of socioeconomic topics but liberals do so for other issues such as sexual orientation; see Suhay and Jayaratne 2010). Nonetheless, given what I believe are still common stereotypes, scholars should be cognizant of how their work may be invoked.

Another relevant policy matter concerns the explosion of biological-based research and how that work can be used. The 2008 Genetic Information Nondiscrimination Act bars employers and health insurers from discriminating based on genetic information. The politics behind these and other policies are worth study themselves. While this may lie outside the purview of those employing biology to explain political behaviors, it is can be seen as part of the larger agenda.

Finally, as several chapters in the volume make clear, biological approaches introduce a host of methods unfamiliar to most political scientists. It is incumbent on those applying the methods *to make them as transparent as possible and to also follow debates in related fields*. Political scientists have long been importers of new methodologies, and it is clear that one must do more than pick and choose, but rather become fully conversant in the literatures of other fields. Failure to do so can significantly impair progress (see, e.g., Druckman, Kuklinski, and Sigelman 2009). Several chapters in the volume do exemplary jobs at describing the latest approaches in a way that is accessible to those of us who lack any background. There is no doubt that many of the contributors to this volume are thoroughly trained in the methods they employ. Moreover, political scientists have already engaged in serious debate about some of these methodologies (e.g., the equal environment assumption underlying inferences taken from twin studies; see, e.g., Beckwith and Morris 2008, Alford, Funk, and Hibbing 2008, Suhay and Kalmoe 2009).

Having read this volume, I can confidently say that these issues are being considered and addressed by those working on biology and politics. While the volume has not entirely eliminated my aforementioned dissonance about biological approaches and rigorous social science, it has very much shaped my thinking and left me excited about future research and debates.

References

Alford, J. R., C. L. Funk, and J. R. Hibbing. 2008. Twin studies, molecular genetics, politics, and tolerance: A response to Beckwith and Morris. *Perspectives on Politics* 6:793–97.

Beckwith, J., and C. A. Morris. 2008. Twin studies of political behavior: Untenable assumptions? *Perspectives on Politics* 6:785–91.

Coyle, D. 2009. *The talent code.* New York: Random House

Druckman, J. N., J. H. Kuklinski, and L. Sigelman. 2009. The unmet potential of interdisciplinary research: Political psychological approaches to voting and public opinion. *Political Behavior* 31:485–510.

Feltovich, P. J., M. J. Prietula, and K. A. Ericsson. 2006. Studies of expertise from psychological perspectives. In *Cambridge handbook of expertise and expert performance*, ed. K. A. Ericsson, N. Charness, P. J. Feltovich, and R. R. Hoffman, 39–68. Cambridge: Cambridge University Press.

Freese, J. 2008. Genetics and the social science explanation of individual outcomes. *American Journal of Sociology* 114 (Suppl.): S1–S35.

Lynch, Z., with B. Laursen. 2009. *The neuro revolution: How brain science is changing our world.* New York: St. Martin's Press.

McDermott, R., D. Tingley, J. Cowden, G. Frazzetto, and D. D. P. Johnson. 2009. Monoamine oxidase A gene (MOA) predicts behavioral aggression following provocation. *Proceedings of the National Academy of Sciences* 106:2118–23.

Suhay, E., and T. E. Jayaratne. 2010. Does biology justify ideology? Political ideology and the "nature v. nurture" debate. Unpublished paper, Lafayette College, Easton, Pa.

Suhay, E., and N. P. Kalmoe. 2009. Violations of the equal environment assumptions in twin studies of political traits. Unpublished paper, Lafayette College.

Acknowledgments

We would like to thank Michael Gazzaniga at the Sage Center for the Study of the Mind at the University of California–Santa Barbara for hosting the conference in February 2009 which served as the foundation for this book project. We are very grateful for his support. We also thank those additional participants whose contributions greatly enriched the conference, and whose ideas infuse this volume, especially Leda Cosmides, John Tooby, Sarah Medland, Allan Stam, and Anthony Lopez. In addition, we would like to thank David Pervin at the University of Chicago Press for his tireless and insightful efforts in support of this volume. And we are grateful to Therese Boyd for her careful copyediting of the entire manuscript. All errors remain our own.

INTRODUCTION

Peter K. Hatemi and Rose McDermott

Why do people do what they do? Why do they want what they want? How do they know what they want, and how do they go about trying to get it? These are questions we—those who examine human behavior—all attempt to answer in some form or another. The traditional approach in political science has been to explore the "environmental" dimensions, whether by social learning or happenstance, to determine where political preferences come from and why we want what we want and do what we do. In this view, preferences are based on socialization or personal experiences. However, what we typically measure as "preferences" only reflect the end result or outcome; they show the expressed attitude or preference and do not explain the origin of the preference or the process by which these preferences are developed, interpreted, maintained, and expressed.

As scientific advances have progressed at an increasingly rapid pace over the last half century, the ability to drill deeper into the processes involved in human decisionmaking and preference formation has become more available. Over the last three decades, we have witnessed the emergence of neurological, biological, endocrinological, and physiological paradigms for the study of human behavioral differences. Psychological and characterological differences that were once construed in purely social terms are no longer understood without reference to the role of what it is to be human and how extraordinarily biologically and genetically diverse we are. In this volume, we present evidence from powerful new techniques with which to explore political behavior; in so doing, we show that political behaviors are no different than other human behaviors, subject to the interaction of biology and environment. Politics and political decisionmaking include the way that people process information and make choices about all kinds of important aspects of their lives, even when those dynamics do not appear "political" in the classic meaning regarding governance. Politics occurs when siblings expect parents to arbitrate fights and when lovers argue. Politics encompass much of what people think of as "gossip" when they talk about who did what to whom and why. And politics are certainly brought to bear when we think about the performance of any coalitional groups, including sports teams, police and fire departments, fraternity houses, and terrorist cells. Yet research in political behavior incorporates as much biology, physiology, or neurology as it does political science. We accept that this position represents a radical departure from traditional models of political science, which have been, until quite recently, agnostic if not antagonistic about the biological organism that supports our social and political lives.

Thus, the goal of this volume is to offer an introduction to scientific advances in the study of the human behavior that may influence political preferences. In doing so, we offer a theoretical, methodological, and empirical guide for scholars interested in learning how to incorporate biological approaches into their own future investigations of political and social attitudes, preferences, and behavior. We provide an overview of some of the fundamental theoretical and methodological aspects of biology, endocrinology, evolution, genetics, neurology, and physiology and describe their utility to the discipline of political science in a series of independent but interrelated empirical studies. This approach can be invoked to study many enduring problems of pervasive concern to political scientists. Such issues include topics such as prejudice and discrimination, and how such attitudes toward out-groups might also manifest in public policy choices on issues such as immigration and segregation. Research related to conflict, cooperation, bargaining, and negotiation might also be approached from this perspective, examining dispositional differences in orientations to risk, among other forces. These provide just a few examples of the kinds of topics authors in this volume explore using this particular theoretical and methodological lens. Our purpose is both to encourage scholars to undertake such work themselves and to provide clear directions for how interested practitioners new to the field might go about doing and evaluating this kind of work. Toward this goal, certain chapters contain detailed methodological steps that interested scholars can follow to explore traits of their own interests.

By focusing on particular substantive topics related to political attitudes and behavior, we aim to provide a clear and unbiased overview of the nature of this emerging area of research. We believe that a broader integration of "biological" work into political science will encourage greater interdisciplinary discourse and a deeper understanding of the behaviors we seek to explicate, and will help open new doors for political scientists who may wish to embark on collaboration with those in other areas whose substantive interests overlap and coalesce with our own. In this way, we hope to further encourage the growing movement within the discipline, already widely prevalent across other disciplines, which emphasizes the critical contribution of biological factors toward explaining individual differences in political and social behaviors.

Traditional work in political science has focused on environmental, institutional, and structural features to account for human political behavior and has proved critical for understanding the myriad ways in which environmental cues and triggers help shape and guide human political behavior. Promoting the use of biology, neurology, or physiology in no way diminishes the importance of any past or future contributions of environmental-only models. Yet, however extensive and nuanced our understanding may be of environmental influences, we argue that it is important to combine a subtle understanding of biological factors, in interaction with environmental forces, in order to provide a comprehensive understanding of political behavior. Importantly, the more we know about biology, the more informed we become about the sophisticated nature of environmental contingencies and interactions. In this way, increased knowledge can help refine existing models of socialization as well as develop new models regarding the potential influence of biology on political outcomes of interest.

In no way do we reify an outdated juxtaposition between nature and nurture; that horse has been beaten dead long ago. Rather, we support the dominant interpretation across sciences which assumes the inextricable interaction between biology and environment in determining the growth and development of any living organism within a particular ecological context. The atavistic dichotomy between nature and nurture only preoccupies social scientists who retain a philosophical interest in the point; any credible scientist employing standard approaches appreciates that any such posited dualism remains absurd on its face. Complex biological predispositions only know when and how to emerge based on particular environmental cues, and environmental triggers can only manifest through a physical and biological agent of action. Regarding human behavior, there is no either/or between biology and environment; both factors remain codependent and interactive in determining complex social and political behaviors. We acknowledge that the theoretical and methodological differences between those who fundamentally privilege socialized processes and those who stress biological ones remain real and deep. We suggest that this need not be the case, and we support and encourage an active dialogue between those who study processes of socialization and those who investigate more biologically based phenomena in order to achieve a more comprehensive, complementary, and unified appreciation of the complexity of human social and political behavior in its multifaceted and flexible expression.

Past work seeking to examine the biological bases of political action often faltered on a nature–nurture approach, the lack of empirical analyses, limits of data, or the restrictions in the scientific methods available at the time. We are more fortunate in that recent explosions in the technology surrounding the study of the human brain and human genetics in particular have opened new venues for exploration at much deeper levels of analysis than previously possible. While we remain agnostic about the extent to which current work at the intersection of biology and political behavior will stand up to future efforts at replication, we nonetheless assume that the next generation of more sophisticated scholars will surpass what we do here, with more advanced statistics and methodologies. We believe it is likely that it will take many generations to fully uncover the operation and interaction of such variables in the more complex aspects of human behavior, but this is all the more reason why such efforts should begin sooner rather than later. Political scientists can take heart from the vast strides that fields like psychiatric genetics have been able to make in their understanding of the etiology and treatment of serious mental illness in the span of little more than a decade. While a long journey remains on the road to cures, enormous progress has been accomplished in understanding the processes of human behavior. And just because the trip is long and arduous does not render the destination insurmountable or un-rewarding. Humans would never have reached the moon if everyone believed the task to be impossible from the outset.

In assessing the utility of any novel paradigm, one of the critical points of evaluation surrounds the extent to which biological models provide useful roadmaps to unexplored questions, posing previously unrecognized conundrums, or pointing to areas for potential unrealized gains. In this area, the advantages appear myriad and obvious. Biological approaches can provide scholars with an endogenous source of preferences upon which to build and support rational actor models that currently depend on such notions without a clear ontological foundation for understanding their nature or appearance. Further, biological factors can help elaborate and refine the number and kind of variables used to explore significant social and political phenomena of interest. Endogenous forces can help explicate the nature and manifestations of individual variance, helping illuminate why some people who are socialized the same way behave differently, just as some who are raised in obviously different environmental circumstances can respond the same way to similar challenges. In short, understanding more about the biological basis of behavior also illuminates the nature of environmental effects and helps elucidate which kinds of situations affect which types of individuals in what specific ways. Finally, insights drawn from biological and genetic factors can help aid in informing policy debates, providing mechanisms for potential positive interventions to alleviate suffering.

In addition, techniques drawn from other areas can be assessed according to the degree to which these new methods have proved successful in other fields and allow the exploration of unresolved issues in previously unexamined ways within political science. Employing this standard highlights the important theoretical contributions that models of evolutionary development, combined with methodological techniques from magnetic resonance imaging, physiological monitoring, and behavior genetics can make to a more comprehensive understanding of political preferences and behavior.

Whether looking at hormone levels, cognitive functioning, emotion reactivity, physical reactions, or genome-wide scans, the growing movement across disciplines that includes measures of intrinsic sources of preferences for political behavior has reached a point that necessitates a volume that both introduces biology and makes it accessible to the greater political science community.

It is our belief that this is a critical time for the discipline. Many in our field remain unaware that our discipline's topics have been co-opted to a great extent by other fields of study. Just about every discipline except political science has been exploring the importance of biological markers for *political* phenotypes and making great strides in discovery and scholarship on topics such as ideology and racism, which have traditionally fallen under the purview of political science scholarship. This is no longer the case and we provide a brief summary of some of these studies in the following chapters. Unfortunately, these scholars, having no training in our field, seldom if ever address the field of literature in political science on those very topics.

On the one hand, the attraction seems inevitable and obvious, since politics certainly present much more fascinating questions and problems to explore on average, than, let's say, cell division. On the other hand, political scientists are losing an important collaborative opportunity to help inform and define the next generation of empirical work involving political topics, simply as a consequence of insularity and neglect as much as anything else. We hope to begin to remediate those limitations with this volume.

Of possibly even more concern than our discipline being largely ignored when it comes to the scientific investigation of biological aspects of political behavior is the fact that some of the best work from political scientists is being published outside the discipline as well. Over the last five years, the most profound discoveries regarding the foundations of political behaviors have not been published in political science journals. Rather, they are seen in the pages of the *New England Journal of Medicine* (Fowler and Christakis 2008), *Science* (Oxely et al. 2008; Fowler and Schreiber 2008), *Nature* (Fowler 2005; Fowler, Johnson, and Smirnov 2005; Fowler et al. 2007), the *Proceedings of the National Academies of Science* (McDermott et al. 2009), and *Proceedings of the Royal Society of London B (Biological Science)* (Johnson et al. 2006) among other journals.

While a growing group of scholars explores the use of biological elements, they are still somewhat insulated, and most political science editors and reviewers are still unfamiliar with the methods and scientific advances in these areas that have inspired such works, creating a vacuum of individuals competent to evaluate and review such manuscripts when sent to our political science journals. This is in part due to the separation of the research programs that the biological and social sciences have traditionally used to examine behavior. Such historical institutional barriers can be hard to overcome. With the exception of a handful of scholars, these research projects have remained independent of one another. The integrated interdisciplinary group of scholars at Caltech provides a notable exception worthy of emulation in this regard.

The dual and potentially overlapping research agendas of biology and social science had the potential to contribute to another incarnation of the ongoing philosophical tensions within social science, but so far this has not materialized. By chance, design, or intellect, and to our benefit, political science seems to have sat on the sidelines during the nature/nurture debates that took place from the 1970s to the 1990s. Indeed, in political science most of the epistemological debate occurred between the rational individualistic economic models of behavior and the more socially constructed sociological views of human agency. In one way, this waiting period proved quite useful, as both the theory and methods used in biological explorations have grown more advanced, testable, and accessible in recent years, and our discipline does not carry the same scars of the fights that ripped other disciplines asunder and led to the wholesale bifurcation of some departments and fields, such as those between neuropsychology and psychology or between cultural and biological anthropology. However, in another way, we are now far behind many other disciplines in exploring our own traits and interests.

Common Themes

Several important themes permeate the background of the discussion in the chapters that follow. Before providing an overview of each of the contributions, we briefly discuss these critical issues. We first note the orienting assumption of enduring stability within the framework of heritable transmission and then we challenge the reductionist fallacy that has been leveled against such work. The following section outlines each of the chapters and describes their relationship to one another.

Cause and Transmission

In any investigation into large-scale behavioral phenomena, the question of cause remains central. In exploring the relative contribution of endogenous factors to an understanding of political and social behavior, the burden of proof requires a demonstration that such forces matter in systematic and predictable ways in determining the outcomes we seek to explain. In order to demonstrate such an effect, scholars must first demonstrate that biological factors do in fact exert an effect on the behavior we are interested in explaining and this behavior differs across humans in some systematic and predictable way. In addition, they need to examine whether or not such aspects of behavior emerge idiosyncratically, or whether they derive in some systematic way from heritable components that remain subject to generational transmission across time, just as eye or hair color, height or intelligence appear influenced by such forces.

In the chapters that follow, contributors share an orienting assumption that biological factors may help shape and guide important social and political behaviors. Uncovering the precise ways in which particular genes, hormones, psychological mechanisms, or other biological factors inform and direct such behavior motivates the specific explorations in which each author engages. Again, this work does not deny the critical role played by environmental factors in determining outcome, but rather seeks to more precisely explicate the specific environmental cues that help trigger particular biological responses within certain circumstances and not others. This delicate and subtle interplay requires not only an understanding of the process of socialization to which an individual organism is exposed, but also a precise delineation of the intrinsic factors, including prenatal development factors, all of which may differ across individuals, which are brought to bear in any given situation.

The standard criticism of this perspective characterizes this approach as reductionist in nature. This accusation remains specious because the very nature of any scientific enterprise writ large requires at least some reductionist reasoning at root. It becomes untenable to examine systematic patterns in the larger world without reducing at least some of these central elements into more tractable pieces for analysis. In addition, to the degree that such an exercise appears reductionist to those who prefer to concentrate on larger social and political processes, note that such alternative directions of approach need not remain mutually exclusive or contradictory. Those moving from the "outside in" can eventually meet those moving from the "inside out" somewhere in the middle without either side having to resort to exclusionary dismissal of the other style.

Further, concerns about reductionism limiting the utility of biological approaches fall prey to the typical "is/ought" fallacy. Just because hormones or genes themselves may prove immutable in any given individual, this does not mean that the effects of such factors themselves remain immutable across a population. For example, genetic mutations clearly occur across generations, but not every individual will inherit any given trait or characteristic. But more important, knowledge can affect our ability to reason about and change our reactions in response to such recognitions. Humans remain the only species whose understanding of ourselves allows us to change our own evolutionary trajectory and in so doing exhibit the ability to globally change our environment. Medical interventions alone interfere with outcomes that range from fertility to death every day. To the extent that those who study environmental factors wish to use their knowledge to intervene to improve the course of human nature, they benefit from those whose approach begins from a more basic biological research agenda.

At a more pragmatic level, the methods and data utilized by those who study biology, neurology, genetics, or physiology can in no way be interpreted as reductionist, given the many thousands of people who are employed in any typical study. Such studies certainly remain less reductionist than typical so-called large number quantitative studies that rely on at most a few hundred cases in order to draw their inferences about state behavior over time.

Chapter Outlines

The volume begins with a chapter by Peter Hatemi and Rose McDermott which provides a brief introduction to evolutionary theory, concentrating on its relevant applications to the study of political behavior. This chapter establishes how and why certain behavioral influences are naturally innate and why it is that we should have evolved trait universals as well as individual differences. In addition, this chapter discusses why traditional rational choice and behaviorism only tell part of the story of human political behavior and why there is a need for a more nuanced and encompassing theory of politics built on evolutionary principles.

The second chapter, by Darby Proctor and Sarah Brosnan, uses work on primates, in particular chimpanzees, to both illustrate and inform our understanding of the evolutionary bases of human political behavior. Oleg Smirnov and Tim Johnson then present an evolutionary game theoretic model to explore distinct arenas of human political behavior in chapter 3. Using civic involvement and political corruption as an example, the authors show how an evolutionary approach is just a light twist on theoretical and simulation models already common in many areas of political science, including analyses of Congress or mass political behavior.

Lindon Eaves, Peter Hatemi, Nicholas Martin, and Andrew Heath then discuss the genetic transmission and model the biological and cultural inheritance of political attitudes. This chapter introduces the methods by which parental transmission occurs and specifically addresses kinship designs and applications that illustrate the principal patterns of inheritance for socially significant outcomes. This chapter includes the importance of mate selection for the transmission of social and genetic information and addresses this critical aspect of nonenvironmental transmission. They discuss the fundamental domains on which spouses choose one another.

Jason Boardman extends the models presented in the previous chapter by displaying the importance of gene-environment interaction in population-based studies. In doing so, Boardman makes a strong case for why such approaches will prove most amendable for political science.

James Fowler, Peter Loewen, Jamie Settle, and Christopher Dawes discuss cooperation and political participation as a specific example of how to use genetic applications to explore political behavior. The level of cooperation among humans is quite unique and constitutes one of the most basic of human group functions. This topic thus provides an important arena in which to search for heritable contributions to the stability of this behavior across generations.

Moving from genetics to physiology, Kevin Smith and John Hibbing outline their work on physiological relationships and political behavior. This chapter describes the process by which genes operate through brain development to affect heart rate and other physiological processes, such as eye blinks.

The next two chapters explore the ways in which endocrinology can infuse political behavior. The first chapter, by Rose McDermott, describes how genes help build hormonal dynamics, which in turn influence behavior. This chapter provides a theoretical review of the literature and explains why it is critical to include these factors in discussions of endogenous influences on political outcomes. This overview includes detailed discussion of a number of specific hormones and their putative effects on particular behaviors, which may encompass political consequences, such as aggression. The sequential chapter, by Coren Apicella and David Cesarini, offers an empirical exploration of a particular hormone, testosterone, and details its effects on an important electoral outcome.

Finally, Darren Schreiber provides a description of some of the neurological processes that influence behavior. Genetic processes encode proteins that ultimately inspire neurochemical releases as individuals respond to the stimuli they confront. One method to capture differences in neuroanatomy comes from neuroimaging. This chapter provides an overview of how we go from genes to brains, and how this process can be investigated through the use of functional magnetic resonance imaging (fMRI) technology.

Conclusion

In the following chapters, the authors paint a diverse canvass of what is currently going on in a variety of areas involving the exploration of endogenous factors in political behavior. Specifically, these authors examine evolutionary psychology, behavior genetics, physiology, and brain imaging, all with an eye toward illuminating some of the physical basis for political and social preferences, attitudes, and actions. In so doing, they remain profoundly aware of the essential role played by environmental forces in guiding and structuring such expressions. In addition, they remain suitably humble about the extent to which we can offer any definitive conclusions about the specific nature of genetic-environmental determinants on political behaviors of interest. But they also remain devoted to furthering the investigation so that those who come after us can progress beyond us to achieve more sophisticated understandings of the origins and manifestations of human political choice. In so doing, all the authors join the majority of political scientists in sharing an interest in understanding how individuals come to develop and exhibit the diverse political styles they manifest. In the conclusion of the volume, we provide a broader sense of where we see this work developing and how we hope it might progress in the future.

References

Fowler, J. 2005. Second order free rider problem solved? *Nature* 437. doi:10.1038/nature0420.

Fowler, J., and N. Christakis. 2008. The collective dynamics of smoking in a large social network. *New England Journal of Medicine* 358 (21): 2249–58.

Fowler, J., C. Dawes, R. McElreath, O. Smirnov, and T. Johnson. 2007. Egalitarian motives in humans. *Nature* 446:794–96.

Fowler, J., T. Johnson, and O. Smirnov. 2005. Egalitarian motives may underlie altruistic punishment. *Nature* 433. doi:10.1038/nature03256.

Fowler, J. H., and D. Schreiber. 2008. Biology, politics, and the emerging science of human nature. *Science* 322 (5903): 912–14.

Johnson, D. M., J. Cowden, E. Barrett, R. Wrangham, and S. Rosen. 2006. Male overconfidence and war. *Proceedings of the Royal Society of London B (Biological Science)* 273:2513–20.

McDermott, R., D. Tingley, J. Cowden, G. Frazzetto, and D. Johnson. 2009. Monoamine oxidase A gene (MAOA) predicts behavioral aggression following provocation. *Proceedings of the National Academy of Sciences* 106 (7): 2118–23.

Oxley, D. R., K. B. Smith, J. R. Alford, M. V. Hibbing, J. L. Miller, M. Scalora, P. K. Hatemi, and J. R. Hibbing. 2008. Political attitudes vary with physiological traits. *Science* 321 (5896): 1667–70.

1

EVOLUTION AS A THEORY FOR POLITICAL BEHAVIOR

Peter K. Hatemi and Rose McDermott

Political science covers a broad range of meaningful human behavior from attitudes to warfare. Traditionally, political behavior has long been dominated by two distinct approaches, one that might be called situational, and the other that is more individual in its orientation. However both are considered "environmental" or at least environmentally influenced. The former might include, for example, models of voting behavior based on parental socialization, while later models include rational-choice theories of decisionmaking, which posit that changing a (usually financial) incentive structure should prove sufficient to shift the direction of individual choice. In their most reduced form, behavioral models argue that all behavior results from social conditioning (Campbell et al. 1960), while rational-choice models assume preferences are exogenous, fixed, and given, and remain agnostic, if not unconcerned, about their source (Bueno de Mesquita 1983). In essence, both models represent environmental theories—if the socialization or incentive structures change, then the behavior is supposed to change as a result.[1]

The Limits of Socialization and Rational Choice

Behavioralist and rational-choice theories form the core of political behavior, yet as an explanatory framework for human behavior these theories are widely considered implausible as uniform explanations of human behavior outside of political science (Green and Shapiro 1994; Robson and Kaplan 2003). Numerous challenges from economics, psychology, neuroscience, and other fields have found that not all people are socialized to act the same way; rational-choice models also hold limited explanatory capacity by remaining almost exclusively focused on choices motivated by unrealistically narrow conceptions of self-interest (Dawes and Thaler 1988; Tversky and Thaler 1990; Fehr and Gächter 2000; Gintis 2000; Henrich et al. 2001; Fehr and Fishbacher 2004).

While rational-choice models allow idiosyncratic preferences to drive choice among options, such work fails to interrogate the fundamental basis or cause for such preferences, or why they may differ among individuals. Rather, analyses begin from such preferences and seek to understand the nature of subsequent choice behavior. Yet just as some people may be driven by the incentives such as money or status or power, others appear more focused on sex, food, and travel. These differences may result not only from different levels of biological drives states, but also because not everyone is socialized in the same manner, and not everyone learns to associate rewards from the environment in the same way. We suggest both such domains of difference remain well worthy of further investigation.

The political implications of the origins of such differences appear obvious. For example, conflict and cooperation are often conceptualized as opposition forces rather than two sides of the same whole. Yet the same person can be deeply cooperative, even loving, to an in-group member, while retaining murderous intent toward out-group members. The political motives that undergird such behavior deserve examination, elucidation, and explication.

Evolutionary models provide insight precisely in the theoretical lacunae in which rational choices remain silent and where socialization models fail to account for differences in behavior when socialized the same: on the origin of preferences. The process of natural selection is based upon adaptive traits beginning at a much earlier period in human development, where pure economic power-seeking and self-interest were not the only potential adaptive traits, if such abilities were adaptive at all. Certainly many important human social and political traits, including detecting kin, selecting mates, foraging for food, avoiding predators, and detecting cheaters, evolved in a context prior to modern market conditions.

Few better examples can be found than the central role cooperation and trust play in human evolution. Collaboration is an adaptive trait, particularly for related individuals. Numerous studies show that it takes enormous incentives to motivate one to "sell out" in-group and family members, particularly those with whom a person shares a significant amount of genes (Trivers 1971; Axelrod and Hamilton 1981; Kruger 2003). Trust can prove adaptive in many situations and, though strongest for family members, also allows for cooperation with those to whom we are not related. Gintis et al. (2003) finds humans maintain a predisposition to cooperate with others and punish those who violate the norm of cooperation, even at a personal cost or when there is no expectation that they will recover the cost of punishing.

Yet people must be careful in their judgment concerning who to trust, and keep careful track of those who violate trust in order to maximize opportunities for successful cooperation over time with those who share similar values and goals. With the exception of vampire bats, the ability to track others behaviors and know who and when to trust, and when to punish, is unique to humans and certain primates (Wilkinson 1984). The human capacity to "identify a large number of individuals and to keep score of its relations with them, detecting the dishonest or greedy and taking vengeance, even at some cost to itself" is an evolved one (Gintis et al. 2003).

Certainly, the evolution of our species directly results from our success as a collective, but our universal or individual genetic adaptive traits may likely have little bearing on modern-day individual success within our society. We cannot confuse our species' success with individual success, nor can we confuse our species' source of evolved attitudes with individual ones.

Rational choice appears primarily interested in choices as "revealed preferences" or end results. However preferences are modified and developed during the process of making a decision suggests that decisionmaking may involve a creative rather than a revelatory dynamic. Indeed, from a functional perspective, in many cases it would be maladaptive to have fixed preferences. In addition, rational-choice models cannot account for certain behaviors, such as acts of pure altruism or suicide, and ultimately such an argument can lead to a tautological method in its "thin" form, since any action, even an irrational one, can be explained by hidden "preferences" (Landemore 2004). However, preferences often remain absent, relative, volatile, and based upon nonobservable internal processes. Most important, rational choice ties all outcomes to preferences, but offers no explication for the preceding logical step, "where do preferences come from?"

One potential place to look for explanations of the origins of preferences resides in animal ethology. Brosnan and de Waal (2004) provide a very simple example of the fallibility of absolute gains and rationality in an experiment where they taught monkeys to receive tokens as a reward and then barter them for food. The monkeys learned to be content to swap tokens for cucumber, but if the researchers gave one of the monkeys a grape, a better-tasting food, the other monkeys would act irrationally and refuse to hand over their tokens for cucumber; in some instances, they would exchange their tokens for cucumber but refuse to eat it. The monkeys clearly paid attention to what other monkeys were doing and acted differently when other monkeys received a better reward; thus relative gains proved more important to monkeys than absolute gains. In another demonstration of seemingly irrational decisionmaking, Chen et al. (2006) showed that capuchin monkeys displayed different levels of reference dependence and loss aversion when confronted with risky gambles. Both studies not only illustrate a primate basis for seemingly irrational economic and social behavior, but also point to individual differences in the behavior of nonhuman animals.

In one of the most intriguing experiments, Glimcher and Rustichini (2004) isolated a single neuron to determine its relevance in decisionmaking. They trained a monkey to recognize that by looking a certain direction when prompted to make a decision, the monkey would receive a well-liked juice reward 40 percent of the time, but by looking the opposite direction the monkey would receive the juice 60 percent of the time. Examining the brain activity during this decision process revealed that during the learning period significant brain activity was present, but after the learning period the monkey exhibited no activity in any part of the brain outside of the single neuron in the eye when faced with the decision task. In other words, after the training period, the monkey's optical neuron appeared to encode a defined expected utility and, in turn, the monkey reacted in anticipation of a preferred outcome without ever accessing the brain!

While most evidence finds that primates, including humans, often do not always act in a utility maximizing way, especially because emotional constraints prohibit or supersede decisionmaking capability, Platt and Glimcher's (1999) experiment provides evidence that in certain situations a single neuron can act rationally (unbeknownst to the individual), even if the brain and the larger conscious person does not (also see Glimcher and Rustichini 2004). That is, even when the rules of the game changed (new information), the monkey had already been cued to stay on course in its pre-preprogrammed decision. What possible purpose could this serve? From an energy-saving biological perspective, once a task is learned, ignoring new information could be adaptive because it saves energy. Based on these findings, it could be hypothesized that this conservation of cognitive energy may constitute part of the reason why many people have a difficult time changing their opinions once formed. Staying the course may simply be an energy-saving tactic, so new information need not be processed unless severe pressures requires relearning. So while rationality exists, and behavior can be trained or socialized, it is not the rational-choice or socialization conceptions of behavior that scholars in political science promote, nor is it the kind of choice humans may always be aware of; rather, rationality may emerge prior and subsequent to environmental stimuli. *Thus, rationality exists at a biological, not merely cognitive, level.*

Outside of political science, rational choice is even questioned on the grounds that rational action is self-serving. Gintis (2000) emphasizes that "[i]n neither the everyday nor the narrower economic sense of the term does rationality imply self-interest." Indeed, interest can be defined in myriad ways and what appears logical at the level of the individual may not actually prove beneficial for reproductive success, for example. Those who fight to ensure the security of their families and communities may die, but still improve their relative prospects for passing their genes along into the next generation. *The source of our preferences and the processes of accessing preferences are biologically influenced and dependent in part on biological mechanisms.* In a remarkable way, biology does not challenge rational action; instead, biology can be used to help fill in the lacuna within the "black box" of individual preferences.

Nature and Nurture

The nature–nurture debate does not remain an open question. It has become widely accepted in science that human behavior is not predetermined, nor is it uninfluenced by our biology; outcomes of interest, including preferences and actions, result from a combination and interaction of both environment and biology. In our view and the view of a growing number of scholars, there is no intellectual line in the sand or juxtaposition of biological and environmental approaches as polar opposites. Rather, the environment constitutes a central component of biology; situational cues and triggers elicit, define, and shape the emergence and representation of our underlying genetic structure and physiological makeup. Indeed, reactions to the environment ultimately drive human behavior and variation in these propensities pass through offspring and population shifts. But individuals react differently to the same stimuli, and the source of such variation remains a continually intriguing puzzle which can best be addressed by constructive collaboration across disciplinary boundaries. As E. O. Wilson (2002) stated, "The boundary between the natural sciences on one side and humanities and humanistic social sciences on the other is not an epistemological fault line, but a broad domain of poorly understood material phenomena that invites cooperative exploration from both sides." This book constitutes an empirical attempt to overcome just such a divide by manifesting such an integrated enterprise.

A majority of political science essentially embraces the standard social science model, which posits that humans come into the world as a tabula rasa, possessing only a general-purpose learning instinct, and focuses only on the present environment without reference to the variability of the biological organism under observation (Lopreato and Crippen 1999; Alford and Hibbing 2004). Simply put, our current theories and examinations largely assume that all people are biologically the same when it comes to politics, which is a radical notion considering how remarkably diverse humans are in virtually every other domain.

For example, consider typical models of vote choice. Researchers gather several important social indicators, such as sex, race, age, income, religion, education, ideology, and so forth, observe individual-level voters using a large sample, employ one of the many accepted statistical techniques, examine the significance and coefficients, and make generalizations. These models provide insight into why people at large vote for the candidates they choose. Yet taking a look at the majority of the literature, the R-squares are often fairly low. Thus, while significant predictors are identified, in many cases the models are not predicting very much (Matsusaka and Palda 1999).[2] Specifically, traditional models do not provide explanations as to why, when faced with different stimuli, individuals make the same choices or, when faced with similar stimuli, individuals often choose radically different paths of action, outside the tautological recourse to "preference" being invoked. If a significant portion of individual variation in behavior is explained by nonenvironmental influences, then our current models are limited in their ability to accurately predict political behavior. The only way this would be false is if we believe all humans are the same. Such a position is often taken, though even a passing examination of any given individual bears false witness to such a claim. While all people may share certain similarities, each person remains indelibly unique as well.

Using traditional theories and models, the most critical cause of behavior is left unanswered: that is, where do those preferences come from? It is a question political behavior scholars have not been able to fully answer by invoking only environmental factors. For instance, even though males and females are biologically different, the majority of the social science literature accounts for sex differences as socialized gender differences (Gilligan 1982; Chodorow 1978, 1995). In political science the biological difference is rarely considered (for an exception see Hatemi, Medland, and Eaves 2009; Thayer 2000). Indeed, political-behavior research considers "gender" the same as "sex"! While it may be possible to socially influence one's sexual identity or gender roles, it is certainly impossible to socialize ovaries and childbearing onto a male, or sperm production onto a female. Using biology and the human organism as a potential starting point for universal human similarities as well as individual differences, a biological model can offer an answer for why sex provides variation in addition to "gendered" socialization, and why we find further variation in a given subgroup when all other environmental considerations remain constant.

Taking this argument further, environmental models also do not clearly distinguish between different sources of environmental variation. For instance, numerous studies attempt to determine if voting is primarily based upon familial influence as suggested by Campbell et al. (1960), or more uniquely driven by individual rational action (Downs 1957). Variables are labeled as "familial" (e.g., religion) or "personal" (e.g., occupation), but this is an almost arbitrary categorization. Without considering a third biological layer and controlling for familial heredity and in utero influences, it is not possible to parse out the different sources of variation for each variable and examine their effects on the dependent variables of interest (e.g., Eaves et al. 2008).

At the center of this discussion is the longstanding philosophical question regarding the nature of basic human preferences and motivations. Countless theories of human wants and desires have been offered over the centuries: Aristotle's "virtue," Rousseau's "social contract," Hobbes's *Leviathan*, or Maslow's "hierarchy of needs," to name a few. However, these preference structures continue to provide an almost arbitrary account of human nature. They lack a unifying theory for why these various needs and desires exist, or how they might be connected to one another. Human preference structures can be more profitably approached from a biological and evolutionary perspective that incorporates our past development and immediate ancestry as precursors to explaining our current political preferences.

Evolution as a Model for Human Political Behavior

As long as different theories are seen as in opposition to each other, the goal of integration will be impossible. Such models, while useful in their own environmental or cultural domains, tell only a portion of the "human" story. None directly incorporate the innate part of the equation regarding human biological development: that is, why humans developed as they have, and how their political preferences and social actions may be decisively influenced by their biological needs and drives. Research on human political behavior will be incomplete until it takes into account the evolutionary, neurological, physiological, and genetic foundations of human traits that are universal along with those that vary across groups and individuals. These foundations of individual variance provide some of the most important bases of preference formation, including the propensity to share resources; attitudes, including those toward justice, tolerance, and inequality; perceptions of fairness, which can be influenced by framing; and at the most basic level, why humans form groups and make sharp distinctions between in- and out-groups that manifest themselves in a range of ways, such as political parties, racism, and war. A more complete theory of human decisionmaking and preference structures incorporates *both* the endogenous and environmental sources of behavior.

In this chapter, we introduce the theory of evolution and argue that evolution offers a potential foundation for a unifying theory of political behavior, and, in concert with the methods and models introduced by biology, genetics, epidemiology, and physiology, among other cognitive and behavioral sciences, a means to empirically test hypotheses that address the combination of sociological, evolutionary, and biological influences. We recognize the classic levels of analysis problem imposed by focusing on decisionmaking at an individual level with a theory seemingly based on human universals, with less emphasis on the nature of individual variance. Evolutionary theory may rest on a foundation of human universals for those design features that have proven particularly adaptive for survival of offspring. And this basis becomes transferred across generations, at least in part, by genetic encoding. However, constant mutation, along with equilibrium strategies for complex social behaviors that can privilege a mix of strategies depending upon the *local* environment, ensures that individual variance continues. In this way, human universals structure our understanding of the basic mechanism, but individual differences can accrue and aggregate into population differences across regions and cultures and help explain human political differences.

To be clear, evolutionary models offer insight into the nature and development of human universals; however, the carriers of such universals across generations lies in genetic and biological structures that do vary across individuals, at least at the margins, due to mutual and other factors. These differences can be examined and explored using methods and models from the realm of behavior genetics, thus affording a comprehensive glimpse in the nature of individual difference within the context of universal structures. To provide a simple analogy, most people may live in structures that have walls and windows and a roof; such foundations provide the basis of housing. However, the inside decorations in any one unit may differ drastically, revealing personal reflections of an individual's taste and values; such accoutrements reflect the nature of individual difference. Similarly, we all live in a human body, but the inside social and psychological fabrications may differ drastically across individuals. Therefore, it becomes possible to examine the ways in which various models and methods, all drawn from a biological foundation, can be employed to explore the interaction between individual variance, human universals, and populations across various levels of analysis.

Using this approach, we can examine the ways in which individual differences in political disposition represent an instantiation of universal strategies evolved to respond effectively to the threats and opportunities commensurate with group living. Thus, an evolutionary approach argues that our brains are organized in certain ways, and indeed humans tend to think in particular patterns, but tremendous individual variance remains within those broader patterns. We seek to investigate the nature of this variation within this particular evolutionary context.

Through this exploration, we seek to combine the parsimony of evolutionary models for explaining the emergence of human universals with the powerful methods of the cognitive and behavioral sciences that help explain the emergence, purpose, and manifestation of individual differences within the context of those universals. We thus explore the nature of individual difference in the context of human universals to create a synthesis of the ways in which universality and variance interact to produce the expression of political attitudes, preferences, and behavior we all witness acting throughout the world every day in myriad institutional contexts. To achieve this goal, it remains beneficial to explore the neurocomputational psychological mechanisms that underlie human behavior in interaction with their specific genetic precursors. Such an approach provides greater purchase toward understanding and uncovering the sources of human political and social motivations when faced with a certain decision or environmental challenges.

Theoretically, this means that many investigations begin with the study of complex adaptive behaviors, which are assumed to have evolved as a function of natural selection. The goal of investigating how mutations can develop into species typical designs then focuses the exploration of how functional adaptations can evolve into specific psychological mechanisms. Variations in response to particular environmental or ecological inputs provide the basis for such an adaptationist approach to the emergence of individual differences. A good analogy for individual variance within the context of universal species typicality is provided by cars. All cars share a similar function, namely that of taking the driver and passengers from one point to another. That said, the ride provided by a Ferrari bears almost no relation whatsoever to the experience of driving, say, a Ford Pinto. In this way, the function of transportation remains universal; the individual variance of the experience varies enormously. Similarly, evolution continues to operate on all living things all the time, much like trying to fix your car while it is still running, posing similar biological challenges to survival.

Below we provide an overview of evolutionary theory and how it might be applied to consequential political attitudes, choices, and actions. We outline how to move from a study of human universals to an examination of individual variance and demonstrate how evolutionary models, in combination with methods drawn from other sciences, can tie these disparate research agendas together into a synthetic theory that can not only incorporate the models and lessons learned from environmental approaches, but also provide a serious foundation for future empirical work in preference formation and other crucial aspects of human political and social attitudes and behavior. We then describe how biology has been used to examine some work in the past. Next, we move to a substantive discussion of how this model informs four classic concerns in political science: nature and nature; conflict and cooperation; the origin of preferences, a problem that remains of key concern to rational-choice theorists; and choice and preference formation. Following this, we note some challenges and limitations to evolutionary models. Summing up, we describe how to look at political behavior, broadly construed, from an evolutionary perspective. We conclude with some final thoughts.

Evolution serves as the foundation of biology and represents a broad theory for individual, societal, institutional, and natural development and existence. Evolutionary theory is widely espoused by nearly all branches of science as the theoretical underpinning of scholarly work, whether in geology, climatology, primatology, or oncology (*Economist* 1997; Werner 1999; Alexander 2004; Wilson 2002; Ramaswany et al. 2006). The evidence that evolution exists and is widespread across species is overwhelming. The models and methods available are expanding in breadth and depth, and are increasingly interconnected across almost all disciplines of study, including economics, the discipline that once championed rational choice (Axelrod and Hamilton 1981; *Economist* 1997; Quammen 2004; Robson and Kaplan 2003; Wilson 1987). The main tenets are not restricted to biologists; rather, evolution as a theory can be invoked by any discipline with minimal investment (Wilson 2002).

For purposes relevant to political scientists, the main concepts of evolution refer to natural selection as the means driving evolution; thus, traits are passed down from our ancestors. The existence of natural selection no longer prompts great debate; it is an assumed reality among those in the scientific, medical, and professional fields and is accepted as mainstream thought in the public, mass media, pop culture, and academic circles (Aach et al. 2001; Buss 1995; Futuyma 1985, 1986; Lander et al. 2001).[3] There is considerable evidence that genetic differences play a significant role in explaining differences in personality traits, willingness to take risks, and attitudes toward time. Given the importance of these characteristics, and others, in political behavior, it is somewhat curious that examining the impact natural selection has on political traits and how political preferences may be transmitted genetically remains relatively novel. There is no reason to believe a priori that the robust findings that evolution and genetics influence human behavior *generally* should not apply to human *political* behavior specifically. The important thing is that the amount or significance of genetic transmission can be empirically tested on a trait-level basis and can account for individual variation in political outcomes of interest. Such work can, in turn, undergird the development of an empirically accurate model encompassing elements of universal political preference formation while also fully recognizing the ways in which individuals remarkably differ. Thus an evolutionary foundation can better inform socialization and rational actor models.

Charles Darwin (2003) proposed that individuals who differ from others in their species in ways that increase their relative number of offspring will inevitably leave a greater number of descendants in the following generations with those same (heritable) traits. The concept is that small, random, heritable differences among individuals result in different chances for survival and reproductive success. The development of such heritable differences led to a process of gradual species change that is "evolution by natural selection." Natural selection is ultimately a matter of reproductive success and species survival, but it is a severe misconception to suggest that natural selection favors the "fittest" in the common sense of the word, or that evolution by natural selection implies progress to a superior form of life (Badcock 1991).

Generally, natural selection only asserts that heritable tendencies leading to greater reproductive success are enough to explain evolution. However, evolutionary theory is not solely about reproduction in the narrow as opposed to the broader sense. In other words, evolution does not privilege the life of an individual over the life of that individual's offspring. As long as a person lives long enough to reproduce, strategies like courage may be selected for even if they lead to differentially high rates of mortality in their possessors, as long as those who possess it are more likely to be able to reproduce than those bereft of the given trait. Any psychological mechanism could offer a potential means for reproductive advantage depending on how successful it becomes in the *current and specific environment*. Stronger preferences for warfare or cooperation, although likely to appear opposite, could be used in different circumstances within the same individual or community to pursue the goal of survival or mating and therefore be considered adaptive (Badcock 1991; Gat 2000; Quammen 2004). Consider how successful a balance between out-group warfare and in-group cooperation might be in promoting survival against neighbors in an environment defined by scarce resources. If those environments existed long enough, then over generations there would be a gradual shift in the populations toward the more advantageous traits. Thus, over time, the number of organisms in that species who possess the particular advantageous reproductive traits will increase. And *over generations*, the relative percentage of organisms without the advantageous reproductive traits will decline in a commensurate fashion. In its simplest sense, organisms that possess heritable traits for reproductive success will inevitably indirectly ensure that their offspring are more plentiful than others who do not possess those heritable traits for reproductive success in a given environment.

In most species, natural selection will eventually "phase" out genotypes or traits that minimize reproductive success. However, highly successful organisms such as humans are not necessarily forced to confront this scenario. Humans represent the most adaptable and successful sentient organism on the planet and have been able to both adapt to various environments and to alter their environment on local and global scales (birth control, medical advancements, global warming, migration, and so on). As such, humans appear to have the greatest within-species genetic variation and thus are not as readily subject to the phasing out of traits. Because of human adaptability, a variety of different traits may prove successful within particular ecological contexts, which in turn increases genetic variability. Moreover, a variety of tendencies on some traits, such as cooperation, for example, may produce stable equilibriums over time (Orbell et al. 2004). Of further interest is how human culture has shaped genetic transmission; adhering to modern social norms, humans have been able to alter their evolutionary design by ensuring those with suboptimal survival traits survive in greater numbers, or by making changes to their diet (lactose tolerance) through cultural and environmental change, again furthering genetic variation (e.g., vaccinations or domestication of cattle).

An important and common misperception is that Darwin's theory of evolution by natural selection inevitably and principally predicts contemporary "survival of the fittest." In fact, this term was coined by Herbert Spencer. Darwin adopted the phrase to summarize the process of natural selection, but not to define it. The individual organism is not adapting, nor is it the "fittest." Rather, the species as a whole is changing over generations. Filtering would be more accurate than adaptation in certain ways. Not all heritable traits involve survival, fitness, or reproductive traits; rather, genes are linked in countless ways and individuals can inherit genetic sources for numerous preferences, behaviors, and physical conditions that do not represent optimal survival traits in a given environment, such as the current one, or relate to modern reproduction or fitness (offspring). It is quite likely that only certain genetic markers remain relevant for survival or fitness, while a large number of other genotypes are also passed down, thus providing endless variations in behavioral and physiological traits that have little influence on species survival.

Of further importance is that humans migrate. The intermingling of peoples from vastly different regions, which led to different traits supporting optimal adaption for those different environments, has given rise to even greater variation. Evolution is not focused on individual survival, but species success. Differential reproductive success linked to differences in heritable traits for a specific environment, not differential individual survival success, is the core of natural selection. Survival is important to the extent that it is required for reproduction, but individual survival does not represent the primary foundation for natural selection (Buss 1989). No individual is immortal, but any given gene remains potentially immortal depending on its advantage in aiding its transporter to reproduce.

Evolutionary theorists assert preferences have inherent elements; as such, we would thus expect political behavior to be influenced by heritable genetic traits that are the product of our species' evolutionary past. As our evolutionary past has made us highly adaptable, humans are able to integrate or overlay the social context of the day from the past. Indeed, humans' adaptability is itself one of our most critically important evolved traits. Thus, behavior results from a function of genes passed down through generations in interaction with the current environment. Unquestionably, evolutionary theorists acknowledge the importance of environmental cues because human adaptations occur precisely in reactions to particular environmental contingencies. Thus, in the face of similar genetic traits, humans often manifest different preferences and behaviors, especially if they experience divergent eliciting triggers for behavior. In other words, individuals with different traits may respond differently to the same trigger, just as individuals with the same trait may respond similarly to different cues. In essence, part of an individual's trait may include inclinations in how best to interpret the environment; some individuals will see threat where others see opportunity. This explains one of the ways in which individual variance can occur in the context of human universals, along with genetic noise, variation, or mutation.

Evolutionary theories are consistent with social science research designs that locate the source of current behavior in environmental forces. Neither the genetic component nor the environmental component alone can account for behavioral variability (Corning 1971; Eaves, Eysenck, and Martin 1989), even though statistical models partition sources of influence into these discrete elements. Only within particular environments can certain preferences be expressed; for example, the desire for sex will not likely emerge under conditions of serious immediate threat, as when a predatory animal is chasing a person. *Evolution is intrinsically rational, dependent on the environment, but biologically rational in nature.* This is vital to understanding the importance of heritability; proponents of evolutionary theories do not advocate the dismissal of rational choice or behaviorism. Rather, evolutionary models posit that the current environment represents only part of the equation instead of the whole story.

By utilizing the theory of evolution, and incorporating inherited traits to examine political attitudes, political scientists can incorporate a theory and methodology that have motivated and continue to produce some of the most important scientific findings. Employing evolutionary models can also help to bridge the gap between the social and hard sciences (Wilson 1987; *Economist* 1997; Kurzban, Tooby, and Cosmides 2001; Kurzban and Leary 2001; Ridley 2003; Quammen 2004). Central to this integration remains the intrinsic intertwine between endogenous and environmental factors in generating political attitudes and behaviors of interest.

Consider the following thought experiment. Humans are by nature driven to do certain things: we must eat, drink, and sleep. As a species, we strive to learn, procreate, communicate, have relationships, cooperate, and so on (Wilson 1980). We are social beings and are designed to interact with one another. We do not do these things because our current environment forces us to do so. We do not need to eat only because there is food; no matter what the environment offers, we must eat. Certain behaviors and attitudes are inherent regardless of stimuli. But how these manifest themselves depends considerably on the context, because it is the context that influences human choices. Few, if any, human traits are completely biologically determined, and for many traits "biology" only plays a relatively minor role, while environmental factors shape every choice we have. We need to eat, and we have an evolved preference for sweet- over bitter-tasting foods, but what if we have a choice? How do we explain why one person chooses cauliflower over chocolate? The need and desire to eat is biological, even though what we experience to be tasty (sweet) is not socially determined (Bufe et al. 2005). But the choice of what to eat is partly biological and partly environmental—we cannot choose what is tastier to us, we cannot choose our need to eat, but we can choose to eat the tastier food, or the healthier one, if provided with options (environment).

If we are observing a given subject in this scenario and we do not possess any information concerning the nature or source of the subject's inherent taste preference structure, and what is biologically healthier, then we would not answer why a subject chose to eat chocolate versus cauliflower in a particular case; observing the person eating chocolate would not tell us anything about the reason for the choice or the real source of the preference being observed. It would be considered strange if observers thought that people actually consciously chose or could be raised to have physical reactions to certain foods (e.g., lactose intolerance, allergic reactions, hives, visceral responses).

Both the past and present environments are important mediators of genetic expression. In other words, evolutionary theories of behavior grant more consideration to the impact of the environmental than popularly understood. The environment affects humans' internal sources of preferences, as well as the external expression of those preferences. Primarily environmental models such as rational choice or behaviorism only tend to include current environmental influences, and neglect past environmental influences outside general-purpose learning, and either discount all inherent properties or assume them as given without any explanation for variation across individuals.

Moving from Human Universals to Individual Differences

Population universals only tell part of the story. As noted earlier, humans are remarkably individually diverse. Our genetic code varies to a greater degree than any other species (see Aach et al. 2001 for results from the Human Genome Project). If we take off our scholarly hats for moment and ask ourselves whether someone with Down's syndrome processes information and behaves the same as the "average" person when evaluating political information or making everyday choices, we would know that this characterization is not accurate. Yet Down's syndrome results from just a relatively small genotypic and biological variation, a relatively small difference that can alter an entire set of social and physical behaviors (Antonarakis et al. 2004). Considering that we have endless small genetic differences across the entire population, the logical assumption would be that these differences also affect attitudes and behaviors, including political preferences. Using biological models, we can test to see if small individual differences influence specific responses to external stimuli or otherwise affect social conditions that in turn help influence or determine political choices and behaviors.

Earlier Approach to Incorporating Evolution as a Theory of Preferences

We are, of course, not the first to introduce evolutionary models into analyses of political behavior; such concepts have been introduced before. However, many of these approaches either discussed evolution more as metaphor than model, or allowed deficiencies because of their exclusive focus on human universals to the exclusion of a sufficient appreciation of individual variance. Yet the modern instantiation of evolutionary models we provide and discuss here actually includes a full accommodation of individual difference. This is where behavior genetics and evolutionary psychology meet to provide a more comprehensive understanding of the development of human political and social attitudes, behaviors and social preferences, than would be possible using either perspective alone.

The use of evolution as an explanatory theory for human social behavior has been gaining steady momentum since the 1970s, with increased attention beginning in the 1990s. It has taken different forms depending on its origin in psychology, sociology, biology, or ecology, but each variant uses a common foundation based upon evolution and natural selection (Buss 1995; Cosmides and Tooby 1997; Barber 2005). In analyzing social and psychological behaviors, evolutionary psychology has represented the most common theoretical variant.

Evolutionary psychology (EP) asserts preferences are not simply inherent, but inherent because of our ancestors' ability to solve repeated adaptive problems, which impacted our survival as a species. Therefore, our cognitive architectures results from an interaction of our genetic structure with our environment over generations. These propensities are then passed on to our offspring, who utilize these inherent abilities in their day-to-day actions in an almost unconscious way. Our simple tasks (e.g., optical transmission) only seem simple because our proficiency in solving them is genetically transmitted and largely goes unnoticed. The most useful of these effortless abilities typically evolve into a convergent universal, species typical functional design.

Evolutionary psychology theorists posit that 99 percent of our history as humans developed in hunter-gatherer (HG) societies and this period helped shape the human decision making cognitive architecture with which we live today (Cosmides and Tooby 1997; Gat 2000). Thus our ability to mitigate the problems of today are only adaptations of skills evolved from the past HG way of life that shaped human behavior over approximately 2 million years of development (Tooby and Cosmides 1990; Barkow, Cosmides, and Tooby 1992; Buss 1989, 1995). Evolutionary psychology utilizes the HG hypotheses to generate predictions about human behaviors by specifying physiological and psychological systems that might have developed to solve earlier repeated adaptive problems that impacted reproductive fitness. EP starts with the adaptive problem to be solved and then infers the particular functional physiological or psychological requirements that would be needed to solve it, generating experimental tests for the existence of such mechanisms in the modern mind along the way. As EP utilizes these standards for examining evolutionary hypothesis regarding personality, social scientists can also use these ideas to do the same for political behaviors. Such a model would potentially provide insight into the need for humans to have political preferences as derived or mediated by our evolutionary adaptive traits.

The earliest proponents of evolutionary behavior theories claim every personality phenomenon is analyzable as one of the following: (1) an adaptation; (2) a by-product of an adaptation; (3) noise in the system; or (4) some combination thereof (Symons 1979; Cosmides and Tooby 1994). Therefore, EP tends to largely focus on identifying cross-cultural universals of human behavior, not individual subgroup differences. However, EP recognizes that "both the psychological universals that constitute human nature and the genetic differences that contribute to individual variation are the product of the evolutionary process" (Tooby and Cosmides 1990, 1992). Indeed, universal human characteristics may have different expressions in different societies dependent upon culture and other differences in environmental cues.

Experiments with flies as well as population differences between people in Asia versus South America show the evolution of such variance clearly (Harpending and Cochran 2002). Patterns of genetic variation in HG groups such as the !Kung and African Pygmies exhibit low genetic diversity within the population coupled with higher frequencies of DNA types not found in surrounding population groups, thus suggesting long-term isolation, small population sizes, and strong heritable and evolved development. *Humans did not all evolve the same*, just mostly the same.

It is important to clarify that although many evolved traits still work in the best interest of human survival and reproduction today, not all evolved traits maintain their usefulness over time. For example, the human preference for high-sugar, high-fat, and high-calorie foods was definitely adaptive in prehistoric life since such preferences helped humans survive in times of famine, and access to this type of food was not commonplace as it is today. Yet in modern human societies, large intake of high-fat and high-sugar foods is largely maladaptive, leading to health problems such as obesity, high blood pressure, high cholesterol, and diabetes (Bjorklund and Pellegrini 2002; Johansen and Edgar 1996; Kaplan et al. 2000; Tattersall 1998).

Evolutionary psychology has developed considerably since its inception, but in its earlier inception, and still most common form, was subject to significant empirical and theoretical challenges (e.g., Kurzban and Haselton

2005; Rose and Rose 2000; Machery and Barrett 2006). From the perspective of political behavior, the most critical problem revolves around temporal concerns. If the majority of human existence took place in the HG (Pleistocene) period, then we must look for the source of modern universal human preference structures from this early period. Although we may not know for certain how hunter-gatherers lived, archeological, anthropological, and contemporary observations of modern-day HG societies serve as models of human communities prior to the development of agricultural societies, and thus provide populations for examination in the areas of interest (Oota et al. 2005). The Pleistocene period was stable for a very, very long time, whereas our current environment changes rapidly. Thus, following the logic of EP, there is too much time needed to observe real-time empirical evidence of human evolution in progress. In the EP view, the enduring legacy of past psychological infrastructure does not change easily or quickly even in the face of a rapidly changing external environment. In this way, watching evolution in action is like trying to fix a car while it is running.

Using anthropology and evolutionary literature, it might be possible to construct a theme of basic attitudes and behaviors that would represent putatively adaptive traits for the social environments in which they putatively evolved. However, any attempt to examine if evolutionary selection pressures have a relationship to modern political attitudes would require a sample of humans in the HG mold. This would allow a test of some hypotheses about which behaviors HG humans would have needed to negotiate their social and political world successfully in a way that would have also exerted an impact on reproductive fitness. However, findings in the evolutionary literature with regard to selection pressures are often imprecise, as is the knowledge of the environments that HG societies typically faced. While the theory of natural selection remains relatively straightforward, linking current behaviors and attitudes to past selection pressures is not. Some behaviors may not exert any reproductive advantage and thus would not be expected to be heritable; others may exist as by-products of designs that evolved for other purposes (i.e, mate selection). Other preferences may represent genetic noise or mutation. Separating out these effects as they manifest in the modern world poses complex theoretical and empirical challenges. Clearly our society is much more complex than that faced by our earlier hunter-gatherer ancestors and therefore it is not always readily apparent how we can empirically answer how it is that yesterday's brain is solving today's problems. Thus linking every possible contemporary individual attitude and behavior to a past selection pressure is not plausible and would be highly speculative at best.

Regardless, even if we could perform tests of such hypotheses, these types of examinations would likely add very little explanatory capacity to addressing such specific questions as why someone votes the way he or she does. In effect, if the designs prove universal, as is the larger focus of EP, they provide little additional edifice upon which to build a model to explain individual variance in political preference. In other words, while the most recent version of the theory promotes the importance of individual and cultural variation, the empirical focus has concentrated on uncovering human universals, not on explicating individual variations—which is what political scientists typically emphasize. Thus, EP has been often criticized as simply a nice foundation upon which to generate hypotheses or, at worst, a better "just so" story. This does not mean that explorations of EP remain without merit, but rather that evolutionary psychology's focus on human universals provides formidable roadblocks in seeking to explain stable individual political differences.

In addition, the vast majority of EP limited evolutionary pressures and changes to the Pleistocene or to a very long period of development (tens of thousands of years), and often does not consider more modern cases of human evolution. Studies of organisms in laboratory settings provide strong evidence that certain representations of EP miscategorized the potentially rapid pace of evolutionary change. There is considerable evidence that in modern life evolution is taking place at a much quicker pace in the face of environmental change than typically posited by the greater EP literature (e.g., Lenski, Winkworth, and Riley 2003; Rice and Chippendale 2001).

These concerns presented a considerable problem for political scientists seeking to use EP, as it appeared to assume that stability in the environment slowed down evolution, or at least assumed evolutionary change always proceeded at a slow pace. Indeed, this is the opposite of what evolution is, what evolution does, and how evolution operates. Species evolve as their environment evolves; as modern day human environments evolve rapidly, so should the humans who interact with them similarly experience relatively more rapid changes and shifts. While it is true that the Pleistocene was stable for tens of thousands of years, there is little evidence that evolution only takes place in spans just as long. Rather, as noted above, evidence to the contrary exists.

So how does political science utilize evolution and biology to empirically examine human political behavior? How can we test the evolution of political behaviors and the biological sources of political preferences? Modern revisions and extensions of EP, driven by new experimental and biological methods, have emerged (e.g., Burns 2004; Keller 2008; New, Cosmides, and Tooby 2007; Zietsch et al. 2008). These approaches are geared toward addressing the other half of the heuristic not initially addressed by Tooby and Cosmides (1990); that is, they focus on individual differences. If evolution is to provide a universal theory for political behavior, the ability to explain the similarities humans share through population studies must be followed by attempts to explain subgroup and individual variations within and among these universal themes (Flinn and Low 1986). Specifically, it is in variation within these universal themes, often likely to influence reproductive fitness, where we should find a genetic relationship to political behaviors. Modern biological methods and statistical techniques allow for empirical testing of individual variation within the universal themes of human behavior. By adding genotypic, hormonal, and neurological analyses, it becomes possible to make individual level inferences concerning political behaviors. The relation between the environment, culture, and individual variability is mediated by one's underlying genetic makeup, which at a population level has been formed by past selection forces, but at an individual level by that person's direct ancestors and environment, which vary to a great degree within a given population (e.g., Wilson 1975).

Merging Human Universals with the Study of Individual Differences

Early explorers were faced with the daunting problem of how we might go about examining these individual differences from an empirical position within the theoretical paradigm of evolutionary modeling. Fortunately, due to modern science, new methods have emerged; technology now enables more appropriate testing of the theories' predictions. Early proponents of evolutionary psychology did not apply the lens of their empirical scrutiny onto modern political attitudes. However, the theory, combined with recent methods used in genetics, psychology, neuroscience, endocrinology, and biology, now offers testable hypotheses to identify predictors of political behavior (e.g., Eaves and Eysenck 1974; Eaves 1977; Eaves et al. 1978; Dawson, Shell, and Filion 2007; Jinks and Fulker 1970; Knutson et al. 2006; Kordon, Pfaff, and Christen 2008; Madsen 1985; Neale and Cardon 1992; Oxley et al. 2008; Pfaff, Tetel, and Schober 2008).

One of the more promising recent developments in this area tests models of political behavior derived from work in behavior genetics (Eaves, Eysenck, and Martin 1989; Eaves et al. 1999; Eaves et al. 2008; Hatemi et al. 2007; Martin et al. 1986; Truett et al. 1994). Modern biometrical theory and methods focus on *individual differences* and provide a means to partition out environmental variance into that which is common to members of a family or social group (both social and genetic) and that which is unique to the individual, thus allowing political scientists a technique to examine different environmental and biological sources of preferences. The methods focus on both individual genetic variation as well as population norms (Neale and Cardon 1992).

Using both family studies and genotypic data matched with behaviors, behavior genetic methods offer a means to test whether certain behaviors and attitudes are in fact heritable. Once genotypic data is collected, it becomes possible to link particular behaviors to specific genes, which can be used as potential statistical predictors of behavior (e.g., Bouchard and McGue 2003; Mattick 2004). It has been widely accepted that a significant number of physical, physiological, and behavioral traits ultimately result from a complex interaction between inheritance (genes) and the environment (Bailey et al. 1993; Eaves and Eysenck 1974; Eaves 1977; Happonen et al. 2002; Jansson et al. 2004; Jang, Livesley, and Vemon 1996; Olson, Vernon, and Jang 2001; Saudino 1997; Truett et al. 1994).

The central problem EP and evolutionary designs faced in the past was the challenge of linking behavior to evolved traits, and while difficult to match current behavior with grandiose hypothesized selection pressures, behavior genetics can begin to show that certain behaviors and attitudes are passed on from our direct ancestors (heritable), thus providing powerful evidence that evolution in its simplest form (political traits passed on from our ancestors specifically) is empirically both feasible and falsifiable. Behavior genetics offers a means to provide the empirical link between evolutionary theory and political behavior. Furthermore, these methods make it possible to confirm theories based on evolutionary survival traits. It could simply be that the genetic sources of certain political preferences are side effects of genes intended primarily for other purposes, such as immune system strength or longevity (Pfaff, Vasudevan, and Kow 2008). Or we may come to find that genetic sources of political preferences are not a side product but rather designed to support preferences intended for group survival mechanisms, which in modern cultures are represented as political behaviors.

Initial studies utilizing twins and family members found that political traits are in fact genetically transmitted. That is, some underlying latent trait influenced by genes was indirectly influencing modern preference structures for certain political outcomes (Martin et al. 1986; Eaves, Eysenck, and Martin 1989; Alford, Funk, and Hibbing 2005; Hatemi, Funk et al. 2009; Fowler, Baker, and Dawes 2008). Additional research suggested that these genetic differences were moderated by sex (Hatemi, Medland, and Eaves 2009). More advanced work looked at the importance of spousal selection in the genetic transmission of political preferences, noting that political preferences were among the strongest indicators of spousal similarity in a very wide variety of social and behavioral traits (Hatemi et al. 2007). Using molecular samples, Hatemi (2008) reported that several genetic markers located within a chromosomal region that significantly predicted political preferences were related to olfactory and pheromone receptor activity. These pheromone and olfactory receptors were similar to those discovered in animal studies of mate selection involving bacteria in mice. While it is far too early to state with any certainty, it is quite possible that the genetic sources of political preferences are simply intended for spousal selection and cohesion, in a similar manner to the way that mice mate selection is largely influenced by the immune system's exigencies (Kavaliers et al. 2006). In other words, mate selection, which clearly exerts a direct influence on reproductive fitness through sheer parental investment strategies, may operate at least partly on the basis of similarities in values and characteristics that manifest in the modern world as political preferences. The political tendencies affecting mate selection reflect not only proclivities toward parental investment, but may also help ensure sufficient genetic diversity in offspring as well as provide a basis for social cohesion within the context of cross-sex dyadic interaction that might otherwise be governed by conflicting sexual incentive structures.

In essence, genetics offers the beginning of an understanding of innate sources for political preferences by identifying latent factors that are transmitted genetically, by identifying specific genes that have a mean effect on a given trait, and by tying those genes to other human behavioral, hormonal, neurological, and physiological systems. Combined with environmental methods, the umbrella of evolution has the potential to better explain human political behaviors than extant models such as rational choice which appear leakier in their theoretical coverage of the empirical evidence. Along with genetics, an evolutionary model offers a way to help uncover and explain individual difference within the context of human universals.

Looking at Political Behavior from a Biological Perspective

If environmental theories such as rational choice and behaviorism are incomplete, and biology provides additional insight into human behavior, then it is necessary to clarify how evolution and biology mesh with the study of political behavior. Although the number of scholars adding to the literature continues to rise, evolutionary politics and the biology of political preferences remain a relatively small part of political science scholarship (Fowler, Baker, and Dawes 2008; Fowler and Dawes 2008; Hatemi 2008; Hatemi, Hibbing et al. 2009). However, while the field is relatively small, the amount of research undertaken and the importance of the findings have grown in considerable magnitude over the last five years (see Fowler and Schreiber 2008; Oxley et al. 2008). Recent studies have shown that political behaviors are in part heritable and subject to evolutionary designs (Alford, Funk, and Hibbing 2005; Fowler, Baker, and Dawes 2008; Hatemi et al. 2007). Opinions regarding "abortion on demand," immigration, death penalty, euthanasia, conservatism, and authoritarianism as well as behaviors such as being a leader, religiosity, educational attainment, voter participation, and political intensity have been found to be genetically influenced, while religious affiliation and political partisanship appear primarily environmental (Martin et al. 1986; Eaves, Eysenck, and Martin 1989; Crelia and Tesser 1996; Eaves et al. 1999; Fowler and Dawes 2008; Olson, Vernon, and Jang 2001; Bouchard and McGue 2003; Bouchard et al. 2003; Hatemi, Funk et al. 2009; Hatemi, Hibbing et al. 2009). The findings that shared genes can explain up to 50 percent of the variance in political attitudes was a stunning revelation to the discipline (see Alford, Funk, and Hibbing 2005; for an earlier version see Eaves et al. 1999). *Environment is not everything.*

Examples of such work abound. Neuroscientists such as Amodio (et al. 2007), and Zamboni (et al. 2009), have been using fMRI technology to explore the different brain activity of those on the left and right. Psychologists such as Jesse Graham and Jonathan Haidt (Haidt and Graham 2007) have been focusing on the importance of disgust and ideology, and Jacob Vigil has been exploring facial expression and processing of liberals and conservatives. Psychiatrists such as Drew Westen have also focused on brain imaging, looking at swing voters. Cognitive scientists such as George Lakoff have focused on mortality and conservatism. And, of course, geneticists such as Lindon Eaves and Nick Martin have done seminal work on the heritability of social attitudes, which literally set the stage for the introduction of these variables into political science. Even entomologists such as Gene Robinson have used bees to explore social behavior. These are just a few of the countless examples across disciplines of scientists exploring political topics without contribution from political scientists, whether in economics, biology, anthropology, psychology, or behavior genetics. In simple terms, our discipline's exclusive focus on environmental-only effects has left the door open for us to be raided by other fields!

Adding a biological component to the study of political preferences and accepting that voter preferences are not simply a function of one's issue positions, party affiliation, or level of information, but rather reflect elements influenced by one's genetic makeup, has inspired a movement to redress the examination of political behavior as a whole. Introducing a more nuanced model that includes both environmental and biological factors may help further explain why some people vote, others stay home, why some people choose different issue positions in the face of similar environmental or social stimuli, and why others choose the same position in the face of divergent environmental triggers. One such example is a recent exploration of voting preference; Hatemi et al. (2007) found that which party one votes for is genetically influenced, but only indirectly through attitudes about social welfare.

Research in the area of psychiatric behavior genetics has developed a series of advanced epidemiological methods we advocate and apply for exploring political behaviors. They ask questions such as: why do some people raised in the same environment, faced with a competitor, choose violence, while others choose cooperation? Could it be that some people simply have an inherently higher or lower threshold for using violence than others? Could this tendency be related to other aspects of individual variance, such as personal physical strength in organized systems of covariation (Sell, Cosmides, and Tooby 2009)? Do mechanisms in our brain and internal chemical reactions mitigate, mediate, or moderate our reactions to external stimuli in systematic, yet contingent, ways? Looking beyond the political science scholarship, the answer is a profound "yes" (e.g., Coolidge, Thede, and Jang 2004; Meyer, Houle, and Sagrati. 2004; Lesch 2005; McDermott et al. 2009).

However, biological or genetic processes are not static, nor do they predetermine behavior. For example, in 2002, Avshalom Caspi and others examined a large sample of male children from birth to adulthood to determine why only some abused children develop antisocial (violent) behavior, whereas others do not. They found that a variant of the gene encoding the neurotransmitter metabolizing enzyme Monoamine Oxidase (MAO) moderates the effect of childhood abuse. Abused children with the genotype that promoted higher levels of MAO activity appeared less likely to become abusers than abused children with the genotype that resulted in lower levels of MAO. Several additional studies verified their findings, thus partly explaining why not all abused children grow up to victimize others, although others have more recently called their findings into question. Nonetheless, genotypes can moderate our sensitivity to environmental stimuli along such pathways.[4]

The recognition of biological differences as an important explanatory and predictive factor requires the integration of a wide array of empirical observations into a more cohesive theoretical frame. While social psychological theories pull together the majority of the methods and models that rely on sociological determinants (e.g., familial upbringing), and rational-choice models encompass the economic, utility-maximizing, and self-interest themes, neither theory in its current form allows the potential for locating innate sources of preference. An evolutionary theory of political behavior, which builds from previous efforts, allows for the combination of familial socialization, cultural norms, environmental stimuli, rational action, and endogenous or innate influences, which not only provides a comprehensive illumination of the origins of preferences, but also allows predictive power regarding how individuals vary in their pursuit of such objectives.

In order to justify a model of political preferences that includes biology, we need to understand the ways in which genetics, hormones, cognitive function, or physiology may influence the development and manifestation of political attitudes and behavior, either through a process of evolved variation, as a by-product of such an evolved mechanism, or as noise, depending on topic and domain. We all know that individuals espouse diverse political attitudes and behavior, and these differences in political orientation often remain quite stable over the life course despite changing environmental circumstances (Hatemi, Funk, et al. 2009). How is it that we can witness stable individual differences in preferences within the context of a species typical universal design in humans? Why should political attitudes and beliefs coalesce along such predictable patterns, such as the left-right spectrum, which seems to emerge across cultures and regions? We suggest that this may occur because such clustering might provide an adaptive advantage in solving repeated problems that humans encountered throughout their species development. These preferences may inculcate strategies that help people negotiate the complex social and political problems they confront. We can then interrogate and examine the nature of these mechanisms and how they manifest within the modern political context. In so doing, it becomes possible to explore how dimensions of variation in the ancestral world map onto the process of developing stable individual political preferences and ideologies within population groups encompassing a variety of such belief patterns .

Conclusions

Introducing an empirically driven biological approach to political behavior offers a firm intellectual foundation based upon human development. Political behavior scholars can use biology and evolution to construct empirically falsifiable hypotheses and thus expand the discipline's explanatory capacity.

Including biology and evolution simply offers a more complete explanation of humanity by including humans' physical being into our understanding of political behavior at the individual level.

E. O. Wilson (2002) stated that "the boundary between the natural sciences on one side and humanities and humanistic social sciences on the other is not an epistemological fault line, but a broad domain of poorly understood material phenomena that invites cooperative exploration from both sides." We agree. The use of evolutionary theory has been previously introduced into the political psychology literature but with limited success (e.g., Sidanius and Kurzban 2003). Instead, the use of evolutionary models tends to evoke strong negative reactions. "In effect, social scientists treat the life sciences as enclosed within impermeable walls. Inside these walls, evolutionary thinking is deemed capable of producing powerful and astonishing truths; outside them, in the realm of human behavior, applications of evolutionary thinking are typically treated as irrelevant and often as pernicious, wrong, or downright dangerous" (Lustick 2005).

However, the last several years have witnessed increasing acceptance of evolutionary models in a variety of domains, as evidenced by its emergence within the flagship journals in political science, funding from political science arms of the National Science Foundation, and panels devoted to the topic in the discipline's main conferences. The introduction of the theory of evolution to build a model of human political behavior is one that attempts to explain human behavior by considering how evolution acts through genes, and how it exerts an influence on the relationship between genes and the environment in reciprocal fashion. More contemporary research has moved far away from the nature/nurture debate, which has driven animosity toward evolution. Rather, if anything, it is clear that environment is as much a part of the process of evolution as the inheritance of genes. Insofar as political preferences are concerned, culture is largely driving genetic transmission, as spouses tend to sort on political preferences above almost all other traits, and then pass down those genes that have some influence in social behavior in greater amounts than under random mating (Eaves et al. 2008; Hatemi et al. 2010).

The most important attitude for political scientists to take toward the influence of endogenous factors on political attitudes and behavior is not to think in unchangeable rules of fixed elements with fixed effects on behavior, but to treat the entire paradigm as testable, with specific cultural and environmental constraints. Certainly, proclivities toward certain behaviors are inherited to varying degrees, and likely so are many preferences, but not all individual differences in behaviors or preferences may be subject to evolutionary pressures or genetic influence, and in some societies little individual variation is present or allowed. For example, it appears that for the specific nature of group affiliation, whether religious or political party, genes appear to have no significant influence on individual differences, and parental socialization is almost all that matters (Hatemi, Funk et al. 2009). Thus, the goal is not to find the "genes" for a certain behavior, but rather to identify both environmental and innate determinants of behavior and to ascertain how they interact, if at all, and to achieve a clearer and better defined set of biological and environmental mechanisms to explore the extent to which they are relevant to specific modern political behaviors. In this way, the more we learn about our genetic dispositions, the more we learn about the importance and specific influence of the environment.

Biology may give us the beginning of understanding why we want what we want and delineating the internal processes and preferences we have, while our lives, upbringing, society, and personal experience alter those things to varying degrees. How we go about making decisions, although not uninfluenced by our biology, is a matter of personal will, but the preferences for those choices, and the processes by which we go about making such choices, are mediated by our internal and external conditions. Behavior is not predetermined, but influenced by many factors from both within and outside the body. Emile Durkheim (1982) claimed the study of social behaviors was a distinct and independent discipline; social behaviors could only be explained by social indicators. We disagree. While Durkheim's view remains dominant among the majority of political scientists, the effective identification and inclusion of biology as a source of human behavior has largely debunked such claims.

Evolution accepts the importance of the environment as encompassing heritable adaptations that exist, and are activated, in reaction to specific environmental contingencies. Thus, in the face of similar genetic traits, humans often have different preferences and behaviors in response to divergent cues and triggers. As a populace, we possess certain similar inherent characteristics; as individuals, we share certain genetic traits. The question for political scientists is whether the combination of these factors within the context of the modern environment translates into identifiable predictors of political attitudes, behaviors, and preferences. To examine the individual variation within our species using biological paradigms we need to find genetic similarities that correlate with observed or self-identified preferences. Without biological methodologies, our options for behavioral research remain limited to studying the social processes and institutions that have preoccupied the discipline for decades. This work, while undoubtedly useful, enlightening, and often accurate, nonetheless represents only part of the story of human development and expression. However, by incorporating biological models and methods, political behavior research has the opportunity to examine the biological, physical, *and* environmental sources of political preferences and behaviors, for both a given population and at an individual level.

By presenting a theoretical framework that allows for empirical testing, one that ties together a group of literature and models, and remains open to change and modification when new results provide evidence that deem it necessary, evolutionary theory offers the beginnings of a more complete and fruitful theoretical underpinning for the empirical exploration of political behavior. The following chapters seek to apply methods specifically designed for this theory to explicate important processes of social and political behavior.

Notes

1. Constructivist models posit social interaction as the source of identities and interests (Wendt 1999).

2. Utilizing more than three dozen variables in multiple models of survey data for four national election years, Matsusaka and Palda (1999) find that demographic and contextual variables provide significant effects on the probability of voting, but the models do not predict who votes more accurately than random guessing.

3. The evidence to support natural selection and evolution in general is vast (see Aach et al. 2001, for results from the Human Genome Project). Also see Gunter and Dhand (2002) editor's note on the mouse genome effort, where they find that 99 percent of house mice genes have direct counterparts in humans. For natural selection examples, see Rice and Chippendale's (2001) lab experiments involving scores of generations of the fruit fly; also see Lenski et al.'s (2003) experiment involving 20,000 generations of the bacterium *Escherichia coli*.

4. Another example of the interaction between genotype and environmental factors can be found in the form of traumatic early life events. Such events emerge as a key precursor to sparking the manifestation of adult predilections toward physical violence. Frazzetto et al. (2007) demonstrated that, significantly, the timing of such assaults matter as well in predisposing affected youth to physical aggression in later life; trauma during puberty portended much more poorly than negative events experienced at other times. Similar experiments examining depression, suicide and alcoholism provide converging evidence (Meyer et al. 2004; Kendler et al. 2005; Newman et al. 2005). For human behavior, genes not only matter, but in certain cases and under certain social conditions they also exert a profound difference.

References

Aach, J., M. L. Bulyk, G. M. Church, J. Comander, A. Dertik and J. Shendure. 2001. Computational comparison of two draft sequences of the human genome. *Nature* 409:856–59.

Alexander, R. D. 2004. Evolutionary selection and the nature of humanity. In *Darwinism and philosophy,* ed. V. Hosel and C. Illies, 424–95. Notre Dame, Ind.: University of Notre Dame Press.

Alford, J., C. Funk, and J. Hibbing. 2005. Are political orientations genetically transmitted? *American Political Science Review* 99 (2): 153–67.

Alford, J. R., and J. R. Hibbing. 2004. The origin of politics: An evolutionary theory of political behavior. *Perspectives on Politics* 2 (4): 707–23,

Amodio, D. M., J. T. Jost, S. L. Master, and C. M. Yee. 2007. Neurocognitive correlates of liberalism and conservatism. *Nature Neuroscience* 10 (10): 1246–47.

Antonarakis, S. E., R. Lyle, E. T. Dermitzakis, A. Reymond, and S. Deutsch. 2004. Chromosome 21 and Down syndrome: From genomics to pathophysiology. *Nature Reviews Genetics* 5 (10): 725–38.

Axelrod, R., and W. D. Hamilton. 1981. The evolution of cooperation. *Science* 211 (4489): 1390–96.

Badcock, C. 1991. *Evolution and individual human behavior: An introduction to human sociobiology.* Cambridge, Mass.: Blackwell.

Bailey, J. M., R. C. Pillard, M. C. Neale, and Y. Agyei. 1993. Heritable factors influence sexual orientation in women. *Archives of General Psychiatry* 50:217–23.

Barber, N. 2005. Educational and ecological correlates of IQ: A cross-national investigation. *Intelligence* 33:273–84.

Barkow, J. H., L. Cosmides, and J. Tooby. 1992. *The adapted mind: Evolutionary psychology and the generation of culture.* New York: Oxford University Press.

Bjorklund, D. F., and A. D. Pellegrini. 2002. *Origins of human nature: Evolutionary developmental psychology.* Washington, D.C.: American Psychological Association.

Bouchard, T., Jr., and M. McGue. 2003. Genetic and environmental influences on human psychological differences. *Journal of Neurobiology* 54:4–45.

Bouchard, T., N. Segal, A. Tellegen, M. McGue, M. Keys, and R. Krueger. 2003. Evidence for the construct validity and heritability of the Wilson-Patterson Conservatism Scale: A reared apart twins study of social attitudes. *Personality and Individual Differences* 34:959–69.

Brosnan, S. F., and F.B.M. de Waal. 2004. Monkeys reject unequal pay. *Nature* 425:297–99.

Bueno de Mesquita, B. 1983. The costs of war: A rational expectations approach. *American Political Science Review* 77:347–57.

Bufe, B., P.A.S. Breslin, C. Kuhn, D. R. Reed, C. D. Tharp, J. P. Slack, U.-K. Kim, D. Drayna, and W. Meyerhof. 2005. The molecular basis of individual differences in phenylthiocarbamide and propylthiouracil bitterness perception. *Current Biology* 15 (4): 322–27.

Burns, J. K. 2004. An evolutionary theory of schizophrenia: Cortical connectivity, metarepresentation, and the social brain. *Behavioral and Brain Sciences* 27:831–85.

Buss, D. 1989. Sex differences in human mate preferences: Evolutionary hypotheses tested in 37 cultures. *Behavioral and Brain Sciences* 21:1–49.

———. 1995. Evolutionary psychology: A new paradigm for psychological science. *Psychological Inquiry* 6 (1): 1–30.

Campbell, A., P. E. Converse, W. E. Miller, and D. E. Stokes. 1960. *The American voter.* New York: Wiley.

Caspi, A., J. McClay, T. Moffitt, J. Mill, J. Martin, I. Craig, A. Taylor, and R. Poulton. 2002. Role of genotype in the cycle of violence in maltreated children. *Science* 297:851–53.

Chen, K., V. Lakshminarayanan, and L. Santos. 2006. How basic are behavioral biases? Evidence from capuchin monkey trading behavior. *Journal of Political Economy* 114:517–37.

Chodorow, N. 1978. *The reproduction of mothering.* Berkeley: University of California Press.

————. 1995. Gender as a personal and cultural construction. *Signs* 20 (3): 516–44.

Coolidge, F. L., L. L. Thede, and K. L. Jang. 2004. Are personality disorders psychological manifestations of executive function deficits? Bivariate heritability evidence from a twin study. *Behavior Genetics* 34 (1): 75–84.

Corning, P. 1971. The biological bases of behavior and some implications for political science. *World Politics* 23 (2): 321–70.

Cosmides, L., and J. Tooby. 1994. Better than rational: Evolutionary psychology and the invisible hand. *American Economic Review* 84 (2): 327–32.

————. 1997. Evolutionary psychology: A primer. Center for Evolutionary Psychology, University of California–Santa Barbara. http://www.psych.ucsb.edu/research/cep/.

Crelia, R., and A. Tesser. 1996. Attitude heritability and attitude reinforcement: A replication. *Personality and Individual Differences* 21 (5): 803–8.

Darwin, C. 2003. *The origin of species and the descent of man*. New York: The Modern Library.

Dawes, R., and R. Thaler. 1988. Anomalies: Cooperation. *Journal of Economic Perspectives* 2 (3): 187–97.

Dawson, M. E., A. M. Shell, and D. L. Filion. 2007. The electrodermal system. In *Handbook of psychophysiology*, ed. J. T. Cacioppo, L. G. Tassinary, and G. G. Berntson, 159–81. New York: Cambridge University Press.

Downs, A. 1957. *An economic theory of democracy*. New York: Harper.

Durkheim, E. 1982. *Rules of sociological method*. New York: Free Press.

Eaves, L., A. Heath, N. Martin, H. Maes, M. Neale, K. Kendler, K. Kirk, and L. Corey. 1999. Comparing the biological and cultural inheritance of personality and social attitudes in the Virginia 30 000 study of twins and their relatives. *Twin Research* 2:62–80.

Eaves, L. J. 1977. Inferring the causes of human variation. *Journal of the Royal Statistical Society* 140 (3): 324–55.

Eaves, L. J., and H. J. Eysenck. 1974. Genetics and the development of social attitudes. *Nature* 249:288–89.

Eaves, L. J., H. J. Eysenck, and N. G. Martin. 1989. *Genes, culture and personality: An empirical approach*. London: Academic Press.

Eaves, L. J, P. K. Hatemi, E. C. Prom, and E. L. Murrelle. 2008. Social and genetic influences on adolescent religious attitudes and practices. *Social Forces* 86 (4): 1621–46.

Eaves, L. J., K. A. Last, P. A. Young, and N. G. Martin. 1978. Model-fitting approaches to the analysis of human behavior. *Heredity* 41:249–320.

Economist. 1997. Darwin revisited. *Economist* 344 (8032): 59–61.

Fehr, E., and U. Fischbacher. 2004. Third party punishment and social norms. *Evolution and Human Behavior* 25:63–87.

Fehr, E., and S. Gächter. 2000. Cooperation and punishment. *American Economic Review* 90:980–94.

Flinn, M. V., and B. S. Low. 1986. Resource distribution, social competition and mating patters in human societies. In *Ecological aspects of social evolution*, ed. D. I. Rubenstein and R. W. Wrangham, 217–43. Princeton, N.J.: Princeton University Press.

Fowler, J. H., L. A. Baker, and C. T. Dawes. 2008. Genetic variation in political participation. *American Political Science Review* 102 (2): 233–48.

Fowler, J. H., and C. T. Dawes. 2008. Two genes predict voter turnout. *Journal of Politics* 70 (3): 579–94.

Fowler, J. H., and D. Schreiber. 2008. Biology, politics, and the emerging science of human nature. *Science* 322 (5903): 912–14.

Frazzetto, G., G. D. Lorenzo, V. Carola, L. Proietti, E. Sokolowska, A. Siracusano, C. Gross, and A. Troisi. 2007. Early trauma and increased risk for physical aggression during adulthood: The moderating role of MAOA genotype. *PLoS ONE* 2 (5): e486.

Futuyma, D. J. 1985. *Science on trial: The case for evolution.* New York: Pantheon Books.

———. 1986. *Evolutionary biology.* Sunderland, Mass.: Sinauer Associates.

Gat, A. 2000. The human motivational complex: Evolutionary theory and the causes of hunter-gatherer fighting, part 1. Primary somatic and reproductive causes. *Anthropological Quarterly* 73 (1): 20–34.

Gilligan , C. 1982. *A different voice: Psychological theory and women's development.* Cambridge: Harvard University Press.

Gintis, H. 2000. Strong reciprocity and human sociality. Working paper. University of Massachusetts Amherst, Department of Economics. http://www.umas.edu/economics/publications/econ2000_02.pdf.

Gintis, H., S. Bowles, R. Boyd, and E. Fehr. 2003. Explaining altruistic behavior in humans. *Evolution and Human Behavior* 24:153–72.

Glimcher, P., and A. Rustichini. 2004. Neuroeconomics: The consilience of brain and decision. *Science* 306:447–52

Green, D., and I. Shapiro 1994. *Pathologies of rational choice theory: A critique of applications in political science.* New Haven, Conn.: Yale University Press.

Gunter, C., and R. Dhand. 2002. Human biology by proxy. *Nature* 420 (6915): 509.

Haidt, J., and J. Graham. 2007. When morality opposes justice: Conservatives have moral intuitions that liberals may not recognize. *Social Justice Research* 20:98–116.

Happonen, M., L. Pulkkinen, J. Kaprio, J. Van der Meere, R. J. Viken, and R. J. Rose. 2002. The heritability of depressive symptoms: Multiple informants and multiple measures. *Journal of Child Psychology and Psychiatry* 43 (4): 471–47.

Harpending, H., and G. Cochran. 2002. In our genes. *Proceedings of the National Academy of Sciences* 99 (1): 10–12.

Hatemi, P. K., J. Alford, J. Hibbing, N. Martin, and L. Eaves. 2009. Is there a "party" in your genes? *Political Research Quarterly* 62 (3): 584–600.

Hatemi, P., C. Funk, H. Maes, J. Silberg, S. Medland, N. Martin, and L Eaves. 2009. Genetic influences on social attitudes over the life course. *Journal of Politics* 71:1141–56

Hatemi, P.K. , J. Hibbing, S. Medland, M. Keller, J. Alford, K. Smith, N. Martin, and L. Eaves. 2010. Not by twins alone: Using the extended family design to investigate genetic influences on political beliefs. *American Journal of Political Science* 54 (3): 798–814.

Hatemi, P. K., S. E. Medland and L. J. Eaves. 2009. Genetic sources for the gender gap? *Journal of Politics* 71 (1): 1–15.

Hatemi, P. K., S. E. Medland, K. I. Morley, A. C. Heath, and N. G. Martin. 2007. The genetics of voting: An Australian twin study. *Behavior Genetics* 37:435–48.

Henrich, J., R. Boyd, S. Bowles, C. Camerer, E. Fehr, H. Gintis, and R. McElreath. 2001. In search of *Homo economicus*: Experiments in 15 small-scale societies. *American Economic Review* 91 (2): 73–78.

Jang, K. L., W. J. Livesley, and P. A. Vemon. 1996. Heritability of the Big Five Personality Dimensions and their facets: A twin study. *Journal of Personality* 64:3.

Jansson, M., M. Gatz, S. Berg, B. Johansson, B. Malmberg, G. McClearn, M. Schalling, and N. L. Pedersen. 2004. Gender differences in heritability of depressive symptoms in the elderly. *Psychological Medicine* 34:471–79.

Jinks, J. L., and D. W. Fulker. 1970. Comparison of the biometrical, genetical, MAVA, and classical approaches to the analysis of human behavior. *Psychological Bulletin* 73:311–49.

Johansen, D., and B. Edgar. 1996. *From Lucy to language.* New York: Simon and Schuster.

Kaplan, H. S., K. R. Hill, J. B. Lancaster, and A. M. Hurtado. 2000. A theory of human life history evolution: Diet, intelligence, and longevity. *Evolutionary Anthropology* 9:156–85.

Kavaliers, M., E. Choleris, A. Ågmo, W. Braun, D. Colwell, L. Muglia, S. Ogawa, and D. W. Pfaff. 2006. Inadvertent social information and the avoidance of parasitized male mice: A role for oxytocin. *PNAS* 103 (11): 4293–98.

Keller, M. C. 2008. The evolutionary persistence of genes that increase mental disorder risk. *Current Directions of Psychological Science* 17:395–99.

Kendler, K. S., J. W. Kuhn, J. Vittum, C. A. Prescott, and B. Riley. The interation of stressful life events and a serotonin transporter polymorphism in the prediction of episodes of major depression: A replication. 2005. *Archives of General Psychiatry* 62 (5): 529–35.

Knutson, K. M., J. N. Wood., M. V. Spampinato, and J. Grafman. 2006. Politics on the brain: An fMRI investigation. *Social Neuroscience* 1 (1): 25–40.

Kordon, C., D. Pfaff, and Y. Christen. 2008. *Hormones and social behavior*. Heidelberg: Springer-Verlag.

Kruger, D. J. 2003. Evolution and altruism: Combining psychological mediators with naturally selected tendencies. *Evolution and Human Behavior* 24 (2): 118–25.

Kurzban, R., and M. G. Haselton. 2005. Making hay out of straw: Real and imagined controversies in evolutionary psychology. In *Missing the revolution: Darwinism for social scientists*, ed. J. H. Barkow, 149–61. Oxford: Oxford University Press.

Kurzban, R., and M. R. Leary 2001. Evolutionary origins of stigmatization: The functions of social exclusion. *Psychological Bulletin* 127 (2): 187–208.

Kurzban, R., J. Tooby, and L. Cosmides. 2001. Can race be erased? Coalitional computation and social categorization. *Proceedings of the National Academy of Sciences USA* 98 (26): 15387–92

Landemore, H. 2004. Politics and the economist-king: Is rational choice theory the science of choice? *Journal of Moral Philosophy* 1 (2): 177–97.

Lander, E. S., L. M. Linton, B. Birren, C. Nusbaum, M. C. Zody, J. Baldwin, K. Devon, et al. 2001. Initial sequencing and analysis of the human genome. *Nature* 409 (6822): 860.

Lenski, R. E., C. L. Winkworth, and M. A. Riley. 2003. Rates of DNA sequence evolution in experimental populations of Escherichia coli during 20,000 generations. *Journal of Molecular Evolution* 56 (4): 498–508.

Lesch, K.-P. 2005. Alcohol dependence and gene x environment interaction in emotion regulation: Is serotonin the link? *European Journal of Pharmacology* 526 (1–3): 113–24.

Lopreato, J., and T. A. Crippen. 1999. *Crisis in sociology: The need for Darwin*. Somerset, N.J.: Transaction.

Lustick, I. 2005. Daniel Dennett, comparative politics, and the dangerous idea of evolution. *Comparative Politics Newsletter* 16 (2): 19–24.

Machery, E., and C. Barrett. 2006. Debunking adapting minds. *Philosophy of Science* 73: 232–46.

Madsen, D. 1985. A biochemical property relating to power seeking in humans. *American Political Science Review* 79 (2): 448–57

Martin, N. G., L. J. Eaves, A. C. Heath, R. Jardine, L. M. Feingold, and H. J. Eysenck. 1986. Transmission of social attitudes. *Proceedings of the National Academy of Sciences* 83:4364–68.

Matsusaka, J. G., and F. Palda. 1999. Voter turnout: How much can we explain? *Public Choice* 98 (3–4): 431–46.

Mattick, J. 2004. The hidden genetic program of complex organisms. *Scientific American* (October): 60–67.

McDermott, R., D. Tingley, J. Cowden, G. Frazzetto, and D. Johnson. 2009. Monoamine Oxidase A gene (MAOA) predicts behavioral aggression following provocation. *Proceedings of the National Academy of Sciences* 106 (7): 2118–23.

Meyer, J. H., S. Houle, S. Sagrati, A. Carella, D. Hussey, N. Ginovart, V. Goulding, J. Kennedy, and A. Wilson. 2004. Brain serotonin transporter binding potential measured with carbon 11-labeled dasb positron emission tomography: Effects of major depressive episodes and severity of dysfunctional attitudes. *Archives of General Psychiatry* 61 (12): 1271–79.

Neale, M. C., and L. R. Cardon. 1992. *Methodology for genetic studies of twins and families.* Dordrecht: Kluwer Academic.

New, J., L. Cosmides, and J. Tooby. 2007. Category-specific attention for animals reflects ancestral priorities, not expertise. *Proceedings of the National Academy of Sciences* 104 (42): 16593–603.

Newman, T. K., Y. V. Syagailo, C. S. Barr, J. R. Wendland, M. Champoux, M. Graessle, S. J. Suomi, J. D. Higley, and K. P. Lesch. 2005. Monoamine oxidase: A gene promoter variation and rearing experience influences aggressive behavior in rhesus monkeys. *Biological Psychiatry* 57 (2): 167–72.

Olson, J., P. Vernon, and K. Jang. 2001. The heritability of attitudes: A study of twins. *Journal and Personality and Social Psychology* 80 (6): 845–60.

Oota, H., B. Pakendorf, G. Weiss, A. von Haeseler, S. Pookajorn, W. Settheetham-Ishida, D. Tiwawech, T. Ishida, and M. Stoneking. 2005. Recent origin and cultural reversion of a hunter–gatherer group. *PLoS Biology* 3 (3): e71.

Orbell, J., T. Morikawa, J. Hartwig, J. Hanley, and N. Allen. 2004. "Machiavellian" intelligence as the basis for the evolution of cooperative dispositions. *American Political Science Review* 98: (1): 1–15.

Oxley, D. R., K. B. Smith, J. R. Alford, M. V. Hibbing, J. L. Miller, M. Scalora, P. K. Hatemi, and J. R. Hibbing. 2008. Political attitudes vary with physiological traits. *Science* 321 (5896): 1667–70.

Pfaff, D. W., M. Tetel, and J. Schober. 2009. Neuroendocrinology: Mechanisms by which hormones affect behaviors. In *Handbook of neuroscience for the behavioral sciences*, ed. G. Berntson and J. Cacioppo, 99–118. New York: Wiley.

Pfaff, D., N. Vasudevan, and L.-M. Kow. 2008. Sexual behavior and arousal: Neuroendocrine and genomic controls. In *The encyclopedia of neuroscience*, ed. L. R. Squire et al. Oxford: Elsevier.

Platt, M. L., and P. W. Glimcher. 1999. Neural correlates of decision variables in parietal cortex. *Nature* 400:233–38.

Quammen, D. 2004. Was Darwin wrong? *National Geographic* 206 (5): 1–24.

Ramaswany, V., M. D. Schwarzkopf, W. J. Randel, B. D. Santer, B. J. Soden, and G. L. Stenchikov. 2006. Anthropogenic and natural influences in the evolution of the lower stratosphere cooling. *Science* 311:1138.

Rice, W. R., and A. K. Chippindale. 2001. Sexual recombination and the power of natural selection. *Science* 294 (5542): 555.

Ridley, M. 2003. *Nature via nurture.* New York: HarperCollins.

Robson, A. J., and H. S. Kaplan. 2003. The evolution of human life expectancy and intelligence in hunter-gatherer economies. *American Economic Review* 93 (1): 150–69.

Rose, H., and S. Rose. 2000. *Alas poor Darwin: Arguments against evolutionary psychology.* New York: Harmony Books.

Saudino, K. J. 1997. Moving beyond the heritability question: New directions in behavioral genetic studies of personality. *Current Directions in Psychological Science* 6:86–90.

Sell, A., L. Cosmides, and J. Tooby. 2009. Formidability and the logic of human anger. *Proceedings of the National Academy of Sciences* 106 (35): 15073–78.

Sidanius, J., and R. Kurzban. 2003. Evolutionary approaches to political psychology. In *Handbook of political psychology*, ed. D. O. Sears, L. Huddy, and R. Jervis, 146–81. Oxford: Oxford University Press.

Symons, D. 1979. *The evolution of human sexuality*. New York: Oxford University Press.

Tattersall, I. 1998. *Becoming human: Evolution and human uniqueness*. New York: Harcourt Brace.

Thayer, B. A. 2000. Bringing in Darwin: Evolutionary theory, realism, and international politics. *International Security* 25 (2): 24–51.

Tooby, J., and L. Cosmides. 1990. On the universality of human nature and the uniqueness of the individual: The role of genetics and adaptation. *Journal of Personality* 58:17–67.

Trivers, R. L. 1971. The evolution of reciprocal altruism. *Quarterly Review of Biology* 46:35–57.

Truett, K. R., L. J. Eaves, E. E. Walters, A. C. Heath, J. K. Hewitt, J. M. Meyer, J. Silberg, M. C. Neale, G. M. Martin, and K. S. Kendler. 1994. A model system for the analysis of family resemblance in extended kinships of twins. *Behavior Genetics* 24:35–49.

Tversky, A., and R. Thaler. 1990. Anomalies: Preference reversals. *Journal of Economic Perspectives* 4 (2): 201–11.

Wendt, A. 1999. *Social theory of international politics*. New York: Cambridge University Press.

Werner, D. 1999. Evolution: Implications for epistemology and cultural variation. In *The Darwinian heritage and sociobiology*, ed. J.M.G. van der Dennen, D. Smile, and D. Wilson, 83–100. Westport, Conn.: Praeger.

Wilkinson, G. S. 1984. Reciprocal food-sharing in the vampire bat. *Nature* 308:181–84.

Wilson, D. S. 1980. *The natural selection of populations and communities*. Menlo Park, Calif.: Benjamin Cummings.

Wilson, E. O. 1975. *Sociobiology: The new synthesis*. Cambridge, Mass.: Belknap Press.

———. 1987. *On human nature*. Cambridge: Harvard University Press.

———. 2002. On the relation of science and the humanities. Presentation given at Harvard University, December 11, 2002.

Zamboni, G., M. Gozzi, F. Krueger, J.-R. Duhamel, A. Sirigu, and J. Grafman. 2009. Individualism, conservatism, and radicalism as criteria for processing political beliefs: A parametric fMRI study. *Social Neuroscience* (June 26): 367–83.

Zietsch, B. P., K. I. Morley, S. N. Shekar, K.J.H. Verweij, M. C. Keller, S. Macgregor, M. J. Wright, J. M. Bailey, and N. G. Martin. 2008. Genetic factors predisposing to homosexuality may increase mating success in heterosexuals. *Evolution and Human Behavior* 29:424–33.

2

POLITICAL PRIMATES

What Other Primates Can Tell Us about the Evolutionary
Roots of Our Own Political Behavior

Darby Proctor and Sarah Brosnan

A group of high-ranking males gathered around two particularly animated males, who were vocalizing wildly. The postures of all the males revealed the situation to be quite tense and that an escalation from vocalized threats to physical violence was very real. In the middle of the males was the resource they all apparently desired. Initially there was close contact among the males along with some minor physical aggression. However, this aggression eventually escalated into all-out violence with the males hitting each other repeatedly in the head and body. This aggression lasted approximately one minute before the males calmed down and distanced themselves from one another.

This was a real scenario among primate males that was caught on video. Specifically, these were human males, at the Bolivian congress in 2007 (Live Leak.com 2007). The limited resource was a podium at which a heated debate was raging. The men engaging in this behavior were not hoodlums or crazed sports fanatics, but elected officials engaging in normal primate male behavior. We find scenarios like this unfolding in many parts of the world. From the Ukrainian parliament descending into egg throwing and fist fighting (Silverberg 2010) to a physical altercation between a councilman and mayor in Mississippi (Mamrack 2010), power struggles among primates are ubiquitous.

This chapter examines the political behavior of nonhuman animals, particularly the primates, in an effort to understand the roots of human political behavior. We focus in particular on the chimpanzee, as our closest relative and a species for which much is known. Our goal is to determine how these species' behaviors may elucidate the evolutionary trajectory that led to modern political behavior in humans. We start with an examination of how the human ideals of politics and political behavior can be translated into useful concepts for other species, following which we discuss the logic of the comparative approach to behavior. We then discuss both laboratory and field results that illuminate political behavior in other primates. We end with a discussion of what this means for human political behavior.

Defining Political Behavior

Studying any behavior requires an operational definition that allows us to focus on the specific behaviors of interest. In particular, it is important to have a definition that spans different contexts and, in this case, different species; otherwise the broader connections are missed (for example, we wouldn't define being human as requiring a particular experience, such as college or hunting experience, a particular trait, or living in a particular place or time period, as this would obscure the underlying commonalities of being human). With this in mind, we find the most useful definition of politics to be Lasswell's (1936) classic description as who gets what, when, and how. This definition describes a series of observable and measurable phenomena in both humans and nonhumans. In the opening example of this chapter, the males were attempting to gain the podium (what) to express their views before those of others (when) through physical aggression (how).

Thus we follow Laswell, and define political behavior as the actions of an individual or individuals that influence the distribution of resources. Throughout this chapter, we discuss how behaviors we can observe, such as aggression, reciprocity, and social interactions, as well as the context of those behaviors, allow us explain who gets what. We begin, however, with a discussion of why the study of other species is important for a better understanding of human political behavior.

Behavioral Phylogeny

One of the most powerful tools in the evolutionary arsenal is the comparative method. In essence, the comparative approach allows us to compare the behaviors of different species with the goal of elucidating underlying similarities in behaviors across species. These similarities may include not only the manifestation of the behavior, but also the conditions that elicit the behavior and hence are likely to have been important in selection of the behavior. Critically, this comparison allows us to illuminate the evolutionary function of a behavior; that is, how did it increase the fitness of those individuals who possessed it? Note that the power of this approach is that by understanding similarities and differences, we can determine why a behavior evolved.

Charles Darwin (2003) initially proposed two major tenets related to the evolution of species. First was that species are related by some common genealogy, and second was that the traits of those organisms are influenced by the environment in which they developed evolutionarily. Darwin's idea of natural selection was not limited to physical forms, but extended to behaviors as well. Thus, one can compare the behavior of related species in order to trace the evolution of a behavior, an idea known as behavioral phylogeny (Brosnan 2007; Wrangham and Peterson 1996; Preuschoft and van Hooff 1995; Boehm 1999).

Similarities between species can arise in two different ways, through homology or convergence. Phylogenetic continuities, or homologies, occur when shared behaviors evolved in a common ancestor and were maintained through subsequent speciation events. Thus, the trait exists because of shared ancestry and may not actually reflect shared selective pressures in the current time period (and in fact if the environment becomes too different, one or more species will undergo selection to diverge from the ancestral trait). On the other hand, convergent evolution occurs when individuals with a similar set of selective pressures share a behavior that was not shared by their common ancestor. Thus, these behaviors are similar despite occurring in different lineages. For example, complex eyes, which are one very useful mechanism for improving interactions with one's environment, appear to have evolved independently numerous times across many lineages (Land and Nilsson 2002) and many species form coalitions and alliances (Harcourt and de Waal 1992). Recognizing convergences can help in identifying which selective pressures are the most important for a trait to evolve. It is important to understand the distinction between homology and convergence, as an understanding of whether common descent or common selective pressures led to the trait in question can help to elucidate the evolutionary function of a given trait.

In studying the development of human political behavior, both the closely related apes and the more distantly related monkeys may provide information through either of these two evolutionary mechanisms. In other words, if we find a behavior that is similar between ourselves and the other apes, this trait may have been present in our last common ancestor, indicating that it may have emerged to support social interactions long before humans emerged. If the trait is also present in monkeys, who are more distantly related, then the behavior is even more evolutionarily ancient. This allows us to understand when traits evolved and the degree to which traits that are uniquely human, such as our advanced cognitive capacity, are truly required. However, if there are human traits that we do not see in the other primates, we may be able to conclude that those traits evolved after the humans and apes diverged from their common lineage, or common evolutionary past.

Perhaps more interesting is convergent behaviors. If we share behaviors with some primates, but not others, then this implies first that the behavior is not uniquely selected for humans and second that there is some common feature, either in social behavior or ecology, which led to selection for the behavior. Finding this commonality allows us to extrapolate the function it evolved to serve. Note that in both homology and convergence, a fuller understanding of how the trait evolved allows for a fuller understanding of the characteristics that are or are not associated with the trait and, hence, its evolutionary function.

The evolutionary pressures that lead to adaptations, whether they are due to phylogenetic continuities or convergent evolution, are analyzed on two levels, the proximate and the ultimate. The proximate level of analysis addresses the mechanisms by which the behavior operates in the immediate sense within the individual, while ultimate level of analysis addresses why a behavior was selected in evolutionary history (e.g., why it is adaptive). Note that for any given trait, there are both proximate and ultimate explanations. For instance, animals have sex. Among the proximate reasons are the hormones that influence behavior and development in ways that lead to copulation, and that the act stimulates nerves that cause reward areas to be activated in the brain. The ultimate reason is the individual passes on its genetic material to the next generation. Note that all of these reasons are correct—and not mutually exclusive—explanations for why animals have sex, but utilize different rationales. Many times conflicts between competing explanations for behavior are actually due to the utilization of different levels of analysis, not mutually exclusive explanations (Alcock and Sherman 1994). Thus it is important to understand these different levels of explanation when making evolutionary arguments.

To make any of these comparisons, an understanding of primate phylogeny is essential. Briefly, humans (*Homo sapiens*) are part of the primate order. The primate order consists of four taxa: apes (including humans), Old World monkeys, New World monkeys, and prosimians. The extant species to which humans are most closely related are the sister *Pan* species, chimpanzees (*P. troglodytes*) and bonobos (*P. paniscus*), followed by the other apes, then Old World monkeys, then New World monkeys, then prosimians (for a more in-depth review of the dates of divergence in the primate lineage see Steiper and Young 2006 and Ho et al. 2005). Studying the behavior of the other primates allows us to extrapolate to what may have influenced behavioral adaptations in the evolutionary past to emerge into the behaviors that we see in humans today (e.g., Brosnan, Newton-Fischer, and van Vugt 2009).

Who Gets What and How, Part 1: Experimental Studies

Schreiber (this volume) notes that decisionmaking or choice under some constraint is fundamental to the study of politics. This is an ideal area for studies of nonhuman animals to contribute, as much experimental work with animals is done on decisionmaking under varying degrees of constraint, and much of the research shows that humans and other species often have similar reactions and reach similar outcomes. This section of the chapter will focus on the experimental evidence for determining who gets what and how in several different contexts.

Cooperation among Primates

Cooperation is arguably the basis for much political behavior. Cooperation consists of individuals working together to increase their evolutionary fitness (Brosnan and Bshary in press), and as such allows for a dramatic expansion in the number of ways in which individuals can attempt to acquire more resources. Humans represent the extreme of the continuum; we are capable of cooperating to the degree that literally our survival depends on others. For example, in modern Western cultures, few individuals provide their own food supply, and no one individual is responsible for providing food to the rest. In this (oversimplified) example, farmers produce food, which then goes through intermediary companies that process and deliver the food to grocery stores, where we go to buy our food; yet few of us consider the degree of interrelationship that went in to getting it there (Seabright 2010). Among other species, only those that have been domesticated are able to survive without knowing how to acquire their own basic necessities.

Nonetheless, other species do cooperate, even if not to the degree to which humans are capable. Over the past thirty years there has been an emergence of literature on cooperation in animals (Brosnan and Bshary 2010; Dugatkin 1997), showing that cooperation exists literally across the animal kingdom. Given that natural selection is about the promotion of individual fitness, an evolutionary account of cooperation must explain how working together with another individual can lead to increased fitness for both individuals. There are currently three explanations for this behavior—mutualism, kin selection, and reciprocal altruism—although more recent thought emphasizes the necessity of broadening this approach (Brosnan and Bshary 2010).

In the case of mutualism, individuals work together for a joint reward that is received immediately, meaning that cooperating in this case yields an immediate individual benefit to both participants. Kin selection can benefit individuals in two ways. First, they can increase their own fitness and, second, they can increase the fitness of their relatives, as this is a second mechanism for passing one's own genetic material to the next generation. Hamilton (1967) refined this into a simple equation embodying the idea that as long as the degree of benefit to a relative, multiplied by their degree of relatedness, outweighs the cost to the actor, then the behavior will be selected. Finally, Trivers (1971) followed this a few years later with the recognition that individuals could benefit in the long term from a cost paid now. This, called reciprocal altruism, explains how cooperation can be selected in groups of individuals who interact with each other over time.

Although these theories provide ultimate explanations for cooperation, they still do not explain how animals are able to successfully cooperate in their day-to-day lives or the proximate mechanisms for cooperation. We here focus on the experimental evidence for how nonhumans cooperate. Experimental studies of cooperation are typically done by putting individuals in a situation in which they must work together in order to obtain food rewards. Moreover, most of these studies focus on mutualism tasks (in which both individuals benefit).

A common methodology for studying cooperation involves a barpull device, which consists of a weighted tray on which food can be placed out of reach of the animals being tested. Two bars extend from the tray to the subjects. If both animals pull on their bars together, the tray moves closer and they can then reach the food reward (Nissen and Crawford 1936). The barpull setup is so useful because it can be manipulated to investigate variables such as visual contact, reward distribution, and physical contact.

A series of studies have been done on capuchin monkeys, which provide a great deal of evidence about what contingencies of the barpull task these monkeys are able to understand (see Brosnan in press for more details). First, the monkeys pull more often when their partners are present rather than absent, indicating that they recognize the need for a partner. This indicates that the animals understand that they are working together, as opposed to simply working independently on the same task (Mendres and de Waal 2000). Moreover, capuchins are hesitant to participate in the barpull if the reward is easily monopolizable by one of them, even on the first trial (i.e., this hesitation has no learned component), demonstrating that the monkeys take into account the likelihood of competition over the food reward (de Waal and Davis 2003). However, if only one individual is rewarded, cooperation is more likely if the recipient shares some of the spoils, suggesting that this can be overcome (de Waal and Berger 2000). A critical caveat of this research is that for experiments to induce cooperative behaviors the experimental task must be intuitive; otherwise, cooperation never occurs (Brosnan and de Waal 2002). The barpull apparatus mimics the natural behavior of pulling food toward oneself (e.g., fruit on a tree branch), and provides kinesthetic feedback about the partners' activities. Experiments that lack a naturalistic component with feedback do not elicit cooperation (Visalberghi, Quarantotti, and Tranchida 2000; Chalmeau, Visalberghi, and Gallo 1997; Brosnan and de Waal 2002).

Although the above contingencies indicate that the monkeys do understand cooperation and are able to manipulate the situation to their gain, they are also sensitive to their partners' outcomes, even when the outcomes all result in an absolute gain. Monkeys refuse to cooperate with individuals who do not share the best outcomes, regardless of the fact that the interaction results in an absolute gain for both (Brosnan, Freeman, and de Waal 2006). To test this, monkeys were allowed to freely move between either bar, in essence forcing them to choose among themselves which bar each would pull in. In some trials, one side of the tray had a less valuable reward than the other. In this way, one monkey could dominate the better food rewards. The researchers found that the reward the monkeys received on any given trial was not as important as the partner's behavior over the entire interaction. That is, the monkeys would pull in the tray even if they were getting a less good reward. However, this was only true if both individuals had roughly equal access to the better rewards. Rates of successful cooperation were almost three times as high when the monkeys alternated who got the better reward, as compared to situations in which one monkey consistently dominated the better food. What this suggests is that capuchin monkeys do not mind short-term inequity during a cooperative interaction *as long as* the gains over the long term are approximately equal. This is particularly significant as it is rare that every cooperative outcome will lead to exactly equal payoffs, and so opens the door for the establishment of long-term cooperation even when such variation in payoffs exists (Brosnan, Houser et al. 2010). This has significant implications for natural behaviors such as group hunting in which prey must be divided among the hunting group.

There is evidence from one wild study site, the Täi forest, that chimpanzees hunt cooperatively with a relatively equal distribution of prey that is caught (Boesch 2002). In this particular case, chimpanzees take on specific roles in order to drive and capture prey, and it appears that the chimpanzees recognize the roles of the other hunters, anticipate the direction the prey will travel, and engage in the hunt accordingly. Once the prey is caught, all the hunters get a share of the prey, suggesting a reward for effort schema for distributing the prey. What makes this particularly interesting is that this sort of distribution is not the same in all chimpanzee groups. At another site, Gombe, the hunter that ends up with the prey dictates the distribution of the food, sharing primarily when harassed by other chimpanzees (Gilby 2006). The difference in these two distribution patterns seems to be based on the ecology of the hunting sites. At Täi, the forest canopy is contiguous, such that monkeys can more easily escape, and the chimpanzees must work together, while at Gombe, with a more fragmented canopy, a single chimpanzee has approximately the same success as a group. Thus, the sharing at Täi may have evolved because each chimpanzee needed the help of the others in order to have any success at all (Boesch and Boesch 1989). This provides further evidence that cooperation is selected because it benefits all partners, not in spite of it.

Finally, chimpanzees, at least, are very sensitive to the role of the partner in a cooperative interaction and adjust their willingness to cooperate accordingly. Using another barpull task, Melis and colleagues (Melis, Hare, and Tomasello, "Chimpanzees" 2006) explored the conditions under which chimpanzees would recruit a collaboration partner. They found that chimpanzees did not recruit a partner when they could get the food reward alone, but did so when they were unable to work the barpull by themselves. Moreover, when given a choice between two potential partners with whom they had previous experience, the chimpanzees selected the partner who had been more tolerant (e.g., shared food more readily) in previous interactions. When partners were chosen for the chimpanzees, the rate of spontaneous cooperation was dependent upon the subjects' relationships; those pairs that were more socially tolerant were more likely to cooperate than those which were less tolerant (Melis, Hare, and Tomasello, "Engineering" 2006). These results suggest that chimpanzees not only recognize when cooperation partners are needed, but recognize which partners are more beneficial for their long-term outcomes.

Thus when answering the critical question "who gets what," it is clear that this need not always be a free-for-all brawl, as described in the opening example. In many cases, political behavior is highly cooperative, and everyone wins. However, among humans, as well as other species, it is important to keep in mind the constraints. First, cooperation breaks down if not all partners benefit, a lesson that is just as important for humans as capuchins. Moreover, there are differences between humans and other primates. Chimpanzees are heavily influenced by their personal relationship with potential collaboration partners (Melis, Hare, and Tomasello, "Engineering" 2006) while humans will collaborate in a variety of contexts, including with anonymous partners or strangers (Henrich et al. 2002). This willingness to cooperate with unknown individuals appears to have evolved after the human divergence from the rest of the apes, making it a uniquely human trait.

Punishment

One problem with cooperation is that individuals can cheat. Therefore, there must be some mechanisms for detecting cheaters; otherwise, cheating would be the rule rather than the exception (Cosmides and Tooby 1992) and cooperation would cease. Indeed, we see punishment of cheaters, in the form of aggression, in several cooperative species, including chimpanzees, wasps, and naked mole rats. However, punishment is not restricted solely to cooperative contexts. Clutton-Brock and Parker (1995) list five contexts in which punishment has been observed in animals: the enforcement of cooperative behaviors, establishment and maintenance of dominance relationships, theft, parasitism and predation, mating and courtship, and parent-offspring conflict.

In fact, some of the best evidence for punishment comes from outside of the primates, indicating that the mechanisms for punishment are evolutionarily ancient. Cleaner fish (*Labroides dimidiatus*) males punish their partners for cheating during the process of feeding on their client fish; punishment occurs when one individual takes a bite of the client's mucus and scales rather than restricting itself to parasites, which causes the client to flee and thus end the feeding session (Raihani, Grutter, and Bshary 2010).

This example also directly addresses the issue of third-party punishment (Fehr and Gächter 2002), which has been so difficult to explain because of the lack of a selective advantage for the punisher, who seems to gain nothing from the interaction. Although this is third-party punishment, as it is the client fish who suffers the most, this punishment also benefits the punisher, providing a suggestion for how third-party punishment may have evolved. Since client fish leave if they are cheated on, by punishing a cheating partner, the punisher may increase his future benefits (Raihani, Grutter, and Bshary 2010). This may represent a step toward the third-party punishment; it may have evolved first in a context in which both the punisher and the third party gained fitness, providing a self-serving outcome as one of the original functions of the behavior.

In human egalitarian societies, such as the !Kung, group ostracism and group punishment of social deviants form the basis for punishment (Boehm 1999). This is particularly striking as individuals with lower status can band together to keep higher-status individuals in line. Boehm argues that this is a flattened, or upside down, form of hierarchy as weak individuals band together to dominate the strong. This allows for a form of collective power among the weaker individuals that guarantees a greater access to resources by keeping dominant individuals in line. Examining how small-scale egalitarian societies handle punishment can help us understand human political behavior as these were likely the type of groups that humans first formed.

A similar form of group punishment has been observed in chimpanzees. Even though among chimpanzees males are the most dominant members of the group (the alpha male outranks the alpha female), in at least some circumstances females have some control over which male takes the alpha position and can collectively punish the male for socially unacceptable behavior. This collective female power allows them to outmaneuver individuals who are dominant to them (de Waal 1986).

Sapolsky and Share (2004) document a similar phenomenon in a wild-living group of baboons. All the most dominant (and thus most aggressive) males in this group were killed by bovine tuberculosis from a human waste dump they visited. None of the females or less-dominant males (and, hence, less aggressive) could get past the other baboon group in whose territory the dump resided, so they were unaffected. Following the dominant males' deaths, there was significantly less aggression in the group. Years later, after all of the original males were gone, the males of this particular group remained markedly less aggressive than is typical, yet there was no evidence of genetic change. Share and Sapolsky speculate that this is due to the influence of the females, who exerted collective power to force the males to maintain their lower rates of aggression. Despite males dominating females, females exerted sufficient collective power to ensure the males maintained their lower rates of aggression. Thus, in both monkeys and apes this collective power of lower-ranking individuals can ensure both that dominant individuals stay in check and that there is an improved access to resources for weaker individuals.

Decisionmaking

All individuals of all species make decisions. They decide where to go, with whom to mate, what to eat, where to find shelter, and so forth. However, decisionmaking may also be more complex, as individuals decide how to handle their property and whether to take into account others' gains. In the following section we discuss decisionmaking in both of these contexts, with the goal of showing how individuals make decisions which affect who gets what.

DECISIONMAKING ABOUT PROPERTY AND POSSESSIONS Humans are alone among primates with regards to maintaining personal property. This is due in part to the lack of objects for other primates to own. Their food items (mostly fruit) are perishable and their tools are abundant and easily acquired. However, there are behaviors that suggest that nonhuman primates have a concept of possession including, among some species, allowing individuals to maintain possession of a desirable item (see Brosnan in press for a review). The relative dearth of property in the wild makes it difficult to study; however, there is experimental evidence that possession and associated behaviors are quite important.

One beneficial aspect of possessions and property are that you can trade them to get more possessions and property. As recognized centuries ago (Smith 2000), a very successful way to acquire more resources is to trade what you have a surplus of with another who has a surplus of something else you would like to have. Humans are the only species that engages in habitual trade; however, the behavior does occur in other species. Many primates easily learn the basics of exchange, to trade a token with an experimenter to get a food reward (Brosnan in press; Brosnan and de Waal 2004, 2005). This allows them to trade a nonuseful object for a useful one. However, humans typically consider trade to involve the exchange of two useful objects, so how do individuals respond when given the option to exchange one useful item for another? Chimpanzees are willing to do so, showing that they are capable of giving up an item with value—not an easy thing to do (Brosnan et al. 2008; Lefebvre 1982; Lefebvre and Hewitt 1986). Moreover, they do so rationally; they trade foods they like less well for foods they like better, but not the other way around. They have even been observed to do so spontaneously on occasion (Paquette 1992).

However, while this regards exchange, it does not answer the question about trade. To do this, we set up an experiment to see if chimpanzees would barter tokens with one another (Brosnan and Beran 2009). Earlier work had shown that chimpanzees would use symbols to request tools from other chimpanzees (Savage-Rumbaugh, Rumbaugh, and Boysen 1978), so for this study subjects could trade with each other tokens displaying well-known symbols for favored foods, which could then be cashed in for the represented food. The chimpanzees were then put in situations in which each had tokens representing foods the other could obtain, to see if they would learn to trade their tokens to obtain more foods. When the experimenters mediated the interaction, requiring the subjects to trade with each other prior to cashing in, the subjects did very well, trading tokens that their partner needed over tokens that were useless to their partner. However, when experimenter mediation was removed, subjects quit trading with each other within a single session, and instead reverted to autarky, collecting only those foods that they could acquire on their own. Thus, while chimpanzees are capable of exchange, they do not seem inclined to do so. One likely reason is that without narrative language, chimpanzees lack the means to solicit third-party support and the control mechanisms (e.g., the legal system) to enforce interactions, making trade too risky and too inherently costly to be under selection (Brosnan and Beran 2009).

Nonetheless, despite the apparent lack of propensity to trade, several primates exhibit cognitive biases related to trade behaviors in humans. A notable example is the endowment effect, in which an individual prefers the item in its possession over one which it normally prefers, which could be obtained through trade (Kahneman, Knetsch, and Thaler 1990). Although this has been treated as a cognitive quirk in the human literature, it is likely that the behavior was selected because, prior to the advent of human control mechanisms, maintaining property was a far better way to increase fitness than attempting to trade it for other items, which risks losing both of the items (Jones and Brosnan 2008). In fact, other species act in similar ways when given the chance to trade one item for the other, indicating that this may be a beneficial and evolutionarily ancient behavior.

In an initial study, chimpanzees showed an endowment effect of similar magnitude to that of humans (Brosnan et al. 2007). Using a procedure from the human literature (Knetsch and Sinden 1984), the chimpanzees were given items and allowed to immediately trade them for other items. In the case of foods, subjects showed a preference for keeping items even when given a chance to trade for others they preferred in separate preference tests. The same results have been found now in orangutans (Flemming et al., in revision) and capuchin monkeys (Lakshminarayanan, Chen, and Santos 2008).

Intriguingly, while endowment effects were found for food items, this was not the case for nonfood items, possibly indicating that the endowment effect varies dependent upon the context of the interaction (Brosnan et al., in review).

In short, other species have some ability to understand the concept of possessions and to use items in their possession to obtain other ones. What the nonhuman primates do not seem to do is actively engage in barter to better their own outcomes. In fact, this may be an excellent example of a failure of political behavior outside of humans; lacking any ability to communicate others' inappropriate actions or to solicit support for acts not observed by another, individuals have little leverage in influencing others' behavior beyond that which is immediately observable. Thus, in this context, who gets what is much more dependent upon one's own actions than anything else.

DECISIONS UNDER CONDITIONS OF INEQUITY Sometimes decision-making isn't affected by one's own outcomes, but rather by comparison with those of others. In several primate species, individuals refuse to accept food rewards if they receive a lower value food than a partner performing the same task (Brosnan and de Waal 2003; Brosnan, Schiff, and de Waal 2005; van Wolkenten, Brosnan, and de Waal 2007); this topic is covered in depth elsewhere (for details please see Brosnan 2009; Brosnan, Talbot et al. 2010). This differs from situations in which they simply see better rewards, but no one else gets them. In this latter case, they happily accept the lower-value rewards. Thus, the reaction seems to be based on a social comparison; how do my outcomes look compared to those of others? From the traditional economic standpoint, this decision by the monkeys not to participate under a condition of inequity makes no sense. The monkeys should accept any reward that they are willing to work for regardless of what their partner receives. Yet, this is clearly not the case in monkeys or humans (Yamagishi et al. 2009).

The evidence for inequity is widespread in primates (see reviews above) and in dogs (Range et al., "Absence" 2009; Range et al., "Effort" 2009), suggesting either an ancient evolutionary origin for this mechanism or a widespread convergence. In fact, one hypothesis is that the evolutionary function of the behavior is to promote cooperation (Fehr and Schmidt 1999; Brosnan 2006). There are several ways in which this might occur. First, recognizing inequity would allow individuals to determine when their partners are not responding in kind. Such recognition allows them to find a new partner with whom the joint efforts are matched by joint rewards (van Wolkenten, Brosnan, and de Waal 2007). Another possibility is that responding negatively to inequity may function as a commitment device (Frank 1988), allowing individuals to send a signal to their partners that they will not tolerate this sort of behavior (Yamagishi et al. 2009) and thus improving outcomes in future interactions.

Thus it is clear that in many cases interactions are not simply about what one gets, but what one gets in comparison with everyone else. To go back to the initial example, the politicians were not satisfied with the fact that they would eventually get to present their views, but wanted to do so immediately, before anyone else. This makes sense using the logic of evolution; a selective advantage comes not from what you have, but from what you have *in comparison with everyone else*. Thus an important consideration for political science is to consider not just what outcomes are, but how they compare to others'.

DECISIONMAKING AND SOCIAL INFLUENCES Many animals, including primates, learn information socially from one another (Fragaszy and Perry 2003). This is a powerful mechanism by which individuals can gain knowledge from more experienced individuals without the potential costs of individual exploration. The lack of any apparent teaching in most contexts has led to the hypothesis that social learning functions primarily through a process that is similar to the master-apprentice relationship in which the apprentice learns only by observation, as opposed to actively being taught (Matsuzawa et al. 2008). Learning some skill, like nut-cracking in chimpanzees, from another individual is also a mechanism by which the behavior does not have to be invented from scratch in each generation.

Recently, it has come to light that the animals do not choose who to copy blindly, but instead select a model based on proficiency (Ottoni, de Resende, and Izar 2005), dominance rank (Pongracz et al. 2008) and social affiliation (de Waal 2001; Menzel 1973; Bonnie and de Waal 2006; Horner 2010). For instance, chimpanzees prefer to copy the behavior of high-ranking individuals with previous experimental history over lower-ranking individuals with less experience, even though the rewards for copying one or the other model are identical and no aggression or coercion occurred. Taken together, these demographic features outline a concept very similar to what we would refer to as prestige (Horner et al. 2010). In humans, the individuals with demonstrated knowledge and/or skills, or prestige, disproportionately influence the behavior of others (Barkow 1975). Since both humans and chimpanzees copy prestigious individuals, this trait was likely present in our last common ancestor. While the reasons for this mechanism need to be explored more fully, there is adaptive value to copying successful individuals as their success is an honest indicator of their ability and knowledge with respect to acquiring resources.

Who Gets What and How, Part 2: Observational Studies

In the previous section, we focused on how we could understand individuals' behavior through controlled experiments. Experiments have many advantages, not the least of which is an ability to control extraneous factors and thus derive causal, rather than correlational, results. On the other hand, most interactions between primates do not take place in preset pairings with a mediator who is not even of the same species (e.g., the human experimenter), so it is also important to consider behaviors related to politics in more natural contexts. In the following section, we discuss a variety of behaviors in either natural or more naturalistic settings, and their relevance for who gets what and how.

Power, Dominance, and Political Behaviors in Nonhuman Primates

Some of the most readily observable features of political behavior in primates involve dominance and power. Although these concepts are only a part of the suite of political behaviors that we see in the nonhuman species, they are fundamental to an understanding of political behavior. Dominance is so important in primates because of the fitness advantages experienced by dominant individuals. They have greater access to food (Sapolsky 2005; Boehm 1999), more influence over others (Horner et al. 2010; Pongracz et al. 2008), better health (Whitten 1983; Sapolsky 2005), greater access to mates (de Waal 1982; Boehm 1999), and increased survival of offspring (Currie 2009; Sapolsky 2005). Because these are the most critical factors affecting evolution, there is strong positive selection for dominance behavior.

In nonhuman primates, dominance relationships are typically conceived with respect to a dominance hierarchy. For dominance hierarchies to be effective, the individuals in the hierarchy need to know their position relative to the others with whom they interact. This often includes signals of either dominant status or subordinance. Signals of dominance can include an increased physical size (Fedigan 1993) or accentuated feature (Kuze, Malim, and Kohshima 2005), both of which are metabolically costly and thus require a significant resource investment (Vogel 2005), making them hard to fake. Signals of subordination are found throughout the primate order and often take the form of a ritualized greeting (de Waal 1978, 1982; Hinde and Rowell 1962; Whitham and Maestripieri 2003; Smuts and Watanabe 1990). This stabilizes day-to-day interactions by reducing the need for the dominant to "remind" group members each day of his or her status. Humans, too, show such ritualized greetings which take into account power differences (Schottman

1995; Morsbach 1988; Duranti 1992; Argyle 1990). While these greetings serve to remind individuals of the social order, they can also be used as a subtle way to manipulate that order (Morton 1988; Whitham and Maestripieri 2003). For instance, prior to an attempted overthrow of an existing alpha male chimpanzee, a lower-ranking male will sometimes stop giving submissive vocalizations to the alpha (Goodall 1986), thus altering the typical social greeting.

A discussion of political action in nonhuman primates would be incomplete without giving some attention to aggression, as this topic has a long history of being the focus of scientific research (see Zuckerman 1932 as an example). Even though scientists now recognize that there is more to dominance than physical aggression (de Waal 1982, 1990), it does play a central role in the lives of many primates, including, of course, humans. Intraspecies competition revolves around access to limited resources, including food and mates. Using physical aggression or the threat of aggression can allow individuals to gain access to those resources and maintain their position in the dominance hierarchy (Isbell 1991; Sapolsky 2005; Silk 1983).

Although aggression may be violent, such as hitting or biting, much aggression is less severe. Threats are a type of aggressive interaction that stop short of physical violence. Threat vocalizations and gestures, such as threat yawning in baboons (see fig. 2.1), may replace direct physical violence, reducing both the energetic costs of fighting and the associated risks of injury

FIGURE 2.1. *Left*: An adult male chacma baboon (*Papio ursinus*) threat-yawning, presumably in an attempt to discourage competition from other males. Right: An adult female chacma baboon yawning in a situation that does not require a threat. While there is no distinction in the literature between the facial movements associated with "regular" yawns and threat yawns in baboons (Altmann 1967; Redican 1975), this distinction has been documented in other monkey species (Deputte 1994). In this population of baboons it appears that nonthreat yawns were characterized by covering the teeth with the lips. Group members are able to distinguish between these yawns and respond appropriately to threats versus a tired baboon. Cape Point group, Cape Point, South Africa. Photo by Darby Proctor.

(Harper 1991). In fact, Henrich and Gil-White (2001) argue that the threat of possible aggression is sufficient to enforce social rules.

Social Maneuvering

Social maneuvering is another strategy by which individuals gain access to resources. For example, male chimpanzees engage in grooming other individuals (Foster et al. 2009), which plays an important role in regulating relationships (Goodall 1986), resolving conflict (de Waal and Aureli 1999), and increasing access to resources (de Waal 1997; Hockings et al. 2007). Such affiliative relationships, called friendships, may be formed by a male with a female and her offspring (Smuts 1985; Smuts and Gubernick 1992). Although this would certainly be a way for the male to increase his fitness if the offspring are his (Altmann et al. 1996), in many cases they are not (Curie-Cohen et al. 1983). Instead these friendships seem to be a mechanism for gaining future mating benefits with the female by providing services (e.g., food, support, and infant care) now (Smuts 1985; Smuts and Gubernick 1992; Palombit, Seyfarth, and Cheney 1997; Palombit et al. 2000). One species, bonobos, has extended affiliative relationships, in the form of non-conceptive sex (Wrangham 1993), to relationships between individuals of almost every demographic, indicting the degree to which affiliative relationships can be used as a social tool (de Waal 1995; Idani 1991; Parish 1994; White 1989).

Physical tools can also be used as a mechanism to climb in social status. Goodall (1968) reported that one aspiring alpha male made himself appear more formidable by banging empty kerosene cans during displays. Despite the fact that the cans were available to all of the chimpanzees, only he was able to use this resource and thus achieved the alpha position.

However, being in power typically does not give individuals free rein to behave in any way that they want. As noted earlier, even dominant individuals are subject, at times, to the collective social power of nondominant individuals (Boehm 1999; Sapolsky and Share 2004). In some species, the social rules seem to be maintained by third-party interventions, such that others will intercede if the dominant becomes overly aggressive (de Waal 1982). The risk of retaliation or ostracism helps to keep powerful individuals in check, as well as increasing access to resources for less-powerful individuals (Boehm 1999).

Coalitions and Alliances

Power may also be achieved through the use of alliances, in which two (or more) individuals participate in a long-term coalition, which may last for years (Harcourt and de Waal 1992). For instance, in one particularly long-lasting alliance, two male chimpanzees jointly maintained the alpha position over a stronger male for several years, sharing the benefits of the position (e.g., mating opportunities). The power of the alliance became clear when the allies had a fight and the third male took over almost instantly (de Waal 1982).

Alliances may also involve more than dyads. For instance, male dolphins form super alliances, in which distinct alliances band together in larger groups (Connor, Heithaus, and Barre 1999). There are even reports of humans and dolphins engaging in mutually beneficial and helpful fishing relationships (Orams 1997), which may suggest a cross-species alliance, a behavior that has been seen between humans and several species (e.g., Isack and Reyer 1989). Humans also operate in complex coalition and alliance networks, with several nested levels common in political organizations (Falger 1992; Boehm 1992; Boulton 1995; Wilson 2007). The phylogenetic diversity of this behavior indicates that selection for alliances occurred in large-brained, socially complex species in a variety of different ecologies.

Who Gets What and How—Conclusion

So what makes humans different? It is often the case that differences between us and the other primates are of degree rather than kind. For instance, although all primates are cooperative, as mentioned earlier, humans take cooperation to the next level by cooperating with strangers, including in anonymous situations. Similarly, we see punishment and ostracism in other primates, but only humans are known to have institutionalized forms of punishment. Humans also use language to negotiate interactions and support property and possession rights in ways that other species do not.

Perhaps the largest difference comes in the number of individuals that can be dominated. Primate groups seem to be limited to a few hundred individuals or fewer, possibly due to the limits of maintaining social relationships without language (Dunbar 1993). Language frees humans to interact with multiple individuals simultaneously (e.g., speaking to a crowd) and to interact remotely via written or oral communication, which dramatically increases the size of our groups. This implies that nonhuman primates could never form the extensive groups or nation-states that humans have created, in which an individual is dominant over thousands or millions, while personally knowing only a small fraction of them. Rulers do not need to individually know their citizens because they have laws, institutions, and armies, all based on the power of language, to back up their personal power (Mann 1986; Rose and Miller 1992).

One commonality in all of these distinctions is that they seem not to indicate differences in how individuals make decisions and negotiate access to resources, but instead in how they may use language to assist. Thus it seems likely that humans and other primates' political strategies are based on a similar foundation, but that humans have added an enhanced ability to communicate, particularly about distant times, places, and people, to their interactions. In this way, language allows for an expansion of political behavior to a degree that may seem on the surface to be functionally different, but is instead simply an extension of behaviors that humans already had in common with many other species.

Lasswell (1936) likely did not realize that his definition of politics would be so broadly applicable beyond humans. However, many species, including other primates, deal with these issues of power and resource distribution on a daily basis. The same evolutionary pressures that acted on the other primates were also at work in humans. We are not alone in being political animals and can learn much about our own behavior from a comparative study with other primates.

Acknowledgments

We thank Rose McDermott and Peter Hatemi for inviting us to participate in this volume and for many insightful comments. We further thank an anonymous reviewer for very helpful comments, and David Pervin for extended discussion which led to many new ideas in this chapter. Funding to SFB was provided by a National Science Foundation Human and Social Dynamics Grant (SES 0729244) and an NSF CAREER Award (SES 0847351).

References

Alcock, J., and P. Sherman. 1994. The utility of the proximate-ultimate dichotomy in ethology. *Ethology* 96 (1): 58–62.

Altmann, J., S. C. Alberts, S. A. Haines, J. Dubach, P. Muruthi, T. Coote, E. Geffen, et al. 1996. Behavior predicts genetic structure in a wild primate group. *Proceedings of the National Academy of Sciences* 93:5797–5801.

Argyle, M. 1990. *Bodily communication.* 2nd ed. London: Methuen.

Barkow, J. 1975. Prestige and culture: A biosocial interpretation. *Current Anthropology* 16:553–72.

Boehm, C. 1992. Segmentary "warfare" and the management of conflict: Comparison of East

African chimpanzees and patrilineal-patrilocal humans. In *Coalitions and alliances in humans and other animals*, ed. A. H. Harcourt and F.B.M. de Waal, 137–73. Oxford: Oxford University Press.

———. 1999. *Hierarchy in the forest: The evolution of egalitarian behavior.* Cambridge: Harvard University Press.

Boesch, C. 2002. Cooperative hunting roles among Täi chimpanzees. *Human Nature* 13 (1): 27–46.

Boesch, C., and H. Boesch. 1989. Hunting behavior of wild chimpanzees in the Täi National Park. *American Journal of Physical Anthropology* 78:547–73.

Bonnie, K. E., and F.B.M. de Waal. 2006. Affiliation promotes the transmission of a social custom: Handclasp grooming among captive chimpanzees. *Primates* 47:27–34.

Boulton, M. J. 1995. Playground behaviour and peer interaction patterns of primary school boys classified as bullies, victims and not involved. *British Journal of Educational Psychology* 65 (2): 165–77.

Brosnan, S. F. 2006. Nonhuman species' reactions to inequity and their implications for fairness. *Social Justice Research* 19 (2): 153–85.

———. 2007. Fairness and other-regarding preferences in nonhuman primates. In *Moral markets: The critical role of values in the economy*, ed. P. J. Zak, 77–104. Princeton, N.J.: Princeton University Press.

———. 2009. Responses to inequity in nonhuman primates. In *Neuroeconomics: Decision making and the brain*, ed. P. W. Glimcher, C. Camerer, E. Fehr and R. Poldrack, 285–302. Amsterdam: Elsevier.

———. In press. Property in nonhuman primates. *New Directions in Child and Adolescent Behavior.*

Brosnan, S. F., O. D. Jones, M. Gardner, S. L. Pavonetti, and S. Schapiro. In review. The impact of object usefulness on the endowment effect highlights the context dependence of cognitive biases.

Brosnan, S. F., and M. J. Beran. 2009. Bartering behavior between conspecifics in chimpanzees, *Pan troglodytes. Journal of Comparative Psychology* 123:181–94.

Brosnan, S. F., and R. Bshary. 2010. Cooperation and deception: From evolution to mechanisms. *Philosophical Transactions of the Royal Society B* 365:2593–98.

Brosnan, S. F., and F.B.M. de Waal. 2002. Variation on tit-for-tat: Proximate mechanisms of cooperation and reciprocity. *Human Nature* 13 (1): 129–52.

———. 2003. Monkeys reject unequal pay. *Nature* 425 (6955): 297–99.

———. 2004. A concept of value during experimental exchange in brown capuchin monkeys. *Folia Primatologica* 75:317–30.

———. 2005. A simple ability to barter in chimpanzees, *Pan troglodytes. Primates* 46:173–82.

Brosnan, S. F., C. Freeman, and F.B.M. de Waal. 2006. Partner's behavior, not reward distribution, determines success in an unequal cooperative task in capuchin monkeys. *American Journal of Primatology* 68:713–24.

Brosnan, S. F., M. Grady, S. Lambeth, S. Schapiro, and M. J. Beran. 2008. Chimpanzee autarky. *PLoS ONE* 3 (1): e1518.

Brosnan, S. F., D. Houser, K. Leimgruber, E. Xiao, T. Chen, and F.B.M. de Waal. 2010. Competing demands of prosociality and equity in monkeys. *Evolution and Human Behavior* 31:279–88.

Brosnan, S. F., O. D. Jones, M. C. Mareno, A. S. Richardson, S. P. Lambeth, and S. J. Schapiro. 2007. Endowment effects in chimpanzees. *Current Biology* 17:1–4.

Brosnan, S. F., N. E. Newton-Fisher, and M. van Vugt. 2009. A melding of the minds: When primatology meets personality and social psychology. *Personality and Social Psychology Review* 13 (2): 139–47.

Brosnan, S. F., H. C. Schiff, and F.B.M. de Waal. 2005. Tolerance for inequity may increase with social closeness in chimpanzees. *Proceedings of the Royal Society B: Biological Sciences* 1560:253–58.

Brosnan, S. F., C. Talbot, M. Ahlgren, S. P. Lambeth, and S. J. Schapiro. 2010. Mechanisms underlying the response to inequity in chimpanzees, *Pan troglodytes*.

Chalmeau, R., E. Visalberghi, and A. Gallo. 1997. Capuchin monkeys, Cebus apella fail to understand a cooperative task. *Animal Behaviour* 54 (5): 1215–25.

Clutton-Brock, T. H., and G. A. Parker. 1995. Punishment in animal societies. *Nature* 373: 209–16.

Connor, R. C., M. R. Heithaus, and L. M. Barre. 1999. Superalliance of bottlenose dolphins. *Nature* 397:571–72.

Cosmides, L., and J. Tooby. 1992. Cognitive adaptations for social exchange. In *The adapted mind: Evolutionary psychology and the generation of culture*, ed. J. Barkow, L. Cosmides and J. Tooby, 163–228. New York: Oxford University Press.

Curie-Cohen, M., D. Yoshihara, L. Luttrell, K. Benforado, J. W. MacCluer, and W. H. Stone. 1983. The effects of dominance on mating behavior and paternity in a captive troop of rhesus monkeys (*Macaca mulatta*). *American Journal of Primatology* 5 (2): 127–38.

Currie, J. 2009. Healthy, wealthy, and wise: Socioeconomic status, poor health in childhood and human capital development. *Journal of Economic Literature* 47 (1): 87–122.

Darwin, C. 2003. *The origin of species by means of natural selection of the preservation of favoured races in the struggle for life*. New York: Signet Classic.

de Waal, F.B.M. 1978. Exploitative and familiarity-dependent support strategies in a colony of semi-free-living chimpanzees. *Behaviour* 66:268–312.

———. 1982. *Chimpanzee politics: Power and sex among apes*. 25th anniversary ed. Baltimore: Johns Hopkins University Press.

———. 1986. The integration of dominance and social bonding in primates. *Quarterly Review of Biology* 61 (4): 459–79.

———. 1990. *Peacemaking among primates*. Cambridge: Harvard University Press.

———. 1995. Sex as an alternative to aggression in the bonobo. In *Sexual nature, sexual culture*, ed. P. R. Abramson and S. D. Pinkerton, 37–56. Chicago: University of Chicago Press.

———. 1997. The chimpanzee's service economy: Food for grooming. *Evolution and Human Behavior* 18 (6): 375–86.

———. 2001. *The ape and the sushi master: Cultural reflections of a primatologist*. New York: Basic Books.

de Waal, F.B.M., and F. Aureli. 1999. Conflict resolution and distress alleviation in monkeys and apes. In *The integrative neurobiology of affiliation*, ed. C. S. Carter, I. I. Lederhendler, and B. Kirkpatrick, 119–40. Cambridge, Mass.: MIT Press.

de Waal, F. B. M., and M. L. Berger. 2000. Payment for labour in monkeys. *Nature* 404:563.

de Waal, F.B.M., and J. M. Davis. 2003. Capuchin cognitive ecology: Cooperation based on projected returns. *Neuropsychologia* 41:221–28.

Dugatkin, L. A. 1997. *Cooperation among animals: An evolutionary perspective*. Oxford: Oxford University Press.

Dunbar, R.I.M. 1993. Coevolution of neocortical size, group size and language in humans. *Behavioral and Brain Sciences* 16 (4): 681–735.

Duranti, A. 1992. Language and bodies in social space: Samoan ceremonial greetings. *American Anthropologist* 94 (3): 657–91.

Falger, V.S.E. 1992. Cooperation in conflict: Alliances in international politics. In *Coalitions and alliances in humans and other animals*, ed. A. H. Harcourt and F.B.M. de Waal, 323–48. Oxford: Oxford University Press.

Fedigan, L. 1993. Sex differences and intersexual relations in adult white-face capuchins (*Cebus capucinus*). *International Journal of Primatology* 14 (6): 853–77.

Fehr, E., and S. Gächter. 2002. Altruistic punishment in humans. *Nature* 415:137–40.

Fehr, E., and K. M. Schmidt. 1999. A theory of fairness, competition, and cooperation. *Quarterly Journal of Economics* 114 (3): 817–68.

Flemming, T. E., O. D. Jones, T. S. Stoinski, L. Mayo, and S. F. Brosnan. In revision. Endowment effects in orangutans. *Animal Cognition*.

Foster, M. W., I. C. Gilby, C. M. Murray, A. Johnson, E. E. Wroblewski, and A. E. Pusey. 2009. Alpha male chimpanzee grooming patterns: Implications for dominance "style." *American Journal of Primatology* 71:136–44.

Fragaszy, D., and S. Perry, eds. 2003. *The biology of traditions: Models and evidence*. Cambridge: Cambridge University Press.

Frank, R. H. 1988. *Passions within reason: The strategic role of the emotions*. New York: W. W. Norton.

Gilby, I. C. 2006. Meat sharing among the Gombe chimpanzees: Harassment and reciprocal exchange. *Animal Behaviour* 71 (4): 953–63.

Goodall, J. 1968. The behaviour of free-living chimpanzees in the Gombe Stream Reserve. In *Animal behaviour monographs*, 161–311. London: Bailliere, Tindall and Cassell.

———. 1986. *The chimpanzees of Gombe: Patterns of behavior*. Cambridge, Mass.: Belknap.

Hamilton, W. D. 1967. Extraordinary sex ratios. *Science* 156:477–88.

Harcourt, A. H., and F. B.M. de Waal, eds. 1992. *Coalitions and alliances in humans and other animals*. Oxford: Oxford University Press.

Harper, D.G.C. 1991. Communication. In *Behavioural ecology*, ed. J. R. Krebs and N. B. Davies, 364–97. Oxford: Blackwell.

Henrich, J., S. Bowles, R. Boyd, A. Hopfensitz, P. J. Richerson, K. Sigmund, E. A. Smith, F. J. Weissing, and H. P. Young. 2002. The cultural and genetic evolution of human cooperation. In *Genetic and cultural evolution of culture*, ed. P. Hammerstein, 445–68. Cambridge, Mass.: MIT Press.

Henrich, J., and F. Gil-White. 2001. The evolution of prestige: Freely conferred deference as a mechanism for enhancing the benefits of cultural transmission. *Evolution and Human Behavior* 22:165–96.

Hinde, R.A.R., and T. E. Rowell. 1962. Communication by postures and facial expressions in the Rhesus monkey. *Proceedings of the Zoological Society of London* 138:1–21.

Ho, S. Y. W., M. J. Phillips, A. Cooper, and A. J. Drummond. 2005. Time dependency of molecular rate estimates and systematic overestimation of recent divergence times. *Molecular Biology and Evolution* 22 (7): 1561–68.

Hockings, K. J., T. Humle, J. Anderson, D. Biro, C. Sousa, G. Ohashi, and T. Matsuzawa. 2007. Chimpanzees share forbidden fruit. *PLoS ONE* 2 (9): e886.

Horner, V. 2010. The cultural mind of chimpanzees: How social tolerance can shape the transmission of culture. In *The mind of the chimpanzee*, ed. E. V. Lonsdorf, S. Ross and T. Matsuzawa, 105–15. Chicago: University of Chicago Press.

Horner, V., D. Proctor, K. E. Bonnie, A. Whiten, and F.B.M. de Waal. 2010. Prestige affects cultural learning in chimpanzees. *PLoS ONE* 5 (5): e10625.

Idani, C. 1991. Social relationships between immigrant and resident bonobo (*Pan paniscus*) females at Wamba. *Folia Primatologica* 57:82–95.

Isack, H. A., and H. U. Reyer. 1989. Honeyguides and honey gatherers: Interspecific communication in a symbiotic relationship. *Science* 243 (4896): 1343–46.

Isbell, L. A. 1991. Contest and scramble competition: Patterns of female aggression and ranging behavior among primates. *Behavioral Ecology* 2 (2): 143–55.

Jones, O. D., and S. F. Brosnan. 2008. An evolutionary perspective on the endowment effect. *William and Mary Law Review* 49:1935–90.

Kahneman, D., J. L. Knetsch, and R. Thaler. 1990. Experimental tests of the endowment effect and the Coase theorem. *Journal of Economic Perspectives* 98:1325–48.

Knetsch, J. L., and J. A. Sinden. 1984. Willingness to pay and compensation demanded: Experimental evidence of an unexpected disparity in measures of value. *Quarterly Journal of Economics* 99:507–21.

Kuze, N., T. P. Malim, and S. Kohshima. 2005. Developmental changes in the facial morphology of the Borneo orangutan (*Pongo pygmaeus*): Possible signals in visual communication. *American Journal of Primatology* 65:353–76.

Lakshminarayanan, V., M. K. Chen, and L. R. Santos. 2008. Endowment effect in capuchin monkeys. *Proceedings of the Royal Society of London B (Biological Science)* 363:3837–44.

Land, M. F., and D. E. Nilsson. 2002. *Animal eyes*. Oxford: Oxford University Press.

Lasswell, H. D. 1936. *Politics: Who gets what, when and how*. New York: McGraw-Hill.

Lefebvre, L. 1982. Food exchange strategies in an infant chimpanzee. *Journal of Human Evolution* 11:195–204.

Lefebvre, L., and T. A. Hewitt. 1986. Food exchange in captive chimpanzees. In *Current perspectives in primate social dynamics*, ed. D. M. Taub and F. A. King, 476–86. New York: Van Nostrand Reinhold.

LiveLeak.com. 2007. Bolivian congress breaks into massive fist fight. August 22. http://www.liveleak.com/view?i=f75_1187836313 (accessed July 30, 2009).

Mamrack, K. 2010. Councilman plans public statement on fist fight with mayor. *The Dispatch* (Columbus, Miss.), April 3. http://www.cdispatch.com/news/article.asp?aid=5584 (accessed July 2, 2010).

Mann, M. 1986. *The sources of social power*. Vol. 1. Cambridge: Cambridge University Press.

Matsuzawa, T., D. Biro, T. Humle, N. Inoue-Nakamura, R. Tonooka, and G. Yamakoshi. 2008. Emergence of culture in wild chimpanzees: Education by master-apprenticeship. In *Primate origins of human cognition and behavior*, ed. T. Matsuzawa, 557–74. New York: Springer.

Melis, A. P., B. Hare, and M. Tomasello. 2006. Chimpanzees recruit the best collaborators. *Science* 311:1297–1300.

———. 2006. Engineering cooperation in chimpanzees: Tolerance constraints on cooperation. *Animal Behaviour* 72 (2): 275–86.

Mendres, K. A., and F.B.M. de Waal. 2000. Capuchins do cooperate: The advantage of an intuitive task. *Animal Behaviour* 60:523–29.

Menzel, E.W.J. 1973. *Precultural primate behavior*. Basel: Karger.

Morsbach, H. 1988. Nonverbal communication and hierarchical relationships: The case of bowing in Japan. In *Cross-cultural perspectives in nonverbal communication*, ed. F. Poyatos, 189–99. Toronto: Hogrefe.

Morton, J. 1988. "Sakanab": Greetings and information among the Northern Beja. *Africa: Journal of the International Africa Institute* 58 (4): 423–36.

Nissen, H. W., and M. P. Crawford. 1936. A preliminary study of food-sharing behavior in young chimpanzees. *Journal of Comparative Psychology* 22:383–419.

Orams, M. B. 1997. Historical accounts of human-dolphin interaction and recent developments in wild dolphin based tourism in Australia. *Tourism Management* 18 (5): 317–26.

Ottoni, E. B., B. D. de Resende, and P. Izar. 2005. Watching the best nutcrackers: What capuchin monkeys (*Cebus apella*) know about others' tool-using skills. *Animal Cognition* 24:215–19.

Palombit, R. A., D. Cheney, J. Fischer, S. Johnson, D. Rendall, R. Seyfarth, and J. B. Silk. 2000. Male infanticide and defense of infants in chacma baboons. In *Infanticide by males and its implications*, ed. C. P. van Schaik and C. Janson, 123–52. Cambridge: Cambridge University Press.

Palombit, R. A., R. Seyfarth, and D. Cheney. 1997. The adaptive value of "friendships" to female baboons: Experimental and observational evidence. *Animal Behaviour* 54 (3): 599–614.

Paquette, D. 1992. Object exchange between captive chimpanzees: A case report. *Human Evolution* 7 (3): 11–15.

Parish, A. R. 1994. Sex and food control in the "uncommon chimpanzee": How bonobo females overcome a phylogenetic legacy of male dominance. *Ethology and Sociobiology* 15:157–79.

Pongracz, P., V. Vida, P. Banhegyi, and A. Miklosi. 2008. How does dominance rank affect individual and social learning performance in the dog (*Canis familiaris*)? *Animal Cognition* 11:75–82.

Preuschoft, S., and J.A.R.A.M. van Hooff. 1995. Homologizing primate facial displays: A critical review of methods. *Folia Primatologica* 65 (3): 121–37.

Raihani, N. J., A. S. Grutter, and R. Bshary. 2010. Punishers benefit from third-party punishment in fish. *Science* 327 (5962): 171.

Range, F., L. Horn, Z. Viranyi, and L. Huber. 2009. The absence of reward induces inequity aversion in dogs. *Proceedings of the National Academy of Sciences* 106 (1): 340–45.

Range, F., L. Horn, Z. Virányi, and L. Huber. 2009. Effort and reward: Inequity aversion in domestic dogs? *Journal of Veterinary Behavior: Clinical Applications and Research* 4 (2): 45–46.

Rose, N., and P. Miller. 1992. Political power beyond the state: Problematics of government. *British Journal of Sociology* 43 (2): 173–205.

Sapolsky, R. M. 2005. The influence of social hierarchy on primate health. *Science* 308 (5722): 648–52.

Sapolsky, R. M., and L. J. Share. 2004. A pacific culture among wild baboons: Its emergence and transmission. *PLoS Biology* 2 (4): 0534–0541.

Savage-Rumbaugh, E. S., D. M. Rumbaugh, and S. Boysen. 1978. Symbolic communication between two chimpanzees (*Pan troglodytes*). *Science* 201 (18): 641–44.

Schottman, W. 1995. The daily ritual of greeting among the Baatombu of Benin. *Anthropological Linguistics* 37 (4): 487–523.

Seabright, P. 2010. *The company of strangers: A natural history of economic life.* Rev. ed. Princeton. N.J.: Princeton University Press.

Silk, J. B. 1983. Local resource competition and facultative adjustment of sex rations in relation to competitive abilities. *American Naturalist* 121 (1): 56–66.

Silverberg, D. 2010. Ukraine's parliament descends into egg-throwing smoke bomb chaos. *Digital Journal.* http://www.digitaljournal.com/article/291259.

Smith, A. 2000. *The wealth of nations.* Modern Library Classics. New York: Random House.

Smuts, B. 1985. *Sex and friendship in baboons.* Edison, N.J.: Transaction Publishers.

Smuts, B., and D. Gubernick. 1992. Male-infant relationships in nonhuman primates: Paternal investment or mating effort? In *Father-child relations: Cultural and biosocial contexts,* ed. B. Hewlett, 1–30. New York: Aldine de Gruyter.

Smuts, B., and J. Watanabe. 1990. Social relationships and ritualized greetings in adult male baboons (*Papio cynocephalus anubis*). *International Journal of Primatology* 11 (2): 147–72.

Steiper, M. E., and N. M. Young. 2006. Primate molecular divergence dates. *Molecular Phylogenetics and Evolution* 41:384–94.

Trivers, R. L. 1971. The evolution of reciprocal altruism. *Quarterly Review of Biology* 46:35–57.

van Wolkenten, M., S. F. Brosnan, and F.B.M. de Waal. 2007. Inequity responses of monkeys modified by effort. *Proceedings of the National Academy of Sciences* 104 (47): 18854–59.

Visalberghi, E., B. P. Quarantotti, and F. Tranchida. 2000. Solving a cooperation task without taking into account the partner's behavior: The case of capuchin monkeys (*Cebus apella*). *Journal of Comparative Psychology* 114 (3): 297–301.

Vogel, E. R. 2005. Rank differences in energy intake rates in white-faced capuchin monkeys, *Cebus capuchinus*: The effect of contest competition. *Behavioral Ecology and Sociobiology* 58:333–44.

White, F. J. 1989. Ecological correlates of pygmy chimpanzee social structure. In *Comparative socioecology: The behavioural ecology of humans and other mammals,* ed. V. Standen and R. A. Foley, 151–64. Boston: Blackwell Scientific.

Whitham, J., and D. Maestripieri. 2003. Primate rituals: The function of greetings between male Guinea baboons. *Ethology* 109:847–59.

Whitten, P. L. 1983. Diet and dominance among female vervet monkeys (*Cercopithecus aethiops*). *American Journal of Primatology* 5 (2): 139–59.

Wilson, G. 2007. The legal, military and political consequences of the "coalition of the willing" approach to UN military enforcement action. *Journal of Conflict and Security Law* 12 (2): 295.

Wrangham, R. W. 1993. The evolution of sexuality in chimpanzees and bonobos. *Human Nature* 4:47–79.

Wrangham, R. W., and D. Peterson. 1996. *Demonic males.* Boston: Houghton Mifflin.

Yamagishi, T., Y. Horita, H. Takagishi, M. Shinada, S. Tanida, and K. S. Cook. 2009. The private rejection of unfair offers and emotional committment. *Proceedings of the National Academy of Sciences* 106 (28): 11520–23.

Zuckerman, S. 1932. *The social life of monkeys and apes.* New York: Harcourt Brace.

3

FORMAL EVOLUTIONARY MODELING FOR POLITICAL SCIENTISTS

Oleg Smirnov and Tim Johnson

Given their common application to nonhuman entities, evolutionary models seem an odd tool for political scientists. Yet, evolutionary models have a history in political science and, in fact, some of the most engaging work in the discipline has an evolutionary tinge. Consider the central postulate of David Mayhew's *Congress: The Electoral Connection* (1974). Members of Congress aggressively pursue reelection by providing constituents particularized benefits, because those who don't get voted out of office. Something akin to evolution is going on here (Fiorina 1989, 37). All the mechanisms of an evolutionary process— *variation, selection*, and *retention*—operate in Mayhew's explanation of Congress members' behavior. First, Mayhew posits that, conceivably, there is *variation* in the behaviors politicians employ while in office: politicians could pursue personal goals that frustrate constituents, but most engage in activities designed to ensure reelection (37). Second, politicians' behaviors are subject to *selection*: voters choose politicians based on whether or not they distribute particularized benefits (49–77). Third, politicians perceive a link between their past (electorally motivated) behavior and their successful reelection campaigns; thus they retain—that is, continue to engage in—the reelection-minded behaviors that allowed them to pass voters' selective filter (37–38). In sum, although an occasional politician might refuse to pass particularized benefits to constituents, such politicians won't last long in Congress since voters will kick them out of office and, in retrospect, politicians can see this. Viewed thusly, Mayhew's theory is an evolutionary one.

So too is the logic presented by Larry Sabato in *Feeding Frenzy: How Attack Journalism Has Changed American Politics* (2007). Sabato discusses two populations, one of journalists and another of potential public officeholders. Each, it turns out, is subject to evolutionary processes. First, *variation* exists in both populations. Journalists *vary* in their reporting strategies as they can either focus reporting on investigations of politicians' peccadilloes or they can focus their work on "faithfully reporting what's happening day by day" (Hume, quoted in Sabato 2007, 575). Potential public officeholders, on the other hand, *vary* in their arrogance, which influences their willingness to endure the slings and arrows of public life. Each population also exerts *selective pressure* on the other: journalists can reduce the benefits of public office by placing excess scrutiny on politicians personal lives; politicians—by "adopting" severe character flaws—can create incentives for reporters to dig into their foibles. In turn, these selective pressures lead to the *retention* of distinctive behaviors. That is, the better one generation of journalists is at exposing politicians' foibles, the fewer the number of respectable individuals entering public life in the subsequent generation (i.e., character flaws are retained in the politician population) and, subsequently, these flaws encourage future generations of journalists to investigate politicians' personal lives (i.e., the journalist population retains the investigative strategy). Like Mayhew's theory of congressional activity, Sabato's theory explains this undesirable state of affairs with reasoning that pairs fully with the mechanisms of Darwinian evolution.

The theories presented by Mayhew (1974) and Sabato (2007) indicate that evolutionary reasoning can illuminate important political phenomena, even though those political phenomena do not involve the type of objects (e.g., genes) on which evolutionary models normally focus. In order to encourage others to build on informal applications of evolutionary theory in the study of politics, we present a basic introduction to formal evolutionary modeling—such as evolutionary game theory and computational modeling—in this chapter. Although there exist many thorough treatments of evolutionary modeling (see, e.g., Weibull 1995; Samuelson 1997; Gintis 2000; Nowak 2006), few introductions anchor themselves in the content and problems of political science. Our chapter does exactly that—it aims to illustrate how political scientists can identify evolutionary processes so that they can then build and analyze evolutionary game theoretic models that illuminate questions about government and politics. By pursuing this goal, we also hope to clarify current conceptual confusion.

First, our discussion of formal evolutionary modeling will help political scientists distinguish when evolutionary modeling, as opposed to conventional rational-choice modeling, should be used to capture political phenomena. Some informal rational-choice models—for example, the ones mentioned above—can be modeled using the concepts of evolutionary theory, since they embody all the main aspects of evolutionary theory and seem to posit that agents in their model are *retrospectively* (as opposed to prospectively) rational.

Second, our presentation of formal evolutionary theory will illuminate the difference between the literal use of the term *evolution*—that is, to describe a process closely approximating Darwinian selection—and its figurative usage. That is, political theorists and proponents of historical institutionalism often use *evolution* to describe change over time, thus employing the term synonymously with *development* (see, e.g., Thelen 1999). Although we do not object to such uses (language, after all, is the quintessential decentralized evolutionary process that utterly resists command and control), we offer information that will help scholars identify when the term is appropriate. However, *evolution* has a more specific meaning used figuratively and when it is used to describe an evolutionary process involving variation, selection, and retention. Indeed, to help navigate this current conceptual overlap, we will use the terms *formal evolutionary modeling* and *formal evolutionary theory* to emphasize the distinctiveness of this line of theory from both *formal theory* (e.g., rational-choice theory) and the *evolutionary theory* common in both the historical institutionalism and political theory literatures.

Yet, primarily, we aim to provide information that will help political scientists use evolutionary modeling to study theory that can accurately describe many phenomena of political import and contribute to a better understanding of politics and government. The chapter is organized as follows. We begin by conceptually delimiting evolution. In order to prevent confusion resulting from the myriad uses of the term *evolution*, we pin down exactly what we mean by that word and, in so doing, we foreshadow the various components of an evolutionary model. Next, we motivate our primer on evolutionary modeling by discussing its use in fields outside of political science (Bowles 2004) and, as well, its use within political science to study issues of collective action (Bendor and Swistak 1997). This discussion highlights two important features of evolutionary modeling: (1) it can model nonrational behavior that more closely approximates psychological models of judgment and choice, and (2) it can capture out-of-equilibrium dynamics in a manner that standard game theoretic models cannot. With the case made for evolutionary modeling, we then introduce a simple model that casts new light on both the principal-agent problem (Miller 2005) and the influence of civil society on political outcomes. Using this model, we elaborate upon the necessary infrastructure for an evolutionary model, and we illustrate how to study the model for equilibria and characterize out-of-equilibrium dynamics. With this analytic model specified and studied, we then show how computational modeling procedures can be used to extend and explore the model. Following that section, we conclude by pointing toward future applications of evolutionary modeling in political science.

What Is Evolution?

Given that most classes on evolutionary theory are taught in biology departments, many people learn about evolution as a phenomenon that operates on "biological entities"—that is, genes, plants, and animals. Yet, for those who have encountered formal evolutionary theory in, say, a computer science or mathematics course, evolution is a more general, substrate-independent phenomenon (Dennett 1995). Just as evolutionary pressures can affect genetic change across generations, they can also operate on units such as voters, politicians, parties, ideas, technologies, norms, and institutions (see, e.g., Richerson and Boyd 2005). Indeed, evolution can occur—and thus formal evolutionary theory can be used to model—any situation that possesses the following features:

1. *Population:* There exists an identifiable population of agents.
2. *Variation:* Agents in the population vary along some dimension (or, for ease of exposition, we might say that agents are of varying "types").
3. *Selection:* The dimension along which agents vary determines the agents' welfare or *fitness.*
4. *Retention:* A mechanism determines how agents' fitness alters the proportion of different types of agents, in the population, and in the subsequent generation.

When these four conditions exist, evolutionary processes can work. Why? The import of each feature results from the feature following it—a fact that highlights the interdependence of mechanisms that create an evolutionary system.

The first condition emphasizes that evolutionary analysis studies populations, not individuals. This condition is important because individuals—to the extent that they are defined by their unique, stable qualities—cannot vary as populations can. An individual, at any one point in time, cannot at once have brown hair *and* blond hair, or be a Democrat *and* a Republican. Sure, an individual might have sandy-blonde hair and hold centrist values that borrow from both the Democratic and Republican platforms, but that doesn't mean she can vary in these traits at any one time. A population, on the other hand, can exhibit *variation*: two-thirds of the population might have blond hair and one-third might have brown hair; one-half might align with the Democrats and the other half might support Republicans.

Such variation is necessary in order for the selective mechanism of evolution to carry any consequence. That is, evolution occurs because different types in the population replicate at different rates. If there are no different types, then there is no evolution. Mutation, which is the phenomenon in which entities in the population randomly switch types, ensures that variation exists in the population. Differential replication is what is meant by *selection*. The extent to which one trait replicates more rapidly than another trait is the extent to which that trait is selected for over the other trait. So, for instance, if political consultants choose a campaign strategy each election cycle and they adopt strategies in proportion to their success in the previous election cycle, then the extent to which certain campaign strategies are adopted more frequently than other strategies is the extent to which those campaign strategies are selected for over their rivals.

Although that logic seems simple, this concept can be challenging due to the active connotation associated with the word *selection*. The selection process is actually passive—it results either from the differential reproduction of entities possessing certain traits or from mutation (random adoption of a trait), not from any one entity "choosing" one trait over another one. Notice in the above hypothetical case that it is not any one political consultant doing the "selecting": political consultants are simply following a deterministic program stipulating that they adopt more (as opposed to less) successful campaign strategies. It is the success of campaign strategies—which might be the product of, say, voter preferences—that is responsible for "selection," not the preferences or motives of political consultants. Note also that selection results from *relative* comparisons. A campaign strategy needn't be the best imaginable strategy in order to be adopted (see Elster 1979 on this point). The adoption of strategies occurs in proportion to their success; this means that underperforming strategies will eventually cease to be employed and overperforming strategies will grow more common.

The fourth condition, which stipulates that successful variants in the population are retained, illuminates the mechanism underlying selection. It specifies that variants must be transmissible from t, the time period in which selection occurs, to $t + 1$, the following time period. This adds weight to the concept of selection; without transmissible units, selection would not alter the frequency of any trait in the population. Although this condition seems trivial, it has spurred much debate. With respect to biological applications of evolutionary theory, the identification of transmissible genetic units (e.g., DNA) provided important support for Darwin's theory. In the realm of social science applications of evolutionary theory, the notion of retention has sparked controversy because it raises two issues. First, are there nonbiological heritable units that help explain cultural change and, if so, what are they (Dawkins 1989)? Second, how are evolutionary processes modified by the fact that humans have the ability to acquire (or dispense with) seemingly heritable traits (e.g., learned technologies) during the course of a generation (Boyd and Richerson 1985; Richerson and Boyd 2005)? As we will discuss below, these questions have enriched evolutionary models and provided theorists with powerful ways of modeling dynamic phenomena.

Before addressing those extensions, however, it is worth reiterating the core message of this section. Namely, evolution can occur whenever a population of agents exhibits variation along some dimension, traits varying along that dimension replicate across time, and replication occurs in such a way that some traits replicate more frequently than other traits. Note that we have stated these conditions without referring to any "biological entities" such as DNA. This feature of our discussion emphasizes the fact that evolutionary processes can operate on any substantive content so long as the above conditions are present.

Formal Evolutionary Models

The wide range of substantive topics amenable to evolutionary modeling indicates one form of evolutionary modeling's generality. The diverse categories of evolutionary models, each aimed at capturing subtle differences in selective processes, offer another example of the generality of formal evolutionary models. In this section we outline the various methods of modeling evolutionary processes and discuss their applicability to various research topics.

The most general tool for formally modeling the evolution of social behaviors is *evolutionary game theory*. We focus considerable attention on this avenue of formal evolutionary modeling later in this chapter, but we present its basic contours here in order to show its relationship with other forms of formal evolutionary models. Evolutionary game theory studies one or more populations of agents interacting over a series of generations. Agents in the population follow a behavioral program, labeled a strategy, which dictates how they will play a fully specified game each generation. Agents draw these behavioral programs from a finite set of strategies that can dictate either discrete (e.g., cooperate or defect) or continuous (e.g., contribute a fraction of the pie to the public good) behaviors. The game agents play determines the payoffs that result from the combination of choices made by interacting strategies; these payoffs, in turn, translate into agents' fitness at the end of each generation. A replication rule, specified in advance by the researcher, then determines how agents' fitness in the present generation alters the frequency of strategies that agents adopt in the subsequent generation.

Evolutionary game theoretic models such as these are investigated to understand (1) whether or not a strategy (or combination of strategies) is evolutionarily stable—that is, whether or not a population of agents using a given strategy will continue to do so when a small portion of the population chooses to adopt a competing strategy—and (2) what the combination of strategies in the population will be in a subsequent generation, given the current constitution of the population. For those familiar with conventional game theory, the first purpose of these models should be familiar; studying evolutionary stability is analogous to investigating the equilibrium of a game—both are interested in understanding when interacting agents find themselves engaging in behaviors from which they have no incentive to deviate. The second purpose for studying evolutionary game theoretic models, however, is novel and will be discussed more in subsequent sections of this chapter. It allows agents to move beyond the static portrait provided by conventional game theory in order to understand how agents arrive (or fail to arrive) at equilibrium when engaging in out-of-equilibrium behaviors.

Models of *adaptive learning* are a subset of evolutionary models describing the alteration of population-level behavior across time, but they explicitly allow for intragenerational alteration in behavior and rational strategy updating by agents. For this reason, models of adaptive learning are often employed to understand processes of cultural evolution in which agents can transmit behaviors "vertically" (across generations from parent to child) or "horizontally" (between members of the same generation). The selective forces in models of adaptive learning behave similarly to (and, in some instances, exactly the same as) the replication rules in evolutionary game theoretic models. In models of adaptive learning, agents assess the returns to their own and others' behaviors at set points in time. Individuals then choose the most profitable behavior given the past behavior of other individuals in the population. Specifically, an individual follows the history of how other players have played in the past and chooses a strategy for the future that is a best response to the past play of others (Gintis 2000). This can be regarded as a "more intelligent" selection mechanism that resembles a form of Bayesian learning absent any rational expectations about others. Thus, agents can be regarded as *retrospectively* rational since they reasonably respond to past outcomes, but not *prospectively* rational as in conventional game theoretic models where they make optimal choices based on the possible future actions of their game partner. Such models are often most appropriate for nonsocial situations in which outcomes do not depend on the actions of others (for instance, some forms of technology adoption).

Models of *evolutionary imitation* are similar to models of adaptive learning except agents in these models adopt strategies myopically. Instead of choosing behaviors that are a best response to the past actions of others, agents simply choose the behavior that produced the greatest return in the previous time period. Again, such behavior can be modeled in evolutionary game theoretic models via rules of replication that stipulate myopic strategy switching.

Finally, *computational evolutionary models*, which are defined more by their implementation than their content, represent a broad category of evolutionary models. One branch of computational evolutionary models consists of computational implementations of the models described above. That is, any of the models described in previous paragraphs can be implemented computationally and they often are when models become analytically intractable. Some computational models are unique, however, in that they use the principles of natural selection in order to find rough solutions for well-defined, but intractable, optimization problems. Genetic algorithms, which search a solution space by trying out various solutions, gauging the quality of each solution, and then retaining the most successful solutions (or subcomponents of a solution), are perhaps the most diverse and widely employed example of this category of computational model. However, unlike computational implementations of evolutionary game theoretic models, genetic algorithms are less used for theoretical study than for practical applications in, say, engineering or the medical sciences.

Also, in discussing computational evolutionary models, it is important to note that these models represent a subset of *agent-based models* (Gilbert and Troitzsch 1999; Epstein 2007). Agent-based models, put roughly, are simulations used to study the actions of computer-generated agents. Thus, all computational evolutionary models are agent-based models in the sense that they, too, simulate the actions of computer-generated agents. Yet, not all agent-based models are evolutionary models, since many agent-based models do not study evolutionary processes.

Still, with that distinction noted, the menu of evolutionary models remains diverse. This allows scholars to find the correct fit between substantive content and modeling approach. For the purposes of the political scientist, we believe that evolutionary game theoretic models and models of adaptive learning probably offer the greatest potential for addressing questions about politics and government, given their focus on interactive decisionmaking and their ability to model various degrees of agent rationality.

Formal Evolutionary Modeling in Political Science

With the components of evolution spelled out and the diverse range of evolutionary models enumerated, the question now becomes: how can we apply these tools to political phenomena? If other social sciences are any indication, evolutionary theory carries great potential. Over one hundred years have passed since Veblen (1898) applied evolutionary principles in the realm of economics and, during the last half-century or so, other scholars have followed suit (Alchian 1950; Becker 1962; Bowles 2004). These initial forays have led, over the past decades, to a renaissance of formal evolutionary modeling (Maynard Smith 1982; Weibull 1995; Samuelson 1997; Gintis 2000; Nowak 2006). Building on the intellectual foundation of conventional game theory (von Neumann and Morgenstern 1944), formal evolutionary modeling has provided an overarching framework to analyze how social behaviors change over time (Rousseau and van der Veen 2005; Gintis 2006).

In political science, these tools have not been applied as broadly. Rather, evolutionary models have focused almost exclusively on problems of collective action (Axelrod and Hamilton 1981; Axelrod 1986; Bendor and Swistak 1997; Orbell et al. 2004). Nevertheless, specific applications of evolutionary game theory to political phenomena are easier to find in economics, for example, in evolutionary game theoretic models of voting (Conley, Toossi, and Wooders 2001), fairness considerations (Guth and Pull 2004), and cultural dynamics (Vega-Redondo 1993). In this section, we add to this nascent literature by creating an evolutionary game theoretic model of civil society. Not only does the model illustrate how to construct and analyze a simple evolutionary model, but it also offers some empirical predictions about the dynamics of civic engagement and politician behavior.

At the core of the model rests the principal agent problem (Miller 2005): a population of citizens delegates governing authority to a population of public officials. Through their governing efforts, public officials can provide benefits to the population of citizens, but they also can abuse public funds for personal gain. In response to the latter possibility, citizens can either incur costs to scrutinize the activity of public officials or they can remain "rationally ignorant"—as Downs (1957) put it—by failing to take notice of public

officials' actions. If citizens choose to scrutinize public servants and, in so doing, incur the costs of learning about public officials' behavior, then they can
expose corrupt practices and create disutility for public officials who engage
in such unsavory activity. On the other hand, if citizens stay ignorant, they
can forego the cost of learning about public officials' behavior; doing such,
however, allows public officials to reap the benefits of corruption without
paying any costs. Those are the basic features of the model that we will construct and explore in this section.

Yet, why not use conventional rational-choice modeling to study this politically salient situation? Since the pioneering work of Arrow (1951), Downs
(1957), Olson (1965), and Buchanan and Tullock (1962), students of politics have
used rational choice theory to explain and analyze political scenarios of this
sort (Shepsle and Bonchek 1997). The original motives of these practitioners
help explain our choice of methodology. Departing from traditional political theory—which sought to answer the question, "how *should* the political
world be organized to achieve [insert moral objective here]?"—the enterprise
initiated by early rational-choice theorists aimed to answer "why" questions,
such as "why do efforts of collective action often fail?" (Shepsle and Bonchek
1997). To do this, scholars forged a theory founded on the assumption of rational choice and equilibrium analysis. These pillars, however, do not allow
scholars to develop a complete explanation of social, economic, or political
phenomena.

First, the assumption of individual rationality does not correspond with
empirical evidence concerning human judgment and choice. Humans, for
instance, do not reason through all nodes of a game tree using backward in-
duction, nor do they exhaustively gather information to make informed judgments. Instead, individuals rely on simple rules that have proven to work
well in previous, comparable-choice scenarios. These alternative-choice procedures, moreover, do not warrant treating human behavior "as if" it were
rational as they often lead to distinctive predictions from rational choice
theory. Evolutionary models, however, allow scholars to model a wider range
of behavioral and psychological dispositions that more closely resemble reality (Tversky and Kahneman 1982; Simon 1985; Gigerenzer and Todd 1999;
Camerer 2003).

Second, as students of rational choice widely agree, equilibria rarely obtain in the day-to-day world (Chamberlain 1948). It takes time for agents to
converge upon equilibrium or to learn equilibrium behaviors. For instance,
sometimes individuals make mistakes and sometimes parameters of the game
change (Greif and Laitin 2004). For all these reasons, equilibria can come

undone or can take time to emerge; either way, the static portrait of conventional rational choice fails to explain these situations. Evolutionary models, however, can help scholars understand the path to equilibrium by tracing the out-of-equilibrium dynamics of a population.

For these two reasons, formal evolutionary models allow scholars to capture aspects of the social and political world that cannot be studied using conventional game theoretic models. Of course, this bold statement should be demonstrated, not just stated, and, thus, in the next section, we specify the evolutionary model of civil society that we informally introduced above. In so doing, we hope to demonstrate not only the methods of developing and analyzing evolutionary models, but also the intellectual dividends that such models produce for political science.

Specifying an Evolutionary Game Theoretic Model

Evolutionary game theoretic models simulate the processes of evolution—that is, variation, selection, and retention—via five basic components: (1) agents, (2) the strategies agents can adopt, (3) the rules governing agent interaction, (4) the payoffs resulting from game interactions, and (5) the replication process.

Agents in the model exist in either a population or populations. In a single-population model, all agents share the same underlying characteristics—such as the set of game strategies available to them—and they reproduce according to one set of rules. In a multipopulation model, members of each population may have a different strategy set available to them and, as well, they may be subject to dissimilar replication processes.[2]

For instance, in the model of civil society that we develop, we study two populations—(1) citizens and (2) public officials. Each population has two strategies available to them. Citizens can either remain rationally ignorant, thereby avoiding the costs of monitoring public officials, or they can incur costs investigating the deeds of public servants. Public officials, on the other hand, can choose to pursue personal benefits at a cost to citizens, or they can act dutifully by complying with citizens' wants. An agent adopts a strategy at the beginning of a generation and once an agent—whether a citizen or a public official—chooses a strategy, it abides by that strategy for the duration of a generation. Thus, practitioners of evolutionary game theory often refer to different strategies as "types"—just as you might refer to a reliable person as "the type of person on which you can rely."

Strategies represent the variation on which selective forces operate. The fixed strategy adopted by an agent specifies exactly what it will do over the course of a generation. These behaviors can either be straightforward (e.g., always cooperate, always monitor, always attack) or conditional (e.g., cooperate with those who use the same strategy, monitor every other round, attack if you have been attacked in a previous game). Most important, the strategy represents an exhaustive plan of all possible contingencies in the game that agents play.

The third component of an evolutionary model is the rules of interaction. The standard evolutionary game theoretic approach is to assume random matching: each agent in the population is equally likely to be paired with any other agents in the population. This assumption of random matching, however, is frequently relaxed in order to model real-world phenomena—such as ethnic markers or the built environment—that influence the probability of agents encountering each other. For instance, Riolo, Alexrod, and Cohen (2001) have examined how arbitrary tags allow agents playing Prisoner's Dilemma games to sort themselves in such a way that cooperators are more likely to interact with each other than with defectors, thereby limiting defection and allowing cooperation to easily evolve. Similarly, spatial structures have been shown to facilitate cooperation by allowing cooperators to form prosocial neighborhoods whose fitness greatly exceeds that obtained by groupings of defectors (Langer, Nowak, and Hauert 2008). In both types of models, the mechanism responsible for cooperative success is the same: the frequency of interaction.

In the baseline evolutionary game theoretic model we construct, we assume that agents are randomly paired. That is, there is an equally likely chance that any citizen gets "paired" with a given public official. One can interpret that pairing, substantively, by imagining that each citizen—if they were to investigate political corruption—would choose a given public official who may or may not be corrupt. Of course, it would be interesting to examine how changing the frequency of interaction—say, so that investigative citizens would be more apt to scrutinize shady politicians—would alter the model's results. This and other alternative assumptions can be examined analytically in a simple evolutionary game theoretic model or, if necessary, in a more complex computational model.

When referring to such results—including those of the previous investigations of nonrandom pairing—we primarily mean an analysis of the relative payoffs, obtained by different strategies, in the modeled population or populations. In order to study payoffs, however, one first needs to specify them. Payoff specification is thus the fourth crucial component of an evolutionary game model. Specification of payoffs in an evolutionary game theoretic model is similar to that in a standard game theoretic model. Payoffs in the evolutionary model carry a different interpretation. Instead of the notion of "utility," evolutionary game theoretic models use the notion of "fitness." Outcomes are not measured by the satisfaction they give agents, but, rather, by the number of replicants produced by the agent.

The rate of replication—the fifth and final necessary component of a game theoretic model—is determined by rules that detail how the composition of types in the population changes from one generation to another due to the payoffs earned in game encounters. A standard approach is to use a replicator dynamics model, which stipulates that the proportions of types in a population (or subpopulation) change proportional to the average fitness of types (we provide a formal definition below). If the fitness difference is large, the proportions change fast; if the fitness difference is zero, the proportions of types in the population do not change at all. Other mechanisms of replication are possible, however. For instance, as other texts discuss in great detail (see, e.g., Weibull 1995 or Samuelson 1997), the rules of replication can be changed to model social biases (e.g., conformism: the rate at which agents switch to a certain type increases as the proportion of that type grows in the population). As well, in social science models, we may wish to alter the rules of replication so that agents may change types within their lifetime depending on the types' payoffs relative to other types. Such procedures model intragenerational learning, for instance, and are also widely discussed in other texts (e.g., Richerson and Boyd 1985). Regardless of the replication rules, however, notice that types "compete" only within each population and never across. For instance, in the model of civil society that we develop, citizens choose strategies only by comparing their payoffs to those of other citizens and, then, switching their strategy (on average) based on whether or not other their present strategy is performing worse than the strategy employed by other citizens. The same holds for public officials—they only compare their payoffs with agents in the same population. This feature of the model makes intuitive sense. Although individuals often try to "keep-up-with-the-Joneses," few would do so if the Joneses happened to be landed aristocrats who inherited uncountable fortunes. Most folks make comparisons within an appropriate reference class and formal evolutionary game theoretic models take into account this fact.

Together, the components listed in this section create an evolutionary game theoretic model. Yet, this is only the first part of using evolutionary models to better understand political phenomena. Once a model is constructed, it begs to be studied; in the next section, we show how this can be done.

Studying an Evolutionary Game Theoretic Model

Scholars produce evolutionary game theoretic models in order to draw predictions from them; those predictions result from careful study that aims to understand the equilibrium and out-of-equilibrium behavior of the population (or populations) in the model. To illustrate how one studies an evolutionary game theoretic model, we again return to our model of civil society.

Our model consists of two infinitely large populations, each having two strategies that agents in the respective population can adopt. For the population of citizens, two strategies are available—citizens can either be a "learner" (L) or an "ignoramus" (I). Public officials, on the other hand, can either be "honest" (H) or "corrupt" (C). Furthermore, each strategy, in each population, carries associated costs and benefits. For citizens who adopt the "learner" strategy, a cost $c > 0$ of learning about the activity of public officials is incurred. However, the public benefit to a citizen, whenever a corrupt official is exposed by a "learner," is $b > 0$. When a corrupt public official is exposed, the public servant suffers a punishment x such that $x > 0$. Public officials, however, earn profits from corruption and we represent the values of these profits by y, which always is a positive value: $y > 0$. Moreover, we model the proportion of types in the population using the following notation. The proportion of learners in society is p where $0 \leq p \leq 1$, meaning that the proportion of citizens employing the "ignoramus" strategy is $1 - p$. The proportion of public officials adopting the "honest" strategy is q where $0 \leq q \leq 1$, meaning that the proportion of corrupt public officials is $1 - q$. Combining this information, we arrive at the payoff matrix displayed in table 3.1.

The first step in studying this model—and any other evolutionary model—is to identify any equilibrium or equilibria. We first examine the model for Nash equilibria since these equilibria will help us delimit the conditions in which a strategy might be evolutionarily stable. From conventional game theory, we know that a strategy is a Nash equilibrium if no player obtains greater payoffs by unilaterally switching her strategy. Following from this definition, we can see that if the cost of learning is greater than the public benefit ($b < c$), the game has a unique pure strategy Nash equilibrium: all

TABLE 3.1. Two-population evolutionary game (citizens and public officials)

		Public officials	
		Honest, q	Corrupt, $(1-q)$
Citizens	Learner, p	$b - c, 0$	$b - c, -y$
	Ignorant, $(1 - p)$	$b, 0$	$0, x$

citizens stay ignorant and all public officials are corrupt. No player—whether citizen or public official—would obtain greater benefits by pursuing an alternative strategy to those constituting this Nash equilibrium. However, in a more plausible case, when $b > c$ (that is, where investigating public officials is actually worthwhile), there is only a mixed strategy Nash equilibrium (p^*, q^*). Citizens choose to learn with a probability $p^* = x/(x+y)$ and politicians are honest with a probability $q^* = (b-c)/b$.

Although the Nash solution concept provides us some insight into the equilibrium properties of the model, it does not tell us whether the equilibrium or equilibria it identifies are robust to arbitrary fluctuations in the population composition. This is a very subtle, but important point. Conventional game theoretic analysis asks the question, "What actions would individuals have to take for them to have no incentive to deviate from those actions?" Evolutionary game theoretic analyses, on the other hand, ask the question, "If a population of individuals engages in a stable combination of actions across time, how substantially would that combination of actions have to change in order for the population *not* to return to the original, stable combination of actions?" In order to answer the latter question, which highlights the import of out-of-equilibrium dynamics in evolutionary models, we begin by evaluating the model for evolutionary stable strategies (ESS)—that is, strategies that resist subtle changes in population composition.

Formally, we can define an ESS by considering conditions in which a strategy, Z_i, cannot be invaded by another strategy Z_j. Following convention (Nowak 2006), we denote the fitness of Z_i, resulting from an interaction with Z_j, as $\pi(Z_i, Z_j)$. A strategy Z_i obtains the ESS designation if the following condition holds for all $j \neq i$:

(1) $$\pi(Z_i, Z_i) > \pi(Z_j, Z_i)$$

or

(2) $$\pi(Z_i, Z_j) = \pi(Z_j, Z_i) \text{ and } \pi(Z_i, Z_j) > \pi(Z_j, Z_j).$$

Notice the similarity of this definition to that of a Nash equilibrium:

(3) $$\pi(Z_i, Z_i) \geq \pi(Z_j, Z_i)$$

All ESS are Nash equilibrium, as (1) and (3) indicate, but not all Nash equilibrium are ESS. Condition (1) states that one way for Z_i to be ESS is if the payoff to strategy Z_i, when interacting with a member of the population employing the same strategy, exceeds the payoff to Z_j when interacting with Z_i. This makes sense once you remember that we are considering the situation in which strategy Z_i is ubiquitous and Z_j represents a minute portion of the population. With that in mind, this condition is intuitive: (i) since a very large portion of the population consists of agents using Z_i interactions between two agents employing Z_j is highly unlikely; (ii) given (i), the payoffs accruing to Z_i and Z_j will mainly result from interactions with Z_i; and, thus, (iii) if Z_i does better when encountering another Z_i than does Z_j it makes sense that no agents in the population would want to switch to using Z_j as they would be worse off for doing so.

Condition (2) suggests that we need to look at what happens between invaders if it turns out that the invading strategies do equally well as the incumbent, ubiquitous strategy. That is, when the payoff to Z_i when playing against Z_j equals the payoff that Z_i gets when playing against Z_i, then the only way that selection could favor Z_i is if Z_i earned more playing against invaders than Z_j earn playing against other invaders. Again, this makes sense intuitive sense. A population would want to switch strategies if it found out that another strategy yielded greater returns. Thus, if the population is using the incumbent strategy, then it first wants to know if the incumbent strategy is doing better than the invading strategy or strategies when it is playing against the incumbent strategy. If the incumbent strategy's payoff is the same as that earned by the invader(s) playing against it, then it is unclear if it is worth switching. Thus, the population would want to check if the "small" portion of the fitness function matters; that is, in the small number of encounters strategies have with mutant invaders, how well, relatively, is each strategy doing? If it turns out that invaders do better against themselves than the incumbent strategy does against invaders, then it makes sense to switch—there are no conditions in which the incumbent is doing strictly better. However, if the incumbent strategy does better than the invading strategy or strategies, then it makes sense to remain using the incumbent strategy since one does not increase fitness by switching. In this latter instance, the strategy is ESS. As you may have surmised, the relationship between Nash equilibria and ESS can be inferred from condition 2. A Nash equilibrium obtains even when the second half of condition 2 (the portion after the "and") doesn't hold, but, for an ESS to obtain, the second half of condition 2 must hold (for the reasoning specified above).

Working through a simple example, prior to returning to the two-population model, may help to reinforce this reasoning. Consider a model

TABLE 3.2. One-population evolutionary game (citizens)

	Investigate	Ignore
Investigate	4, 4	3, 5
Ignore	5, 3	0, 0

consisting solely of a population of citizens who can either investigate politicians (α) or remain ignorant (β) of those politician's activities. Substantively, this can be interpreted as a situation in which it *always* pays to monitor politicians. That is, unlike in the two-population model, in this model there are no honest politicians, only charlatans who need to be watched. We assume that investigating politicians involves costs but produces information that yields a benefit. Moreover, those benefits are greatest when agents can collaborate on an investigation by joining disparate pieces of information (for example, citizen 1: "the politician is embezzling government funds"; citizen 2: "the politician's mistress is wearing a new diamond bracelet"). Together, these assumptions yield a preference ordering consistent with the payoff matrix displayed in table 3.2. We use a numerical example here.

To examine if a strategy is ESS, we first check for Nash equilibria because we know that if there is an ESS it must satisfy the conditions of this "simpler" solution concept. Examination of the payoff matrix indicates that no strategy is a pure Nash equilibrium: informally, we can state that it pays to investigate politicians when your game partner ignores them, and vice versa. There is, however, a mixed-strategy Nash equilibrium. Setting each player's payoff function against the other and solving for p, we find:

(4) $$4p + 3(1-p) = 5p \Rightarrow p = 0.75$$

The algebra in (4) indicates that in a mixed strategy Nash equilibrium, players investigate politicians with probability 0.75 and they ignore politicians' activities with probability 0.25. This mixing strategy can be interpreted directly in an evolutionary game theoretic context as a strategy (γ) that varies its play consistent with the proportions specified in the mixed Nash equilibrium. Is such a strategy an ESS?

To address this question, we want to examine if the mixing strategy can resist an invasion by an infinitesimally small proportion of citizens playing the investigate strategy. We compare the payoffs of the mixing strategy versus itself—viz. $\pi(\gamma, \gamma)$—with those of the investigative strategy versus the mixing strategy—$\pi(\alpha, \gamma)$:

(5.1) $\pi\,(\gamma,\,\gamma)=0.75(0.75*4+0.25*3)+0.25(0.75*5+0.25*0)=3.75$

(5.2) $\pi(\alpha,\,\gamma)=0.75*4+0.25*3=3.75$

Since $\pi\,(\gamma,\,\gamma)=\pi(\alpha,\,\gamma)$, we then check if $\pi(\gamma,\,\alpha)>\pi(\alpha,\,\alpha)$:

(6.1) $\pi(\gamma,\,\alpha)=0.75*4+0.25*5=4.25$

(6.2) $\pi(\alpha,\,\alpha)=4$

Therefore, the mixing strategy resists invasion by a small fraction of citizens who switch their strategy to investigate. The same can be found when analyzing an invasion by those using the ignore strategy. First we examine if $\pi(\gamma,\,\gamma)$ $>\pi(\beta,\,\alpha)$:

(7) $\pi(\beta,\,\alpha)=0.75*5+0.25*0=3.75$

Again, since $\pi(\gamma,\,\gamma)=\pi(\beta,\,\gamma)$, we then check if $\pi(\gamma,\,\beta)>\pi(\beta,\,\beta)$:

(8.1) $\pi(\beta,\,\alpha)=0.75*3+0.25*0=2.25$

(8.2) $\pi(\beta,\,\beta)=0$

Once more, we find that the mixing strategy resists invasion. In general, an ESS resists invasion of mutant pure as well as mixed strategies.

Not all games have an ESS, however, and, indeed, in the two-population model we study there is no ESS. Remember that in our model there is a population of citizens that can either be a "learner" (L) or an "ignoramus" (I) and a population of public officials that can either be "honest" (H) or "corrupt" (C). Moreover, when interacting, each type earns the payoffs specified in table 3.1, such that there exists a mixed Nash equilibrium (p^*, q^*). Citizens choose to learn with a probability $p^*=x/(x+y)$ and politicians are honest with a probability $q^*=(b-c)/b$.

The fitness payoff of learners is $\pi_L=b-c$, while the average citizen fitness is

(9) $$\pi_c = p(b-c) + (1-p)bq.$$

According to a simple continuous replicator dynamics model, the proportion of learners grows at a rate $\dot{p} = p(\pi_L - \pi_c)$, or

(10) $$\dot{p} = p(b-c-(p(b-c)+(1-p)bq)).$$

The fitness of honest officials is $\pi_c = 0$, while the average public official has a fitness of

(11) $$\pi_p = (1-q)(-xp+y(1-p))$$

Thus, the growth rate of honest politicians is

(12) $$\dot{q} = q(1-q)(xp-y)(1-p))).$$

We can verify that for the mixed strategy Nash equilibrium $(p^\star, q^\star)$, the growth rates for both populations are zero, that is, $\dot{p} = 0$ and $\dot{q} = 0$ for $p^\star = y/(x+y)$ and $q^\star = (b-c)/b$. In the evolutionary model, however, the equilibrium has minimal empirical relevance. For an asymmetric evolutionary game, an evolutionary stable strategy profile must be a strict Nash equilibrium (all populations must be monomorphic, e.g., all citizens are learners and all politicians are honest). Otherwise, no strategy profile can be evolutionary stable (Gintis 2000, 211). Specifically, Gintis (2000, 212) proves the following theorem: "In the asymmetric evolutionary game in which each player has two pure strategies, a mixed strategy Nash equilibrium $(p^\star, q^\star)$ is either unstable or an evolutionary focal point. In the latter case, all trajectories are closed orbits around the fixed point." Thus, evolutionary analysis tells us that the mixed-strategy Nash equilibrium prediction is essentially meaningless in a two-population model since there is a strong tendency toward oscillations as opposed to convergence. The exact nature of the oscillations can be seen in a replicator dynamics phase diagram, which we describe below. The replicator dynamics can be represented graphically in the form of a phase diagram (3.1).

Payoff matrix parameters: $b = 4, c = 1, x = 3, y = 1$. The proportion of learners in the population is p; the proportion of honest politicians is q. Arrows in the phase diagram indicate how the proportions of types change for any given composition of types in the population. The length of arrow indicates the speed of selection, which is directly proportional to fitness differences among types.

Creating a phase diagram is similar to plotting a complex function. For a 2×2 evolutionary game theoretic model, we can create a two-dimensional phase diagram with horizontal axis representing the proportion of honest public officials q and vertical axis representing the proportion of learners p. For any given combination of p and q, we can find $\dot{p}$ and $\dot{q}$, which describe the direction and speed of evolutionary selection (or an "evolutionary trajectory"). Notice that in order to find numerical values for $\dot{p}$ and $\dot{q}$, we will need to assign numerical values to the set of model parameters.

Consider the following example. Assume the following model parameters: b=4, c=1, x=3, y=1. Let us find, the evolutionary trajectory $[\dot{p},\dot{q}]$ for p=0.5 and q=0.5, which corresponds exactly to the center of the phase diagram. Using equations (2) and (4) above we can find that for these parameters $\dot{p}$=0.25 and $\dot{q}$=0.25. In other words, if 50% of citizens are learners and 50% of public officials are honest, we would expect selection to increase the proportions of learners and honest officials. On the other hand, consider the case of p=0.8 and q=0.8. Now the evolutionary trajectory becomes $\dot{p}$= −0.032 and $\dot{q}$=0.352. While the proportion of honest officials continues to grow, the proportion of learners declines, albeit a slow rate. These examples can be verified in figure 3.1 representing the phase diagram for the parameters specified above.

While it is straightforward, if laborious, to create a phase diagram manually, it is much easier to use a computer program. The latter typically requires only specification of the payoff matrix and, in some cases, the types of evolutionary mechanism with replicator dynamics being the most common one. The phase diagram in figure 3.1 was created by means of the Dynamo package for Mathematica 5 (Sandholm and Dokumaci 2007).

If we want to model the evolutionary dynamics in discrete time, with each time period representing a generation, we can modify the replicator dynamics for a discrete temporal scale. According to this model, to find the change in the proportion of a type, we divide the fitness of the type by the average population fitness, i.e.:

(13.1)
$$P_{t+1} = P_t\left(\frac{b-c}{p(b-c)+(1-p)bq}\right),$$

(13.2)
$$q_{t+1} = q_t\left(\frac{K}{K+xp-y(1-p)}\right),$$

where K is a constant making the nominator payoff positive. The discrete-time version is especially convenient if we want to examine the model using

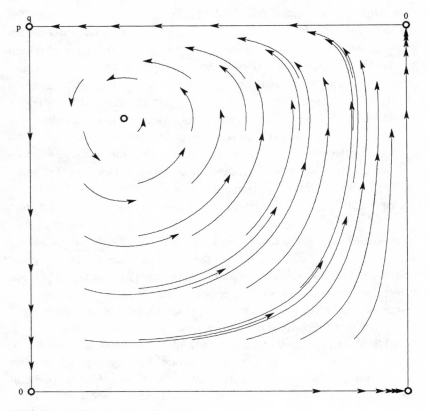

FIGURE 3.1. Replicator dynamics phase diagram.

computer simulation with explicitly specified time steps. In the next section we build such a model.

The evolutionary game theoretic model above provides us with some general insights into the operations of civil society. If one agrees with the assumptions our model is founded upon, then it becomes apparent that the strategies under study are self-limiting. The relative gains to monitoring, for instance, decline as the scrutiny of "learners" wipes out corrupt public officials; in turn, the decline of corrupt officials increases the payoffs of "rationally ignorant" citizens, who enjoy the benefits of honest politicians without having to incur the costs shouldered by "learners." As these "ignoramuses" proliferate, however, the lack of scrutiny placed on public officials allows corrupt officials to prosper, thereby reducing the benefits of "rational ignorance" and creating greater relative returns to monitoring. So, in sum, the model predicts that fluctuations in citizen involvement and public official honesty will character-ize civil society.

This finding engages with the argument put forth by Sabato (2007 [1991]), which we discussed in the opening of this chapter. Sabato describes a socially detrimental evolutionary process between a population of journalists (similar to the population of citizens in our model) and a population of politicians. He claims that increased media scrutiny selects for brazen politicians who pos-sess undesirable peccadilloes. In turn, when journalists expose those politi-cians' faults, they receive benefits and those benefits select for investigative journalism strategies that further select for brazen political types. Our model suggests that the downward spiral Sabato identifies might be self-limiting, if one modifies some of the assumptions he makes. That is, Sabato seems to assume that the investigative strategy yields a cost to honest politician types, not just to corrupt types; this cost keeps honest types out of the public sphere, but it does not deter corrupt types. We don't make that assumption. Rather, we hold that investigating a squeaky-clean public figure imposes no costs on the politician (only the citizen conducting the investigation incurs costs). Un-der that assumption, we find that the investigative strategy drives down the proportion of corrupt types in the politician population. Yet, as fewer corrupt types enter the political sphere, the benefits to the investigative strategy de-cline and this reduces the number of citizens investigating politicians. With fewer citizens monitoring politicians, shady individuals can again regain po-litical office. Future efforts might profitably explore the relationship between our model and the interesting ideas Sabato presents. A careful effort to for-malize the informal model put forth by Sabato, coupled with an extension of our model, might yield new insights and empirical predictions concerning the interplay of civil society and public official integrity.

Creating and Studying a Computational Evolutionary Model

By themselves, the insights offered by our evolutionary game theoretic model provide baseline predictions about how civic involvement and political cor-ruption might fluctuate, across two populations, over time. Those predictions might not provide sufficient guidance for empirical analyses, however.

For one, any simple theoretical model may sacrifice important compo-nents of the phenomenon under study in order to achieve analytic tractabil-ity. When theorists take such an approach, they intentionally trade off verisi-militude for parsimony and, in so doing, they knowingly limit their model's ability to guide empirical analyses. This approach pays dividends for some research questions (for instance, when theoretically exploring the *possibility* of a phenomena—say, given acceptable assumptions about democratic politics, is it *possible* for a democracy to incarcerate the majority of its citizens?), but it may not be appropriate if one seeks to develop a descriptive model that makes empirical predictions.

Second, abstract theoretical models may not draw enough attention to the specific phenomena that obtain when model parameters take realistic values. For instance, in the model we study in this section, it may be that the actual composition of, say, the populations of citizens and public officials in the United States closely approximates the mixed strategy Nash Equilibrium identified in our analysis. If that is the case, then we would expect to see, over time, much smaller fluctuations in the composition of each respective population than we would expect if we examined the modal generation-to-generation fluctuation displayed in the phase diagram. Although the model provides the information we need in order to make predictions, it provides additional information that may distract empirical analysts from realizing the predictive potential of the model.

To develop a more realistic model that produces better empirical predictions, scholars can resort to the computational modeling of evolutionary processes. Computational models allow agents to introduce additional populations, types, and variables into the model since analytical tractability is of little concern. These computational models then produce simulated data that can be compared with actual data in order to understand both the phenomenon under study and the reliance of the initial theoretical model on its simplifying assumptions.

Fortunately, formal evolutionary models can be programmed in a very intuitive way. See the appendix for a generic example of a complex evolutionary game theoretic model programmed in R (modified from Smirnov et al. 2010). The construction of this model follows a series of simple procedures. First, since computational processes require numerical input, the first task is to specify the model parameters (e.g., $b=4$, $c=1$, $x=3$, $y=1$) as well as important simulation parameters such as the population size and the number of generations (i.e., how long the simulation will run). Instead of using an abstract parameter, computational methods model the population as a data array that is used to record how the proportions of types change from one generation to another. Thus, the size of the array will be defined as the number of generations multiplied by the number of types. In order to implement replicator dynamics we will need to introduce additional arrays describing each type's population proportion and fitness. The population array will have a size equal to the number of agents multiplied by two. The two variables describing each agent are fitness and type.

To execute random matching, each generation each agent is randomly assigned to another agent. All agents play exactly one game per generation—an assumption that is easy to relax. In order to implement the replicator dynamics, we need to calculate the average population fitness (AFP). Thus, for each type, we will need to calculate the average fitness of all agents belonging to the type i ($AF[i]$). This allows us to find the new proportions of types ($P[i]$) in the population for the next generation. To create a new population of players given $P[i]$, we can use R's multinomial random number generation function. The probability that a newborn agent is assigned to a type i will be $P[i]$. Notice that new proportions of types in the population may be slightly different from the values of $P[i]$ given the multinomial random number generation. This approach is an example of stochastic replicator dynamics.

This basic model can be easily modified and made more complicated with extra features and modeling assumptions. For example, agents may interact on a spatial landscape instead of random matching (cf. Epstein 2007). Agents may interact with others selectively based upon certain attributes such as tags or reputation (cf. Riolo, Axelrod, and Cohen 2001). Agents may be endowed with mindreading capacities being able to recognize the type of the opponent with a certain probability (cf. Orbell et al. 2004), and so on. The complexity makes the evolutionary model analytically not tractable and, therefore, the computational method becomes a necessity.

While these particular methods illustrate the basic contours of crafting a computational evolutionary model, there exist innumerable ways to implement such models. Further source materials to determine the most efficient means of model construction for their specific substantive interests can be found in Baeck, Fogel, and Michalewicz (1997), for instance, who provide a comprehensive and accessible treatment of the subject. Through such works one should be able to craft models that further explore analytic investigations and produce empirically relevant results.

Conclusion

Formal evolutionary modeling provides political scientists with a novel toolkit in order to understand a broad range of political phenomena. Evolutionary analyses focus on aggregate changes in behavior (as is often the case in political science research—e.g., survey research) without sacrificing methodological individualism. Evolutionary models also allow students to study out-of-equilibrium dynamics that make predictions about political changes over long time scales. In sum, these models open up new opportunities for political scientists, without closing the door on traditional analyses involving the study of individual behavior in equilibrium.

Indeed, for students comfortable with the technology of conventional rational choice, these tools should appear attractive in that they allow for rigorous analysis that addresses the criticism that rational choice can tell us little about political change occurring over time and out-of-equilibrium (see discussion in Katznelson and Weingast 2007). On the flip side of that coin, evolutionary modeling allows students interested in political change to refine their discussion of temporal dynamics; via evolutionary modeling, scholars can pin down exactly what processes underlie the historical events that importantly determine political outcomes. And, on a related note, gaining familiarity with formal evolutionary modeling will allow political science students to recognize evolutionary processes when they see them. Such capabilities will allow for more appropriate model selection and, as a result, will facilitate a deeper understanding of the political phenomena under study.

As well, given the impressive list of empirical findings on display in this volume, a thorough, formal understanding of evolution will caution scholars against causally devising "just so stories" that frame empirical data in armchair evolutionary theories. By studying evolution rigorously, scholars gain appreciation for the counterintuitive and complex phenomena that can result from the rote churning of variation, selection, and retention. Such surprising directions are at once humbling and exciting, an admonition against careless speculation and an invitation to use the tools of formal evolutionary analysis to better illuminate the world of politics and government.

Appendix: Example of an Evolutionary Game Theoretic Model in R

```
#replace simulation parameters with own relevant values
#population size, number of generations
N=400; G=200;
#payoff matrix for a symmetric (one population) game with five types
GAME=t(array(c(1,2,1,1,1,
1,1,2,1,1,
1,1,1,2,1,
```

```
1,1,1,1,2,
2,1,1,1,1),dim=c(5,5)))
      #data array to record proportions of types for each generation
data=array(0,dim=c(G,5))
#arrays for type operations: total players, proportion, average type fitness
Tot=array(0,dim=c(5));p=array(0,dim=c(5));AF=array(0,dim=c(5))
      #population array: fitness, type
pop=array(0,dim=c(N,2))
#initial proportions of types (must sum to one)
p=c(0.2,0.2,0.2,0.2,0.2)
      #transposed multinomial random number generation
pop[1:N,2]=max.col(t(rmultinom(N,1,c(p[1],p[2],p[3],p[4],p[5]))))
      #generations start
for (g in 1:G) {
          #random matching and player (x,y) interaction
          match=sample(1:N)
          for (i in seq(1,N,2)) {
              x=match[i]; y=match[i+1]
              pop[x,1]=pop[x,1]+GAME[pop[x,2],pop[y,2]]
              pop[y,1]=pop[y,1]+GAME[pop[y,2],pop[x,2]]
          }
          #average population fitness
          AFP=sum(pop[1:N,1])/N
              #proportions and fitness of the types
          for (i in 1:5) {
              Tot[i]=sum(pop[1:N,2] = i)
              p[i]=data[g,i]=Tot[i]/N
              if (Tot[i]>0) AF[i]=sum(pop[pop[1:N,2]=i,1])/Tot[i]
                  #stochastic discrete replicator dynamics
              p[i]=p[i]*(AF[i]/AFP)
          }
      #individual types given aggregate level proportions (here: probabilities)
pop[1:N,2]=max.col(t(rmultinom(N,1,c(p[1],p[2],p[3],p[4],p[5]))));
      #reset starting fitness
pop[1:N,1]=0;
      #generations end
}
plot(data[,1],type="l",col="red",ylim=c(0,1))
```

```
lines(data[,2],col="blue"); lines(data[,3],col="green"); lines(data[,4],col="brown");
lines(data[,5])
    #remove comment to save 'data'
    #write.csv(data, file="sim_data.txt")
```

References

Alchian, A. 1950. Uncertainty, evolution, and economic theory. *Journal of Political Economy* 58:211–21.

Arrow, K. J. 1951. *Social choice and individual values.* New York: Wiley.

Axelrod, R. 1986. An evolutionary approach to norms. *American Political Science Review* 80:1095–1111.

———. 1997. *The complexity of cooperation: Agent-based models of competition and collaboration.* Princeton, N.J.: Princeton University Press.

Axelrod, R., and W. D. Hamilton. 1981. The evolution of cooperation. *Science* 211 (4489): 1390–96.

Baeck, T., D. B. Fogel, and Z. Michalewicz. 1997. *Handbook of evolutionary computation.* Oxford: Oxford University Press.

Becker, G. S. 1962. Irrational behavior and economic theory. *Journal of Political Economy* 70:1–13.

Bendor, J., and P. Swistak. 1997. Evolutionary stability of cooperation. *American Political Science Review* 91 (2): 290–307.

Bowles, S. 2004. *Microeconomics: Behavior, institutions, and evolution.* New York: Russell Sage.

Boyd, R., and P. J. Richerson. 1985. *Culture and the evolutionary process.* Chicago: University of Chicago Press.

Buchanan, J. M., and G. Tullock. 1962. *The calculus of consent: Logical foundations of constitutional democracy.* Ann Arbor: University of Michigan Press.

———. 1990. *The calculus of consent.* Indianapolis: Liberty Fund.

Camerer, C. F. 2003. *Behavioral game theory.* Princeton, N.J.: Princeton University Press.

Chamberlain, E. H. 1948. An experimental imperfect market. *Journal of Political Economy* 56 (2): 95–108.

Conley, J. P., A. Toossi, and M. Wooders. 2001. Evolution and voting: How nature makes us public spirited. The Warwick Economics Research Paper Series 601. Department of Economics, University of Warwick, England.

Dawkins, R. 1989. *The selfish gene.* 2nd ed. Oxford: Oxford University Press.

Dennett, D. C. 1995. *Darwin's dangerous idea.* New York: Touchstone.

Downs, A. 1957. *An economic theory of democracy.* Boston: Addison Wesley.

Elster, J. 1979. *Ulysses and the Sirens: Studies in rationality and irrationality.* Cambridge: Cambridge University Press.

Epstein, J. M. 2007. *Generative social science: Studies in agent-based computational modeling.* Princeton, N.J.: Princeton University Press.

Fiorina, M. P. 1989. *Congress, keystone of the Washington establishment.* New Haven: Yale University Press.

Gigerenzer, G., and P. M. Todd. 1999. Fast and frugal heuristics: The adaptive toolbox. In *Simple heuristics that make us smart,* ed. G. Gigerenzer, P. Todd and the ABC group, 3–34. Oxford: Oxford University Press.

Gilbert, N., and K. Troitzsch. 1999. *Simulation for the social scientist*. Philadelphia: Open University Press.

Gintis, H. 2000. *Game theory evolving*. Princeton, N.J.: Princeton University Press.

———. 2006. A framework for the integration of the behavioral sciences. *Behavioral and Brain Sciences* 30:1–61.

Greif, A., and D. Laitin. 2004. A theory of endogenous institutional change. *American Political Science Review* 98 (4): 14–48.

Guth, W., and K. Pull. 2004. Will equity evolve? An indirect evolutionary approach. *European Journal of Political Economy* 20:273–82.

Langer, P., M. A. Nowak, and C. Hauert. 2008. Spatial invasion of cooperation. *Journal of Theoretical Biology* 250:634–41.

Mayhew, D. R. 1974. *Congress: The electoral connection*. New Haven: Yale University Press.

Maynard Smith, J. 1982. *Evolution and the theory of games*. Cambridge: Cambridge University Press.

Miller, G. J. 2005. The political evolution of principal-agent models. *Annual Review of Political Science* 8:203–25.

Nowak, M. A. 2006. *Evolutionary dynamics*. Cambridge, Mass.: Belknap Press.

Olson, M. 1965. *The logic of collective action*. Cambridge: Harvard University Press.

Orbell, J., T. Morikawa, J. Hartwig, J. Hanley, and N. Allen. 2004. Machiavellian intelligence as a basis for the evolution of cooperative dispositions. *American Political Science Review* 98:1–16.

Richerson, P. J., and R. Boyd. 2005. *Not by genes alone*. Chicago: University of Chicago Press.

Riolo, R. L., R. Axelrod, and M. D. Cohen. 2001. Evolution of cooperation without reciprocity. *Nature* 414:441–43.

Rousseau, D. L., and A. Maurits van der Veen. 2005. The emergence of a shared identity: An agent-based computer simulation of idea diffusion. *Journal of Conflict Resolution* 49 (5): 686–712.

Sabato, L. J. 2007. Feeding frenzy. In *The Lanahan readings in the American polity*, ed. A. Serow and E. C. Ladd, 574–81. Baltimore: Lanahan.

Samuelson, L. 1997. *Evolutionary games and equilibrium selection*. Cambridge, Mass.: MIT Press.

Sandholm, W. H., and E. Dokumaci. 2007. Dynamo: Phase diagrams for evolutionary dynamics. Software suite. http://www.ssc.wisc.edu/~whs/dynamo.

Shepsle, K. A., and M. S. Bonchek. 1997. *Analyzing politics: Rationality, behavior, and institutions*. New York: W. W. Norton.

Simon, H. 1985. Human nature in politics: The dialogue of psychology with political science. *American Political Science Review* 79:293–304.

Smirnov, O., C. Dawes, J. H. Fowler, T. Johnson, and R. McElreath. 2010. The behavioral logic of collective action: Partisans cooperate and punish more than non-partisans. *Political Psychology* 31 (4): 595–616.

Thelen, K. 1999. Historical institutionalism in comparative politics. *Annual Review of Political Science* 2:369–404.

Tversky, A., and D. Kahneman. 1982. Judgment under uncertainty: Heuristics and biases. In *Judgment under uncertainty: Heuristics and biases*, ed. D. Kahneman, P. Slovic, and A. Tversky, 3–20. Cambridge: Cambridge University Press.

Veblen, T. B. 1898. Why is economics not an evolutionary science? *Quarterly Journal of Economics* 12 (3): 373–97.

Vega-Redondo, F. 1993. Competition and culture in an evolutionary process of equilibrium selection: A simple example. *Games and Economic Behavior* 5:618–31.

von Neumann, J., and O. Morgenstern. 1944. *Theory of games and economic behavior.* Princeton, N.J.: Princeton University Press.

Weibull, J. W. 1995. *Evolutionary game theory.* Cambridge, Mass.: MIT Press.

4

MODELING THE CULTURAL AND BIOLOGICAL INHERITANCE OF SOCIAL AND POLITICAL BEHAVIOR IN TWINS AND NUCLEAR FAMILIES

Lindon J. Eaves, Peter K. Hatemi, Andrew C. Heath, and Nicholas G. Martin

The dominant paradigm in the social and political sciences embodies the theory that the origin and transmission of behavioral differences is social. Indeed, Emil Durkheim's (1895) view that social behaviors could only be explained by social indicators has only recently been challenged. Lumsden and Wilson (2005) refer to this as the theory of the "Promethean genotype," that is, that human evolutionary history has emancipated humans entirely from the influence of their genes. Thus, the effects of genetic inheritance on social and political behavior can safely be ignored and the social sciences can proceed with little reference to biology.

Notwithstanding several publications in the life and behavioral sciences that have explored the role of genetic differences in normal and abnormal human behavior, including social, religious, and political attitudes and behaviors (Eaves and Eysenck 1974; Eaves et al. 1978; Martin and Jardine 1986; Martin et al. 1986; Eaves, Eysenck, and Martin 1989; Truett et al. 1994; Tesser 1993; Eaves et al., "Comparing" 1999; Eaves et al., "Biological" 1999; Bouchard et al. 1990; Bouchard and McGue 2003; Eaves et al. 2008), political science had remained largely unaware of or immune to such work. Recent exceptions to this trend (Alford, Funk, and Hibbing 2005; Dawes and Fowler 2009; Fowler, Baker, and Dawes 2008; Fowler and Dawes 2008; Hatemi et al. 2007; Hatemi, Medland, and Eaves 2009; Hatemi, Funk et al. 2009; Hatemi, Hibbing et al. 2009; Hatemi et al. 2010) suggested that political scientists were beginning to consider the implications of an alternative paradigm, grounded in the theory that, even in the domain of their primary interest, political science cannot entirely ignore the effects of genetic influences.

The current chapter is intended to provide a theoretical and empirical framework for evaluating the roles of biological and cultural inheritance in the transmission of human social and political behavior. Our final goal is the substantive scientific understanding of significant features of human variation in social and political behaviors. However, our approach is expository and purposefully more didactic than usual in the hope that it *will introduce political scientists to a significant and long-standing corpus of method and theory* that may be helpful in their own work. We provide a step-by-step account of formulating, fitting, and testing a series of competing and complementary models for the causes and familial transmission of individual differences in six key domains of human behavior and attributes: group affiliation ("party ID"), ideology (conservative-liberal attitudes), religiosity (church attendance), education (educational attainment), personality (neuroticism), and physical appearance (stature).

Theoretically we take the position echoed by the life and social sciences that there can be no organism without both genes and environment and that the study of *individual* differences, which includes the roles of genes and environments, rather than differences between larger geographical, ethnic, or cultural groups, may provide great insight about the ontogeny of human differences. In any specific case, "social" and "genetic" theories are often treated initially as competing models that should be evaluated in terms of their ability to account for data on patterns of variation and correlation between relatives. Ultimately, however, elements of both models are required. Our methodological perspective relies on the ability of empirical observations about the transmission of individual differences in human families to determine which model is to be preferred with what quantitative parameter values.

Empirically, we divide our treatment into three principal themes: (1) modeling the effects of biological and cultural inheritance on human differences and family resemblance; (2) exploring some alternative mechanisms for mate selection; and (3) illustrating the unfolding role of the family and individual environment in attitude development.

Thus, in this chapter we apply representative models of cultural and biological inheritance to a selected range of human physical, behavioral, and socially significant variables: stature; neuroticism; liberalism-conservatism; church attendance; educational attainment, and political preference. The data comprise the correlations between relatives derived for two very large studies of twins and their relatives in the United States and Australia (N = c. 50,000 adult subjects). We explain how theories of biological and cultural inheritance can be formulated and tested in different constellations of family relationships. We show that no single model (biological or social) is adequate to explain the pattern of inheritance for all of the traits selected to illustrate the approach. Rather, different outcomes, for different traits, illustrate different combinations of genetic and social influences with the implication that a far more nuanced understanding of both will be needed for a comprehensive understanding of human political behavior. We show remarkable consistency in the differential inheritance of different traits in the two cultural contexts.

We also conduct a preliminary analysis of some possible mechanisms of mate selection in the attempt to determine how far similarity between spouses is due to their own choice of partners like themselves for the behavior measured ("phenotypic assortative mating"), or selection based on a correlated variable, such as family and social background ("social homogamy"), or simply a function of social interaction between partners after they establish their relationship ("spouse interaction"). Assortative mating is of considerable potential significance because it affects the distribution of genetic and cultural resources within a population and it restricts intergenerational recombination of genetic and cultural differences. Again, we do not pretend to offer an exhaustive treatment of all the subtleties and models of mate selection but we hope we present enough data to illustrate how data on marriages of family members can be used to resolve some of the principal mechanisms. Although the data are not definitive, the analyses we present suggest that for the traits we explore, spousal similarities are consistent with phenotypic assortative mating (as assumed in the previous paragraph above) rather than social homogamy or spousal interaction.

Finally, we examine the developmental trajectory of genetic and environmental influences on the development of liberal/conservative social attitudes across the lifespan. The analysis demonstrates how the contributions of genes and environment change with age, most markedly at about the time when most children leave home, and illustrates the cumulative longitudinal influence of the social environment on the development of social attitudes during adolescence. The analysis shows that a dynamic understanding of the interplay between individuals and their social milieu is essential for a theory of social behavior.

The current treatment is designed to help the newcomer gain some sense of a way of thinking that may be unfamiliar and constitutes an invitation to deeper study. We are conscious of steering a difficult course between appeal to intuition and rigor. The best way to become engaged in a new discipline is to think about real data. We, thus, devote a lot of space to "looking at the numbers" in preparation to developing and testing more formal models. In many places, we have chosen to sacrifice some statistical purity in our methods of estimation and model-testing in the interests of making the connection between the data and results more transparent.[1]

Family Clusters and Individual Differences

Behavior genetic and epidemiological techniques have developed in an attempt to understand why individuals in a population differ from one another. Focusing on individual differences allows us to identify a range of factors that are otherwise hard, even impossible, to resolve in studies of differences between groups that almost inevitably differ biologically and socially. Thus, by *focusing on individual differences rather than group differences* we may begin to explore to what extent differences between individuals express their genetic or environmental individuality and/or the clustering of these effects by social group of which, in many if not most communities, the family is the primary group around which many other effects are clustered. Although *group* characteristics comprise a convenient device for summarizing population data and trends, and even for developing more cost-effective strategies for targeted manipulation and intervention, it is ultimately the *individual* who is the locus of action and decision, so it the individual who comprises the ultimate unit of analysis even when he or she is subject to social influences as part of a family or larger social group.

Family clusters differ from one another genetically and socially. Thus there are *between family* and *within-family* genetic and environmental differences (see, e.g., Cattell 1960 and critique by Loehlin 1965). Furthermore, the effects of genes and environment may correlate within and between families. The environments of individuals may be created by or arise in response to their own genetic differences. They might reflect the genetically influenced behavior of their relatives (e.g., parents and siblings). Our treatment focuses only on that genotype-environment correlation that arises because parents may exercise an environmental influence on their offspring. Insofar as parents are sources of both genetic and social advantage (or disadvantage), Jencks et al. (1972) refer to this type of genotype-environment correlation as a "double advantage" phenomenon. In a paper that is now regarded as a classic in behavioral genetics, Jinks and Fulker (1970) pointed out that the underlying simplicity of Mendelian genetics, following Fisher, allowed for many of Cattell's genetic parameters to be redefined in terms that required far fewer parameters that reflected how clusters of genes (polygenes) affected the behavioral phenotype. They further showed that the model-fitting methods already established in statistical genetics at that time (e.g., Nelder 1960) made it possible to estimate model parameters reliably and provide a basis for the statistical comparison of alternative models for the same data.

Thus were born the elements of a decomposition of the variance between individuals into a relatively small number of parameters: genetic differences between and within families of differing genetic relationship could be expressed in terms of the additive and nonadditive effects of genes. Those due to the environment partitioned into those due to differences *between* family clusters (also referred to as the "shared" or "common" environment) and those due to differences between individuals *within* families (also called the "unique," "nonshared," or "specific" environment). The reader of this literature from the 1970s encounters a frustrating series of different notations and coefficients that largely reflected the academic allegiance of the authors. Now the notation for the variance components has largely been standardized, especially for the study of twins and randomly mating populations (see Neale and Cardon 1992). These days, it is typical to refer to the components of variance thus: A = additive genetic component; D = dominance (nonadditive) genetic component; C = shared ("common") family environment; E = unique (within-family) environment. In much of the literature, especially that following the school established by Douglas Falconer (Falconer and Mackay 1995) these parameters are referred to as V_A, V_D, $V_{EC,}$ and V_E respectively. In the absence of genotype-environment interaction and correlation the total variance in the population may be expressed as the simple sum of the variance components $V_p = A + D + C + E.$[2]

Regarding the data used in the current study on kinship structures, figure 4.1 summarizes the pedigrees that form the core of the data set exploited in our illustrative analyses. We refer to such pedigrees as "extended twin kinships" (ET) because they are constructed around pairs of twins. There are five types of twins featured in the ET kinships: monozygotic (MZ) male and female pairs, and dizygotic (DZ) male, female, and unlike-sex pairs. Twins form the core of our ability to identify critical genetic effects. However, the ET study is extended to include other constellations of relationships including the parents, spouses, siblings, and (adult) children of the original twins

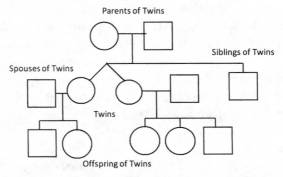

FIGURE 4.1. Idealized kinship structure in Virginia 30,000 and Australian 20,000. *Note:* Circles represent women. Squares represent men. The figure illustrates the idealized pedigree constructed around female monozygotic twins. Similar pedigrees are constructed around male (MZ) twins, male, female, and male-female dizygotic (DZ) pairs.

(see Eaves et al., "Comparing" 1999). If we allow for the five types of twins, and distinguish the various compositions of relative pairs by sex (e.g., mother-daughter, father-son) the ET kinships comprise some 80 unique biological and social relationships (ignoring relationships that span more than two generations since there are relatively few kinships in which we can obtain direct measures on all three generations of adults at the same time; see Keller et al. 2009). Pedigrees can be extended further (and sample sizes increased) by using reports provided by relatives about others in the family but the number and detail of measures that can be obtained this way is limited and such data raise additional analytical problems of reporting bias so will not be considered here.

The richness of the ET kinships can be appreciated by a brief consideration of the implications of some potential comparisons. For example, the spouses of MZ and DZ twins (and of sibling pairs) provide an unparalleled opportunity to resolve subtleties of mate selection including the roles of measured phenotype, interaction between spouses, and latent genetic and social differences in mate selection (e.g., Eaves 1979; Eaves and Heath 1981; Heath et al. 1985; Heath 1987; Grant et al. 2007). The offspring of male and female twins provide a powerful opportunity to explore the environmental effects of genetic differences between parents (e.g., Nance and Corey 1976; Heath et al. 1985; D'Onofrio et al. 2003, 2007; Eaves et al. 2005; Silberg and Eaves 2004; Silberg, Maes, and Eaves 2010; Keller et al. 2008). The monozygotic co-twin of a parent is genetically related to his/her nephew niece as a biological parent, but is

TABLE 4.1. Sample sizes for Virginia and Australia

Relationship	Australia			Virginia		
	Male	Female	Total	Male	Female	Total
Twins	3,459	6,098	9,557	5,325	9,436	14,761
Parents of twins	1,418	1,956	3,374	913	1,447	2,360
Spouses of twins	1,547	823	2,370	2,515	1,876	4,391
Children of twins	925	668	1,593	1,890	2,910	4,800
Siblings of twins	1,554	2,032	3,586	1,260	1,924	3,184
Total	8,646	11,834	20,480	11,903	17,593	29,496

socially an uncle/aunt. Such relationships illustrate the unique opportunity that these kinships offer to resolve genetic and environmental effects that are typically confounded in studies of ordinary kinships. For the purposes of this analysis we confine ourselves to data that comprise the relationships in nuclear families (spouses, parent-offspring, and siblings) and the five types of twin pairs.

The families that comprise our illustrative were obtained as part of two parallel studies, conducted in the greater Virginia (United States) area and from Queensland Australia.[3] The studies are referred to as the Virginia 30,000 (VA30K) and the Australian 20,000 (OZ20K) respectively in this chapter. Ascertainment of the samples and zygosity determination for the twins is described by Lake et al. (2000). The structure of the sample is summarized for individual twins and their relatives in table 4.1. The structure of the sample with respect to the relationships chosen for the present analysis is summarized in table 4.2. The Ns in table 4.2 reflect the number of pairs that can be reconstructed from the sample to yield estimates of the correlation. The same individual may enter into several correlations, so the correlations are not independent and their sampling errors may be inflated with respect to the values expected if the pairs had been independent. Typically, the lack of independence inflates estimates of the sampling errors of model parameters but does not lead to significant bias (McGue, Wette, and Rao 1984). Numerous comparisons of the Australian samples to the general public have shown the sample to be remarkably similar in attitudes, personality, and somewhat similar in income, educational attainment, and religiosity. The Virginia sample, which more than half the sample is drawn from across the United States, has higher levels of income and education than the general public but is quite similar in attitudes, personality, and religiosity in comparison to the general public.

TABLE 4.2. Sample sizes (number of pairs of relatives) for participating families

Relationship	Virginia			Australia			Total median
	Min.	Max.	Median	Min.	Max.	Median	
Spouses	4525	4930	4865	2569	3474	3422	8287
Mother-daughter	3994	4667	4549	2882	4291	4208	8875
Mother-son	2724	3138	3045	2001	2948	2861	5906
Father-daughter	2675	3095	3010	2009	3005	2947	5957
Father-son	1962	2247	2174	1552	2859	2224	4398
Total parent-offspring			12778			12240	25018
Male siblings	1368	1551	1523	1105	1586	1540	3063
Female siblings	3203	3645	3588	2139	3288	3228	6816
Male-female siblings	3858	4395	4331	3131	4562	4487	8818
Total siblings			9442			9255	18697
Male DZ twins	505	583	575	285	476	380	955
Female DZ twins	1022	1183	1151	624	955	826	1977
Male-female DZ twins	1147	1334	1310	629	1070	878	2188
Total DZ Twins			3036			2084	5120
Male MZ twins	721	790	774	482	723	632	1406
Female MZ twins	1657	1885	1843	1032	1469	1374	3217
Total MZ Twins			2617			2006	4623

Note: Variation occurs in the number of pairs for different variables because of patterns of missing variables. For the purposes of this analysis values are assumed to be missing at random.

Choice of Measurements

The measures used to illustrate the approach to family resemblance are selected to illustrate a range of different types of causes for human variation and family resemblance. At one pole, we select stature as representative of a physical trait that might be expected to illustrate relatively simple biological inheritance (see Fisher 1918). The personality dimension of neuroticism was selected as a relatively simple and widely studied behavioral trait that is often regarded as reflecting differences in fundamental, relatively primitive features of the nervous system (see Eysenck 1966). Other variables, such as political affiliation, represent traits that could not be conceived without a highly developed capacity for social behavior and language that, if anything, are likely to represent the Promethean liberation of human behavior from its genetic history.[4]

Family resemblance for each of the variables was summarized by computation of the correlations between relatives for each of the variables using every possible pair that could be derived for each relationship in each sample.

Product moment correlations were used to summarize data for stature, conservatism and neuroticism. Polychoric correlations were generated for church attendance, political affiliation and educational attainment. The correlations are given in table 4.3. Each was stored for analysis along with the number of pairs on which it was based for each variable. These are not reported individually, but summarized in table 4.2 (above).

Application to Twins and Nuclear Families

An ideal analysis would focus on the entire set of 80 correlations for each variable including those for more remote relationships (see, e.g., Eaves et al., "Biological" 1999; Keller et al. 2009). However, it is informative to conduct the analysis in stages that reveal the kinds of model and information that can be obtained from different kinds of data.

With this in mind we conducted three separate analyses using: (1) correlations between members of nuclear families only (spouses, parents and offspring, and siblings); (2) MZ and DZ twins; (3) twins and nuclear families jointly. Each analysis illustrates different elements of the modeling process and illuminates the strengths and weaknesses of different constellations of relatives. The analysis of twin data (2) was conducted with and without the correlation between mates in order to exemplify the effect of assortative mating on conclusions from the analysis of twin data. The full data set comprise 13 unique correlations for each variable (cf. table 4.3 above).

Non-Twin Nuclear Family Resemblance: The Data

The data on nuclear family resemblance comprise eight unique correlations between relatives: spouses; mother-daughter; mother-son; father-daughter; father-son; male siblings; female siblings; unlike-sex siblings (e.g., see Eaves and Hatemi 2008). The data comprise a total of approximately 8,000 spouse pairs, 25,000 parent-offspring pairs, and 18,000 sibling pairs (cf. table 4.2). The raw correlations (table 4.3) show a variety of different patterns for different variables even within nuclear families. The pattern of correlation between mates differs markedly across variables in both countries. All the correlations between spouses are positive, confirming a repeated finding that spousal correlations are frequently zero but seldom, if ever, negative. That being said, the correlation between mates for neuroticism is very close to zero in both samples. This pattern is typical for the principal personality dimensions (see Eaves, Martin, and Heath 1990; Eaves et al., "Comparing" 1999) and implies

TABLE 4.3. Correlations between relatives for illustrative variables in United States and Australia

Variable	Country	Spouse	Mo-Da	Mo-So	Fa-Da	Fa-So	Sib M	Sib F	Sib MF	DZM	DZF	DZMF	MZM	MZF
Stature	US	0.223	0.430	0.446	0.411	0.439	0.432	0.429	0.411	0.483	0.502	0.432	0.850	0.855
	AU	0.208	0.455	0.424	0.399	0.424	0.391	0.421	0.371	0.415	0.501	0.441	0.872	0.827
Conservatism	US	0.619	0.456	0.369	0.396	0.410	0.341	0.405	0.328	0.379	0.432	0.310	0.593	0.637
	AU	0.683	0.469	0.409	0.437	0.443	0.423	0.488	0.408	0.513	0.562	0.464	0.612	0.691
Neuroticism	US	0.092	0.157	0.148	0.127	0.134	0.109	0.172	0.137	0.178	0.224	0.097	0.353	0.410
	AU	0.059	0.150	0.111	0.139	0.162	0.145	0.137	0.111	0.108	0.197	0.115	0.360	0.429
Church attendance	US	0.819	0.566	0.565	0.574	0.585	0.496	0.531	0.456	0.608	0.603	0.488	0.722	0.714
	AU	0.754	0.434	0.412	0.383	0.379	0.344	0.397	0.372	0.437	0.459	0.352	0.536	0.653
Political affiliation	US	0.642	0.434	0.378	0.382	0.400	0.377	0.316	0.329	0.444	0.491	0.404	0.509	0.563
	AU	0.831	0.742	0.716	0.686	0.739	0.605	0.532	0.561	0.767	0.643	0.611	0.790	0.753
Educational attainment	US	0.568	0.472	0.427	0.449	0.502	0.539	0.573	0.534	0.623	0.673	0.549	0.880	0.854
	AU	0.508	0.294	0.234	0.303	0.294	0.385	0.469	0.340	0.490	0.543	0.443	0.706	0.746

Notes: Correlations are based on all possible pairs for each relationship so the same person may contribute several times to one correlation or to several correlations. Product-moment correlations are used for stature, conservatism and neuroticism. Polychoric correlations were computed for church attendance, political affiliation and educational attainment.

that services that seek to match partners for personality may be capitalizing on information that most potential mates regard as relatively unimportant in choosing their partners in the real world. Similarly, the correlation for stature is also small, though significant. Neither personality nor stature plays such a marked role in the choice of mate as the more "social" and "political" dimensions and are expected to have less impact on the transmission of differences from one generation to the next. The correlations between mates are much higher for conservatism, church attendance, political affiliation, and educational attainment, especially so for church attendance and political affiliation in Australia. All these correlations are among the highest documented for human traits and are expected to have a major impact on individual differences and similarity between relatives. By itself, a spousal correlation may be due to one of several processes individually or jointly including convergence due to interaction between mates ("spousal interaction"); matching on the measured phenotype ("phenotypic assortment"); and matching for correlated features of family and social background ("social homogamy"). We assume initially that assortment is based directly on the measured traits (i.e., phenotypic assortment). This assumption is explored further below.

The correlations between biological relatives in nuclear families—parent-offspring and siblings—reveal a heterogeneous picture of family resemblance. The pattern for stature is very close to that expected from a highly heritable polygenic trait, with modest assortative mating with additive and cumulative genetic effects. These correlations are very similar in both the United States and Australia and reminiscent of those published by Pearson and Lee more than a century ago that comprised the foundation for Ronald Fisher's (1918) analysis of family resemblance. In the absence of assortative mating, a completely heritable additive polygenic trait produces correlations of 0.5 between first-degree relatives. Assortative mating and vertical cultural transmission (e.g., social training/learning) tend to inflate parent-offspring correlations relative to those for siblings. This is clearly not the case for stature. Thus the pattern of correlations for nuclear families, including that between spouses, is consistent with a model of substantial genetic influence with little genetic consequence of assortative mating or large additional impact of nongenetic inheritance from parent to child. Genetic "dominance" arises when individuals who carry only one variant copy of a form ("alleleomorph") of a gene resemble those who carry two copies.[5] In nuclear family data, large amounts of genetic dominance tend to inflate the correlation between siblings relative to those between parents and offspring. The same is also true of additional environmental factors shared by siblings that do not depend directly on the measured parental phenotype. The U.S. and Australian correlations for stature give little *prima facie* hint of dominance, though we add the qualification that a modest amount of assortative mating may offset the apparent effects of dominance on the correlations between relatives, reinforcing the overall pattern of polygenic additivity. The fact that the correlations between first-degree relatives for stature hover around 0.4 rather than 0.5 implies that other random, nongenetic influences create differences between individuals within families. These may include random developmental effects, or specific developmental effects, such as nutritional differences during development and errors of measurement.

We devote substantial space to the discussion of stature because it is a benchmark of a trait that appears to be influenced substantially by genetic factors and offers a point of departure for the comparison of other traits of greater interest to social and political scientists. Indeed, even the most ardent supporters of environment-only models do not refute the importance of heritability for height. Despite one of the authors' many attempts, to include hanging from the closet bar for long periods, one cannot socialize height effectively absent lack of nutrition in development. At the other end of the spectrum of interest lie the correlations for neuroticism. Along with extraversion, and more recently, "openness to experience," neuroticism ("N") is perhaps the most studied of personality traits largely because of the ease of measurement by self report and broad validation against clinical and epidemiological data on depression and anxiety disorders. Our correlations for N in Virginia and Australia, based on very large samples, are typical of those reported by other investigators over a long period in numerous western contexts (see Loehlin and Nichols 1976; Floderus-Myrhed, Pedersen, and Rasmuson1980; Martin and Jardine 1986; Lake et al. 2000). The correlations between spouses, though statistically significant in these large samples, are so small as to be of little account in describing the social process of mate selection on family resemblance. The correlations between first-degree biological relatives are all very small in both samples, implying that a large part of the variation between individuals for this aspect of personality is due to random environmental influences unique to individuals, not shared with family members. These effects may include the long-term consequences of individual experiences and the shorter-term fluctuations of mood that characterize individual day-to-day changes. The pattern for N is shared by several other related traits, including liability to depression and anxiety disorders and other measured dimensions of personality, including extraversion.

The results for stature and neuroticism serve to highlight the marked differences between these relatively simple traits and those of greater interest to social and political scientists. The parent-offspring and sibling correlations for conservatism, church attendance, political affiliation, and educational attainment are all large and resemble those for stature more than neuroticism. For all these outcomes, there is considerable, even extreme resemblance between mates that is far in excess of that seen here for stature, or for most other behavioral or dispositional traits such as IQ (Vandenberg 1972; Eaves 1973; Rao et al. 1975; Mascie-Taylor and Vandenberg 1988). *Whether correlations between spouses reflect mate selection, spousal interaction or a mixture of both, it is quite clear that partners who care little about physical stature and personality invest heavily in partners resembling themselves for religious behavior, social attitudes, educational attainment and political commitment.* The same is clearly true for intergenerational transmission. Whether its cause be genetic or social or some function of both, differences between pairs of parents are transmitted to their offspring with considerable fidelity such that the new generation is not *creation ex nihilo* but heavily dependent on influences from the previous generation. No more extreme example of this process may be seen than that for voting preference in Australia for which the correlations between first-degree relatives exceed even those for stature! (see table 4.3 above). The excess of the parent-offspring correlation over that for siblings is consistent with the intergenerational transmission of differences between families established by the very high degree of assortative mating for political commitment. In theory, this effect will be apparent whether intergenerational transmission is genetic, cultural, or both. Further analysis (see below) allows us to tease apart these theoretically significant alternatives (for a full discussion on spousal similarity, and testing models of assortment see appendix A). Whatever the cause, marked resemblance between spouses has more than passing significance for the transmission of political attitudes.

Although the small fluctuations in the correlations as a function of the sexes of the relatives are highly significant statistically with these very large samples, the broad trend of the correlations challenges many popular psychological myths about the effects of parents on their children. The correlations between unlike-sex parents and children are generally little smaller than those for like-sex pairs. This effectively excludes notions of children modeling their behavior more on that of their like-sex parent. Likewise, there is no consistent evidence that mother-offspring correlations exceed father-offspring correlations. Indeed, neither mothers nor fathers appear to play a predominant role in the transmission of these aspects of behavior to the next generation. A variety of biological and social mechanisms are thus excluded as vital features of the transmission of behavior. From a genetic perspective, the data exclude large contributions of sex-dependent transmission such as sex-linkage (which predicts much-reduced father-son resemblance, e.g., Mather and Jinks 1983), environmental effects of the maternal genotype (predicting larger mother-offspring correlations; ibid.) or sex-dependent gene expression such as sex limitation (which predict greater correlations between like-sex pairs than unlike-sex pairs; Eaves 1977). Although there are some statistically significant differences between sibling correlations as a function of sex, these tend to have no consistent pattern and confirm that, smaller effects notwithstanding, the same basic principles of family resemblance, whether genetic or social, apply to both sexes and that there is no overall tendency for men and women raised in the same home to share different, etiologically salient, familial effects. At least as far as shared genetic and environmental influences are concerned, the broad first impression is that sons and daughters experience and respond in a similar way to common features of their family background.

Nuclear Family Resemblance: Models for Cultural and Biological Inheritance

The discussion so far has concentrated on purely visual inspection of the data to describe the principal contours of family resemblance for the chosen variables in these two contexts. We now turn to a more rigorous mathematical treatment by developing and testing elementary models for genetic and non-genetic inheritance. There is, of course, no one model or set of models. Those we describe have some heuristic value and capture many essential features of the processes and theories we seek to evaluate. However, other investigators may and should develop their own models to test more specific alternatives, dependent upon the trait and theoretical foundation they seek to explore. The key to any model is ultimately not merely its ability to characterize a current given data set, but also to generate predictions that may be tested with other kinds of data and in other contexts.

We present two initial path models for nuclear family resemblance. The first (fig. 4.2) is a model for nongenetic transmission. The second (fig. 4.3) is a simple model for additive genetic transmission. The models are illustrative and neither exhaustive nor mutually exclusive.[6]

Single-headed arrows represent hypothetical directions of causation. The variables u_m, v_f and so on, are the path coefficients, standardized regressions of the consequences on their assumed causes. Double-headed arrows (such as

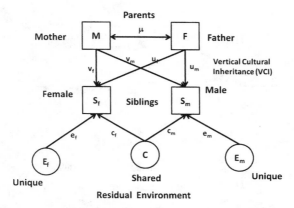

FIGURE 4.2. Elementary model for nongenetic inheritance in nuclear families.

that labeled μ in the path diagram) reflect correlations for which now direction of cause can be attributed. Most models for family resemblance involve manifest variables such as the measured trait values of parents (M and F) and siblings (S_f and S_m) and latent variables that are not measured explicitly (such as residual shared, C, and specific environmental influences on males and females, E_m and E_f). The task of modeling consists primarily in (1) estimating the paths and correlations between manifest and latent variables for a given model and set of correlations, and (2) assessing the goodness of fit, that is, addressing the ability of any model to account for the data.

The nongenetic model assumes assortative mating is based on the measured phenotypes of mothers and fathers (M and F) and that the marital correlation is μ. Parent-offspring transmission occurs by the direct effect of the measured phenotypes of mothers and fathers on the phenotypes of their children. The paths u_m and u_f reflect the environmental impact of fathers on their male and female children, respectively. Similarly paths v_m and v_f reflect the environmental impact of mothers on their sons and daughters. The model also incorporates two nongenetic residual sources of variation. We postulate that siblings also share environmental influences, C, that do not depend directly on the manifest variables of their parents. These may have a different influence on male (c_m) and female (c_f) offspring.

In addition, we anticipate that residual nongenetic influences are specific to individual offspring that are not shared with their siblings so are uncorrelated between siblings. These are denoted in the diagram by the latent variables E_m and E_f for men and women respectively. The paths from the unique, specific environments of siblings are e_m and e_f. Since we are working with

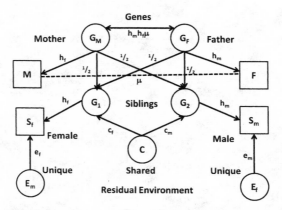

FIGURE 4.3. Elementary model for genetic inheritance in nuclear families. *Note*: Model assumes no cultural transmission from parent to offspring. Assortative mating is assumed to be based primarily on parental phenotype.

correlations and there is no theory of differences in variance in this application, we assume that all latent and manifest variables are standardized to unit variance.

The basic genetic model (fig. 4.3) has structural similarities with the model for vertical cultural inheritance (fig. 4.2). Both models allow for residual nongenetic effects of the shared and nonshared environment (C and E). Both also allow for phenotypic assortative mating, represented by μ in the diagram. However, the mechanism of transmission is assumed to be different. In the genetic model, intergenerational transmission depends on latent genetic variables, G, rather than on the manifest phenotypes. Fisher's exposition of polygenic Mendelian inheritance shows that the intergenerational paths between the latent genetic components are all the same and have an explicit prior value ($\frac{1}{2}$) that follows from Mendel's first law of segregation regardless of the sex of the parent or recipient. The same may not be said, however, for the effects of the genes on the phenotype. These may depend on sex. Thus the model allows for different paths, h_m and h_f, from latent genetic effects to manifest outcomes in males and females respectively.

Although the "genetic" model assumes that assortment is based primarily on the phenotype of the spouses, the fact that the phenotypes are only an unreliable indicator of the latent genotype means that the correlation between the genetic effects of spouses will be attenuated by nongenetic effects. Following Fisher (1918), we note that primary phenotypic assortment induces a correlation between spouses' genetic effects that depends on the marital correlation, μ, and the paths, h_m and h_f, from additive genetic effect to phenotype.

TABLE 4.4. Expected correlations between members of nuclear families under models for phenotypic (fig. 4.2) and genetic (fig. 4.2) inheritance

	Transmission model	
Correlation	Phenotypic (Cultural)	Genetic
Spouses	μ	μ
Mother-daughter	$v_f(1 + u_f)$	$\frac{1}{2} h_f(h_f + h_m\mu)$
Mother-son	$v_m(1 + u_m)$	$\frac{1}{2} h_m h_f(1+\mu)$
Father-daughter	$u_f(1 + v_f)$	$\frac{1}{2} h_m h_f(1+\mu)$
Father-son	$u_f(1 + v_m)$	$\frac{1}{2} h_m(h_m + h_f\mu)$
Male sibling	$u_m^2 + v_m^2 + 2\mu u_m v_m + c_m^2$	$\gamma h_m^2 + c_m^2$
Female sibling	$u_f^2 + v_f^2 + 2\mu u_f v_f + c_f^2$	$\gamma h_m h_f + c_m c_f$
Male-female sibling	$u_m u_f + v_m v_f + \mu (u_m v_f + u_f v_m) + c_m c_f$	$\gamma h_f^2 + c_f^2$
Total variance (male)	$u_m^2 + v_m^2 + 2\mu u_m v_m + c_m^2 + e_m^2 = 1$	$h_m^2 + c_m^2 + e_m^2 = 1$
Total variance (female)	$u_f^2 + v_f^2 + 2\mu u_f v_f + c_f^2 + e_f^2 = 1$	$h_f^2 + c_f^2 + e_f^2 = 1$

Note: γ is the genetic correlation between siblings. $\gamma = \frac{1}{2} (1 + h_m h_f \mu) = \frac{1}{2}$ when mating is random ($\mu = 0$).

Fisher considers other possible mechanisms of assortative mating, including assortment for a (genetically) correlated variable and assortment based primarily on genotype rather than phenotype. These mechanisms are considered below. Both the genetic and nongenetic models assume that the effects of genes and environment are not modulated by age. This assumption appears to be approximately true for adults insofar as it has been tested. Hatemi, Funk et al. (2009) consider application of models for age-dependent expression of genetic and environmental factors in the development of conservative-liberal attitudes (also see Eaves et al. 1997). Their analysis is summarized below. The current adult sample comprises individuals who are all older than eighteen years.

The rules of linear algebra (e.g., Wright 1921; Duncan 1966; Cloninger, Rice, and Reich 1979; Heath et al. 1985; Truett et al. 1994; Li 1975; Loehlin 2003; Neale et al. 2002; Eaves et al. 2005) allow derivation of algebraic expectations of the correlations in terms of the model parameters. The expectations for the correlations between nuclear families are summarized for the two basic models in table 4.4.

FITTING THE MODEL: COMPUTATIONAL METHOD The nuclear family data comprise eight unique correlations between relatives. The "nongenetic" model involves seven free parameters: the correlation between mates, μ; four parameters for the environmental effects of parents on children, u_f, v_f, u_m, v_f; and the two paths from the residual shared environment, C, to the phenotypes of male and female offspring, c_m and c_f. The remaining paths,

e_m and e_f, are fixed when the others are known by the constraint that the total variance is standardized to unity in males and female. Similarly, the full genetic model has five free parameters: m, h_f, h_f, c_m, and c_f. In principle, estimates of the parameters of both models might now be derived by solving the eight simultaneous equations generated by equating the eight observed nuclear family correlations for each of the variables in table 4.3 to their algebraic expectations under each model in table 4.4. However, this may not be as easy as it seems, especially as the models get more complex. First, there are more equations than unknown parameters, so there is no unique solution for each parameter. Second, the equations are nonlinear, sometimes extremely so, making the algebra very tedious. Third, some models (see below) require the imposition of (nonlinear) constraints on the parameters. In addition, it is preferable that any approach to estimation makes optimal use of the data and allows some statistical assessment of the adequacy of any model and relative predictive value of alternative explanations of the empirical data.

Ideally, we would employ the method of maximum likelihood (ML), which has been used extensively in the analysis of kinship data (see, e.g., Lange, Westlake, and Spence 1976) including the extended kinships of twins (e.g., Maes, Neale, and Eaves 1997; Maes et al. 2009; Silberg, Maes, and Eaves 2010; for ideology see Hatemi et al. 2010). However, this approach requires that the expectations for all the kinship relationships be specified, which are far more numerous than the eight chosen for this application. Although ML makes optimal use of the raw data, in the sense that it yields the most precise estimates attainable with a given data set, and allows likelihood ratio chi-square tests of different subhypotheses, it is less transparent for the purposes of model description because it is applied to the raw data from the extended pedigrees and is harder to use for the partly didactic purposes of this chapter.For the purpose of these analyses we employed a close relative of ML, nonlinear weighted least squares (WLS; see Nelder 1960; Rao, Morton, and Yee 1974).[7]

MODEL-FITTING RESULTS: NONGENETIC MODELS The full model for nongenetic transmission (fig. 4.3) was fitted initially to each of the variables by WLS using code written in *Mx*. Subsequently, reduced models were fitted by setting specific sets of parameters to zero, or imposing constraints on parameter values. The model-fitting results are summarized for the nongenetic model in table 4.5. For most of the variables, the full nongenetic model fits well. As a "rule of thumb" we may, as an approximation, compare the weighted residual sum-of-squares to the chi-square distribution for the same d.f. By this criterion, the largest $\Sigma\delta^2_{(1)}$ for the full model is a highly significant

TABLE 4.5. Parameters of phenotypic transmission in nuclear families

Trait	Country	Mating μ	Father-offspring transmission u_m	u_f	Mother-offspring transmission v_m	v_f	Residual Shared c_m	c_f	Unique e_m	e_f	Model comparison statistics Full $\Sigma\delta^2_{(1)}$	No sex $\Delta\delta^2_{(4)}$	No C $\Delta\delta^2_{(2)}$	No VT $\Delta\delta^2_{(4)}$	No μ $\Delta\delta^2_{(1)}$
Stature	US	0.223	0.359	0.331	0.367	0.356	0.310	0.369	0.582	0.575	0.65	2.20	47.48	2349.62	235.97
	AU	0.208	0.354	0.316	0.352	0.366	0.252	0.335	0.635	0.586	2.12	8.11	27.85	2361.33	146.30
Conservatism	US	0.619	0.307	0.177	0.176	0.348	0.350	0.410	0.686	0.603	2.68	25.37	109.26	2262.05	1882.05
	AU	0.683	0.323	0.209	0.185	0.328	0.414	0.482	0.608	0.523	3.68	15.37	184.39	2449.18	1617.75
Neuroticism	US	0.092	0.121	0.114	0.137	0.147	0.271	0.367	0.890	0.828	0.00	6.74	91.10	267.16	40.78
	AU	0.059	0.157	0.130	0.101	0.143	0.297	0.296	0.875	0.873	1.84	4.16	56.55	250.31	12.10
Church attendance	US	0.819	0.404	0.320	0.236	0.304	0.278	0.411	0.548	0.478	5.62	6.25	62.07	4174.16	3361.87
	AU	0.754	0.158	0.129	0.293	0.336	0.407	0.450	0.654	0.602	0.02	11.85	138.76	2032.32	1952.30
Political affiliation	US	0.642	0.269	0.175	0.204	0.323	0.434	0.325	0.627	0.687	0.11	9.51	87.63	1846.18	1865.69
	AU	0.834	0.464	0.233	0.331	0.535	0.157	0.015	0.395	0.451	1.20	9.16	0.36	4404.42	2012.25
Educational attainment	US	0.568	0.387	0.264	0.206	0.322	0.495	0.546	0.472	0.431	0.48	7.93	275.65	2730.66	1590.63
	AU	0.508	0.250	0.199	0.103	0.195	0.471	0.575	0.679	0.552	13.92	26.22	389.24	966.39	878.04

[a] Cf. fig. 4.2.

Significance levels of χ^2:

d.f.	P (%) 10	5	1	0.5	0.1
1	2.70	3.84	6.63	7.88	10.83
2	4.61	5.99	9.21	10.60	13.82
3	6.25	7.81	11.34	12.84	16.27
4	7.78	9.49	13.28	14.86	18.47

value of 13.92 for educational attainment in the Australian sample. The only other variable to which the model gives a poor fit is church attendance in the United States ($\Sigma \delta^2_{(1)}$ = 5.62). The table also gives the changes, $\Delta \delta^2_{(d)}$, in $\Sigma \delta^2$ for a series of reduced models. The d.f., d, of $\Delta \delta^2$ is equal to the number of additional constraints imposed in the reduced model. Thus, for a model that assumes random mating, one parameter, μ, is fixed at zero so the corresponding $\Delta \delta^2$ has one d.f. A model that equates all parameters across sexes, that is, $u_m = u_f = v_m = v_f$ and $c_m = c_f$, requires four fewer parameters than the full model so $\Delta \delta^2$ has four d.f. (cf. table 4.5, "No Sex" model).

In general, the full model is quite resistant to reduction for most of the variables. In no case is it possible to ignore the effects of assortative mating (i.e., set m = 0). This is true even for neuroticism, for which the marital correlation is very small and reflects the considerable precision resulting from the relatively large samples of spouse pairs in the sample. Similarly, it is not possible to discount parent-offspring transmission for any of the variables because the $\Delta \delta^2$ for testing the effects of vertical cultural inheritance ("No VCI" in table 4.5) are all very large and highly significant. Nor is parent-offspring transmission, though highly significant for all variables, sufficient to explain the correlations between siblings. Thus, estimates of the residual shared environment of siblings are significant ("No C" in table 4.5) for all variables except for political affiliation in Australian families. With this exception, the data show that the causes of family resemblance in complex behaviors cannot be explained simply by reference to the environmental influence of the parental phenotypes but also reflect other environmental factors that cannot be attributed directly to the corresponding variables in parents. Such effects may include other sources of environmental similarity, including other aspects of parental behavior and the social contexts shared by siblings independently of their parents.

The statistics in table 4.5 suggest that the only acceptable simplifications to the most general model involve removing sex differences in the model parameters ("No Sex," $\Delta \delta^2_{(4)}$ in table 4.5). In neither Virginia or Australia is there compelling evidence that the causes of family resemblance depend on sex for stature, neuroticism, or political affiliation. The effects of mothers and fathers on their male and female offspring are all similar in magnitude. There is no support for the view that mothers are more influential than fathers, or vice versa, or that sons or daughters are more or less susceptible to parental influence on these variables. This being said, the data provide compelling evidence for sex effects on patterns of family resemblance in conservatism in both samples and, in Australia but not Virginia, for church attendance and educational

TABLE 4.6. Relative contributions (% total variation explained) of phenotypic familial influences outcome measures

Trait	Source	Males			Females		
		Parents	Shared	Unique	Parents	Shared	Unique
Stature	US	32.2	9.6	58.2	28.8	13.6	57.5
	AU	30.1	5.4	63.5	30.2	11.2	58.6
Conservatism	US	19.2	12.2	68.6	22.9	16.8	60.3
	AU	22.0	17.2	60.8	24.5	23.2	52.3
Neuroticism	US	3.6	7.4	89.0	3.7	13.5	82.8
	AU	3.7	8.8	87.5	4.0	8.8	87.3
Church attendance	US	37.4	7.7	54.8	35.3	16.9	47.8
	AU	18.1	16.6	56.4	19.6	20.2	60.2
Political affiliation	US	18.5	18.8	62.7	20.7	10.6	68.7
	AU	58.1	2.5	39.5	54.9	0.0	45.1
Educational attainment	US	28.3	24.5	47.2	27.1	29.9	43.1
	AU	9.9	22.2	67.9	11.7	33.1	55.2

attainment. Table 4.6 summarizes the relative contributions of the various sources of hypothesized environmental influences in nuclear families for the variables chosen for study.

The table shows that by far the largest contributors to variation in outcome are influences that cannot be predicted by family membership, that is, the influence of parental phenotypes or other, residual contextual effects shared by siblings. In the most extreme case, neuroticism, 80–90% of the total variation *cannot* be explained by reference to parents or the shared environmental influences on siblings. For the other variables, unique nonfamilial influences account for less of the variance, but seldom less than 45% of the total. The data reveal two striking differences in transmission between Virginia and Australia. In Virginia parental influences account for about twice as much of the variation in church attendance compared with Australia. By contrast, in Australia the impact of parents on the political preference of their offspring explains more than 50% of individual variation, almost twice as much as in the Virginia sample. *It appears that parents care more about how their children vote in Australia and they care more about whether or not they go to church in Virginia.* The fact that the contributions of parents to the religious and political behavior of their sons and daughters is so labile across cultures perhaps argues for a greater impact of the cultural environment on these variables than for others, such as stature, for which the relative contributions of the sources of variation are more uniform between the two contexts.

MODEL-FITTING RESULTS: GENETIC MODELS Table 4.7 presents parameter estimates and model comparison statistics for the model that assumes intergenerational transmission is purely genetic. Results are not presented for tests of random mating because they depend almost exclusively on the correlation between mates and differ very little from the corresponding values for the nongenetic model in table 4.5. Most of the features in table 4.7 resemble closely the essentials of their counterparts in table 4.5. Thus, just as it is impossible to delete parent-offspring transmission for the nongenetic model, so it is impossible to remove genetic effects from the genetic model. With few exceptions, the genetic model fits no better or worse ($\Sigma\delta^2_{(3)}$) than its cultural counterpart ("No VT" in table 4.7 ($\Sigma\delta^2_{(1)}$), although the genetic model requires two fewer parameters.

Thus, in general, there is little to choose empirically between genetic and nongenetic explanations of non-twin nuclear family data, a fact appreciated more than a century ago by Francis Galton (1883) and which led to his recognition of the possible significance of twin studies for the resolution of cultural and biological inheritance. By contrast, Karl Pearson (Pearson and Lee 1903) had no compunction in generalizing his conclusions about the inheritance of physical human and animal traits to "the mental and moral characteristics of man" using data on the ratings of sibling pairs by their teachers.

There are some exceptions to the conclusion that non-twin nuclear family data are inherently weak for resolving genetic and social models for transmission. There is little doubt that a purely genetic model cannot explain the transmission of political affiliation in Australia. The residual sum of squares for the cultural model is only 1.20 compared with a much larger value of 30.08 for the genetic model. A nongenetic model is also marginally better supported than its genetic counterpart for conservatism in Virginia and educational attainment in Australia but the difference is not great. Table 4.8 presents the estimated contribution of genetic and environmental factors to differences in the outcomes based on the nuclear family data. These values should be compared with the estimated contributions under the purely "nongenetic" model in table 4.6.

A noteworthy feature of the genetic model is an inherent reduction in estimates of the relative contribution of the unique environment (E). This result is an artifact of the fact that models for genetic effects recognizes that genetic influences that contribute to parent-offspring transmission and to differences *between* family clusters also contribute to variation *within* sibships as a result of the separation of genetic variants into different gametes at meiosis (see glossary). These effects are implicitly estimated from parent-offspring

TABLE 4.7. Parameters of genetic transmission in nuclear families

Trait	Country	Parameter estimates[a]									Model comparison statistics			
		Mating	Genes		Environment				Full		No sex	No C	No genes	VT[b]
					Shared		Unique							
		μ	h_m	h_f	c_m	c_f	e_m	e_f	$\Sigma\delta^2_{(3)}$		$\Delta\delta^2_{(2)}$	$\Delta\delta^2_{(2)}$	$\Delta\delta^2_{(2)}$	$\Sigma\delta^2_{(1)}$
Stature	US	0.223	0.854	0.831	0.001	0.172	0.520	0.530	1.91		0.94	1.77	2348.36	0.65
	AU	0.211	0.808	0.854	0.131	0.000	0.580	0.528	7.55		3.83	0.33	2355.90	2.12
Conservatism	US	0.617	0.657	0.768	0.241	0.000	0.714	0.640	10.12		17.93	3.89	2254.60	2.68
	AU	0.683	0.703	0.744	0.221	0.322	0.676	0.587	7.46		11.59	32.68	2445.40	3.68
Neuroticism	US	0.092	0.479	0.535	0.029	0.159	0.877	0.829	1.16		5.57	1.38	266.00	0.00
	AU	0.061	0.495	0.512	0.143	0.000	0.857	0.859	5.95		0.47	0.47	246.25	1.84
Church attendance	US	0.820	0.797	0.783	0.000	0.260	0.603	0.565	2.33		9.54	9.04	4177.45	5.62
	AU	0.754	0.662	0.697	0.226	0.265	0.715	0.666	5.25		4.40	20.23	2027.09	0.02
Political affiliation	US	0.643	0.681	0.710	0.272	0.033	0.680	0.703	5.66		4.70	5.14	1840.63	0.11
	AU	0.850	0.878	0.844	0.000	0.000	0.479	0.535	30.08		3.10	0.00	4375.54	1.20
Educational attainment	US	0.568	0.768	0.766	0.359	0.421	0.529	0.487	9.08		2.33	122.00	2722.02	0.48
	AU	0.508	0.597	0.625	0.322	0.470	0.735	0.624	20.47		19.67	156.73	959.84	13.92

[a] Cf. fig. 4.3.

[b] Goodness-of-fit test for phenotypic transmission model (see table 4.6).

TABLE 4.8. Relative contributions (% total variation explained) of genetic transmission on outcome measures (nuclear family data)

Trait	Source	Males			Females		
		Genes	Shared E	Unique E	Genes	Shared E	Unique E
Stature	US	£73.0	0.0	27.0	69.0	2.9	28.1
	AU	65.2	1.7	33.0	73.0	0.0	27.0
Conservatism	US	43.1	5.8	51.0	59.0	0.0	41.0
	AU	49.4	4.9	45.7	55.3	10.4	34.3
Neuroticism	US	22.9	0.1	77.0	28.7	2.5	68.8
	AU	24.5	2.1	73.4	26.2	0.0	73.8
Church attendance	US	63.6	0.0	36.4	61.3	6.8	31.9
	AU	43.8	5.1	51.1	48.6	7.0	44.4
Political affiliation	US	46.3	7.4	46.3	50.4	0.1	49.5
	AU	77.1	0.0	22.9	71.3	0.0	28.7
Educational attainment	US	59.1	12.9	28.0	58.6	17.7	23.7
	AU	35.6	10.4	54.0	39.0	22.1	38.9

transmission and a component subtracted from the variance within sibships, assigning any further residual effects to the unique environment (and/or the effects of genetic dominance).

The general conclusion of model-fitting to correlations for nuclear families (without twins) is that parents affect the behavior of their children but, with few exceptions, nuclear family data provide little hard evidence for or against either theory of human differences.

MODELS FOR TWIN RESEMBLANCE As Galton pointed out (1883), twins provide a natural experiment that may facilitate the resolution of biological and environmental influences on human variation. He noted that there were two kinds of twins. Identical twins, Galton theorized, arose by the division of a single fertilized egg into two genetically identical individuals and, hence were termed "monozygotic" (MZ). By contrast nonidentical twins were assumed to arise because two separate ova, released at the same time, were fertilized by separate sperm from the same father. Such twins were thus "fraternal" because they were merely siblings who happened to have undergone gestation and birth at the same time or "dizygotic" because they represent zygotes arising from completely independent events of fertilization. It is intuitively apparent that, *ceteris paribus*, variation within MZ pairs reflects only environmental effects, whereas intra-pair differences for DZ twins reflect both environmental dissimilarity and the effects of genetic segregation.[8]

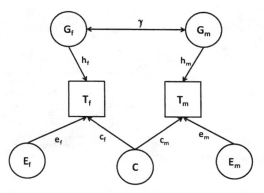

FIGURE 4.4. Model for resemblance between twins. *Note*: The correlation between genotypes of twins (g) is unity for MZ twins and ½ in DZ twins when mating is random and gene action is additive. In the presence of positive assortative mating, g is increased (see text).

Figure 4.4 presents the elements of a simple model for the resemblance of twins. As for our model for nuclear family data, we recognize that the effects of genes and environment may vary across sexes. Thus, the figure represents the model for unlike-sex DZ twins. There are virtually no unlike-sex MZ pairs. The diagrams for like-sex pairs are the same, with the appropriate substitution of the genetic and environmental paths for males and females, *mutatis mutandis*. The diagram embodies a series of assumptions, some of which have been considered in the context of nuclear families above. Gene action is assumed to be additive initially, and to a first approximation we assume that the same genes and shared environmental effects contribute to individual differences within the sexes. However, we do not assume that the genetic and environmental paths are necessarily the same in males and females. The parameter γ is the genetic correlation between twins. Since MZ twins are genetically identical, $\gamma = 1$ for MZ twins. Under random mating, $\gamma = \frac{1}{2}$ for DZ twins. For traits in which assortative mating increases the genetic resemblance between mates (e.g., phenotypic assortment) $\gamma > \frac{1}{2}$. Typically, twin studies do not incorporate data on parents so mating is usually assumed to be random and the genetic correlation between DZ twins fixed at ½ *ex hypothesi*. If there is significant assortative mating and its effects on the genetic similarity of DZ twins (or siblings) are ignored, the genetic consequences of assortative mating inflate estimates of shared environmental effects derived from twin data. This tendency will be illustrated below by analyzing twin data with and without including estimates of the effect of assortative mating.

A further major assumption of the twin model is that the effects of genes

TABLE 4.9. Expected correlations between twins

Correlation	Expectation
Spouses	μ
MZ male	$h_m^2 + c_m^2$
MZ female	$h_f^2 + c_f^2$
DZ male	$\gamma\mu\, h_m^2 + c_m^2$
DZ male-female	$\gamma\, h_m h_f + c_m c_f$
DZ female	$\gamma\, h_f^2 + c_f^2$

Note: Cf. fig. 4.4. If spouses are not available it is assumed that $\gamma = \frac{1}{2}$ (i.e. that mating is random). If $\mu > 0$ but spouse data are not available, the genetic consequences of assortative mating will inflate estimates of the shared environment (c).

and the shared environment are independent. In the event that genetic differences between parents have a direct or indirect effect on the environment of their offspring this will no longer be the case but the effects of genes and shared environment will be correlated. This possibility will be explored explicitly when we attempt to integrate the analysis of twins and nuclear families in a unified model. If the analysis of twins alone, however, such "passive genotype-environment covariance" will be confounded with estimates of the shared environment.

An implication of the "twin" model is that any genetic effects of assortative mating and any environmental effects of the parental genotype contribute to estimates of the shared environment. Thus, in the analysis of twin data, estimates of the shared environment subsume a wide range of ways in which parental phenotypes influence those of their children. In the model for nuclear family data, estimate of the residual shared environment in siblings reflect effects that cannot be predicted directly from the parental phenotypes. Wright's rules for deriving expected correlations from path diagrams generate the expected correlations between twins shown in table 4.9.

If mating is random and genetic effects are additive, so that the genetic correlation between siblings is ½, the correlation between MZ twins is expected to be exactly twice that for DZ twins. The effects of the shared environment and positive assortative mating tend to inflate the DZ correlation relative to that for MZs, so that $2r_{DZ} - r_{MZ} > 0$ (see, e.g., Eaves 1982). Nonadditive genetic effects, including genetic dominance, tend to reduce the DZ correlation relative to MZ and result in $2r_{DZ} - r_{MZ} < 0$. Generally, the power for the test of genetic dominance in twin studies is low (see, e.g., Martin et al. 1978) and very large samples are required to test for it.

Preliminary inspection of the correlations for MZ twins and like-sex DZ twins in table 4.3 suggest that the pattern for stature is close to what is expected under additive gene action in the absence of dominance and the shared environment. The DZ correlations for neuroticism are somewhat less than half those for MZs, suggesting that some genetic effects may be nonadditive. Most of the other variables in the study have DZ twin correlations that exceed half their corresponding MZ correlations, suggesting that the effects either of the shared environment or assortative mating or both are contributing to twin resemblance. The model given in the table was initially fitted to the five twin correlations for each variable in each sample in table 4.3 excluding the correlation between spouses and thus ignoring the effects of assortative mating. Thus, the estimates of the shared environment will be inflated by any genetic consequences of assortative mating.

Weighted least squares estimates of model parameters and model comparison statistics are given in table 4.10 using only the five twin correlations for each variable in each sample. The model thus assumes random mating. The fit of the four parameter model to the five correlations is good in most cases. The main exceptions are neuroticism where the explanation probably lies with the relatively low correlations for unlike-sex DZ twins compared with those for like-sex pairs. One possible explanation of this might be that different genetic or shared environmental effects contribute to variation in males and females. For example, genes with sex-limited effects (i.e., that influence one sex but not the other) might lead to a relatively lower correlation between relatives of opposite sexes. This being said, the fit of the model does not generally get worse when the effects of genes and environment are constrained to be the same in males and females ("No sex" in table 4.10). In the U.S. sample there is some evidence supporting heterogeneity across the sexes for conservatism, neuroticism, and educational attainment. In Australia, the sexes appear to be significantly different with respect to the effects of genes and environment on church attendance. The issue of sex-dependent genetic effects will be considered further below.

With the exceptions of stature and neuroticism, the twin data show that the effects of the shared environment (C) are significant for all the variables chosen for analysis. Thus, C cannot be deleted from the model for conservatism, church attendance, political affiliation, or educational attainment in either population. Removing C from the model ("No C" in table 4.10) worsens the fit significantly and, in many cases, substantially. Since the model assumes random mating, it is possible that some or all of what passes for C in the model may actually be the excess genetic correlation between relatives generated by the correlation between mates. The impact of assortment on these measures will be evaluated below.

TABLE 4.10. Parameters of model for twin resemblance (excluding spouse pairs)

Trait	Country	Parameter estimates[a]						Model comparison statistics			
		Genes		Shared		Unique		Full	No sex	No C	No genes
		h_m	h_f	c_m	c_f	e_m	e_f	$\Sigma\delta^2_{(1)}$	$\Delta\delta^2_{(2)}$	$\Delta\delta^2_{(2)}$	$\Delta\delta^2_{(2)}$
Stature	US	0.917	0.836	0.144	0.393	0.371	0.383	1.20	1.98	6.03	204.20
	AU	0.917	0.811	0.154	0.414	0.367	0.414	0.38	2.90	5.26	146.22
Conservatism	US	0.765	0.630	0.163	0.486	0.624	0.605	2.52	7.71	13.69	88.42
	AU	0.570	0.523	0.541	0.644	0.618	0.559	2.39	4.45	55.35	22.27
Neuroticism	US	0.395	0.642	0.396	0.000	0.829	0.767	4.56	10.18	5.95	69.76
	AU	0.515	0.647	0.224	0.000	0.828	0.762	6.18	5.14	0.37	60.38
Church attendance	US	0.681	0.444	0.531	0.711	0.504	0.555	8.05	2.31	93.79	38.35
	AU	0.000	0.633	0.705	0.504	0.709	0.588	2.35	8.70	20.67	41.64
Political affiliation	US	0.498	0.379	0.520	0.644	0.694	0.664	2.09	3.47	64.23	11.59
	AU	0.000	0.509	0.882	0.706	0.471	0.493	0.35	4.98	91.86	13.28
Educational attainment	US	0.823	0.589	0.468	0.708	0.321	0.390	3.54	6.49	81.80	92.46
	AU	0.751	0.634	0.391	0.583	0.532	0.508	2.12	3.70	32.57	66.80

[a] Cf. table 4.4.

TABLE 4.11. Relative contributions (% total variation explained) of genetic transmission on outcome measures (twin data, without spouse pairs)

Trait	Source	Males			Females		
		Genes	Shared E	Unique E	Genes	Shared E	Unique E
Stature	US	84.1	2.1	13.8	69.9	15.4	14.7
	AU	84.1	2.4	13.5	65.7	17.1	17.2
Conservatism	US	58.5	2.7	38.9	39.7	23.7	36.6
	AU	32.5	29.3	38.2	27.4	41.4	31.2
Neuroticism	US	15.6	15.6	68.8	41.2	0.0	58.8
	AU	26.5	5.0	68.5	41.9	0.0	58.1
Church attendance	US	46.4	28.2	25.4	19.7	50.5	29.7
	AU	0.0	49.8	50.2	40.1	25.4	34.6
Political affiliation	US	24.8	27.0	48.1	14.4	41.5	44.1
	AU	0.0	77.8	22.2	25.9	49.9	24.3
Educational attainment	US	65.8	21.9	10.3	34.7	50.1	15.2
	AU	56.4	15.3	28.3	40.1	34.0	25.8

The fit of the model to the twin data is significantly poorer when genetic effects are dropped from the model for all the variables studied in both populations ("No genes" in table 4.10). The loss of fit is dramatic in the case of stature and significant, though far less so, even for political affiliation providing some evidence, albeit not as strong as for the other outcomes, for the role of genes in political preference. Table 4.11 summarizes the estimated contributions of additive genetic effects, shared environment, and individual unique experience to individual differences in the chosen measures. There is no evidence of genetic effects on church attendance and political preference in Australian males. Stature is indeed the most heritable trait in this set.

Estimates of the shared environmental effect are large for many of the variables of concern to social and political scientists. Indeed, the shared environment is clearly the largest contributor to individual differences in political preference and is comparable to or greater than the estimate of genetic effects in many cases.

Table 4.12 summarizes the model fitting results when the correlations between mates are included in the data and the model is adjusted to reflect the corresponding increase in the genetic correlation between DZ twins, γ. The goodness-of-fit tests of the model tell a similar story, as do the tests for the effects of genetic differences. This finding is expected, because the information about the significance of genetic effects comes from the observed difference between MZ and DZ correlations which is not affected by allowing for

TABLE 4.12. Parameters of model for twin resemblance (including spouse pairs)

		Parameter estimates							Model comparison statistics					
		Mating	Genes		Environment								Sex-specific C	
					Shared		Unique		Full	No Sex	No C	No Genes		
Trait	Country	μ	h_m	h_f	c_m	c_f	e_m	e_f	$\Sigma\delta^2_{(1)}$	$\Delta\delta^2_{(2)}$	$\Delta\delta^2_{(2)}$	$\Delta\delta^2_{(2)}$	$\Sigma\delta^2_{(2)}$	$\Delta\delta^2_{(1)}$
Stature	US	0.220	0.837	0.923	0.342	0.000	0.427	0.384	2.51	3.61	3.16	202.89	133.34	69.55
	AU	0.204	0.903	0.909	0.112	0.000	0.415	0.418	4.80	0.03	0.02	141.80	102.16	39.64
Conservatism	US	0.619	0.620	0.800	0.418	0.000	0.664	0.678	2.68	13.91	9.27	88.26	44.91	43.55
	AU	0.683	0.708	0.598	0.359	0.575	0.607	0.559	1.84	5.00	2.09	22.81	10.94	11.87
Neuroticism	US	0.092	0.384	0.641	0.403	0.000	0.831	0.767	4.71	11.19	6.69	69.61	34.89	34.72
	AU	0.058	0.502	0.646	0.244	0.000	0.829	0.766	6.71	5.46	0.54	59.85	43.89	15.96
Church attendance	US	0.821	0.758	0.857	0.396	0.000	0.607	0.518	2.95	7.73	7.57	43.45	13.24	30.21
	AU	0.754	0.612	0.810	0.411	0.029	0.676	0.587	0.15	12.70	5.10	43.84	21.69	41.15
Political affiliation	US	0.642	0.545	0.396	0.475	0.633	0.691	0.665	1.85	3.71	10.47	11.83	4.53	7.30
	AU	0.831	0.000	0.509	0.822	0.706	0.471	0.493	0.35	4.98	3.54	13.28	4.80	8.48
Educational attainment	US	0.569	0.836	0.933	0.392	0.000	0.383	0.359	4.37	7.08	6.75	91.63	45.14	46.49
	AU	0.509	0.733	0.871	0.317	0.000	0.550	0.491	1.52	4.05	2.18	67.34	37.24	30.10

Note: Cf. fig. 4.5.

TABLE 4.13. Relative contributions (% total variation explained) of genetic transmission on outcome measures (twin data, with spouse pairs)

Trait	Source	Males			Females		
		Genes	Shared E	Unique E	Genes	Shared E	Unique E
Stature	US	70.0	11.7	18.2	85.2	0.0	14.8
	AU	81.5	1.3	17.2	82.5	0.0	17.5
Conservatism	US	38.4	17.5	44.1	64.0	0.0	36.0
	AU	50.2	12.9	36.9	35.8	33.0	31.2
Neuroticism	US	14.7	16.2	69.0	41.1	0.0	58.9
	AU	25.2	0.06	68.8	41.7	0.0	58.3
Church attendance	US	57.4	15.7	26.9	73.4	0.0	26.6
	AU	37.4	16.9	45.7	65.6	0.1	34.3
Political affiliation	US	29.7	22.6	47.7	15.7	40.1	44.2
	AU	0.0	77.8	22.2	25.9	49.9	24.3
Educational attainment	US	70.0	15.4	14.7	87.1	0.0	12.9
	AU	59.8	10.0	30.2	75.9	0.0	24.1

assortment. However, including the correlation between mates reduces the estimates and significance of the shared environmental effects because any genetic effects that might have biased estimates of the shared environment due to assortative mating are now correctly removed and transferred to estimates of the genetic component. Thus, the change in fit due to removing C from the model is much smaller in table 4.12.

Table 4.13 shows the revised estimates of the proportions of variance after including the correlation between mates in the data and allowing for phenotypic assortment in the model. Estimates of the unique environmental contribution (E) barely change because these are almost entirely determined from the differences within monozygotic twin pairs. As expected, allowing for assortative mating tends to increase estimates of the genetic contribution and reduce the apparent influence of the shared environment.

Correcting for assortative mating has relatively little effect on the estimated contribution of the shared environment to political affiliation, since the genetic component is relatively small in the first place. The impact of assortative mating on the genetic correlation between siblings/DZ twins is largest when both the heritability and marital correlation are large. By contrast, allowing for assortative mating for educational attainment all but eradicates the case for shared environmental effects on this trait because the difference between MZ and DZ correlations is far greater in the first place.

INTEGRATING TWIN AND NUCLEAR FAMILY DATA Considered separately, twin and non-twin nuclear family data have their specific strengths and shortcomings. Although there is much variation between the specific conclusions for individual outcomes and samples, the broad picture from nuclear families is that there is substantial and highly significant familial clustering of individual differences between and within generations. Parents and offspring and siblings correlate very highly. That being said, between 30% and 90% of variation does not depend on family clustering but on individual unique random environmental effects and/or the segregation of genetic differences within sibships in accordance with Mendel's first law. Non-twin nuclear family data do not generally help discriminate genetic and cultural models for transmission between parents and children. The fit of both tends to be similar to the identical data. However, models that invoke the genetic transmission of a latent genetic variable tend to be more parsimonious. The most elaborate model for direct phenotypic transmission from parent to offspring tends to lead to larger estimates of the residual shared environmental correlation than a model invoking latent genetic transmission. That is, the "genetic model" for nuclear families explains more, more simply. If genetic transmission is indeed a significant component in family resemblance for social traits, then there is an important implication that explaining transmission genetically also explains part of the residual variation between and within sibships without invoking new principles. *If it were possible to "find the genes" then there is a chance of explaining multiple statistical sources of individual differences by reference to the same underlying mechanism.* Such speculation, however, is unwarranted in advance of a convincing demonstration that the data are not merely consistent with genetic theory but actually demand it. For the most part, the twin data suggest strongly that a genetic explanation of some of the variation is required if the equal environments assumption is justified. The problem of the twin-only study lies with its relatively blunt analysis of the environment. Almost all the variables we studied required a model that involved some shared environmental effects, although their source was not clear. When allowance was made for the genetic consequences of assortative mating, the apparent effects of the shared environment were significantly reduced. This finding is consistent with the conclusion from the nuclear family data that a genetic explanation of parent-offspring correlation, with appropriate allowance for assortative mating, also reduces the apparent residual effects of the shared environment compared with models that assume direct transmission between the measured phenotypes of parents and offspring.

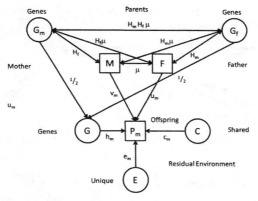

FIGURE 4.5. Combined model for biological and cultural inheritance in nuclear families. *Note:* Diagram is shown for male offspring only. The diagram for females is generated by replacing subscript *m* by *f* on paths where appropriate. Cultural inheritance is assumed to occur directly between the phenotypes of parents and offspring. Other models are possible (see, e.g., Heath et al. 1985)

The principal limitation of the models so far is that they have treated genetic and cultural transmission as *alternative* explanations of parent-offspring transmission. This limitation arises because nuclear family and twin correlations considered separately do not make it possible to consider both mechanisms simultaneously. *A joint analysis of the twin and nuclear family data makes it possible to estimate the genetic and environmental contributions to transmission and variation simultaneously.* Figure 4.5 shows the elements of an integrated model for genetic and vertical cultural inheritance for nuclear families. The diagram only includes parents and a single male offspring. The diagram for female offspring is identical in shape with the substitution of u_f, v_f, h_f, c_f, and e_f for the path coefficients u_m, v_m, h_m, c_m, and e_m respectively. The key to the integrated transmission model lies in the fact that the diagram shows intergenerational paths from parental genotypes and phenotypes to offspring genotype and phenotype (fig. 4.5). Furthermore, the model allows for the correlation between mates and the implications of phenotypic assortative mating for family resemblance. The offspring phenotype, P_m (in males) is the linear sum of the contributions of genes (G_m), parental phenotypes (M and F), and residual shared (C) and unique (E) environmental effects. The diagram may be extended to include a sibling, DZ co-twin, or MZ co-twin. We focus only on one offspring in the diagram to minimize confusion.

An important implication of joint genetic and cultural inheritance is that the *correlations* between genotype and phenotype, H_m and H_f, are not the same as the *path coefficients* between genotypes and phenotypes, h_m and h_f respec-

TABLE 4.14. Expected correlations between relatives under model for joint biological and cultural inheritance

Relationship	Expected correlation
Spouses	μ
Mother-daughter	$v_f + \mu u_f + \frac{1}{2} h_f (H_f + \mu H_m)$
Mother-son	$v_m + \mu u_m + \frac{1}{2} h_m (H_f + \mu H_m)$
Father-daughter	$u_f + \mu v_f + \frac{1}{2} h_f (H_m + \mu H_f)$
Father-son	$u_m + \mu v_m + \frac{1}{2} h_m (H_m + \mu H_f)$
Male siblings	$\gamma h_m^2 + u_m^2 + v_m^2 + 2\mu u_m v_m + h_m[v_m(H_f + \mu H_m) + u_m(H_m + \mu H_f)] + c_m^2$
Female siblings	$\gamma h_f^2 + u_f^2 + v_f^2 + 2u_f v_f + h_f[v_f(H_f + \mu H_m) + u_f(H_m + \mu H_f)] + c_f^2$
Male-female siblings	$\gamma h_m h_f + u_m u_f + v_m v_f + \mu u_f v_m + u_m v_f) + \frac{1}{2} h_m [v_f(H_f + \mu H_m) + u_f(H_m + \mu H_f)] + \frac{1}{2} h_f$ $[v_m(H_f + \mu H_m) + u_m(H_m + \mu H_f)] + c_m c_f$
Male DZ	$\gamma h_m^2 + u_m^2 + v_m^2 + 2\mu u_m v_m + h_m[v_m(H_f + \mu H_m) + u_m(H_m + \mu H_f)] + c_m^2 + t_m^2$
Female DZ	$\gamma h_f^2 + u_f^2 + v_f^2 + 2\mu u_f v_f + h_f[v_f(H_f + \mu H_m) + u_f(H_m + \mu H_f)] + c_f^2 + t_f^2$
Male-female DZ	$\gamma h_m h_f + u_m u_f + v_m v_f + \mu u_f v_m + u_m v_f) + \frac{1}{2} h_m [v_f(H_f + \mu H_m) + u_f(H_m + \mu H_f)] + \frac{1}{2} h_f$ $[v_m(H_f + \mu H_m) + u_m(H_m + \mu H_f)] + c_m c_f + t_m t_f$
Male MZ	$h_m^2 + u_m^2 + v_m^2 + 2\mu u_m v_m + h_m[v_m(H_f + \mu H_m) + u_m(H_m + \mu H_f)] + c_m^2 + t_m^2$
Female MZ	$h_f^2 + u_f^2 + v_f^2 + 2\mu u_f v_f + h_f[v_f(H_f + \mu H_m) + u_f(H_m + \mu H_f)] + c_f^2 + t_f^2$
Where:	$\gamma = \frac{1}{2}(1 + \mu H_m H_f)$
Subject to:	$1 - h_m^2 + u_m^2 + v_m^2 + 2\mu u_m v_m + h_m[v_m(H_f + \mu H_m) + u_m(H_m + \mu H_f)] + c_m^2 + t_m^2$ $+ e_m^2 = 0$
	$1 - h_f^2 + u_f^2 + v_f^2 + 2u_f v_f + h_f[v_f(H_f + \mu H_m) + u_f(H_m + \mu H_f)] + c_f^2 + t_f^2 + e_f^2 = 0$
	$H'_m - h_m + \frac{1}{2} H_m(v_m + \mu u_m) + \frac{1}{2} H_f(u_m + \mu v_m) = 0$
	$H'_f - h_f + \frac{1}{2} H_m(v_m + \mu u_m) + \frac{1}{2} H_f(u_m + \mu v_m) = 0$

Note: The model tabulated does not incorporate genetic dominance or sex-specific genetic and environmental effects.

tively. Thus, from the diagram, it can be seen that, if H_m and H_f are the genotype-phenotype correlations in mothers and fathers, the expected correlation between offspring genotype and (male) phenotype is not h_m but

$$H'_m = h_m + \frac{1}{2} H_m(v_m + \mu u_m) + \frac{1}{2} H_f(u_m + \mu v_m), \text{ similarly } H'_f = h_f + \frac{1}{2} H_m(v_m + \mu u_m) + \frac{1}{2} H_f(u_m + \mu v_m).[9]$$

The algebraic expectations for the correlations between twins and relatives within nuclear families are given in table 4.14. The model as presented in the table makes some simplifying assumption. In particular, it is assumed that the same genes and shared environmental effects affect males and females, although there may be sex differences in the effects of these components on the phenotype. In performing the analysis, we test this assumption by relaxing this constraint and allowing for sex-specific genetic and environmental effects, that is, effects are expressed in one sex but not in the other. The expectations for the more complex model are not tabulated but have been implemented in the general algorithm for model-fitting.

The expectations for the twin correlations contain two additional parameters, t_m and t_f, to allow for the possibility that MZ and DZ twins may share greater environmental similarity than siblings. This parameterization assumes that twins do not experience qualitatively different environments from non-twin siblings but that the residual environments of both types of twins correlate more highly than siblings. Note that this does not deal with the equal environments assumption because the model still assumes that the environments of MZ twins are no more highly correlated than those of DZs. It is apparent from the expectations that there are four nonlinear constraints to be imposed on the parameter estimates. As written, the model assumes that gene action is additive. It is not possible to estimate the effects of dominance at the same time as the shared sibling environment. However, if we are prepared to assume that $c_m = c_f = 0$ their shared environmental parameters may be replace by parameters d_m and d_f to allow for the effects of dominance in males and females. The dominance variance component in MZ twins is d_m^2 in males and d_f^2 in females. The coefficient of the dominance component in siblings and DZ twins is ¼. Dominance does not contribute to parent-offspring resemblance and is not affected by assortative mating in polygenic systems (e.g., Fisher 1918; Falconer and Mackay 1995).

Four equality constraints allow the model to be identified (cf. table 4.14). Two constraints result from the fact that we are analyzing correlations so the total phenotypic variance is constrained to be unity in males and females. The other two follow from the assumption of equilibrium for the correlations H_m and H_f under the combined effects of genetic and nongenetic inheritance in the presence of phenotypic assortative mating. The expectations and constraints were coded for the *Mx* package for structural modeling. The model was fitted simultaneously by weighted least squares to all 12 sets of 13 correlations between relatives. Convergence required 30 seconds CPU time on a Dell Inspiron 1420 laptop computer.

The model in table 4.14 has 11 free parameters that are estimated from 13 correlations for each variable in each sample. Thus, the residual weighted sum of squares for the full model has 13–11 d.f. When allowance is made for sex-specific residual sibling shared environmental and excess shared twin environmental effects two additional parameters are required and the model should fit perfectly ($\Sigma\delta^2 = 0$) unless there are active boundary constraints on one or more parameters. Goodness of fit tests for the full model and for a series of reduced models are shown in table 4.15. In no case does a purely additive

TABLE 4.15. Model comparison statistics: Combined twin and nuclear family data

| | | | Weighted residual SS = $\Sigma\delta^2$ | | | | | | | | | | |
| Trait | | | Stature | | Conservatism | | Neuroticism | | Church attendance | | Political affiliation | | Educational attainment | |
	Model	d.f.	US	AU	US	AU	US	AU	US	AU	US	AU	US	AU
1	Full model: genes +VCI[a]	0[b]	0.00	1.93	0.00	0.00	1.43	9.18	0.00	0.18	0.00	5.79	0.00	0.10
2	No vertical cultural inheritance ("VCI")	4	5.42	12.22	9.08	5.35	3.78	13.77	2.26	6.31	15.49	32.67	9.52	9.25
3	No shared environment/dominance	10	43.81	43.25	38.73	75.07	32.40	41.36	45.58	56.12	49.78	38.60	239.32	341.56
4	No twin or sibling shared environment	6	18.31	15.13	9.77	34.76	14.79	22.51	29.78	7.38	37.61	29.96	161.77	134.89
5	No sibling shared environment	3	2.92	5.49	3.67	28.97	1.44	11.01	10.70	5.10	10.22	5.81	103.89	85.32
6	No twin shared environment	3	6.18	9.42	1.71	8.42	10.63	16.78	10.97	5.45	30.58	28.25	12.06	17.23
7	No genes	2	133.34	102.16	44.91	10.94	34.02	43.89	13.24	21.71	4.53	6.00	45.14	37.24
8	Model 3 plus sex-specific A and D	6	7.81	13.37	5.39	33.13	7.75	8.41	15.68	17.57	42.36	36.87	88.49	109.82

[a] No dominant genetic effects; sex differences in effects of genes and shared environment, but no sex-specific genetic effects.

[b] This model should give a perfect fit in the absence of nonadditive genetic effects.

Significance levels of χ^2:

| d.f. | P (%) | | | | |
	10	5	1	0.5	0.1
2	4.61	5.99	9.21	10.60	13.82
3	6.25	7.81	11.34	12.84	16.27
4	7.78	9.49	13.28	14.86	18.47
6	10.64	12.59	16.81	18.55	22.46
8	13.36	15.51	20.09	21.95	26.13
10	15.99	18.31	23.21	25.19	29.59

genetic model (model 3) account for the pattern of family resemblance. Similarly, the combined data do not generally justify ignoring the role of genetic factors (model 7). *Political affiliation is the only apparent exception to this rule.* A model that excludes genetic factors gives quite a good fit to the correlations for political affiliation ($\Sigma\delta^2_{(2)}$ = 4.53 and 6.00 in Virginia and Australia respectively).

Beyond this basic conclusion, there is clearly no "one size fits all" answer to the question of the relative sizes and types of genetic and environmental effects on the variables included in this investigation. Different variables show different patterns of genetic and environment influence. The goodness of fit tests in table 4.15 suggests a high degree of consistency between the best-fitting models for the different outcomes in the two large samples from Virginia and Australia. The models that seem to give the most consistent acceptable fit in both samples are indicated in bold type in table 4.15. In each case, we identify a model that has the same structure in both populations. Thus, although it is impossible to exclude genes and all sources of shared environmental variance for conservatism, church attendance, and education, a model that eliminates nongenetic parent-offspring transmission (model 2) gives an acceptable fit to these variables. The "best" model for political affiliation does not require genetic inheritance overall (model 7). For stature and neuroticism an adequate model includes the effects of genetic dominance (model 8). The picture is summarized in table 4.16 which shows the parameter estimates for the "best" model for each variable. Blank cells represent parameters that were fixed at zero in the selected reduced models. The models incorporate additional parameters (h'_f, c'_f etc.) to allow for sex-specific effects (see, e.g., Truett et al. 1994; Maes et al. 2009). Zero estimates of these parameters are consistent with the absence of sex-specific effects of the corresponding outcome. The large estimates of d'_f for stature and neuroticism are consistent with sex-specific effects of genetic dominance on these variables.

Although many of the variables provide evidence for significant residual shared environmental resemblance between siblings and twins, perhaps the most striking feature of the overall findings is that the best-fitting models do not generally provide strong support for direct nongenetic influence of parental phenotypes on the phenotypes of their offspring. The only exception is political affiliation in both populations where large parent-offspring correlations and small differences in MZ and DZ correlations conspire to favor a purely environmental explanation of parent-offspring resemblance. Political affiliation also reflects some of the larger effects of other shared environmen-

TABLE 4.16. Parameter estimates for best-fitting models for genetic and environmental components of family resemblance

Parameter		Stature		Conservatism		Neuroticism		Church attendance		Party identification		Educational attainment	
		US	AU	US	AU	US	AU	US	AU	US	AU	US	AU
Additive genetic	h_m	0.853	0.827	0.670	0.697	0.480	0.536	0.797	0.659			0.771	0.583
	h_f	0.817	0.818	0.751	0.747	0.522	0.438	0.788	0.700			0.764	0.638
	h_f^*	0.185	0.286			0.146	0.270						
Sibling shared environment	c_m			0.217	0.304			0.121	0.232	0.438	0.157	0.378	0.428
	c_f			−0.009	0.184			−0.163	0.261	0.313	0.015	0.373	0.278
	c_f^*			0.186	0.274			0.185	0.000	0.106	0.000	0.210	0.387
Dominant genetic	d_m	0.346	0.403			0.332	0.237						
	d_f	0.119	−0.087			−0.010	−0.135						
	d_f^*	0.367	0.221			0.358	0.358						
Twin shared environment	t_m			0.269	0.239			0.299	0.254	0.324	0.420	0.343	0.390
	t_f			−0.067	0.211			0.107	−0.074	0.231	0.124	0.044	0.264
	t_f^*			0.170	0.000			0.191	0.278	0.408	0.384	0.300	0.165
Vertical cultural transmission	u_m									0.268	0.464		
	u_f									0.206	0.331		
	v_m									0.176	0.233		
	v_f									0.321	0.535		
Marital	μ	0.223	0.207	0.618	0.685	0.092	0.060	0.821	0.753	0.642	0.834	0.567	0.507
Goodness-of-fit[a]	$\Sigma\delta^2$	7.81	13.37	9.08	5.35	7.75	8.41	2.26	6.31	4.53	6.00	9.52	9.25
	d.f.	6	6	4	4	6	6	4	4	2	2	4	4
	P%	>10	5–10	1–5	>10	>10	>10	>10	>10	>10	5	1–5	5–10

[a] Probability (P%) assumes weighted residual sum of squares is distributed as chi-square.

tal influences including the increased environmental similarity specific to twins.

Table 4.17 contains the estimated proportions of the total variance attributed to each of the sources in the best-fitting model for each of the outcome measures in males and females. The estimates allow for any effects of assortative mating on the total phenotypic variance.

The estimates for stature provide a benchmark for what is typical of a variable for which family resemblance is entirely genetic. When allowance is made for the modest degree of assortative mating, additive and dominant genetic effects together account for 80–85% of the total variation, the remainder being due to random, unique environmental effects that are uncorrelated between family members. The estimates are remarkably consistent across sexes and between the two populations sampled. The same model fits the data on neuroticism but, for this personality variable, the effects of genetic differences account for only 35–40% of the phenotypic variance. The finding that variation in the major dimensions of personality is only modestly heritable and caused primarily by nonfamilial environmental effects has been long-established in the behavioral genetics literature (e.g., Eaves, Eysenck, and Martin 1989; Plomin, Asbury, and Dunn 2001).

For the purposes of the current investigation, the results for the other variables are challenging and compelling. First, the best model for political affiliation in both populations does not require genetic influences. All the variance is due to the environment. The effects of the environment span all the sources included in the model. Although the basic model is the same, the actual proportions explained by the sources of variance differ greatly between the two contexts. There are small but statistically significant effects of the residual shared environment among sibships (V_{EC}) and excess shared environmental similarity between twins (V_{ET}). Together these effects account for 15–30% of the total variation in outcome. Both populations show large effects of the environment transmitted by parents and influences specific to individual subjects. However, the balance of these contributions is markedly different between the United States and Australia. In the United States, unique environmental effects account for c. 45–50% of the total variance, compared with only 20–30% in Australia, depending on sex. The direct contribution of parents to the political preferences of the adult offspring (V_{CI}) accounts for a much smaller proportion of the variance in the United States (c. 20%) compared with Australia (c. 55–60%). Although it is dangerous to read too much out of such findings, they would suggest that there is far less intergenerational mobility in the political affiliations of Australians than Americans.

TABLE 4.17. Proportions (%) of variance in phenotype attributed to sources in best-fitting model

		Males						Females					
		V_A	V_D	V_E	V_{EC}	V_{ET}	V_{CI}	V_A	V_D	V_E	V_{EC}	V_{ET}	V_{CI}
Stature	US	72.8	11.9	15.3				76.7	14.9	14.4			
	AU	68.3	16.2	15.4				76.2	5.7	18.1			
Conservatism	US	44.8		43.2	4.7	7.2		56.5		36.7	3.5	3.3	
	AU	48.6		36.5	9.3	5.7		55.8		28.9	10.9	4.4	
Neuroticism	US	23.1	11.0	65.9				29.5	11.8	58.7			
	AU	28.7	5.6	65.7				26.6	14.7	58.7			
Church attendance	US	63.5		26.1	2.1	8.9		62.1		27.1	6.1	4.8	
	AU	43.4		44.8	1.5	6.5		49.0		36.0	6.8	8.3	
Political affiliation	US			51.8	19.2	10.5	18.5			46.4	10.9	20.0	20.7
	AU			21.9	2.5	17.6	58.1			28.8	0.0	16.3	54.9
Educational attainment	US	59.4		14.5	14.3	11.8		58.4		14.1	18.3	9.2	
	AU	34.0		32.5	18.3	15.2		40.7		26.9	22.7	9.7	

Note: Sources of variance: V_A = Additive genetic variance; V_D = Dominance genetic variance; V_E = Residual, unique environmental variance within sibships; V_{EC} = Residual shared environmental variance among sibships; V_{ET} = Additional shared environmental variance between twin pairs; V_{CI} = Variance due to nongenetic ("cultural") inheritance from parental phenotype.

At least part of this difference may be due to the fact that the items address somewhat different aspects of political affiliation in the two studies. In the United States, the item comprised a categorical rating of the strength of preference for one or another of the two major political parties. In Australia, subjects were asked to report their voting choice among the principal political parties.

Many social scientists will be surprised by our claim the data are consistent with the contribution of additive genetic factors to individual differences in conservatism, church attendance, and educational attainment. The fact that other variables (stature and political affiliation) support two extremely different models for family resemblance, one purely genetic (stature) and one purely environmental (political affiliation), imply that *the models and methods are not inherently biased against environmental explanations*, contrary to critics claims. Taken at their face value, the results for conservatism, church attendance, and educational attainment imply that much of the evidence for the shared environment from twin studies disappears when allowance is made for the genetic consequences of mate selection and that genetic effects account for c. 35–50% of the total variance depending on measure and context. The effects of residual shared environmental effects on conservatism and church attendance are significant but relatively small (c. 5–16% of the total). For educational attainment the residual shared environmental effects are larger accounting for approximately 30% of the total variance.

Development of Social and Political Attitudes in Childhood

So far, the above analyses deal with differences between *adults*. By the time these studies have begun, the subjects have already passed through two decades or more of biological development and social learning—from their parents, teachers, peers, and media. Infants do not appear with measurable social attitudes. Their world and the perception of it mature and expand as they mature. The world itself changes over time. Contexts and salience change with age. Thus, when we consider differences in behavior, especially differences in social attitudes and behavior, we expect change. Such changes may not merely affect how behavior itself changes over time with age, the so-called main effects of age and secular change, but the actual *causes* of individual differences may change with age and environment. For example, different kinds of environment may be important to different times in the life cycle, different genes may be expressed at different ages or in different social contexts. Thus, it is important to look at the role of social and genetic influences on political attitudes from a life course perspective.

Political socialization research has traditionally focused on how elements of the social environment influence and interact with individual development (Sigel 1989). Within the social environment, familial, and especially parental, influences have long been considered a primary source of political learning over the life course. This focus on the parent seemed well founded as numerous studies have found a strong correspondence between ideological orientations of parents and their children (e.g., Alwin, Cohen, and Newcomb 1991; Jencks et al. 1972; Jennings and Niemi 1982; Miller and Glass 1989). The need to take a developmental perspective extends as much to the study of genetic differences as it does to the effects of socialization. Although the genes may be fixed at conception, the effects of genes are not but emerge as part of an ontogenetic process that extends across the whole of life, with different patterns of expression and regulation arising in response to the adaptive challenges at different times in the lifespan and historical setting. Eaves et al. (2008) found that the genetic and environmental contributions of religious practices and church attendance (religiosity) vary with age. In principle, genetic differences expressed at birth may be eradicated by the cumulative effect of the postnatal environment or they may be imperceptible early on and increase over the lifespan as a result of constant environmental reinforcement (e.g., Eaves, Long, and Heath 1986). Shared environmental factors accounted for the vast majority of variance in children and adolescents, but decreased in importance during late adolescence and young adulthood, while genetic influences on religiosity increase over the same period. This is important as political ideology is believed to stem from a socialization process similar to that affecting religion in that both share the same high levels of parent-child concordance (Niemi and Jennings 1991).

We demonstrate the importance of a more dynamic conception of the roles of genes and environment in social behavior by examining data from published population-based twin surveys that address both the pattern and sources of political attitudes over the life course (see Hatemi, Funk et al. 2009 for details). We combine two studies of twins. The first examines cross-sectional age changes in adult MZ and DZ twin correlations from the Virginia 30,000 (see Eaves et al. 1997 for more details). The second employs longitudinal data on the attitudes of twins gathered as part of a study of cardiovascular risk and function through adolescence.

Figure 4.6 summarizes the correlations for conservatism between MZ and DZ twins in twins from the Virginia 30,000, by age divided into five-year cohorts between 18 and 75+. The individual correlations fluctuate somewhat with age, but the principal feature of the data is that the correlations for MZ

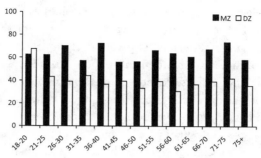

FIGURE 4.6. Twin correlations for conservatism in twins aged 18+.

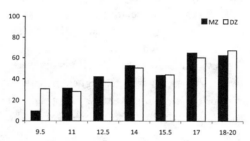

FIGURE 4.7. Twin correlations for conservatism in juvenile twins aged 9–18.

twins are roughly the same across ages and virtually always greater than those for DZs. A simple statistical test of these correlations (see Eaves et al. 1997) shows that variation over ages is largely due to sampling error, while that between MZ and DZ correlations is not. That is, there is consistent evidence for the role of genetic effects on social attitudes in adulthood that does not alter in magnitude through adult life.

Figure 4.7 shows the correlations for a measure of conservatism obtained in a study of juveniles. Note that we have deliberately included twins aged 18–20 in both figures.

The results for juveniles stand in marked contrast to those for adults. In juveniles, the correlations visibly increase with age during adolescence. Furthermore, and very strikingly, there is virtually no difference between the correlations for MZ and DZ twins. The increase in correlation with age and the lack of any significant difference between MZ and DZ correlations in adolescence are both confirmed by a simple statistical test (Eaves et al. 1997). The analysis of the age trends in correlation suggests a remarkable developmental transition in the contributions of genes and environment across the lifespan. Prior to age 20, the pattern is one of purely social determination with no significant hint of genetic effects. After that age, the picture changes with emergence of the marked genetic differences that persist through the rest of adult life. It appears that ages 18–25 reflect a pivotal developmental transition in the contributions of the social environment to social attitudes. Prior to, say, age 21, the overwhelming effects are those of the environment shared by family members. Insofar as these effects depend on parents, they are largely shared and social and not detectably genetic in any form. After age 20, the pattern changes. The abiding effects of parents on their adult offspring seem to be genetic rather than social (exaggerated by the effects of strong assortative mating for social attitudes, see above). As a result, the effects of Mendelian segregation are finally expressed in the adult phenotype, resulting in a sharp and marked reduction in the DZ correlations relative to those for MZs because genes do not only contribute to the resemblance of parents and offspring but also to differences within pairs of dizygotic twins and siblings.

The other impressive feature of the correlations in figure 4.7 is the consistent increase in twin correlation with age, suggesting that the relative effects of the shared environment on twins' attitudes increase with age. In fact, the figure obscures the fact that the increase in the effects of the shared environment is even more marked. The correlations are standardized within each age cohort, so the figure only reflects the contribution of shared influences *relative to the total at each age*. Figure 4.8 summarizes estimates of the absolute amount of variation in conservatism contributed by shared and unique environmental influences across ages.

The figure shows that the *total* variance in conservatism increases almost four-fold between ages 9 and 17. This is not surprising as the items concern issues that are barely salient to younger children and responses likely to be far less structured and organized as they are in older juveniles who are becoming aware of, and influenced by, their social and poltical universe. The vari-

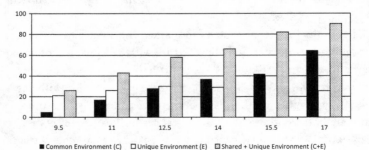

FIGURE 4.8. The relative contributions of shared and unique environmental influences on variation in liberalism-conservatism during childhood and adolescence (Hatemi et al. 2009).

ance contributed by the unique environment (E) fluctuates around the same level (20 units) across the whole age range or shows, at best, only modest accumulation between 9½ and 17. This is consistent with the view that much of what contributes to E is due to relatively short-lived random fluctuation that contribute typically to measurement error. The effects of the shared environment, in contrast, increase from close to zero in the youngest twins to about 60 units in 17 year-olds.

It is tempting to conclude that the effects of the shared environment at any stage during adolescence represent the persistent and cumulative effects of previous environmental experiences. Obviously, this hypothesis cannot be tested with cross-sectional data. However, for this adolescent cohort, we are fortunate that a large part of the sample was studied longitudinally so it is possible to reconstruct how the effects of the shared and unique environment persist and accumulate over time (see Hatemi, Funk et al. 2009). The logic is simple. Just as we can use cross-sectional data on MZ and DZ twins to estimate the contributions of genes and environment to individual differences *within* ages, so we can use the cross-twin correlations *between* ages to estimate the contribution of genes and environment to stability of behavior *between* ages. For example, suppose genetic effects persist over time but the effects of the shared environment are age-specific. Cross-sectional twin data would show that the DZ correlations, while less than the MZ correlations are nevertheless greater than half the MZ correlations (see the above introduction to the analysis of twin resemblance). If the effects of the shared environment are age-specific, however, they will not contribute to the correlation between first twins measured at one age and second twins measured at another. So, for example, in our thought experiment, if genetic effects are stable over time, the correlation between first twins at one age and second twins at another in MZ twins is expected to be twice that for DZ twins. Indeed, we can use the cross-twin cross-age correlations to estimate the extent to which the same genes (or environments) contribute to individual differences at different ages. That is, we can estimate the *genetic correlation* between measures made at different times, an index of the extent to which the same or different genes are expressed at differents ages. Generally, a high genetic correlation implies that a high proportion of the genes affecting a trait are showing effects that are stable over time and age. The same logic can be applied to estimate the *shared environmental correlation* and the *unique environmental correlation* from longitudinal data on MZ and DZ twins. This basic insight allows a variety of models to be elaborated for the effects of genes and environment on development (see Hatemi, Funk et al. 2009 and references in Eaves et al. 2005) and

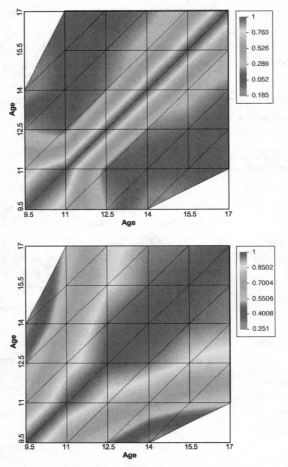

FIGURE 4.9. Cross-age correlations between environmental effects on conservative atttitudes during childhood and adolescence (Hatemi et al. 2009). a. Unique (within-family) environment b. Shared (between-family) environment.

for developmental changes in the effects of genes and environment. Figure 4.9 shows "heat maps" of the cross-age correlations for the effects of the unique (fig. 4.9a) and shared (fig. 4.13b) environment on adolescent liberal-conservative attitudes.

High correlations (close to 1) are shown in red and low correlations (close to zero) in blue. The diagonal (from lower left to top right) represents the correlations between effects for twins of the same age. Obviously these are all unity for both unique and shared environmental effects. The color shades from red to blue as the graph moves from the leading diagonal. As the age differences between the stages of measurement get greater, the correlations get smaller because somewhat different environmental effects operate at different ages. However, the difference between the graphs for the unique and shared environmental effects is very marked. The correlations between the effects of the unique environment fall off very sharply with increasing age difference, rapidly approaching zero. Furthermore, there is very little tendency for the correlations to change as a function of increasing age. Thus, the individual-specific effects of the environment, not shared with co-twins, are relatively transient. They neither persist nor accumulate with age.

The pattern for the shared environment differs greatly. Firstly, the correlations do not decay anything like as rapidly as those for the unique environment, supporting the view that the effects of the shared environment—parents, teachers, peers and media—are far more persistent than those which make individual twins differ within the family. Second, as twins get older, the correlations between measures at different ages also get larger.

This can be seen in the way the band of red and orange in fig. 4.9b spreads out more from the diagonal as the twins approach 17. This finding is consistent with the view that the effects of the shared environment not only persist over time, they also accumulate. Each new occasion may expose each pair to a new set of shared environmental experiences, but these persist throughout adolescence and new shared environmental experiences build up these associations, leading to the pattern we observe of increasing effects of the shared environment with age (fig. 4.8), and high and increasing cross-temporal correlations in the shared environmental components (fig. 4.9b). By contrast the effects of the unique environment show much less dramatic changes over time (fig. 4.8) and are much less stable and accumulate less with age (fig. 4.9a).

The figures are suggestive of a developmental model for social attitudes in which influences of the unique environment are time-specific and short-lived whereas those of the shared environment show continuous, persistent, and cumulative input from before adolescence into early adulthood. These basic ideas can be captured and tested more formally in a variety of linear time series models that specify the input and transmission of environmental influences over time. Hatemi et al. develop and test such a model for the longitudinal twin data we have summarized. Their "best" model, in the sense of that which yields good overall fit without over-elaborating model complexity, is summarized in figure 4.10.

Squares represent the measured trait (conservatism-liberalism) for each age listed. Circles represent latent "input" variables. E is the unique environment. C is the shared or common environment. There are assumed to be specific en-

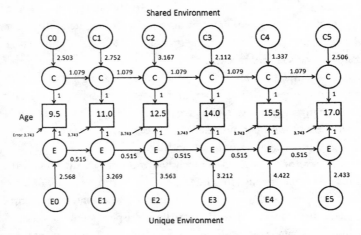

FIGURE 4.10. First-order autoregressive model for the effects of the shared and unique environment on the liberalism-conservatism index during childhood and adolescence (Hatemi and Eaves 2009).

vironmental inputs at each age that are independent of each other over time (Eo . . . E5; Co–C5). Eo..E5 and Co..C5 are assumed to be scaled to unit variance. These effects, however, accumulate through the mediating effects of variables E and C respectively. The paths between successive values of E and C represent the strength of the forward persistence of previous environmental influences. These are allowed to differ between E and C, but are assumed, for simplicity, to be constant over time.

There are assumed to be occasion-specific, individual-specific errors of measurement that do not persist. These are repesented by the arrows labelled "error" in the figure. Hatemi et al. present the results for other versions of the model. The figure presents maximum likelihood estimates of the parameters of their final model for the covariance structure. If anything, the time-specific effects of the unique environments, Eo . . . E5, are somewhat larger than those of the shared environment, Co . . . C5. Thus, at any one time the unique environments are highly variable, perhaps more so than the shared environments. However, the persistence of the unique environment across time (0.515) is far less that that of the shared enviroment (1.079). That is, the effects of the shared environment, once they occur, do not decay over time but persist to the threshold of adult life whereas unique environmental experiences are soon forgotten. Details of the model-fitting process and model-comparison statistics are summarized by Hatemi et al. (2009).

These compelling findings for the development of social attitudes during adolescence also present an abiding problem. Why is it that effects that persist and accumulate so robustly during adolescence are so rapidly dissipated in favor of genetic influences once the young adults leave home? Is our finding for conservatism the footprint of changing roles of social and genetic family influences in the transition from parent-dependent adolescence to adult independence? Late adolescence is seen as the formative phase for establishing social orientations (Inglehart 1977). Our data imply a much more nuanced process where social *orientations* are not established in this period, but social *learning processes* are. The latter comprise the mainspring for the subsequent development of social *orientations*. Only when children leave home do their own longer term orientations manifest themselves. What children may be gaining from their parents is a default heuristic; a process of heuristic acquisition in adolescence which then changes to heuristic application in adulthood, thereby explaining the significant correlation between parents and children but also allowing for idiosyncratic deviations. Thus, offspring begin with the attitudes learned from their parents, but as they leave home, their own experiences and individual genetic disposition interact to modify those attitudes. The underlying mechanisms behind this remarkable transition over a relatively short part of the lifespan remain unclear.

We note in passing that our data on adolescent and adult attitudes present a problem for simple-minded versions of the frequent criticism that MZ twins resemble one another more than DZs because they share more similar patterns of early socialization, with parents and others tending to emphasize the similarities of MZs and the differences in DZs. Proponents of this view have to develop a model that explains why it takes until the twins leave home for these early differences in socialization to occur, yet at the very time they are living together, going to school and playing with friends there is not the slightest hint, at least for the variables in question, that MZ twins are in the least bit more similar than DZs.

Limitations

Within this introductory scope a wide range of themes relevant to the study of genetic and environmental influences on human behavior remain unexplored. Our goal is to provide a basic framework and ideas that, we hope, will engage a new generation of scholars in a way of thinking that may be unfamiliar but worth exploring. However, in this chapter, we do not consider how genes and environment contribute to the patterns of covariation between multiple outcomes ("the genetic analysis of covariance structure"; Martin and Eaves 1977; Behrman, Taubman, and Wales 1977; Neale and Cardon 1992). Many of the more challenging questions involve attempts to characterize the multiple facets of the environment to identify the multiple biological and social pathways from DNA to social behavior. Such studies are inherently multivariate and we hope that the motivated reader will use this chapter as a solid foundation from which to explore models involving the effects of genes and environments on multiple variables. All the models we consider do not model the effects of genotype x environment interaction. That is, the models assume that the behavior ("phenotype") of an individual can be approximated by the sum of his/her individual genetic and environmental deviations from their corresponding population means.

Studies of experimental plants, humans, animals, and microorganisms demonstrate that this is an approximation. Some genes affect the phenotype by increasing or reducing individuals' sensitivity to their environment. Some environments may restrict or facilitate the expression of genetic differences. The more our studies address complex behaviors that rely on the human capacity to evaluate and respond to the world cognitively and emotionally, the more plausible it becomes that such genotype x environment interactions ("GxE") are a significant feature of the genetic architecture of human behavior. Mather and Jinks (1982) provide a basic conceptual framework for the detection, analysis, and significance GxE in experimental organisms. There are several approaches to the analysis of GxE in humans (see, e.g., Jinks and Fulker 1970; Kendler and Eaves 1986; Caspi et al. 2002; Rutter and Silberg 2002; Turkheimer et al. 2003; Eaves et al. 2003) that have met with varying degrees of success in practice. This aspect of the field is still fluid and time will tell how important such interactions are, relative to the main effects of genes and environment, as influences in the development of human behavior.

A theme related to GxE that is especially relevant to political behavior and values is the interaction between the expression of genetic differences and secular change. It is quite conceivable that different epochs facilitate or suppress the expression of genetic differences. Boomsma et al. (1999) offer an intriguing example of the differential expression of genetic differences in juvenile behavior as a function of the difference between a liberal secular upbringing compared with a more conservative religious one. The role of such influences in the social and political arena is extremely plausible. Indeed, recent explorations of gene-environment interplay regarding political attitudes have found that life events, such as losing a job or having financial problems, alter the genetic variance on economic political attitudes (Hatemi 2010).

We have resisted the temptation to address methods for identifying the effects of specific genes on political values and behavior. This is partly a matter of space and partly because the field is still in such a state of flux that it would be premature to say too much. Thirty years of dedicated work, with ever more refined laboratory methods, increasingly large samples, and statistical approaches designed to minimize the effects of data-grubbing in the analysis of horrendously large number of potential predictors are only now reaching a point at which there is an emerging consensus that the number of genes underlying differences in most human traits is very large and their effects, though large in aggregate, appear individually small (Hatemi, Hibbing et al. 2010). There are, of course, exceptions and we never know in advance what those might be, but it seems that for the most part Fisher's original conjecture (1918), borne out by decades of careful study in experimental organisms (see, e.g., Mather and Jinks 1982), is no less true of differences in human behavior, that is, that the number of genes is large and their individual effects are small (see, e.g., Visscher 2008; International Schizophrenia Genetics Consortium 2009).

The extended twin kinship design yields far more correlations between relatives than we chose to illustrate the essentials of the model. Altogether, the studies yield no less than 80 distinct relationships (ignoring three-generational data). These additional relationships not only allow the current model to be tested for its ability to account for a much broader set of kinship relationships but also allow for the development and testing of a richer set of alternatives including different mechanisms of mate selection and intergenerational transmission (see, e.g., Truett et al. 1994; Keller et al. 2009; Maes et al. 2009). The Australian and Virginia samples comprise a far richer set of relationships than those we have chosen to analyze for didactic and illustrative purposes (see, e.g., Eaves et al., "Comparing" 1999; Kirk et al. 1999; Lake et al. 2000). These additional correlations not only generate more data points that provide broader-ranging tests of the generalizability of simpler models but permit a wider range of models, involving greater numbers of parameters, to be fitted and tested (see, e.g., Keller et al. 2009; Maes et al. 2009).

Critics (see Exchange in *Perspectives on Politics*, June 2008 and October 2008) have argued that the reliance of such estimates of genetic contributions on patterns of twin resemblance remains inherently flawed due to the equal environments assumption (EEA). In other words, MZ twins are typically treated more alike than DZs as children (e.g., Loehlin and Nichols 1976) and have more contact with each other as adults (e.g., Kendler et al. 1993). This assumption has been tested for numerous behavioral traits in every fashion the data would allow (for a review see Medland and Hatemi 2009; Hatemi, Hibbing et al. 2009). For example, Posner et al. (1996) showed that the degree of environmental sharing in adult Australian twins is better explained empirically as a consequence rather than a cause of phenotypic differences within MZ and DZ pairs. The analysis of adolescent attitudes discussed above (see Hatemi et al. 2009) have demonstrated that the differences between MZ and DZ correlations for conservatism arise only in adult life and that MZ and DZ correlations are identical during adolescence. These data preclude the obvious implication that additional similarities in the juvenile MZ environment are having a substantial effect on the development of attitudes.

Typically, critics of the EEA have yet to provide a theory of how greater early environmental differences within DZ twin pairs compared with MZs have latent effects that only affect the outcome of interest when the twins leave home. It could still be argued that the persistence of greater MZ similarity in adult attitudes could reflect the abiding greater attachment of MZ twins compared with DZs. The implications of this possibility for adult political and social behavior remain to be explored empirically with the current data. For example, it remains to be explained how the effects of the "MZ special environment" metastasize through entire pedigrees, such as the extended kinships of twins including such a wide range of social and biological relationships as cousins related through MZ and DZ twins, the in-laws of MZ and DZ twins and so forth. That is, if the "special MZ environment" or lasting MZ attachment is a real component of their behavior, then it has to be such that it pervades virtually every feature of adult life, including marriage, mating, and parenting.

Even if such explanations were plausible, in the absence of concrete proposals about their broader implications for family resemblance, they remain an ad hoc refuge of despair in the face of more theoretically grounded genetic models and have the same heuristic value as theories of intelligent design in evolutionary biology. The general consistency of twin data with the growing array of data confirming the contributions of large numbers of identifiable genetic polymorphisms to behavioral outcomes is a further strand in the web of coherent support (cf. Murphy 1997) for the view that parsimonious statistical genetic models, grounded in a wide interwoven history of experimental and observational study, cannot be dismissed so summarily because the conclusions appear counter to our personal preferences (cf. Russell 1946).

Conclusions and Future Directions

We have illustrated the analysis of human family resemblance with two of the largest and potentially most informative datasets available to us, using different constellations of relatives separately and cumulatively. Within limits, the more subtle the models we wish to identify, the greater the range of relationships we need to study. We contrasted, and then combined, models of nongenetic transmission and models that include additive genetic transmission. Our dataset, which is the largest of any genetically informative study on sociopolitical attributes, supports a model that includes genetic transmission for all six traits analyzed except for party identification. Thus, our data from Australia and the United States concur in showing, to a first approximation, that individual differences in party affiliation are due entirely to social and unique environmental influences without any apparent genetic influence. This finding sets party affiliation, along with religious affiliation (see, e.g., Eaves, Martin, and Heath 1990), apart from the majority of traits studied from a genetic perspective almost all of which show at least some contribution of genetic differences. Educational attainment, church attendance, conservatism-liberalism, and party affiliation are all remarkable for the very high correlations between spouses. In this respect, these variables are also distinct from almost all other physical and behavioral traits, including neuroticism and stature, for which the correlations between mates are far smaller if not close to zero. When our models for family resemblance include assortative mating it becomes clear that much of what is assigned to the effects of the shared environment in twin studies may well be a reflection of the genetic consequences of assortative mating. The choice of mate as one of the most significant ways through which humans extend their influence to the next generation.

The actual process that generates spousal resemblance in these initial analyses is moot. It was assumed in the analysis of the twin and nuclear family data that the correlation between mates was a matter of mutual selection of each spouse for the measured phenotype of the other. A series of follow-up analyses exploit the additional information in the patterns of resemblance between the spouses of biological relatives (twins and siblings, in our case) to begin to test alternative hypotheses about the process of mate selection and to discriminate similarity due to assortative mating from that due to spousal interaction (see Alford et al. forthcoming). For those variables where the correlations between mates are large, analysis of the correlations between the spouses of twins and siblings strongly supports the assumption of the initial model-fitting that the principal source of spousal resemblance is indeed the selection of spouses for the actual phenotypes in question and not for aspects of the family background that helped shape them ("social homogamy") or simply due to the mutual social interaction that is expected to occur between spouses.

The adult samples are entirely cross-sectional. Thus, the analyses of these samples only consider the long-term outcome of development. They do not attempt to analyze the ontogenetic process by which attitudes emerge during adolescence. We have summarized the findings of a recent analysis by Hatemi, Funk et al. (2009) in which the development of liberal and conservative attitudes was studied in a longitudinal sample of MZ and DZ twins assessed repeatedly every 18 months between 9.5 and 17 years of age. The results of this analysis are remarkable in showing that, prior to young adulthood, the influences shaping conservative and liberal social attitudes are exclusively environmental and notably the environments that twins share regardless of zygosity. That is, the genetic effects on attitudes expressed in adulthood only emerge in the transition from dependence on parents to relatively independent adult life. During adolescence, the effects of the shared environment are highly persistent and cumulative, whereas those of the individual within-family environment are short-lived and show little, if any, long-term accumulation. A model that elucidates the actual mechanism underlying this apparent "switch" from purely social to partly genetic causation of differences in attitudes will require the careful longitudinal study of a genetically informative sample during this period of transition. Unfortunately, such data are not available to us at this time.

The results of these analyses, based on large sample of informative relatives in two populations addressing a common set of constructs, suggest strongly that the theory of the "Promethean genotype" is not a solid foundation for understanding why people vary in their social and political behavior. Evolution has not entirely emancipated humans from the influences of their biological inheritance. This being said, the results imply a far more subtle understanding than the simple-minded assumption of pure genetic or social inheritance. Although social attitudes and political behavior could not exist without culture, individual differences in the cultural options to which individuals migrate is, at least in part, a function of inherited genetic differences (cf. Martin et al. 1986).

Some may be concerned that our approach raises the specter of genetic determinism. There is no practical or epistemological difference between genetic and environmental accounts of human behavior. Both are inherently determinist because they address "cause." Neither precludes nor necessarily facilitates behavioral change or intervention. Neither precludes human agency as a potent factor in individual or societal transformation. Neither is fixed. The real scientific challenge is to reveal what it is about the phylogeny and ontogeny of human behavior that makes humans capable of transcending perceived biological or social limitations. In this respect, our approach takes the theory of the "Promethean genotype" with complete seriousness, exploring methods that allow it to be tested and charting its empirical merit across a broad range of human sociopolitical differences in two populations.

The conclusion that genetic differences are a significant component underlying variation in some socially and politically important dimensions of human behavior raises the question of the number and genomic location of these heritable differences. Any demonstration that human differences are partly genetic in origin definitely does not imply that there is a single gene, or even a small handful of genes, "for" specific features of complex human behavior. In this respect we concur with Lewontin, Rose, and Kamin (1984). Genetic research in the 90 years since Fisher's (1918) seminal paper, and especially in the last decade, appears to be reaching a consensus that, after analyzing variation throughout the genome on an extraordinarily large number of subjects for a wide range of physical, physiological, and clinical outcomes, the number of genes is very large and their individual effects sometimes vanishingly small (e.g., Visscher 2008; International Schizophrenia Genetics Consortium 2009). Research strategies that recapitulate failed attempts to find individual genes of large effect on other traits are, in the opinion of these authors, unlikely to unlock the underlying biological mechanisms that bridge the developmental gap between the DNA and outcomes of concern to the social or political sciences. Indeed, those who incline toward nongenetic explanations may well agree that the same is true for environmental predictors. The strongest correlations are the empirical correlations between relatives and their resolution into specific material causes remains elusive. Classical twin and family designs provide population estimates of the genetic and environmental components of certain behaviors or attitudes, but they cannot explain why a specific individual has a certain attitude.

How should findings about familial, environmental, and genetic sources of variation be interpreted and incorporated into the research program of political science? The short answer may be "in fear and trembling" because it is very easy to overstate and misrepresent the practical and cultural importance of any scientific conclusion. This being said, the data on family resemblance offer a pressing invitation to address genetic and biological mechanisms underlying some, but not all, aspects of political behavior. Models that incorporate only presumed "environmental" influences may miss one of the most significant factors underlying human motivation and behavioral development. *Individual* differences are paramount in individual behavior and the origin of individual differences is, apparently, not purely social. Political scientists continue to debate whether political preferences and behaviors are matters of social influence or only matters of personal conscious and rational choice. The approach discussed in this chapter makes it possible to explore a third approach, which includes both genetic and social influences within an integrated paradigm that excludes neither *a priori* and allows the data to decide where to focus research in particular contexts. If the effects of the common environments shared by members of different family clusters are small, it is unlikely that differences in socialization of clusters within a given target population can account for individual differences. In the absence of joint analysis of political choices and other predictors it is impossible to know whether genetic influences on social attitudes and choices are expressed through genetic differences in the cognitive functions that lead to the conscious evaluation of individual utility, differences in the innate structure of individual preferences, or inherited variation in adaptive noncognitive emotional functions that bear the long-standing imprint of evolutionary rationality. Resolution or integration of these three perspectives requires the simultaneous collection and analysis of multivariate kinship data.

The vast majority of political scientists, through their analyses, implicitly assume that all people are genetically identical and or that such genetic differences as do exist are irrelevant to the social and political domain. Such a sweeping generalization risks distracting political scientists from a critical component of human behavior. Clustering people by complete genetic identity, as in the case of identical twins, results in far greater empirical similarity than is found for almost any other type of clustering by relationship or context, except possibly for clustering by marriage. The growing appreciation of the scope of genetic variation at the molecular level creates a strong *prima facie* case for taking seriously the possibility that such differences may reach into the social and political domains. Humans vary enormously at the genomic level with molecular variants currently characterized at several million specific locations across long tracts of the human genome. What proportion of these variants translate into manifest phenotypic differences is still uncertain. Current estimates suggest that there are some 20,000–30,000 genes. If individuals are the primary unit of decision and analysis, but vary in ways not captured in any current purely social explanatory model, then any account of their behavior may be seriously deficient. This may be in part why even the best political models of behavior in political science explain less than 30% of the variation (Matsusaka and Palda 1999). Our studies give credence to the view that the best predictors are familial and, in many cases, significantly genetic.

We are under no illusion that the above findings raise more questions than they answer. The models we describe focus on one variable at a time in terms of latent genetic and environmental influences. They do not begin to consider the potential causal pathways between manifest variables, for example between personality or cognitive function and political behavior (e.g., Verhulst, Hatemi, and Martin 2010), that might explain how the latent effects of genes and environment translate into observed differences in political behavior. Statistical-genetic methods and models are available that illustrate how to construct and test multivariate models for genetic and environmental influences (see, e.g., Neale and Cardon 2002) including models that attempt to use genetic information to try to tease apart the nexus of causal relationships between multiple variables (e.g., Heath et al. 1993).

In the context of political science, Hatemi et al. (2007) introduced multivariate genetic models for voter preferences in an Australian population and showed that the genetic variance found on voting is largely accounted for by covariates. Verhulst, Hatemi, and Martin (2010) addressed the importance of personality on political ideology. Utilizing statistical models of twins they have found that certain facets of personality and ideology were related and the greater part of the relationship was due to shared genetic influence. We reiterate that significant estimates of genetic variance do not imply that individual genes have large effects, or correspond to specific behavioral outcomes. Political scientists typically explore voter turnout, vote choice, attitudes, and ideology by trying to assess all relevant predictors, pathways and best-fitting models. An important potential limitation of the models we discuss is that they are linear and additive. The do not take into account possible interactions between genes ("epistasis") or, perhaps more importantly, interactions between genes and environment. In the domain of social and political behavior it is entirely conceivable, yet to our knowledge currently unknown, whether genetic influences on personality (such as differences in sensitivity to reward and/or punishment) or cognitive function modulate the impact of social background and individual situation on political choice. The only barrier to testing for such interactions remains the availability of appropriate data. Our analyses lend credence to a view that incorporating genetic information in models for political behavior may generate further insight and improve prediction. Political behavior did not end with the introduction of Campbell et al.'s *American Voter* (1960) or Downs's *An Economic Theory of Democracy* (1957). It just began again. There are numerous other avenues ripe to explore. Almost every experiment, statistical model, and behavioral trait can be re-explored using these methods, allowing researchers to further pursue their trait of interest with a whole new set of tools, hypotheses, and designs. We look forward to seeing what comes next.

Appendix: Testing Assumptions about Mate Selection

Positive assortative mating can, over relatively few generations, lead to a marked increase in the genetic variance for any trait that contributes to mate selection. The increase arises because assortment engenders covariance between variants at different sites so that the aggregate contribution of a large number of genes (say k) is inflated by an even larger number ($k[k-1]$) of genetic covariances between otherwise unrelated loci. Assortment also increases the correlation between relatives. Thus, the choice of mate is a social event that may have marked genetic consequences. The increase in genetic variance is proportional to the correlation between mates. When the correlation is high, even for moderately heritable traits, the effect of assortment on the distribution and transmission of genetic differences may be large (see, e.g., Crow and Kimura 1970). What is true of genetic influences also applies, *mutatis mutandis*, to environmental influences that contribute to variation in traits for which there is assortative mating.

The consequences of the correlation between mates for the correlations between other relatives and for the family clustering of socially important traits depends significantly on the mechanism underlying spousal resemblance. Our analyses so far make the strong and untested assumption that the correlation between mates is due to assortative mating, that is, that "like tends to marry like" for the traits in question and that the attitudes and behavior of spouses does not converge significantly due to their mutual interaction during their life together. Furthermore, our model has assumed that assortative mating is primarily based on the actual phenotype being measured for the partners themselves (stature, personality, church attendance), and not on some other correlated variable such as income, or even the phenotypes of other family members such as parental or sibling education, political affiliation, or religious belief.

There is no single mechanism or taxonomy of mechanisms of spousal resemblance, nor are they mutually exclusive. Further, there is no one "best" approach for their resolution. An exhaustive treatment is a chapter in its own right. Here we focus on outlining the principal mechanisms and illustrate one approach that allows them to be compared on a common footing with the minimum of complex structural modeling. The integrating framework for our treatment of assortative mating is the recognition that mates select one another for some feature, measured or unmeasured, of their phenotypes. People may choose one another because they prefer people who share their religious, social, or political values or they may be brought together by shared background variables, perhaps including aspects of the homes or neighborhoods in which they grew up. Our treatment of alternative models for assortative mating begins by considering how different selection criteria influence the correlations between relatives and their spouses. If all we were given was a set of correlations between mates, we would find it hard to distinguish between the different processes of mate selection. However, the unique structure of the Virginian and Australian samples allows us to examine the impact of different types of assortment on the correlations between MZ and DZ twins and their spouses, and the correlations between siblings and their spouses. It turns out that these additional relationships can shed significant light on the causes of the observed correlations between mates.

Table 4.A1 summarizes the data that will form the backbone of our analysis of mate selection for the variables chosen to illustrate this introduction. They comprise the correlations between twins, siblings, and spouses for the six illustrative variables and those between the various combinations of in-laws that can be obtained when we include the spouses of siblings and twins in the data set. Correlations are tabulated for both the Virginian and Australian samples.

Ultimately, we want to use all the data for each variable to test alternative theories for the process underlying spousal resemblance between these measures, much as we fitted multiple models for biological and cultural inheritance to the correlations in table 4.3. However, we begin by exploring some of the basic concepts and models that may be used to analyze patterns of spousal resemblance and show how they affect the correlations between twins, siblings and their spouses.

Phenotypic Assortative Mating

Suppose initially that mate selection is based directly on the measured trait under investigation, for example, we measure voting behavior or conservatism in pairs of twins, T_1 and T_2, and their spouses, S_1 and S_2 (fig. 4.A1). The

Spouses of Twins

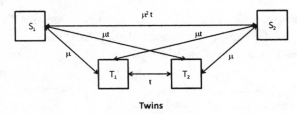

FIGURE 4A.1. Pattern of correlation between twins and spouses when selection is based on measured phenotype.

correlation between twins for the "mate selection" phenotype is t and that between spouses is μ as before. Since mate selection is assumed to depend only on the selection of a spouse by his/her partner and not on characteristics of the other spouse or co-twin, the correlations between a spouse and the co-twin of his/her partner is a secondary consequence of the phenotypes of the partners themselves. Thus, $r_{S_1T_2} = r_{S_2T_1} = \mu t$. Similarly, the correlation between the spouses of twins is expected to be $r_{S_1S_2} = \mu^2 t$ (see Heath et al. 1985, for a more extensive treatment of the correlations between the relatives of spouses under different mechanisms of assortment).

If this simple model is adequate to account for mate selection for a given trait (e.g., "conservatism") then it should be possible to predict the correlations $r_{S_1T_2}$, $r_{S_2T_1}$, and $r_{S_1S_2}$ from the correlations between twins, t, and the correlations between spouses, μ. Thus, if the basic model for assortment is correct, we expect $r_{S_1T_2} = r_{S_2T_1} = r_{T_1T_2}r_{S_1T_1}$ and $r_{S_1S_2} = r_{T_1T_2}r^2_{S_1T_1}$. If the model is wrong, then these expectations will not apply and a better model will be called for.

Consider the case of assortment for church attendance. The correlation between mates in the United States (table 4.A1) is 0.757. In Australia, it is 0.819. The correlations between female siblings are 0.368 and 0.481, respectively. If mating is assortative, we expect the correlation between husbands of female siblings and their sisters-in-law is expected to be 0.757×0.368 = 0.278 in the United States and 0.819×0.481 = 0.394 in Australia. The observed correlations are 0.317 and 0.425 respectively. Although the agreement between the observed correlations and their expected values is not perfect, they lie well within the sampling errors of their differences suggesting, at first sight, that assortment for church attendance may be based on the mutual preference of churchgoers for people like themselves in that respect and not for some other, unmeasured variable that influences mate selection.

Obviously, this is only an illustration to give the idea. In practice, we need

TABLE 4A.1. Raw correlations between married relative pairs in the United States and Australia

Relationship		Stature N	Stature r	Conservatism N	Conservatism r	Neuroticism N	Neuroticism r	Church attendance N	Church attendance r	Political affiliation N	Political affiliation r	Educational attainment N	Educational attainment r
Spouses	US	4850	0.238	4737	0.648	4886	0.087	4831	0.757	4440	0.648	4839	0.565
	AU	3383	0.215	3415	0.666	3446	0.056	3406	0.819	2551	0.832	3379	0.509
Male sibling	US	870	0.415	864	0.397	884	0.116	887	0.356	820	0.369	886	0.567
	AU	866	0.395	871	0.426	876	0.153	859	0.437	648	0.535	895	0.411
Female sibling	US	1871	0.436	1821	0.444	1874	0.202	1866	0.368	1664	0.297	1883	0.586
	AU	2169	0.396	2180	0.441	2222	0.144	2185	0.481	1531	0.487	2208	0.486
Unlike-sex sibling	US	2312	0.407	2283	0.374	2324	0.157	2347	0.378	2096	0.306	2344	0.568
	AU	2678	0.376	2696	0.389	2721	0.122	2669	0.420	1969	0.489	2746	0.354
DZ male	US	337	0.484	324	0.395	330	0.196	337	0.449	303	0.426	329	0.618
	AU	174	0.383	171	0.538	175	0.086	176	0.513	147	0.774	211	0.498
DZ female	US	532	0.550	498	0.480	526	0.331	529	0.435	449	0.436	520	0.689
	AU	520	0.502	508	0.534	528	0.217	517	0.528	420	0.531	579	0.523
DZ unlike-sex	US	690	0.393	645	0.365	682	0.087	679	0.295	589	0.379	684	0.576
	AU	451	0.485	453	0.446	459	0.125	450	0.450	364	0.555	529	0.466
MZ male	US	506	0.841	493	0.600	504	0.372	496	0.476	469	0.480	493	0.865
	AU	324	0.857	323	0.574	327	0.314	317	0.660	269	0.670	363	0.732
MZ female	US	898	0.818	844	0.642	895	0.425	890	0.584	818	0.513	895	0.812
	AU	879	0.851	874	0.648	903	0.431	894	0.656	718	0.671	948	0.766
Spouses of DZM	US	102	0.118	101	0.196	101	-0.024	102	0.482	89	0.319	104	0.203
	AU	35	-0.169	36	-0.313	35	0.201	36	0.507	25	0.718	34	0.173

(Continued)

TABLE 4A.1. (Continued)

Relationship		Stature N	Stature r	Conservatism N	Conservatism r	Neuroticism N	Neuroticism r	Church attendance N	Church attendance r	Political affiliation N	Political affiliation r	Educational attainment N	Educational attainment r
Spouses of DZF	US	126	0.150	126	0.339	124	0.113	123	0.364	115	0.303	124	0.361
	AU	67	-0.121	70	0.294	70	0.013	67	0.630	54	0.360	68	0.254
Spouses of DZMF	US	172	0.045	169	0.194	169	-0.039	166	0.189	156	0.209	169	0.421
	AU	67	-0.114	68	0.426	67	-0.237	66	0.202	40	0.739	67	0.189
Spouses of MZM	US	179	0.195	178	0.338	186	-0.076	181	0.331	169	0.361	184	0.334
	AU	78	0.079	79	0.456	79	0.115	80	0.264	54	0.716	75	0.389
Spouses of MZF	US	306	0.240	295	0.261	302	0.041	305	0.403	287	0.195	305	0.476
	AU	178	0.200	186	0.260	183	0.032	181	0.388	129	0.533	185	0.431
Co-twin-Sp DZM	US	343	0.174	346	0.289	349	-0.058	354	0.311	309	0.404	349	0.392
	AU	151	0.169	147	0.273	152	0.101	153	0.534	115	0.686	159	0.387
Co-twin-Sp DZF	US	449	0.178	436	0.335	445	0.032	445	0.349	399	0.272	447	0.403
	AU	356	0.103	358	0.332	363	-0.011	353	0.517	281	0.169	374	0.291
Co-twin-Sp1 DZMF	US	296	0.154	286	0.220	292	-0.037	290	0.148	258	0.218	291	0.343
	AU	160	0.125	161	0.365	165	-0.093	157	0.324	123	0.463	179	0.277

		N	r	N	r	N	r	N	r	N	r	N	r
Co-twin-Sp2 DZMF	US	334	0.175	316	0.354	332	−0.038	327	0.256	293	0.249	332	0.390
	AU	163	0.128	163	0.432	164	0.093	164	0.340	116	0.531	169	0.467
Co-twin-Sp MZM	US	524	0.300	519	0.476	536	0.077	530	0.393	495	0.358	529	0.475
	AU	296	0.211	295	0.446	301	0.053	296	0.467	217	0.610	303	0.348
Cotwin-Sp MZF	US	888	0.189	842	0.414	886	0.078	884	0.467	825	0.295	886	0.455
	AU	703	0.174	710	0.390	717	−0.006	705	0.442	530	0.451	726	0.498
H of FS-brother-in-law	US	321	0.181	317	0.260	322	0.057	322	0.234	290	0.299	322	0.490
	AU	475	0.148	478	0.396	481	−0.064	468	0.439	329	0.319	481	0.304
H of FS-sister-in-law	US	471	0.138	461	0.231	474	0.082	468	0.317	414	0.075	479	0.504
	AU	702	0.089	715	0.325	721	0.004	701	0.425	493	0.354	715	0.314
W of MS-brother-in-law	US	254	0.143	258	0.360	259	0.033	260	0.164	236	0.138	264	0.342
	AU	266	0.129	274	0.361	271	0.061	265	0.409	190	0.458	266	0.272
W of MS-sister-in-law	US	268	−0.001	268	0.178	272	0.164	274	0.329	239	0.220	272	0.427
	AU	333	0.121	327	0.251	339	0.091	336	0.282	233	0.298	327	0.367

Note: All subjects selected for being married or living with partner. Unmarried subjects excluded from correlations. *Description of relationships involving DZMF pairs.* Co-twin-Sp1 DZMF = male twin, with husband of female co-twin. Co-twin-Sp2 DZMF = female twin, with wife of male co-twin.

to employ all the correlations, including those of other types of sib-pairs and the five kinds of twins. Also, estimates and tests of goodness of fit should embrace all the data, as they did in our analysis of the effects of genetic and cultural inheritance above. However, before doing that, we have to consider how the pattern of correlations might change under different theories of mating.

Phenotypic Assortment for a Latent Trait

Suppose, now, that the correlation between mates is not based on the actual trait that is measured, but that the measured trait is an unreliable index of another trait on which mate selection is truly based according to the model in fig. 4.A1. For example, we may measure the correlations between relatives using an IQ test, but mate selection is not based directly on test scores but on the actual cognitive abilities of the people being tested. We may call this model "phenotypic assortative mating with error" (see Heath et al. 1985). Figure 4.A2 illustrates this model. Mate selection is now based on the latent variables S'_1, S'_2, T'_1, and T'_2 (in circles in the figure) while the actual measured values are S_1, S_2, T_1 and T_2 respectively (in squares). We let the path, r, denote the regression of observed trait on the latent variable ("true score") and $e = (1-r^2)^{1/2}$ the (standardized) path from the residuals, r_{S_1}, r_{T_1}, r_{T_2}, and r_{S_2} respectively (fig. 4.A2). Note that in this case, the residuals are assumed to be uncorrelated. Furthermore, in this simple illustration, we assume that the path r is the same for men and women. The model in figure 4.A2 allows the residuals to be correlated between twins and siblings. This adjustment will allow us to test simple models for social homogamy (see below). However, initially we assume that the twin correlation, u, between residuals is zero.

If we derive new expected correlations from the model parameters we find $r_{S_1T_2} = r_{S_2T_1} = \mu t r^2$ for the correlations between spouses and the co-twins of their partners and $r_{S_1S_2} = \mu r^2$ for the correlation between the spouses of twins. These two correlations cannot now be predicted from the twin and spousal correlations alone since the observed correlation between twins is now expected to be $t r^2$ and that between mates should now be μr^2. A little algebra will show that the correlation between spouses and their partners' co-twins is no longer expected to be $r_{S_1T_2} = r_{S_2T_1} = r_{T_1T_2} r_{S_1T_1}$. Rather, we expect $r_{S_1T_2} = r_{S_2T_1} = \mu t r^2 > r_{T_1T_2} r_{S_1T_1} = \mu t r^4$ and $r_{S_1S_2} = \mu^2 t r^2 > r_{T_1T_2} r_{S_1T_1}^2 = \mu^2 t r^4$. A first guess at the path, r, is thus given by $[(r_{T_1T_2} r_{S_1S_2})/r_{S_1T_2}]^{1/2}$. Substituting the values for the correlations for church attendance in the example above we obtain rough estimates of $r = 0.936$ and 0.905 for the United States and Australian samples respectively. These values are very close to unity, suggesting that reported church attendance is a very reli-

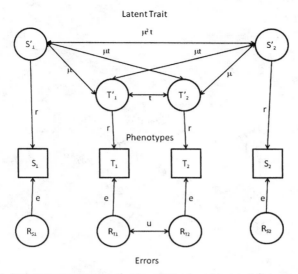

FIGURE 4A.2. Error-prone measurement of mate selection for a latent trait ("phenotypic assortative mating plus error").

able index of the underlying trait for which spouses select one another in this domain. Again, more rigorous analysis would integrate all the correlations in a single analysis.

Social Homogamy

The above model (fig. 4.A2) assumes that the residual twin correlation, u, is zero and that the correlation between twins is less than unity and the twin correlation varies as a function of zygosity. If the latent trait is completely correlated in both MZ and DZ twins (and, for simplicity in siblings) we arrive at the model in figure 4.A3. The model in figure 4.A3 is identical to the previous figure, except that the latent variables in the twins are assumed to be identical. That is, they are assumed to be completely correlated in the same way that the effects of the "shared environment," C, are perfectly correlated in twins. This does not mean that there are no genetic effects on the measured phenotype but, in this simple model, they are assumed to contribute to the correlation between the residuals for biological relatives, u, and not to assortative mating. An important implication of this model is that, regardless of the residual correlation between twins, u, if mate selection is based purely on family background, H in the figure, then the correlation between spouses and their partners is expected to be the same as that between spouses and their

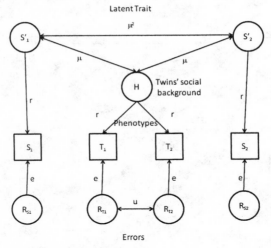

FIGURE 4A.3. Social homogamy in twins and their spouses.

partners' co-twins. That is, under this model for social homogamy, we expect $r_{S_1T_2} = r_{S_1T_1} = \mu r^2$ regardless of the residual twin correlation, u.

Even the most cursory examination of the correlations for church attendance, say, in table 4.A1, are enough to show that the correlations for church attendance between spouses and in-laws are all substantially smaller than the correlations between spouses. Thus, the data from Australia and Virginia provide very little support for a predominant role of purely social homogamy in mate selection for this trait. Indeed, the patterns of correlation for other variables for which there is marked assortative mating (table 4.A1) provide very weak support for predominantly social homogamy in preference to phenotypic assortment.

Spousal Interaction

All the models so far assume that the correlation between spouses is entirely due to assortative mating, that is, to the mutual selection of spouses on the basis of latent or measured phenotypes and not to any mutual interaction after pairing. Thus, it is assumed that once mates have chosen each other, their similarity is fixed forever. They neither converge nor diverge with age or length of marriage. There are, of course, many ways of testing for marital interaction with spouse pairs, including examining the correlations or differences between spouses as a function of age or duration of marriage. This has been done many times, and the effects are modest at best, suggesting that convergence does not occur or that it occurs very rapidly after mate selection so that its effects are already established and completed within an interval that is beyond the resolving power of many cross sectional studies of age change in spousal correlation. Here we follow Heath (1987) and explore an alternative approach that examines the effect of spousal interaction on the correlations between twins (or other biological relatives) and their spouses. In its simplest form, this model assumes only that partners have been together long enough for convergence to be complete. More elaborate forms of the model can take into account variations in the duration of the partnership.

Before examining the algebra of spousal convergence, it may be helpful to think about a simple example. Imagine first that twins are correlated for a trait of interest and that each chooses and interacts with a random partner. Thus, at the start of the relationship, twins will be correlated and spouses will not be. Suppose now that each twin interacts with his/her partner so that, to some extent, each spouse influences and is influenced by the other ("reciprocal spousal interaction"). With the passage of time, two things are expected to happen. One, obviously, is that pairs of spouses will become correlated, even though their correlation was zero initially. The second may not be so obvious, but now each twin is exposed to the influence of a separate randomly chosen environment (the spouse). In so far as the spouses of the twins are not correlated at the start, their effects on the twins will tend to increase the variance of the individual twins and lower their correlation compared with the initial value prior to mate selection.

Figure 4.A4 is an extension of the model in figure 4.A2 to allow for the effects of spousal interaction; the parameter, b, represents the reciprocal influences of husbands and wives on each others' phenotypes. It is not necessary that the influence of husbands on their wives is the same as that of wives on husbands. The basic mathematical treatment of spousal interaction is an application of the general model for the interaction between manifest variables in linear structural ("LISREL") models, such as those developed by Karl Joreskog in the late 1960s.

We begin with the (4x4) correlation matrix, R, between twins and spouses before interaction. If spouses are not correlated at the start of their relationship, R will have the form:

1 0 0 0
0 1 t 0
0 t 1 0
0 0 0 1

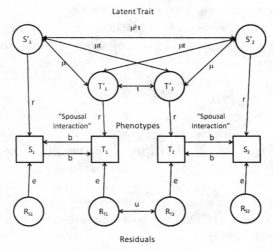

FIGURE 4A.4. Extending the model to include spousal interaction.

where the rows and columns correspond to S1, T1, T2, and S2 respectively. The twin correlation at the start is t. The model then specifies the pattern of interaction between family members. Assuming for simplicity that the only interaction occurs between spouses (we could also allow for interaction between twins; see Carey 1985), and that the coefficient b measures the reciprocal paths between S1 and T1 and between T2 and S2, we form the matrix B thus:

0 b 0 0
b 0 0 0
0 0 0 b
0 0 b 0

The matrix is null except for those cells corresponding to those variables involved in the interaction. Element b_{12} of B denotes the path from the second individual in the family (the first twin in this example) to the first (his/her spouse). b_{21} measures the reciprocal effect of the spouse on the twin. The reciprocal effects do not have to be equal. Indeed, if twins affected their spouses but spouses did not affect their partners, b_{21} would be zero. If spouses reacted against one another, b would be negative.

It may be shown (see, e.g., Carey 1985; Neale et al. 2004) that the covariance matrix between the relatives evolves during interaction to a stable value $\Sigma = (I-B)^{-1} R \, (I-B)^{-1}$ as long as $(I-B)$ is positive definite, when the correlations between twins and their spouses after spousal interaction may be obtained by standardizing Σ. To give an idea of how spousal interaction affects the correlations, assume that the twin correlation, t, is 0.6 at the time of mate selection and that spouses choose each other at random (i.e., the initial correlation between mates is zero). Now allow for the effects of reciprocal interaction with a value of, say, $b = 0.4$. Substituting for t in R and b in B the above matrix multiplication yields the following standardized covariance matrix after spousal interaction:

1.00 0.69 0.21 0.08

0.69 1.00 0.52 0.21

0.21 0.52 1.00 0.69

0.08 0.21 0.69 1.00

That is, the correlation between mates has risen from zero at mate selection to 0.69 after spouses have interacted and the twin correlation has dropped from 0.6 to 0.52. Note also that the other correlations are no longer zero. Twins correlate 0.21 with the spouses of their co-twins and the spouses of twins now correlate 0.08. It is instructive to predict these two correlations under the alternative model that the correlation between mates is purely due to classical phenotypic assortment rather than spousal interaction. In this case, twins are expected to correlate 0.69x0.52 = 0.36 with the spouses of their co-twins and the correlation between the spouses of twins is expected to be 0.69x0.69x0.52 = 0.24. Both these two values are substantially greater than their observed values. The starting values have been chosen to illustrate some of the basic implications of spousal interaction for the correlations between relatives, and suggest how different theories of the correlation between mates predict different correlational patterns for in-laws. Thus, we may use the observed patterns of correlation between in-laws (e.g., the spouses of twins and siblings) to resolve alternative models for spousal resemblance as a precursor to analyzing the mechanisms of transmission within families.

As a rough guide, we suggest asking how the spouse–co-twin correlation and the correlation between the spouses of twins compare with what would be expected if the similarity between spouses were due only to phenotypic assortative mating. The previous treatment suggests that:

1. Phenotypic assortment for a latent variable, including social homogamy, generally produce spouse–co-twin and spouse-spouse correlations that are too high compared with those predicted from the twin and spousal correlations under the hypothesis of phenotypic assortment; and

2. (Positive) spousal interaction leads to spouse–co-twin and spouse-spouse correlations that are too low compared with those predicted under phenotypic assortment.

Fitting Models for Spousal Resemblance

It is helpful for the reader to examine some of the correlations in table 4.A1 to get a basic idea of which of the various models for assortment may best account for the observations. Remember that the sample sizes vary and that confidence intervals of correlations based on small numbers may be surprisingly large. For example, small correlations based on N = 400 have CIs approximately +/− 0.1 so it is important not to overinterpret small differences.

We used the method of weighted least-squares described above to fit a series of models for mate selection to the six sets of correlations in table 4.A1 for the Virginia and Australian samples separately. The models considered are not exhaustive, but embrace some of the principal basic possibilities. They may be enumerated as follows.

1. *No assortative mating or spousal correlation.* This model is included as a baseline. Note that the model includes parameters for the correlations between five types of twins and three types of sibling pairs but assumes that the correlation between mates and all in-laws are zero. The number of free parameters is 8 and there are 24 unique correlations for each sample, yielding 24–16 d.f. to test the goodness of fit, S^2.
2. *Phenotypic assortative mating.* This model corresponds to that in figure 4.A1. All the correlations between in-laws are assumed to be predicted from the marital correlation and the 8 correlations between biological relatives. Thus the model involves 8 + 1 = 9 parameters, yielding 15 d.f. for errors of fitting, and a difference of 1 d.f. (16–15) for comparing the fit of the model of phenotypic assortment with that assuming no assortment from the difference in weighted residual sums of squares, ΔS^2.
3. *Phenotypic assortment plus error.* This model corresponds to that in figure 4.A2. Separate estimates of r are specified for males and females. The residual effects are assumed to be uncorrelated between twins and siblings ($u = 0$). Thus, this model has 9 + 2 free parameters and yields 13 d.f. for testing goodness of fit.
4. *Spousal interaction.* The model for spousal interaction is a reduced version of that in figure 4.A4. It assumes twins and sibling correlations initially take their own value and that all other correlations are zero at the start of

the relationship between spouses. The correlations between mates and in-laws are assumed to result only from the interaction between twins (or siblings) and their spouses. Such an assumption is restrictive. The residual paths are assumed to be zero, and the reciprocal paths between spouses (b) are assumed to be symmetrical.

5. *Social homogamy*. The effects of social homogamy are approximated by the model in figure 4.A3. Mating is assumed to be based on the shared family background, H, which is perfectly correlated in MZ and DZ twins and siblings. Thus, social homogamy contributes equally to all the correlations between first-degree collateral relatives, and any differences among these correlations are explained by differences in the residual correlations between biological relatives. This model, thus, has 10 free parameters: the eight residual correlations between biological variables, the spousal correlation for family background and the path from family background to the outcome.

The above set of models is selected to illustrate the main characteristics of the mate selection process. The models can be made more elaborate by combining multiple elements in a single model, but problems of model identification, that is, what combinations of effects can be estimated reliably, soon arise in this relatively simple data set so we combine ourselves to a restricted set of comparisons. Table 4.A2 summarizes the goodness of fit tests of the selected models. Parameters estimates for conservatism, church attendance, political affiliation, and educational attainment are summarized in table 4.A3. Those for stature and neuroticism are omitted since the correlations between spouses are smaller and there is little to be gained from a more detailed examination of the models for these variables in this context. Also given in table 4.A3 are the P-values associated with a goodness-of fit-test for each of the models on the assumption that the weighted residual sums of squares are approximately distributed as chi-square with their corresponding d.f.

The residual sums of squares are all enormous for models assuming random mating. That is consistent with the results of the models fitting to twins and nuclear families and confirms that the correlations between spouses and pairs of relatives by marriage are all significantly greater than zero on average. Even the residuals for neuroticism are statistically significant under the random mating model, although the spousal correlation is too small to contribute substantially to the overall pattern of family resemblance. All attempts to allow for assortative mating lead to a much better fit than models that assume random mating. However, for none of the variables in table 4.A3 do simple

TABLE 4A.2. Goodness-of-fit statistics (weighted residual sums of squares, S²) for selected models for assortative mating in the United States and Australia

Model		Random mating	Phenotypic assortment (P)	P+Error	Spousal interaction	Social homogamy
d.f.		16	15	13	14	11
Variable	Sample	S²	S²	S²	S²	S²
Stature	US	449.179	31.363	24.423[1]	78.930	28.786
	AU	239.827	12.947	11.817[1]	31.694	25.353
Conservatism	US	2535.373	14.845	12.143	118.266	328.491
	AU	2041.407	31.627	29.669	113.276	239.123
Neuroticism	US	63.371	17.811	See note[2]	20.226	19.458
	AU	28.337	17.444	See note[2]	15.583	22.807
Church attendance	US	3375.872	15.187	12.841	103.042	611.006
	AU	3019.544	22.140	21.548[1]	76.574	403.950
Political affiliation	US	2213.625	22.254	18.500	87.889	429.819
	AU	2337.500	34.183	32.537	70.696	322.685
Educational attainment	US	2477.957	46.210	28.207	243.100	57.774
	AU	1430.440	44.146	18.624	160.747	82.086

[a]Estimated regression of male outcome on latent trait on upper bound (1.000).

[b]This model is poorly identified for Neuroticism because the correlation between mates is close to zero. Stable parameter estimates are not available.

TABLE 4A.3. Models for assortative mating, parameter estimates

Outcome	Conservatism								Church Attendance							
Model	Phenotypic(P)		P + error		Social homogamy		Spousal interaction		Phenotypic(P)		P + error		Social homogamy		Spousal interaction	
Sample	US	AU	US	AU	US	AU	US	AU	US	AU	US	AU	US	AU	US	AU
t_{MZM}	0.645	0.613	0.698	0.655	0.279	0.200	0.840	0.852	0.496	0.610	0.510	0.612	0.252	0.252	0.798	1.000
t_{MZF}	0.637	0.627	0.655	0.658	0.343	0.358	0.793	0.745	0.600	0.614	0.629	0.628	0.284	0.284	0.757	0.847
t_{DZM}	0.411	0.464	0.444	0.487	0.000	0.133	0.541	0.718	0.456	0.575	0.470	0.576	0.000	0.000	0.727	0.958
t_{DZF}	0.498	0.526	0.513	0.554	0.046	0.150	0.604	0.617	0.451	0.575	0.476	0.592	0.018	0.018	0.559	0.768
t_{DZMF}	0.389	0.492	0.411	0.525	0.000	0.000	0.489	0.612	0.288	0.430	0.299	0.436	0.000	0.000	0.413	0.657
t_{SibM}	0.414	0.440	0.462	0.477	0.000	0.000	0.506	0.584	0.335	0.448	0.348	0.448	0.000	0.000	0.508	0.713
t_{SibF}	0.435	0.446	0.450	0.475	0.000	0.000	0.509	0.505	0.374	0.488	0.403	0.505	0.000	0.000	0.442	0.639
t_{SibMF}	0.371	0.402	0.397	0.433	0.000	0.000	0.446	0.493	0.376	0.462	0.398	0.434	0.000	0.000	0.496	0.616
μ	0.657	0.677	0.701	0.721	1.000	1.000	0.000	0.000	0.765	0.819	0.807	0.831	1.000	1.000	0.000	0.000
r_M	1.000	1.000	0.942	0.956	0.745	0.730	1.000	1.000	1.000	1.000	0.978	1.000	0.739	0.739	1.000	1.000
r_F	1.000	1.000	0.982	0.966	0.738	0.740	1.000	1.000	1.000	1.000	0.956	0.980	0.721	0.721	1.000	1.000
$b_{M \to F}$	0.000	0.000	0.000	0.000	0.000	0.000	0.371	0.326	0.000	0.000	0.000	0.000	0.000	0.000	0.397	0.527
$b_{F \to M}$	0.000	0.000	0.000	0.000	0.000	0.000	0.454	0.549	0.000	0.000	0.000	0.000	0.000	0.000	0.650	0.737
P(%)	46.3	0.7	51.6	0.5	<0.1	<0.1	<0.1	<0.1	43.8	10.4	46.0	6.3	<0.1	<0.1	<0.1	<0.1

(Continued)

TABLE 4A.3. (Continued)

| | Political affiliation | | | | | | | | Educational attainment | | | | | | | | |
| | Phenotypic(P) | | P + error | | Social homogamy | | Spousal interaction | | Phenotypic(P) | | P + error | | Social homogamy | | Spousal interaction | |
Model / Sample	US	AU	US	AU	US	AU	US	AU	US	AU	US	AU	US	AU	US	AU
t_{MZM}	0.516	0.715	0.589	0.755	0.094	0.215	0.631	1.000	0.850	0.720	0.922	0.880	0.668	0.548	1.000	0.960
t_{MZF}	0.493	0.638	0.496	0.640	0.208	0.278	0.649	1.000	0.816	0.801	0.959	1.032	0.583	0.606	0.949	0.839
t_{DZM}	0.494	0.807	0.571	0.852	0.000	0.462	0.591	1.000	0.628	0.536	0.682	0.665	0.061	0.154	0.815	0.673
t_{DZF}	0.440	0.433	0.442	0.435	0.083	0.000	0.559	0.727	0.694	0.526	0.821	0.680	0.311	0.197	0.801	0.552
t_{DZMF}	0.377	0.587	0.405	0.605	0.000	0.000	0.476	0.873	0.600	0.501	0.684	0.641	0.013	0.101	0.722	0.580
t_{SibM}	0.352	0.538	0.420	0.580	0.000	0.000	0.419	0.737	0.568	0.418	0.624	0.528	0.000	0.008	0.696	0.528
t_{SibF}	0.280	0.477	0.280	0.478	0.000	0.000	0.345	0.742	0.608	0.493	0.751	0.656	0.082	0.135	0.669	0.520
t_{SibMF}	0.315	0.471	0.348	0.489	0.000	0.000	0.370	0.690	0.585	0.374	0.682	0.489	0.000	0.000	0.675	0.420
μ	0.653	0.824	0.717	0.854	1.000	1.000	0.000	0.000	0.595	0.553	0.664	0.673	0.869	1.000	0.000	0.000
r_M	1.000	1.000	0.894	0.957	0.653	0.761	1.000	1.000	1.000	1.000	0.952	0.882	0.770	0.638	1.000	1.000
r_F	1.000	1.000	1.000	1.000	0.621	0.738	1.000	1.000	1.000	1.000	0.894	0.857	0.741	0.637	1.000	1.000
b_{M-F}	0.000	0.000	0.000	0.000	0.000	0.000	0.420	0.703	0.000	0.000	0.000	0.000	0.000	0.000	0.304	0.153
b_{F-M}	0.000	0.000	0.000	0.000	0.000	0.000	0.376	0.577	0.000	0.000	0.000	0.000	0.000	0.000	0.443	0.504
P(%)	10.1	0.3	13.9	0.2	<0.1	<0.1	<0.1	<0.1	<0.1	<0.1	1.2	13.5	<0.1	<0.1	<0.1	<0.1

Note: Estimates are not given for stature and neuroticism. Estimates for random mating models are omitted from table. In the case of the social homogamy model the twin and sibling correlations refer to the correlations between residuals (i.e., u in fig. 4.A3). Otherwise, the correlations are those between twins and siblings for the manifest or latent variable on which mate selection is based.

models of social homogamy or spousal interaction come close to fitting the data, suggesting that either model, by itself, is not adequate to account for spousal resemblance. Between these two models, invoking social homogamy fits much better, though still extremely badly, for conservatism, church attendance, and political affiliation and assuming spousal interaction does better, though also badly, for educational attainment. In general, the parameter estimates under the social homogamy model are also strange. The estimated correlation between the social backgrounds of spouses is almost always unity, the only exception being that for educational attainment in the U.S. sample. Furthermore, the residual correlations between DZ twins and siblings are often very small and frequently close to zero while those for MZs, while not large are often more than twice those for DZs and siblings. This would arise if the assumption that assortment was based only on the latent *nongenetic* aspects of family background led to overestimation of the contribution of family background to the pattern of family resemblance.

Overall, models that assume phenotypic assortment perform much better, with or without the inclusion of uncorrelated errors of measurement. Assuming that the residuals are distributed as chi-square, the simple model of phenotypic assortment gives an adequate, even "good," fit to conservatism, church attendance, and political affiliation in the U.S. sample, but it is necessary to invoke error components to give a tolerable fit to the Virginia data on educational attainment. Even when allowance is made for errors of measurement in the model for phenotypic assortment, the paths from "true" score to phenotype are typically large suggesting that the measures used provide a good approximation to the traits on which assortment is based. Although, in Australia, models of phenotypic assortative mating give much better fit than those for social homogamy and spousal interaction for all the variables discussed, the fit is still relatively poor for conservatism and political affiliation. Further analysis, perhaps involving elements of more than one model ("mixed homogamy"; Heath et al. 1985) would be needed to see if the fit could be improved further.

The above analyses of the resemblance between spouses, twins and in-laws, suggest that phenotypic assortment, perhaps with some allowance for random residual effects gives a much better account of the correlations between spouses and in-laws than models that assume spousal resemblance results only from their mutual interaction or stratification of the pool of mates by features of the family background. We do not claim that this is a definitive analysis, but it suggests how the study of extended kinships can elucidate the principal features of human mate selection and gives some justification for the assumption of phenotypic assortment in our previous analysis of biological and cultural inheritance.

Notes

1. Methodologically minded readers who have some familiarity with linear modeling and the elements of path analysis should have no problem tracing the details of the argument. Serious students who are coming to genetic ideas and models for the first time may need to get some practice in the basic concepts beyond that offered in the current chapter. We recommend reading some background material to help make the transition to an approach that might seem unfamiliar at first. Some of the more basic principles of modeling from a slightly different perspective are presented in the chapter by Eaves et al. (2005) in the introductory text edited by Kendler and Eaves (2005). The classic introduction to path analysis by Otis Dudley Duncan (1966) is helpful in giving some foundation to applications in territory more familiar to social scientists. David Fulkerís (1979) chapters in Eysenckís volume on intelligence are a didactic masterpiece that translates easily from the analysis of intelligence and socio-economic variables to studies in political science. Greg Carey (2003) has an excellent broader introduction specifically written for students in the social sciences. John Loehlin (2003) offers a characteristically thoughtful and lucid exposition of linear structural modeling. The examples presented in Neale et alís. manual (2002) for the "Mx" program for structural modeling are well tried and tested. These examples, and many others, are available online and have evolved over some 20 years of experience in teaching the elements of genetic modeling to behavioral and social scientists in a series of International Twin Methodology Workshops. Readers are encouraged to use these resources as best suit their needs.

2. The basic components of variance model is used widely in univariate analysis, is easy to understand and extends conveniently to the multivariate analysis of twins and sibship data. However, it does not generalize very well to complex kinship structures, especially when there is both social and genetic inheritance and mating is not random. Thus, while we do not lose sight of the goal of partitioning the total variance into its multiple genetic and environmental components and refer to these often, our actual modeling is conducted in terms of path coefficients that may then be translated into components of variance where needed. Further discussion of this model (with notational differences and limitations) may be found in Jinks and Fulker (1970), Neale and Cardon (2002) and standard texts in quantitative genetics (e.g., Mather and Jinks 1982; Falconer and MacKay 1995). Potential sources of the shared environment include variables such as socioeconomic status, parental influence, religion, and access to education. The distinction between additive ($A = VA$) and dominance ($D = VD$) genetic components of genetic variance was first clarified by Fisher and is a function of the relationship between genotypes and their expression in the phenotypes. Each represents the sum of the individual contributions of separate genetic loci to the phenotype and can be expressed as a function of the frequencies and effects of the different forms ("alleles") of each gene in the homozygous and heterozygous forms. Neale and Cardon (2002, chap. 3) provide a simple derivation and definition of the additive and dominance variance components. Our treatment, and that of most investigators, ignore the effects of higher order interactions between genes, known collectively as "epistasis" or "nonallelic interactions." Although variance components may be defined that represent such effects (see, e.g., Mather

1974) their effects are often largely confounded with those of dominance in most practical applications and will not be considered further here.

3. The investigation that forms the core of this paper was designed in the early 1980s as the culmination of a decade of theoretical analysis and computer-aided design with the goal of identifying constellations of kinships that had a structure, given large enough samples, to test competing theories of biological and cultural inheritance in the presence of assortative mating and to provide estimates of the critical parameters (path coefficients) of such models.

4. Stature was assessed by self report. Scale scores for a general factor of liberalism/conservatism derived from U.S. and Australian modifications of the Wilson-Patterson Conservatism inventory (Wilson and Patterson 1970); arcsin transformed scale scores from 12 neuroticism items selected from the adult form of the longer Eysenck Personality Questionnaire (EPQ, Eysenck 1975) with the aid of Dr. Sybil Eysenck; Ordinal values of church attendance, political affiliation and educational attainment were coded differently in the U.S. and Australian samples to reflect local practice. Thus, in the US, political affiliation was assessed by a five-point scale rating strength of preference for Republicans compared to Democrats. In the Australian sample the scale comprised self-reported voting preference for the three principal parties in their parliamentary system, scored as follows: (o) Conservative (Labor + National coalition) (1) Labor. In the VA30K, educational attainment was coded ordinally using the following categories: (0) 0-7 yrs, (1) 8-yrs, (2) 1-3 yrs High School, (3) High School degree or 4 yrs of High School (4) 1-3 yrs College (5) 4+ yrs college. Educational attainment in the OZ20K was coded: (0) < 7 yrs, (2) 8-10 yrs (3) 11-12 yrs, (4) apprenticeship, diploma, certificate etc. (5) technical or teachers college (6) 4 yr degree (7) post graduate.

5. Genetic dominance was characteristic of the traits analyzed by Mendel in Pisum sativum. One of Fisherís critical insights lay in the recognition that not all genes behaving like Mendelís at the level of gamete formation and transmission behaved like Mendelís examples at the level of expression. That is "dominance is a characteristic of the phenotype, not of the genotype."

6. Both models are well-established in the genetic literature on human family resemblance (see, e.g., Cloninger et al. 1979; Neale and Cardon 2002). The conventions in the figures are similar to those originally developed by Sewall Wright (1921) and expounded for social scientists by Duncan (1966).

7. The numerical analysis requires minimization of the loss-function:

$$i = k$$
$$S^2 = \Sigma \delta^2 = \Sigma \, Ni[r_i - E(r_i)]^2 \ldots\ldots(1)$$
$$i = 1$$

with respect to differences in the p model parameters, q. Summation is applied over all $i = 1 \ldots k$ observed correlations, ri, each based on Ni pairs. The $E(ri)$ are the corresponding expected correlations obtained by substituting current values for the model parameters, m, um, uf, etc. in the algebraic expectations of table 4.4. The weights, Ni, ensure that observations known more precisely (because they are based on larger sample sizes) have proportionally more influence on the final solution. The minimum weighted sum of squared residuals, $Sd2$ is expected to be smaller for models that fit better than those that fit to zero. Sd^2 has $k-p$ d.f. when a model with p free parameters is fitted to k observed correlations.

In comparing WLS to ML in extended kinship design for political attitudes, Hatemi , Funk et al. 2009 (ML) found no differences with Eaves and Hatemi (2008) (WLS). Both ML and WLS can be implemented in well-tried and readily available software for structural modeling. We used Dr. Michael Neale's Mx package (Neale et al. 2002) that has been widely used for fitting models of biological and cultural inheritance to complex pedigrees. Translation of models into code is relatively easy, and especially for WLS, processing is rapid allowing the comparison of series of models for numerous variables to be accomplished relatively quickly. The package uses Gill and Murray's program NPSOL for efficient nonlinear optimization subject to boundary, linear and nonlinear constraints (Gill et al. 1998).

8. An unspoken assumption of the twin method implies that MZ and DZ twins are equally correlated for equally variable environmental influences. The validity of this "equal environments assumption (EEA)" has been widely questioned and tested with a range of results. Frequently, the assumption is violated by measured aspects of the environment that turn out to show little or no correlation with the measured phenotype (e.g., Loehlin and Nichols 1976). Even in the rare instance of when there is a *prima facie* case for violation of the EEA, the direction of causation is ambiguous. This issue is discussed further below.

9. If the intergenerational paths and correlation between mates do not change over time then H'm = Hm and H'f = Hf. These constraints may be imposed numerically when estimating the parameters, allowing identification of the model parameters. Whether or not a given population attains equilibrium under joint biological and cultural inheritance with assortative mating is questionable for traits that are historically labile. However, analytical and simulation studies (e.g., Medland and Keller 2009) show that the approach to equilibrium is quite rapid so violations of the constraint may not be critical. However, there is no single way of parameterizing the same model and no one "best" conception of how environmental transmission should be modeled. For other path models using slightly different conceptions of nongenetic inheritance see, e.g., Heath et al. 1985, Maes et al. 2009. Generally, detailed subtleties of transmission are difficult to resolve with realistic sample sizes.

References

Alford, J. R., C. L. Funk, and J. R. Hibbing. 2005. Are political orientations genetically transmitted? *American Political Science Review* 99 (2): 153–67.

Alford, J., P. Hatemi, J. Hibbing, and L. Eaves. Forthcoming. The politics of mate choice. *Journal of Politics*.

Alwin, D. F., R. L. Cohen, and T. M. Newcomb. 1991. *Political attitudes over the life span: The Bennington women after fifty years*. Madison: University of Wisconsin Press.

Beckwith, J., and C. A. Morris. 2008. Twin studies of political behavior: Untenable assumptions? *Perspectives on Politics* 6:785–92.

Behrman, J., P. Taubman, and T. Wales. 1977. Controlling for and measuring the effects of genetics and family environment in equations for schooling and labor market success. In *Kinometrics: Determinants of socioeconomic success within and between families*, ed. P. Taubman, 35–98. New York: North-Holland Publishing.

Boomsma, D. I., E. J. de Geus, G. C. van Baal, and J. R. Koopmans. 1999. A religious upbringing reduces the influence of genetic factors on disinhibition: Evidence for interaction between genotype and environment. *Twin Research* 2 (2): 115–25.

Bouchard, T., D. Lykken, M. McGue, N. Segal, and A. Tellegen. 1990. Sources of human psychological differences: The Minnesota study of twins reared apart. *Science* 250:223–28.

Bouchard, T. J., Jr., and M. McGue. 2003. Genetic and environmental influences on human psychological differences. *Journal of Neurobiology* 54:4–45.

Campbell, A., P. E. Converse, W. E. Miller, and D. E. Stokes. 1960. *The American voter*. New York: Wiley.

Carey, G. 1986. Sibling imitation and contrast effects. *Behavior Genetics* 16:319–41.

———. 2003. *Human genetics for the social sciences*. Advanced Psychology Texts 4. London: Sage Publications.

Caspi, A., J. McClay, T. Moffitt, J. Mill, J. Martin, I. Craig, A. Taylor, and R. Poulton. 2002. Role of genotype in the cycle of violence in maltreated children. *Science* 297:851–53.

Cattell, R. B. 1960. The multiple abstract variance analysis equations and solutions for nature-nurture research on continuous variables. *Psychological Review* 67:353–72.

Cavalli-Sforza, L. L., and M. W. Feldman. 1973. Cultural versus biological inheritance: Phenotypic transmission from parents to children. (A theory of the effect of parental phenotypes on children's phenotypes.) *American Journal of Human Genetics* 25:18–37.

———. 1981. *Cultural transmission and evolution: A quantitative approach*. Princeton, N.J.: Princeton University Press.

Cavalli-Sforza, L. L., M. W. Feldman, K. H. Chen, and S. M. Dornbusch. 1982. Theory and observation in cultural transmission. *Science* 218:19–27.

Cloninger, R., J. Rice, and T. Reich. 1979. Multifactorial inheritance with cultural transmission and assortative mating II. A general model of combined polygenic and cultural inheritance. *American Journal of Human Genetics* 31:176–98.

Crow, J. F., and M. Kimura. 1970. *Introduction to population genetics theory*. New York: Harper and Row.

D'Onofrio, B. M., L. J. Eaves, L. Murrelle, H. H. Maes, and B. Spilka. 1999. Understanding biological and social influences on religious affiliation, attitudes, and behaviors: A behavior genetic perspective. *Journal of Personality* 67:953–84.

D'Onofrio, B. M., W. S. Slutske, E. Turkheimer, R. E. Emery, K. P. Harden, A. C. Heath, P. A. Madden, and N. G. Martin. 2007. Intergenerational transmission of childhood conduct problems: A Children of Twins Study. *Archives of General Psychiatry* 64:820–29.

D'Onofrio, B., E. Turkheimer, L. Eaves, L. A. Corey, K. Berg, M. H. Solaas, et al. 2003. The role of the children of twins design in elucidating causal relations between parent characteristics and child outcomes. *Journal of Child Psychology and Psychiatry* 44:1130–44.

Dawes, C. T., and J. H. Fowler. 2009. Partisanship, voting, and the dopamine D2 receptor gene. *Journal of Politics* 71 (3): 1157–71.

Downs, A. 1957. *An economic theory of democracy*. New York: Harper.

Duncan, O. 1966. Path analysis, sociological examples. *American Journal of Sociology* 72:1–16.

Durkheim, E. 1895. *The rules of sociological methods*. London: Free Press.

Eaves, L. J. 1973. Assortative mating and intelligence: An analysis of pedigree data. *Heredity* 30:199–210.

———. 1975. Testing models for variation in intelligence. *Heredity* 34:132–36.

———. 1977. Inferring the causes of human variation. *Journal of the Royal Statistical Society* 140:324–55.

———. 1979. The use of twins in the analysis of assortative mating. *Heredity* 43:399–409.

———. 1982. The utility of twins. In *Genetic basis of the epilepsies*, ed. V. E. Anderson, W. A. Hauser, J. K. Penry, and C. F. Sing, 249–76. New York: Raven Press.

Eaves, L. J., S. Chen, M. C. Neale, H. H. Maes, and J. L. Silberg. 2005. Questions, models and methods in psychiatric genetics. In *Psychiatric genetics*, ed. K. S. Kendler and L. J. Eaves, 19–94. Washington, D.C.: American Psychiatric Publishing.

Eaves, L. J., and H. J. Eysenck. 1974. Genetics and the development of social attitudes. *Nature* 249:288–89.

Eaves L. J., H. J. Eysenck, and N. G. Martin. 1989. *Genes, culture and personality: An empirical approach.* London: Academic Press.

Eaves, L. J., and P. K. Hatemi. 2008. Transmission of attitudes toward abortion and gay rights: Effects of genes, social learning, and mate selection. *Behavior Genetics* 38 (3): 247–56.

Eaves, L. J., P. K. Hatemi, E. C. Prom, and E. L. Murrelle. 2008. Social and genetic influences on adolescent religious attitudes and practices. *Social Forces* 86:1621–46.

Eaves, L. J., and A. C. Heath. 1981. Detection of the effects of asymmetric assortative mating. *Nature* 289:205–6.

Eaves, L. J., , A. C. Heath, N. G. Martin, H. H. Maes, M. C. Neale, K. S. Kendler, K. M. Kirk, and L. A. Corey. 1999. Comparing the biological and cultural inheritance of personality and social attitudes in the Virginia 30,000 Study of Twins and their relatives. *Twin Research* 2:62–80.

Eaves, L. J., A. C. Heath, N. G. Martin, M. C. Neale, J. M. Meyer, J. L. Silberg, L. A. Corey, K. Truett, and E. Walters. 1999. Biological and cultural inheritance of stature and attitudes. In *Personality and psychopathology,* ed. C. R. Cloninger, 269–308. Washington, D.C.: American Psychiatric Press.

Eaves, L. J., K. A. Last, P. A. Young, and N. G. Martin. 1978. Model-fitting approaches to the analysis of human behavior. *Heredity* 41:249–320.

Eaves, L. J., J. C. Long, and A. C. Heath. 1986. A theory of developmental change in quantitative phenotypes applied to cognitive development. *Behavior Genetics* 16:143–62.

Eaves, L. J., N. G. Martin, and A. C. Heath. 1990. Religious affiliation in twins and their parents: Testing a model of cultural inheritance. *Behavior Genetics* 20:1–22.

Eaves, L. J., N. G. Martin, A. C. Heath, R. M. Schieken, J. Meyer, J. L. Silberg, M. C. Neale, and L. A. Corey. 1997. Age changes in the causes of individual differences in conservatism. *Behavior Genetics* 27:121–24.

Eaves, L. J., J. L. Silberg, and A. Erkanli. 2003. Resolving multiple epigenetic pathways to adolescent depression. *Journal of Child Psychology and Psychiatry* 44:1006–14.

Eaves, L. J., J. L. Silberg, and H. H. Maes. 2005. Revisiting the children of twins: Can they be used to resolve the environmental effects of dyadic parental treatment on child behavior? *Twin Research* 8:283–90.

Eysenck, H. J. 1966. Personality and experimental psychology. *Bulletin of the British Psychological Society* 19:1–28.

———. 1967. *Dimensions of personality.* London: Routledge and Kegan Paul.

———. 1975. *Manual of the Eysenck Personality Questionnaire (Junior and Adult).* Sevenoaks: Hodder and Stoughton.

Falconer, D. S., and T.F.C. Mackay. 1995. *Introduction to quantitative genetics.* Reading, Mass.: Addison Wesley Longman.

Fisher, R. A. 1918. The correlation between relatives on the supposition of Mendelian inheritance. *Transactions of the Royal Society of Edinburgh* 52:399–433.

Floderus-Myrhed, B., N. Pedersen, and I. Rasmuson. 1980. Assessment of heritability for personality, based on a short-form of the Eysenck Personality Inventory: A study of 12,898 twin pairs. *Behavior Genetics* 10:153–62.

Fowler, J. H., L. A. Baker, and C. T. Dawes. 2008. The genetic basis of political participation. *American Political Science Review* 102 (2): 233–48.

Fowler, J. H., and C. T. Dawes. 2008. Two genes predict voter turnout. *Journal of Politics* 70 (3): 579–94.

Fulker, D. W. 1979. Nature and nurture. In *The structure and measurement of intelligence,* ed. H. J. Eysenck, 102–32. Berlin: Springer Verlag.

Galton, F. 1869. *Hereditary genius: An inquiry into its laws and consequences*. London: Macmillan.

———. 1883. *Inquiries into human faculty and its development*. London: Macmillan.

Garod, A. 1923. *Inborn errors of metabolism*. 2nd ed. London: Henry Frowde and Hodder and Stoughton.

Gill, P. E., W. Murray, M. A. Saunders, and M. H. Wright. 1998. User's guide for NPSOL 5.0: A Fortran package for nonlinear programming. Technical Report SOL 86–2, revised July 30, 1998, Systems Optimization Laboratory, Department of Operations Research, Stanford University, Stanford, Calif.

Goldberger, A. S. 1978. The nonresolution of IQ inheritance by path analysis. *American Journal of Human Genetics* 30:442–48.

Grant, J. D., A. C. Heath, K. K. Bucholz, P. A. Madden, A. Agrawal, D. J. Statham, and N. G. Martin. 2007. Spousal concordance for alcohol dependence: Evidence for assortative mating or spousal interaction effects? *Alcoholism: Clinical and Experimental Research* 31:717–28.

Haley, C. S., J. L. Jinks, and K. Last. 1981. The monozygotic twin half-sib method for analyzing maternal effects and sex-linkage in humans. *Heredity* 46:227–38.

Hatemi, P. K. 2010. The influence of life events on political attitudes: An exploration of gene-environment interaction. Paper presented at the Midwest Political Science Association, Chicago, April.

Hatemi, P. K., et al. 2010. Genome-wide analysis of political attitudes. *Journal of Politics* (Fall).

Hatemi, P. K., J. Alford, J. Hibbing, N. Martin, and L. Eaves. 2009. Is there a "party" in your genes? *Political Research Quarterly* 62 (3): 584–600.

Hatemi, P. K., C. L. Funk, S. Medland, H. M. Maes, J. L. Silberg, N. G. Martin, and L. J. Eaves. 2009. Genetic and environmental transmission of political attitudes over the life course. *Journal of Politics* 71:1141–56.

Hatemi, P. K, J. R. Hibbing, S. E. Medland, M. C. Keller, J. R. Alford, K. B. Smith, N. G. Martin, and L. J. Eaves. 2010. Not by twins alone: Using the extended family design to investigate genetic influence on political beliefs. *American Journal of Political Science* 54 (3): 798–814.

Hatemi, P. K., S. E. Medland, and L. J. Eaves. 2009. Genetic sources for the gender gap? *Journal of Politics* 71 (1): 1–15.

Hatemi, P. K., S. E. Medland, K. I. Morley, A. C. Heath, and N. G. Martin. 2007. The genetics of voting: An Australian twin study. *Behavior Genetics* 37:435–48.

Heath, A. C. 1987. The analysis of marital interaction in cross-sectional twin data. *Acta Geneticae Medicae et Gemellologiae (Roma)* 36:41–49.

Heath, A. C., and L. J. Eaves. 1985. Resolving the effects of phenotype and social background on mate selection. *Behavior Genetics* 15:45–90.

Heath, A. C., K. S. Kendler, L. J. Eaves, and D. Markell. 1985. The resolution of cultural and biological inheritance: Informativeness of different relationships. *Behavior Genetics* 15:439–65.

Heath, A. C., R. C. Kessler, M. C. Neale, J. K. Hewitt, L. J. Eaves, and K. S. Kendler. 1993. Testing hypotheses about direction of causation using cross-sectional family data. *Behavior Genetics* 23:29–50.

Inglehart, R. 1977. *The silent revolution: Changing values and political styles among Western publics*. Princeton, N.J.: Princeton University Press.

International Schizophrenia Genetics Consortium. 2009. Common polygenic variation contributes to risk of schizophrenia and bipolar disorder. *Nature* 460:748–52.

Jencks, C., M. Smith, H. Acland, M. J. Bane, D. Cohen, H. Gintis, B. Heyns, and S. Michelson. 1972. *Inequality: A reassessment of the effect of family and schooling in America.* New York: Basic Books.

Jennings, M. K., and R. Niemi. 1982. *Generations and politics: A panel study of young adults and their parents.* Princeton, N.J.: Princeton University Press.

Jinks, J. L., and D. W. Fulker. 1970. A comparison of the biometrical genetical, classical, and MAVA approaches to the analysis of human behavior. *Psychological Bulletin* 73:311–49.

Keller, M. C., S. E. Medland, L. E. Duncan, P. K. Hatemi, M. C. Neale, H. H. Maes, and L. J. Eaves. 2009. Modeling extended twin family data I: Description of the Cascade model. *Twin Research and Human Genetics* 12:8–18.

Kendler, K. S., and L. J. Eaves. 1986. Models for the joint effect of genotype and environment on liability to psychiatric illness. *American Journal of Psychiatry* 143:279–89.

———, eds. 2005. *Psychiatric genetics.* Washington, D.C.: American Psychiatric Publishing.

Kendler, K. S., M. C. Neale, R. C. Kessler, A. C. Heath, and L. J. Eaves. 1993. A test of the equal-environment assumption in twin studies of psychiatric illness. *Behavior Genetics* 23:21–27.

Kirk, K. M., H. H. Maes, M. C. Neale, A. C. Heath, N. G. Martin, and L. J. Eaves. 1999. Frequency of church attendance in Australia and the United States: Models of family resemblance. *Twin Research* 2:99–107.

Lake, R. I., L. J. Eaves, H. H. Maes, A. C. Heath, and N. G. Martin. 2000. Further evidence against the environmental transmission of individual differences in neuroticism from a collaborative study of 45,850 twins and relatives on two continents. *Behavior Genetics* 30:223–33.

Lange, K., J. Westlake, and M. A. Spence. 1976. Extensions to pedigree analysis. III. Variance components by the scoring method. *Annals of Human Genetics* 39:485–91.

Lewontin, R. C., S. Rose, and L. J. Kamin. 1984. *Not in our genes: Biology, ideology and human nature.* New York: Pantheon Books.

Li, C. C. 1975. *Path analysis: A primer.* Pacific Grove, Calif.: Boxwood Press.

Loehlin, J. C. 1965. Some methodological problems in Cattell's Multiple Abstract Variance Analysis. *Psychological Review* 72:156–61.

———. 2003. *Latent variable models: An introduction to factor, path, and structural equation analysis.* 4th ed. Mahwah, N.J.: Lawrence Erlbaum.

Loehlin, J. C., and R. S. Nichols. 1976. *Heredity, environment, and personality: A study of 850 sets of twins.* Austin: University of Texas Press.

Lumsden, C. J., and E. O. Wilson. 2005. *Genes, mind, and culture: The coevolutionary process.* 25th anniversary ed. Hackensack, N.J.: World Scientific Publishing.

Maes, H. H., M. C. Neale, and L. J. Eaves. 1997. Genetic and environmental factors in body mass index. *Behavior Genetics* 27:325–51.

Maes, H. H., M. C. Neale, L. J. Eaves, K. S. Kendler, J. K. Hewitt, J. L. Silberg, J. M. Meyer, et al. 1998. Assortative mating for major psychiatric diagnoses in two population-based samples. *Psychological Medicine* 28:1389–1401.

Maes, H. H., M. C. Neale, S. E. Medland, M. C. Keller, N. G. Martin, A. C. Heath, and L. J. Eaves. 2009. Flexible Mx specification of various extended twin kinship designs. *Twin Research and Human Genetics* 12:26–34.

Mare R. 1991. Five decades of educational assortative mating. *American Sociological Review* 56:15–32.

Martin, N. G., and L. J. Eaves. 1977. The genetical analysis of covariance structure. *Heredity* 38:79–95.

Martin, N. G., L. J. Eaves, A. C. Heath, R. Jardine, L. Feingold, and H. J. Eysenck. 1986. The transmission of social attitudes. *Proceedings of the National Academy of Sciences* 83:4364–68.

Martin, N. G., L. J. Eaves, M. J. Kearsey, and P. Davis. 1978. The power of the classical twin study. *Heredity* 40:97–116

Martin, N. G., and R. Jardine. 1986. Eysenck's contribution to behavior genetics. In *Hans Eysenck: Consensus and controversy*, ed. R. Modgil and C. Modgil, 13–62. Sussex, England: Falmer.

Mascie-Taylor, C.G.N., and S. G. Vandenberg. 1988. Assortative mating for IQ and personality due to propinquity and personal preference. *Behavior Genetics* 18:339–45.

Mather, K. 1974. Non-allelic interaction in continuous variation of randomly breeding populations. *Heredity* 32:414–19.

Mather, K., and J. L. Jinks. 1983. *Biometrical genetics: The study of continuous variation.* 3rd ed. London: Chapman and Hall.

Matsusaka, J. G., and F. Palda. 1999. Voter turnout: How much can we explain? *Public Choice* 98 (3–4): 431–46.

McGue, M., R. Wette, and D. C. Rao. 1984. Evaluation of path analysis through computer simulation: Effect of incorrectly assuming independent distribution of familial correlations. *Genetic Epidemiology* 1:255–69.

Medland, S. E., and M. C. Keller. 2009. Modeling extended twin family data II: Power associated with different family structures. *Twin Research and Human Genetics* 12:19–25.

Mendel, G. 1865. Experiments in plant hybridization. Translated in *Castle's Genetics and Eugenics* 6 (1916): 353. Cambridge: Harvard University Press

Miller, R. B., and J. Glass. 1989. Parent-child attitude similarity across the life course. *Journal of Marriage and the Family* 51:991–97.

Murphy, N. 1997. *Anglo-American postmodernity: Philosophical perspectives on science, religion, and ethics.* Boulder, Colo.: Westview Press.

Nance, W. E., and L. A. Corey. 1976. Genetic models for the analysis of data from the families of identical twins. *Genetics* 18:69–79.

Neale, M. C., S. M. Boker, G. Xie, and H. H. Maes. 2002. *Mx, Statistical modeling.* 6th ed. Richmond: Department of Psychiatry, Virginia Commonwealth University.

Neale, M. C., and L. L. Cardon. 1992. *Methodology for genetic studies of twins and families.* Dordrecht: Kluwer Academic.

Nelder, J. A. 1960. The estimation of variance components in certain types of experiment on quantitative genetics. In *Biometrical genetics*, ed. O. Kempthorne, 139–56. London: Pergamon Press.

Newman, H. H., F. N. Freeman, and K. J. Holzinger. 1937. *Twins: A study of heredity and environment.* Chicago: University of Chicago Press.

Niemi, R. G., and M. K. Jennings. 1991. Issues and inheritance in the formation of party identification. *American Journal of Political Science* 35:970–88.

Pearson, K. 1903. On the inheritance of the mental and moral characters in man, and its comparison with the inheritance of the physical characters. *Journal of the Royal Anthropological Institute of Great Britain and Ireland* 33:179–237.

———. 1904. On a generalized theory of alternative inheritance, with special references to Mendel's laws. *Philosophical Transactions of the Royal Society of London* 203:53–86.

Pearson, K., and A. Lee. 1903. On the laws on inheritance in man. *Biometrika* 2:356–462.

Plomin, R., K. Asbury, and J. Dunn. 2001. Why are children in the same family so different? Nonshared environment a decade later. *Canadian Journal of Psychiatry* 46:225–33.

Posner, S. F., L. A. Baker, A. C. Heath, and N. G. Martin. 1996. Social contact, social attitudes, and twin similarity. *Behavior Genetics* 26:123.

Rao, D. C., C. J. MacLean, N. E. Morton, and S. Yee. 1975. Analysis of family resemblance. V. Height and weight in northeastern Brazil. *American Journal of Human Genetics* 27: 509–20.

Rao, D. C., N. E. Morton, and C. R. Cloninger. 1979. Path analysis under generalized assortative mating. I. Theory. *Genetical Research* 33:175–88.

Rao, D. C., N. E. Morton, and S. Yee. 1974. Analysis of family resemblance II. A linear model for familial correlation. *American Journal of Human Genetics* 26:331–59.

Russell, B. 1946. *A history of Western philosophy*. London: George Allen and Unwin.

Rutter, M. L., and J. L. Silberg. 2002. Gene-environment interplay in relation to emotional and behavioral disturbance. *Annual Review of Psychology* 53:463–90.

Sigel, R. 1989. *Political learning in adulthood*. Chicago: University of Chicago Press.

Silberg, J. L., and L. J. Eaves. 2004. Analysing the contribution of genes and parent-child interaction to childhood behavioral and emotional problems: A model for the children of twins. *Psychological Medicine* 34:347–56.

Silberg, L. J., H. H. Maes, and L. J. Eaves. 2010. Genetic and environmental influences on the transmission of parental depression to children's depression and conduct disturbance: An extended Children of Twins study. *Journal of Child Psychology and Psychiatry* 51 (6): 734–44.

Sutton, W. S. 1903. The chromosomes in heredity. *Biological Bulletin* 4:231–51.

Tesser, A. 1993. The importance of heritability in psychological research: The case of attitudes. *Psychological Review* 100:129–42.

Truett, K. R., L. J. Eaves, E. E. Walters, A. C. Heath, J. K. Hewitt, J. M. Meyer, J. L. Silberg, M. C. Neale, N. G. Martin, and K. S. Kendler. 1994. A model system for the analysis of family resemblance in extended kinships of twins. *Behavior Genetics* 24:35–49.

Turkheimer, E., A. Haley, M. Waldron, B. D'Onofrio, and I. I. Gottesman. 2003. Socioeconomic status modifies heritability of IQ in young children. *Psychological Science* 14:623–28.

Vandenberg, S. G. 1972. Assortative mating, or who marries whom? *Behavior Genetics* 2:127–57.

Verhulst, B., P. K. Hatemi, and N. G. Martin. 2010. Personality and political attitudes. *Personality and Individual Differences* 49:306–16.

Visscher, P. M. 2008. Sizing up human height variation. *Nature Genetics* 40 (5): 489–90.

Watson, J. D., and F.H.C. Crick. 1953. A structure for deoxyribose nucleic acid. *Nature* 421:397–98.

Wilson, G. D., and J. R. Patterson. 1970. *Manual for the conservatism scale*. London: Academic Press.

Wright, S. 1921. Correlation and causation. *Journal of Agricultural Research* 20:557–85.

5

GENE-ENVIRONMENT INTERPLAY FOR THE STUDY OF POLITICAL BEHAVIORS

Jason D. Boardman

There is fairly consistent evidence that some proportion of political behaviors and attitudes can be traced to genetic differences between people. Voter turnout (Fowler and Dawes 2008), broad political participation (Fowler, Baker, and Dawes 2008), partisan intensity (Hatemi et al. 2009), and political attitudes (Alford et al. 2005) have been shown to be moderately heritable (e.g., $.2 < h^2 < .4$). And there is recent evidence linking candidate genes to political behaviors (Fowler and Dawes 2008). In this volume, Fowler et al. (chapter 6) detail the ways in which genetic factors may both complicate and clarify the otherwise social role of cooperation that is fundamental to political participation. However, the bulk of these studies generally report *main* genetic influences that are believed to be *independent* of environmental factors. Further, environmental and genetic factors are also believed to act in an *additive* manner. That is, genes are not believed to influence environmental effects and environments are not purported to moderate genetic effects. Both of these assumptions are challenged by the gene-environment interplay paradigm (Rutter, Moffitt, and Caspi 2006) that anticipates dependence (e.g., gene-environment correlation [rGE]) and nonadditively (e.g., gene-environment interaction [GxE]) in the effects of genetic and environmental influences on particular outcomes. There is a large body of research dedicated to issues of gene-environment interplay in the fields of epidemiology, social demography, and psychology (Shanahan and Boardman 2009); however, there have been very few efforts in political science to consider the complex interaction between genetic and environmental factors in twin studies or studies using genotypic data. The purpose of this chapter is to describe the gene-environment interplay perspective and to review the limited work that has been done in this area thus far.

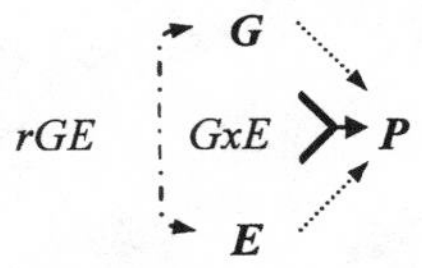

$$rGE \quad \vdots \quad GxE \quad \begin{matrix} G \\ \\ \\ E \end{matrix} \quad P$$

FIGURE 5.1. Gene-environment interplay: conceptual model.

Gene-Environment Interplay: Overview

Conceptualizing the determinants of complex behaviors such as political participation as due to nature or nurture is useful because it simplifies the very complex reality of genetic and environmental influences on the behavior of an individual. However, there is a clear cost associated with this conceptual reduction. That is, individual differences are described as a function of either environmental *or* genetic characteristics rather than the simultaneous influence of genetic *and* environmental factors. The dark arrow in figure 5.1 from G (genetic factors) to P (political behaviors) characterizes the main effects of genotype on political behaviors. Most of the work in this volume has emphasized this type of genetic effect. This section of the book is concerned with the two other forces contained in this figure. If genes and environments are correlated with one another, then efforts must be made by researchers to disentangle these effects from one another. For example, children share one half of their genes with each parent but they are also raised and socialized about political attitudes and behaviors by their parents. Thus genotypes and political behaviors may be correlated but one does not *cause* the other. This can complicate efforts to identify the genetic causes of their attitudes and behaviors.

It is also possible that genes and environments do not influence political behaviors and attitudes in an additive manner. Rather, genetic and environmental influences may be contingent upon their respective levels. For example, an individual may have a genetic profile that is typically linked to increased political activities but that person may reside within a community in which these behaviors are either nonexistent or limited by government institutions. In this case, genotype will not have a strong influence on behavior because of the environmental controls. The gene-environment interaction perspective is illustrated in figure 5.1 by the GxE arrows in the middle of the figure. The next two sections describe the theoretical background for the rGE and GxE frameworks using examples from biological and behavioral sciences.

The Environment

Political behaviors and attitudes have very clear environmental influences; social, cultural, and institutional forces consistently predict voter participation. This is illustrated by the dark arrow from E (environment) to P (political behavior) in figure 5.1. The term "environment" refers to a very broad range of phenomena that may influence political ideology, attitudes, or behaviors. In the social sciences, the environment is typically characterized as organized, enduring patterns of interaction among people, extending from interpersonal relationships to neighborhoods to organizations (such as companies and schools) to communities, societies, and institutions. Thus, there is a multilevel perspective of environmental factors that incorporates the related aspects of *composition* (e.g., the socioeconomic, racial, and demographic characteristics of the population) and *context* (e.g., institutional, environmental, and normative features of the environment). While genetic epidemiologists and behavioral geneticists may characterize the environment as pollutants, toxins, diet, medications, or intrauterine conditions social scientists tend to describe the environment as broadly defined social forces that may limit or enable particular attitudes or behaviors.

Gene-Environment Correlation

Over thirty years ago, Plomin, DeFries, and Loehlin (1977) developed the first typology of rGE in which they describe three forms of correlation: evocative, passive, and active. All three forms of rGE describe a situation in which genotypes and environments are associated with one another but the form of this association of quite different. *Evocative correlation* anticipates that genotype may influence the environment. If people with similar genotypes are more likely than others to evoke the same type of responses from others, then genotype is linked to the environment but the arrow is drawn from G to E. The social context (E) is a response to behaviors with a genetic origin and this association may build over time. The clearest case of evocative correlation is the example of babies with genetic tendencies to be more irritable and fussy are more likely than relatively calm babies children to *evoke* hostility responses from their parents and other caregivers.

Passive correlation occurs regularly because children inherit both genetic and environmental factors from their parents. One of the most common examples of passive correlation is reading ability. Reading ability is a heritable trait but children raised by parents who regularly read themselves are more likely to be raised and socialized in an intellectually stimulating environment that is conducive to the acquisition of reading skills. Children passively inherit *both* the genetic characteristics related to cognitive development *and* the enriching environment.

Finally, *active correlation* most closely resembles a selection process where genotype may influence an individual to choose a particular group of friends, job, residential location, or social activity. It thus describes a situation in which someone's genes influence the type of social environment in which that person chooses to interact. For example, persons who are more vulnerable to nicotine addiction may be more likely to self-select into environments in which more people smoke cigarettes, cigarettes are readily available, and public smoking is not criticized. This is particularly important to social scientists because of the role of human agency; people actively construct their lives by means of those behaviors that they exhibit at different stages. Therefore, gene-environment correlation for children and adolescents is most likely characterized by passive processes within their family because children do not choose their environment and their environment is constrained. However, as children mature they gain increasing discretion in their choice of environments. People at the extremes of the life-course (e.g., the very young and the very old) are less likely to select into social groups as a function of their genes; thus passive or evocative rGE may be more relevant. In contrast, most adults choose their settings. They choose their friends, enroll in organizations, select a job, join organizational memberships, and decide where to live. Therefore, active rGE more likely describes adult behaviors.

Gene-Environment Interaction

The gene-environment interaction (GxE) literature poses four related models: social trigger, social control, social push, and social distinction. These models are described graphically in figure 5.2. The most commonly cited GxE findings are situations in which the social or political environment serves as a *trigger* for genetic influences. The strong triggering perspective anticipates that genetic factors will only matter in the presence of the triggering agent and the weak triggering perspective suggests that genetic factors are heightened in the presence of a triggering agent. Guo and Stearns (2002) find evidence for the weak triggering hypothesis by showing that heritability of verbal IQ is higher among children from families with more economic resources; genetic influence on verbal IQ is higher for adolescents in which both parents

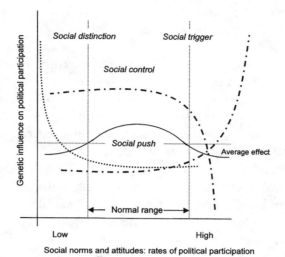

FIGURE 5.2. Genetic influences on political participation in typical and unique environments.

are employed compared to those with at least one unemployed parent. They argue that that employment status also captures family stability and educational resources in the home. These variables reflect fundamental resources that enable genetic factors to be salient. This perspective is central to a social scientific interpretation of gene by environment interaction effects because, as Link and Phelan (1995) argue, the environment should be characterized as a "fundamental cause." That is, although genetic factors are important in child development, the relative influence of these genetic factors may depend on the social environment.

Boardman et al. (2008) use the network-based data of the National Longitudinal Study of Adolescent Health (Add Health) to calculate popularity measures for each student in the school. In addition to a random sample of students from nearly 132 schools in the United States, the Add Health study purposely oversampled twin and sibling pairs for the purposes of behavioral genetic modeling. As described by Eaves et al. in chapter 4, the similarity of siblings as a function of their genetic similarity can be used to identify genetic influences without actually measuring individuals' genes. Because there are multiple pairs within each school, it is also possible to estimate differences in genetic factors *across* the different institutional and social settings of the schools. Boardman et al. (2008) estimate a correlation between popularity and smoking within each school and they argue that schools in which the most popular kids are also the biggest smokers (compared to those schools in which the popular students smoke the least) are more likely to have pro-smoking norms that may influence behaviors. They then show that the genetic influences on smoking are significantly higher for students who attend these pro-smoking schools; the environment enhances genetic tendencies to smoke (weak triggering). To date, the bulk of the evidence supports the triggering hypothesis. In a recent review Reiss and Leve (2007) report : "In virtually all publications reporting positive results for this phenomenon, a substantial association between allele and behavior is observed under adverse environmental circumstances but not under favorable circumstances" (1006–7).

It is also possible that the social environment can limit genetic influences rather than enable them. The *social control model* refers to social norms and institutions that may place limits on the range of behaviors that individuals are able to initiate. Behavioral control is a function of the social structures that are in place to maintain social order (whether for the moral good or not). Control might be a function of laws and legal enforcement, moral codes linked to specific religions, highly organized educational settings, or broad forms of stratification that limit particular individuals' mobility. For example, Timberlake et al. (2006) show that self-rated religiosity dampens the genetic component for smoking onset in which they estimate a heritability of 60%. This estimate becomes negligible for adolescents who report that religion is "more important than anything else" to them because the control swamps genetics. Evidence for the broad social-control model is also presented in two different studies that examined changes in the genetic influences on behavior for men and women over successive birth cohorts. Heath et al. (1985) show significantly lower genetic effects for educational attainment for women compared to men. They argue that this is a function of the social norms and limited opportunities that controlled the educational opportunities more so for women than men. Similarly, Kendler, Thornton, and Pedersen (2000) show that genetic factors consistently predict smoking for men regardless of birth cohort but they do not influence smoking among women born at the turn of the twentieth century. However, by the 1940 birth cohort, the additive genetic effects on regular smoking were indistinguishable for men and women. They argue that social controls limited women's behaviors and subsequently suppressed genetic tendencies that may have influenced the likelihood of smoking. In these cases, the heritability estimates are the smallest among those who are socialized in more controlled social environments with clearly established norms and corresponding sanctions against using substances.

Finally, in some cases, genetic factors may actually become more relevant within social settings in which the behavior is rare or is socially sanctioned.

The social-trigger and social-control models are hypothesized to have a *causal* influence on genetic expression because the social environment either limits or exacerbates genetic influences; shared behavioral expectations and corresponding sanctions *cause* genes to operate differently by either blocking or enabling their expression. But a noncausal model of gene-environment interaction is also possible. The *social push* and *distinction* models are concerned with social environments that minimize "noise" that has the potential to overwhelm and hide these influences. On one hand, genetic associations are most clearly observable in *benign* environments that lack social factors, encouraging genetically influenced addictive behaviors. When social noise is minimized, it allows for "biology to shine through" (Raine 2002, 14). Conversely, when social factors "push" certain behaviors, then biological factors are harder to identify. As Raine makes clear, the social push perspective does not mean that the environment actually causes genes to operate differently. Rather, by adding or eliminating other sources of variation in behavior, the environment hides or highlights the role of genes to scientific observers. Support for this perspective is found in work by Button et al. (2005) who show that the genetic risks for antisocial behavior were the highest among adolescents from families with the lowest levels of family dysfunction. Children from relatively dysfunctional families exhibited a significantly higher risk of antisocial behavior compared to those from integrated and stable families but the cause of antisocial behavior among those from stable and functional families was genetic risk. This perspective can be thought of as "social distinction" because the social environment simply distinguishes genetic influences rather than causing genetic factors to operate differently. Raine (2002) describes a variant of this model that is called the "social push perspective" in which it is claimed that contexts lacking social factors that either encourage or discourage drug use (benign environments) are the most relevant contexts in which to examine genetic associations.

Gene-Environment Interplay and Political Science

Although there are reasons to anticipate social and institutional moderation and mediation of genetic influence on political behavior, to date research on gene-environment interplay has not been the central focus on genetic studies in political science. For example, it is likely the case that there will be relatively low genetic influences on political participation for individuals who are socialized within environments characterized by low rates of political participation. However, genes may effectively differentiate among individuals level of political participation (Fowler, Baker and Dawes 2008) within environments with high rates of political participation, strong norms regarding participation, and institutional support for political participation (social trigger).

In one of the only known papers to examine the simultaneous influence of genetic and environmental factors on political attitudes, Settle et al. (forthcoming) compare self-reported liberalism for those with two copies of the 7 repeat allele at DRD4 to those with either one or no copies of this allele. They also allow the effect of this allele to be moderated by an individual's popularity. Respondents in the first observation of the Add Health study were interviewed in their schools and they were asked to write down the names of their friends. Some people received a large number of nominations while some received none. The authors operationalize this variable as students' popularity scores at their school and they show that DRD4 7R did not differentiate political ideology among students with no friends but was positively associated with liberalism among those with at least one friend. Their findings provide some evidence for the strong version of the social trigger hypothesis; that is, the genetic variant may require some social interactional stimuli to influence this complex phenotype (e.g., political ideology).

In a recent publication, Hatemi et al. (2009) pose the question "Do genes contribute to the 'gender gap'?" Most work on the gender gap in political ideology and participation has focused on the different social contexts, social roles, and social norms that tend to differentiate men from women. These contexts, roles, and norms cause individuals to display different levels of fear, compassion, and sense of community, all of which contribute to political participation and ideology. However, these factors, according to the GxE perspective, may also moderate the influence of latent genetic traits. These researchers examined 27 items tapping political preferences and attitudes, including censorship, gay rights, school prayer, and pacifism. All 27 items were shown to be heritable except for party identification, which was nearly all due to shared environmental influences. Quantitative genetic estimates for all of the items are presented in table 5.1. As shown in this table, additive genetic influences accounted for roughly 30–40% of the variance for most of the items. Of these 26 items, 6 items were shown to be differentially heritable for men and women by more than 10 percentage points ($\Delta a^2 > .10$). Women demonstrated higher heritabilities for two of the items ("live together" and "busing") while men demonstrated higher heritabilities for "divorce," "school prayer," "capitalism," and "abortion." Support for couples living together who are not currently married and support for busing children to different schools to balance the racial and class composition evoke notions of compas-

TABLE 5.1. Quantitative variance components for political and social attitudes

	Model[a]	Females			Males			Δa²	Δc²
		a²	c²	e²	a²	c²	e²		
Live together	ACE[bc]	**.51** (.41–.68)	.16 (.10–.24)	.33 (.30–.37)	**0** (.00–.34)	.48 (.21–.54)	.52 (.52–.58)	.51	.32
Busing	ACE[b]	.31 (.16–.31)	.09 (.08–.20)	.60 (.55–.65)	.12 (.00–.40)	.30 (.06–.45)	.58 (.50–.66)	.19	.21
Divorce	ACE[bc]	.25 (.16–.29)	.23 (.08–.38)	.52 (.47–.57)	.42 (.31–.42)	0 (.00–.07)	.57 (.53–.65)	.17	.23
School prayer	ACE[b]	.32 (.16–.48)	.37 (.22–.51)	.31 (.27–.36)	.47 (.22–.62)	.21 (.09–.41)	.32 (.26–.40)	.15	.16
Capitalism	AE[b]	.47 (.43–.52)	—	.53 (.48–.57)	.61 (.54–.67)	—	.39 (.33–.46)	.14	.00
Abortion	ACE[bc]	.26 (.12–.41)	.41 (.27–.53)	.33 (.29–.37)	.38 (.16–.51)	.19 (.10–.37)	.43 (.36–.50)	.12	.22
Foreign aid	ACE[b]	.40 (.29–.45)	.01 (.00–.10)	.59 (.55–.64)	.31 (.08–.49)	.11 (.00–.31)	.58 (.51–.66)	.09	.10
Women's lib	ACE[bc]	.34 (.18–.49)	.18 (.05–.18)	.48 (.44–.53)	.31 (.23–.39)	0 (.00–.03)	.69 (.61–.76)	.03	.18
Religiosity	ACE[bc]	.48 (.32–.67)	.26 (.09–.41)	.25 (.22–.29)	.47 (.00–.65)	.18 (.04–.56)	.35 (.35–.45)	.01	.08

(Continued)

TABLE 5.1. (*Continued*)

| | | Parameter estimates | | | | | | | |
| | Model[a] | Females | | | Males | | | Δa² | Δc² |
		a²	c²	e²	a²	c²	e²		
Censorship	AE[bcd]	.38 (.33–.42)	—	.62 (.58–.67)	.38 (.33–.42)	—	.62 (.58–.67)	.00	.00
Death penalty	ACE[bd]	.35 (.22–.48)	.21 (.10–.31)	.44 (.40–.48)	.35 (.22–.48)	.21 (.10–.31)	.44 (.40–.48)	.00	.00
Pacifism	AE[bd]	.31 (.27–.35)	—	.69 (.65–.73)	.31 (.27–.35)	—	.69 (.65–.73)	.00	.00
Segregation	AE[bcd]	.37 (.32–.37)	—	.63 (.59–.68)	.37 (.32–.37)	—	.63 (.59–.68)	.00	.00
Draft	AE[bd]	.37 (.32–.41)	—	.63 (.60–.68)	.37 (.32–.41)	—	.63 (.60–.68)	.00	.00
X-rated	AE[bcd]	.51 (.47–.56)	—	.49 (.46–.54)	.51 (.47–.56)	—	.49 (.46–.54)	.00	.00
Modern art	AE[bcd]	.40 (.36–.43)	—	.60 (.57–.64)	.40 (.36–.43)	—	.60 (.57–.64)	.00	.00
Moral Majority	AE[bd]	.42 (.38–.47)	—	.58 (.53–.62)	.42 (.38–.47)	—	.58 (.53–.62)	.00	.00

Issue	Model	a²	c²	e²	a²	c²	e²	Δ	Δ
Property tax	AE[bd]	.42 (.41–.46)	—	.58 (.58–.63)	.42 (.41–.46)	—	.58 (.58–.63)	.00	.00
Socialism	AE[bd]	.38 (.34–.38)	—	.62 (.58–.66)	.38 (.34–.38)	—	.62 (.58–.66)	.00	.00
Immigration	AE[bd]	.46 (.46–.49)	—	.54 (.51–.54)	.46 (.46–.49)	—	.54 (.51–.54)	.00	.00
Party ID	CE[bcd]	—	.81 (.78–.84)	.19 (.16–.22)	—	.81 (.78–.84)	.19 (.16–.22)	.00	.00
Astrology	AE[b]	.47 (.43–.47)	—	.53 (.48–.57)	.47 (.43–.47)	—	.53 (.46–.61)	.00	.00
Gay rights	ACE[bd]	.34 (.24–.45)	.25 (.22–.34)	.41 (.39–.45)	.34 (.24–.45)	.25 (.22–.34)	.41 (.39–.45)	.00	.00
Military drill	AE[bd]	.36 (.31–.40)	—	.64 (.63–.69)	.36 (.31–.40)	—	.64 (.63–.69)	.00	.00
Unions	AE[bd]	.41 (.36–.46)	—	.59 (.54–.64)	.41 (.36–.46)	—	.59 (.54–.64)	.00	.00
Fed housing	AE[b]	.41 (.36–.46)	—	.59 (.54–.64)	.41 (.36–.46)	—	.59 (.54–.64)	.00	.00
Nuclear power	AE[bd]	.34 (.30–.39)	—	.65 (.61–.65)	.34 (.30–.39)	—	.65 (.61–.65)	.00	.00

Note: (a) Only best fitting models shown (thresholds corrected for age). ACE represents a model in which all three variance components are significant; CE represents a model in which common and unique environmental influences are significant; AE represents a model in which genes and unique environment are significant; a^2, c^2, and e^2 represent additive genetic, common environmental, and unique environmental influence respectively; Δ represent the difference between males and females (b) equated thresholds for MZ and DZ pairs (c) equated thresholds for males and females (d) equated variance components for males and females. (Reproduced from Hatemi et al. 2009.)

sion and empathy whereas divorce, school prayer, capitalism, and abortion are all key components of established institutions. These items tap into differences in the socialization and social roles of men and women and may therefore account for the observed gender differences in the relative contribution of genes. In other words, factors responsible for particular forms of socialization (in this case gender socialization) may trigger latent genetic factors that are otherwise "gender neutral." In this case, gender is broadly conceived as an environmental trigger. As with the chapters of McDermott (chapter 8) and Apicella and Cesarini (chapter 9), these emergent findings are providing unique cues about the interaction between biology, social context, and behavior surrounding long-standing differences in the political behavior of men and women.

Gene-Environment Interaction: An Empirical Example

As the two examples above highlight, the "environment" can be thought of as something as broad as gender or as narrow as the number of friends that someone has. In both cases, these aspects are believed to be mechanisms that may serve as indicators of social differences among men and women. However, social scientists often characterize the environment as multidimensional (e.g., normative and institutional), multilevel (e.g., families, neighborhoods, schools, areas of residence), and longitudinal (Lynch and Kaplan 2000). As such, it is important to consider the ways in which these aspects may influence genetic influences. To illustrate the perspective that the environment may moderate genetic influences on political behaviors such as voting, working for a candidate, or attending a political function, I use the multilevel aspect of the sibling and twin design of the Add Health study, a nationally representative sample of adolescents in seventh through twelfth grades (Udry 2003; Harris et al. 2006). In 1994 90,118 adolescents from 134 different schools completed questionnaires about their daily activities, health-related behaviors, and basic social and demographic characteristics. Following the in-school survey, 20,747 respondents were re-interviewed in their homes (wave 1) between the months of April and December of 1995 and then again one year later (wave 2). During wave 3 of the study, respondents who identified that they had a full sibling or a twin during wave 1 were asked to provide saliva specimens to be genotyped. Of the 3,139 individuals that were asked, 83% (n = 2,612) agreed to take part in the study. Researchers then used 11 genetic markers to confirm the reported zygosity of the twin and sibling pairs. After reducing our sample to pairs who resided in the same county during wave 1 of the study, I use a sample of pairs that are comprised of 185 identical twins, 297 fraternal twins, 851 full siblings, 272 half-siblings, and 254 cousins. As described by Eaves et al. (chapter 4), the pair-design makes it possible to calculate quantitative genetic estimates of genetic and environmental influences.

I use a similar technique used by Fowler, Baker, and Dawes (2008) to measure political participation of respondents. In wave 3 of the study, respondents were asked if they had voted in the most recent presidential election and then they were also asked about their involvement in a variety of different political activities. Specifically, they were asked if they had volunteered for a political club or organization, contributed money to a party or a candidate, contacted a government official about a political or community issue, run for public or nonpublic office, or attended a political march or rally. These items produce an internal consistency score (alpha = .60) that is high enough to suggest that these items capture a single latent construct of political participation.

(5.1) $$y_2 = \beta_1 y_1 + \beta_2 g + \beta_3 (y_1 g) + \sum_{k=1}^{K} \beta_K X_K + e_i$$

I decompose the variance of political participation into three quantitative genetic components using a multilevel application of a DeFries-Fulker regression (DeFries and Fulker 1985). This extension provides a parameter estimate that describes the county-level moderation of the heritability of political participation. Because of the role of counties in the voting process, these organized social boundaries capture unique social forces regarding political attitudes. As such, changes in political norms and subsequent behavior may be characterized better at this broad level compared to smaller levels such as the neighborhood. The standard model (see equation 5.1) relies on data obtained from sibling and twin pairs and predicts the outcome of the second sibling of a pair (y_2) as a function of the first sibling's score on the same outcome (y_1), a measure of genetic similarity—average proportion of genes identical by descent for each pair type—(g), and an interaction between genetic similarity and the siblings' score $(y_1 g)$. Because identical twins share all of their genes, these pairs receive a score of $g = 1$, fraternal twins and full siblings a score of $g = .5$. If the similarity of the pair is conditional upon their genetic similarity, then a positive and significant value for b_3 indicates that the degree of similarity for political behaviors among sibling pairs is a function of their genetic similarity. If the distribution of the dependent variable is standard-normal, then the parameter estimates for b_1 and b_3 describe the relative contribution of shared environment (c^2) and heritability (h^2), respectively, and the remaining proportion is due to nonshared environmental characteristics (e^2). This model is quite flexible. It can be extended to include K covariates and it is well suited to complex sampling designs.

$$\underbrace{y_2 = \beta_0 + \beta_1 y_{1ij} + \beta_2 g_{ij} + \beta_3(y_{1ij}g_{ij})}_{\text{Fixed}} + \underbrace{u_{oj} + u_{1j}(y_{1ij}) + u_{2j}(y_{1ij}g_{ij})}_{\text{Random}} + e_{ij}$$

(5.2)

The single-level model has undergone many changes since the original specification (Purcell and Sham 2003) but it is still widely used to estimate quantitative genetic parameters (Rende et al. 2005; Slomkowski et al. 2005). In equation 5.2, I show how to extend this model to a mixed (or multilevel) modeling framework (Rabe-Hesketh and Skrondal 2006). According to the specification in equation 5.2, the ith pair is nested within the jth county and this model includes three level-2 residual components (u_o, u_1, and u_2) that describe the random intercept (average differences in political participation across counties), the random slope for the y_1 covariate (county-level differences in the shared environment influence), and the random slope for the $y_1 g$ covariate (county-level differences in the heritability estimate), respectively. County-level moderation in environmental and genetic influences are detected with a significant level-2 residual estimates (σ^2_{u1} and σ^2_{u2}). Then I will estimate models that include covariates designed to explain this latent factor. This model has been used in previous behavior genetics research (Boardman 2009; Boardman et al. 2008; Rowe, Almeida, and Jacobson 1999).

I then analyze the empirical Bayes estimates for the random effects as a function of county-level factors that are hypothesized to moderate genetic influences on political participation: county-level support for Ross Perot in the 1992 presidential election. I use this example because it allows us to test the social-trigger hypothesis discussed above. As others have shown, there is something unique about the social contexts in which third-party candidates such as Ross Perot have found support. Evidence that political participation may be a stable factor in these areas is shown by comparing the concordance of support for Jesse Ventura and Ross Perot across a relatively large amount of time in Minnesota. Gilbert and Peterson (2001) show that the 1992 support for Ross Perot and the 1998 support for Jesse Ventura in Minnesota counties is .58. More important, Lacy and Burden (1999) provide compelling evidence that Ross Perot's candidacy increased political participation (e.g., voter turnout) by an estimated 3%. They argue that third-party candidates are particularly effective at engaging abstainers into the debate and bringing them out to the polls. As such, counties with a relatively high proportion of Perot support in

TABLE 5.2. Multi- and single-level DeFries-Fulker estimates for political participation among young adults

	Multilevel estimates		DeFries-Fulker estimates	
Intercept	0.05	(−0.25, 0.36)	0.06	(−0.25, 0.36)
Participation Sib 2 (P)	0.07	(0.00, 0.14)	0.11	(0.07, 0.15)
Genetic similarity (G)	−0.07	(−0.21, 0.07)	−0.05	(−0.19, 0.09)
Heritability (P*G)	0.41	(0.02, 0.84)	0.64	(0.38, 0.90)
Age	0.00	(−0.01, 0.02)	0.00	(−0.01, 0.01)
Sex	−0.08	(−0.12, −0.03)	−0.07	(−0.11, −0.02)
Same sex	0.04	(−0.01, 0.09)	0.04	(−0.01, 0.09)
σ_{p*g}	0.62	(0.33, 1.18)		
σ_p	0.14	(0.09, 0.22)		
$\sigma_{int ercept}$	0.12	(0.09, 0.17)		
σ_e	0.56	(0.54, 0.57)		

Note: Data come from wave 3 of the National Longitudinal Study of Adolescent Health. Sibling and twin pairs across counties in the United States are used to calculate these estimates. See methods for more detail.

1992 may be characterized as places that encourage political participation in general. According to the social trigger model, genetic influences on political participation should be higher in areas with pro-participation norms and greater political activity. Therefore, the estimated heritabilities should be higher for those raised in counties that received a relatively high proportion of support for Perot.

I demonstrate the usefulness of this multilevel approach by comparing the estimates from two regression based quantitative genetic models. These estimates are presented in table 5.2. The traditional DeFries-Fulker model provides similar results to other work in this area (Fowler, Baker, and Dawes 2008) and I estimate the heritability of political participation to be 63%, shared environment 11%, and the remaining 26% is due to nonshared environmental influences. I then estimate an identical regression model but I allow the effects for the heritability estimate and the shared environment estimate to vary across counties. The first thing to note is that specifying the residual variance at two levels and allowing for the effects to differ across counties reduces the estimates for the heritability estimate. That is, some of the additive genetic influence on political participation may also contain level 2 gene-environment interaction effects which are absorbed in the level-2 error term. According to these results, political participation has an *average* heritability of 41% and a shared environment estimate of 7%; the remaining 52% is due to nonshared environmental factors. This is important because it suggests that

TABLE 5.3. Range of quantitative genetic parameter estimates for political participation obtained from a multilevel DeFries-Fulker regression model

	Average	Median	1st Q	3rd Q
Heritability	0.41	0.41	0.38	0.45
Shared environment	0.07	0.08	0.04	0.09
Non-shared environment	0.52	0.51	0.49	0.53

Note: Data come from wave 3 of the National Longitudinal Study of Adolescent Health. Sibling and twin pairs across counties in the United States are used to calculate these estimates. See methods for more detail.

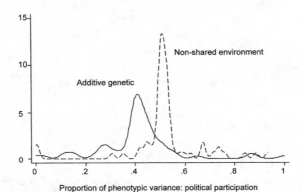

Proportion of phenotypic variance: political participation

FIGURE 5.3. Distribution of additive genetic and nonshared environmental variance estimates across counties in the Add Health study. *Note*: Data come from wave 3 of the National Longitudinal Study of Adolescent Health. Sibling and twin pairs across counties in the U.S. are used to calculate these estimates. See methods for more detail.

environmental moderation may mask variation in quantitative genetic estimates on behavior. That is, the previous findings may have overstated the additive genetic influences on political behavior because they did not explicitly address the possibility of variation due to GxE. This variation is evident in the significant standard deviation estimates for the random factors ($\sigma_{u1} = .62$ and $\sigma_{u2} = .14$) providing empirical support for the gene-environment interaction perspective. Descriptive statistics for the county-level estimates from this model are presented in table 5.3. The range for the heritability estimates includes outlier cases in which the heritability is estimated at 1 or 0; however, the interquartile range suggests a more reasonable range of .38 to .45. The distribution of these estimates is provided graphically in figure 5.3.

The level-2 empirical Bayes estimates were then plotted against county-level support for Ross Perot in the 1992 presidential election (see fig. 5.4). As hypothesized, the latent genetic trait linked to political participation is modestly higher for those who resided in counties receiving relatively higher sup-

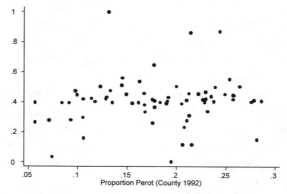

FIGURE 5.4. County-level heritability estimates for political participation as a function of support for Ross Perot in the 1992 presidential election. *Note*: Data come from wave 3 of the National Longitudinal Study of Adolescent Health. Sibling and twin pairs across counties in the United States are used to calculate these estimates. See methods for more detail.

port for Perot. Although the associations were quite modest ($r = .21$, $p < .08$; $b = .56$, $p < .12$), these results provide tentative support for the social trigger hypothesis regarding the genetics of political behavior. As anticipated, support for Ross Perot may also capture a sense of political participation that is shared by the residents of a particular area. Thus, being socialized and raised in an environment like this may trigger tendencies for political participation that have genetic origins.

Conclusion

The gene-environment interplay perspective is a relatively new and exciting area in the social sciences. It has garnered a great deal of attention in the study of physical and mental health and it has begun to shape the work of demographers and sociologists. As an example, the *American Journal of Sociology*, a leading journal for sociologists, recently had an entire issue dedicated to the study of genetic and social explanations for behavior. To date, however, there has been less work from political science involving gene-environment interplay and complex behaviors like voting and political participation or attitudes like conservatism and support for increased taxes. This chapter highlights the limited work that has been done in this area and it makes a strong case for the relevance of this general perspective for political scientists. The case for this perspective rests on the observation that the relative influence of genetic factors on complex political behaviors may be contingent upon the social and political environment in which individuals reside, work, and interact socially. I make the case that the environment should be considered as multidimensional (e.g., contextual features shared by all members, social demographic composition, normative context), multilevel (e.g., families, peer groups, work environment, school environment, residential areas, and regional groupings), and longitudinal. Finally, I stress that gene-environment interaction studies should be structured around hypotheses derived from theory that specifies the forces that trigger, control, push, or distinguish genetic forces. These should be a priori hypotheses based on gene-environment interplay theory.

Although the emerging findings from this body of work offer new and exciting perspectives on the origins of political behaviors, there are still two important factors that should be considered as we move forward. I conclude this chapter by discussing the areas in need of the greatest amount of our attention in this area: gene-environment correlation; and life-course perspective. The GxE models described above assume that genetic composition and environmental conditions are orthogonal to one another. However, as described in the rGE discussion above, there are theoretical reasons to anticipate a correlation between genetic and environment factors. This is a particular concern for GxE researchers investigating specific alleles interacting with specific environments because as Jaffee and Price (2007) point out, "rGE does not have to reach statistical significance to profoundly affect the interpretation of GxE estimates" (437). As an example, one study found an association between the SNP GABRA2 (rs279871) and alcohol dependence (Dick et al. 2006). They also show an association with this SNP and marital status. Those with the risk allele at GABRA2 were less likely to be married because, the authors argue, on average they tended to have had personalities that made them less desirable to others compared to those without this risk allele. As such, an effort to estimate an interaction between this SNP and marital status to predict alcohol dependence would obviously violate the independence assumption and it might bias the GxE parameter estimate.

This is relevant to the study of political science because previous research has shown some evidence for rGE and political attitudes. Coventry and Keller (2005) provide important information about the extent to which rGE may influence quantitative genetic parameter estimates. While not emphasizing political outcomes per se, their study contains items that are of interest to political scientists. They compare estimates from the classic twin design (CTD) model with the extended twin-family design (ETFD) for 16 aspects of attitudes, behaviors, and personality traits. On average, they find very little influence of gene-environment correlation *except* for the limited number of political outcomes in their study. Specifically, they show significant gene-environment covariance for conservatism, attitudes toward the military (males), and attitudes toward taxes (females). In all three cases, the ETFD design provided smaller heritability estimates compared to the CTD. For example, they estimate total genetic variance for attitudes about taxes to be .33 for females using the CTD but this estimate falls to .19 after they show significant gene-environmental covariance ($\sigma_{g,e}$ =.06). These results suggest an important caution regarding rGE when estimating quantitative genetic parameter estimates and this is particularly relevant to the extension of these models to GxE parameter estimates.

Finally, there are reasons to expect that the absolute and relative influence of different forms of rGE and GxE will change over the life course. With few exceptions (see Reiss and Leve 2007), very few efforts have been made to integrate the GxE typology into a life course perspective so that different hypotheses can be constructed for children, adolescents, and adults. Although the effects of genetic factors (measured as heritability estimates) are relatively consistent across adulthood (McGue and Christensen 2003) the same is *not* the case among adolescents and children. Kendler et al. (1993) show that the heritability for major depression among adult women (ages 18–59) is roughly 40% regardless of age or birth cohort. This same consistency across age is also shown for personality (Johnson and Krueger 2004) and cognition (Plomin 1994). However, this is *not* the case among adolescents and children. Genetic influences change across developmental periods, which implicates the rapid environmental changes that occur during a period.

Changes in the social environment among children and adolescents are almost always outside of their control. Changes such as martial stability, residential relocation, and changes in schools are things that *happen to* children and adolescents. Thus GxE models that focus on institutional factors are particularly salient among younger populations. As others have pointed out (Moffitt, Caspi, and Rutter 2006, 12) "the impact of specific environmental influences will be differentially salient at different ages." The same might be said for elderly men and women who reside in large residential-care facilities. No existing work has examined the genetic and social influences on voting behavior among this important and growing part of the population. Furthermore, the exposure to particular work and residential environments linked to particular political attitudes and behaviors are likely to be cumulative. Thus, it is not possible to describe the genetic etiology of some outcome unless an individual's cumulative social profile is understood. As an example in genetic epidemiology, it was the accumulation of stressful life events that served as a strong trigger for a genetic risk compared to single life events (Caspi et al. 2003) even if the single event is very traumatic (Moffitt, Caspi, and Rutter 2006).

In sum, the gene-environment interaction perspective is critical to the study of genetic antecedents to political behavior for a variety of reasons. Perhaps most important, properly specifying environmental moderation of genetic factors may reduce the estimated "genetic effects." That is, as crudely shown in this chapter, by further portioning the additive genetic variance into GxE variance, we saw that the estimated heritability for political behavior decreased by nearly one-third. However, it is also important to note that there remained strong genetic influences on political behavior. These findings support the weak-triggering model and echo the view that complex behaviors such as these require a simultaneous understanding of both genetic and environmental influences.

References

Boardman, J. D. 2009. State-level moderation of genetic tendencies to smoke. *American Journal of Public Health* 99:480–86.

Boardman, J. D., J. M. Saint Onge, B. C. Haberstick, D. S. Timberlake, and J. K. Hewitt. 2008. Do schools moderate the genetic determinants of smoking? *Behavior Genetics* 38:234–46.

Button, T. M. M., J. Scourfield, N. Martin, S. Purcell, and P. McGuffin. 2005. Family dysfunction interacts with genes in the causation of antisocial symptoms. *Behavior Genetics* 35:115–20.

Caspi, A., J. McClay, T. E. Moffitt, J. Mill, J. Martin, I. W. Craig, A. Taylor, and R. Poulton. 2002. Role of genotype in the cycle of violence in maltreated children. *Science* 297:851–54.

Caspi, A., K. Sugden, T. E. Moffitt, A. Taylor, I. W. Craig, H. Harrington, J. McClay, et al. 2003. Influence of life stress on depression: Moderation by a polymorphism in the 5-HTT gene. *Science* 301:386–89.

Coventry, W. L., and M. C. Keller. 2005. Estimating the extent of parameter bias in the classical twin design: A comparison of parameter estimates from extended twin-family and classical twin designs. *Twin Research and Human Genetics* 8:214–23.

DeFries, J., and D. Fulker. 1985. Multiple regression analysis of twin data. *Behavior Genetics* 15 (5): 467–73.

Dick, D. M., A. Agrawal, M. A. Schuckit, L. Bierut, A. Hinrichs, L. Fox, J. Mullaney, et al. 2006. Marital status, alcohol dependence, and GABRA2: Evidence for gene-environment correlation and interaction. *Journal of Studies on Alcohol* 67:185–94.

Fowler, J. H., L. A. Baker, and C. T. Dawes. 2008. Genetic variation in political participation. *American Political Science Review* 102:233–48.

Fowler, J., and C. Dawes. 2008. Two genes predict voter turnout. *Journal of Politics* 70 (3): 579–94.

Gilbert, C. P., and D.A.M. Peterson. 2001. From Ross the Boss to Jesse the Body: Did the Perot phenomenon spawn the Ventura victory? In *Ross for boss: The Perot phenomenon and beyond*, ed. T. Jelen, 143–62. Albany: SUNY Press.

Guo, G., and E. Stearns. 2002. The social influences on the realization of genetic potential for intellectual development. *Social Forces* 80:881–910.

Harris, K. M., C. T. Halpern, A. Smolen, and B. C. Haberstick. 2006. The National Longitudinal Study of Adolescent Health (Add Health) twin data. *Twin Research and Human Genetics* 9:988–97.

Hatemi, P. K., S. E. Medland, and L. J. Eaves. 2009. Genetic sources for the gender gap. *Journal of Politics* 71 (1): 262–76.

Heath, A. C., K. Berg, L. J. Eaves, M. H. Solaas, L. A. Corey, J. Sundet, P. Magnus, and W. E. Nance. 1985. Education policy and the heritability of educational-attainment. *Nature* 314:734–36.

Jaffee, S. R., and T. S. Price. 2007. Gene-environment correlations: A review of the evidence and implications for prevention of mental illness. *Molecular Psychiatry* 12:432–42.

Johnson, W., and R. F. Krueger. 2004. Genetic and environmental structure of adjectives describing the domains of the Big Five Model of personality: A nationwide U.S. twin study. *Journal of Research in Personality* 38:448–72.

Kendler, K. S., M. C. Neale, R. C. Kessler, A. C. Heath, and L. J. Eaves. 1993. The lifetime history of major depression in women—Reliability of diagnosis and heritability. *Archives of General Psychiatry* 50:863–70.

Kendler, K. S., L. M. Thornton, and N. L. Pedersen. 2000. Tobacco consumption in Swedish twins reared apart and reared together. *Archives of General Psychiatry* 57:886–92.

Lacy, D., and B. C. Burden. 1999. The vote-stealing and turnout effects of Ross Perot in the 1992 U.S. presidential election. *American Journal of Political Science* 43 (1): 233–55.

Link, B. G., and J. Phelan. 1995. Social conditions as fundamental causes of disease. *Journal of Health and Social Behavior* 35:80–94.

Lynch, J., and G. Kaplan. 2000. Socioeconomic position. In *Social epidemiology*, ed. L. F. Berkman and I. Kawachi, 13–35. New York: Oxford University Press.

McGue, M., and K. Christensen. 2003. The heritability of depression symptoms in elderly Danish twins: Occasion-specific versus general effects. *Behavior Genetics* 33:83–93.

Moffitt, T. E., A. Caspi, and M. Rutter. 2006. Measured gene-environment interactions in psychopathology: Concepts, research strategies, and implications for research, intervention, and public understanding of genetics. *Perspectives on Psychological Science* 1:5–27.

Plomin, R. 1994. The Emanuel Miller Memorial Lecture 1993: Genetic research and identification of environmental influences. *Journal of Child Psychology and Psychiatry and Allied Disciplines* 35:817–34.

Plomin, R., J. C. DeFries, and J. C. Loehlin. 1977. Genotype-environment interaction and correlation in the analysis of human behavior. *Psychological Bulletin* 84:309–22.

Purcell, S. M., and P. C. Sham. 2003. A model-fitting implementation of the DeFries-Fulker model for selected twin data. *Behavior Genetics* 32:271–78.

Rabe-Hesketh, S., and A. Skrondal. 2006. Multilevel modelling of complex survey data. *Journal of the Royal Statistical Society Series A-Statistics in Society* 169:805–27.

Raine, A. 2002. Biosocial studies of antisocial and violent behavior in children and adults: A review. *Journal of Abnormal Child Psychology* 30:311–26.

Reiss, D., and L. D. Leve. 2007. Genetic expression outside the skin: Clues to mechanisms of Genotype x Environment interaction. *Development and Psychopathology* 19:1005–27.

Rende, R., C. Slomkowski, J. McCaffery, E. E. Lloyd-Richardson, and R. Niaura. 2005. A twin-sibling study of tobacco use in adolescence: Etiology of individual differences and extreme scores. *Nicotine and Tobacco Research* 7:413–19.

Rowe, D. C., D. M. Almeida, and K. Jacobson. 1999. School context and genetic influences on aggression in adolescence. *Psychological Science* 10:277–80.

Rutter, M., T. E. Moffitt, and A. Caspi. 2006. Gene-environment interplay and psychopathology: Multiple varieties but real effects. *Journal of Child Psychology and Psychiatry* 47:226–61.

Settle, J. E., C. T. Dawes, N. A. Christikas, and J. H. Fowler. Forthcoming. Friendships moderate an association between a dopamine gene variant and political ideology. *Journal of Politics* 72 (4): 1189–98.

Shanahan, M. J., and J. Boardman. 2009. Life course sociology and genetics: A promising frontier. In *For craft of life course studies*, ed. J. Z. Giele and G. H. Elder Jr., 215–35. New York: Guilford Press.

Slomkowski, C., R. Rende, S. Novak, E. Lloyd-Richardson, and R. Niaura. 2005. Sibling effects on smoking in adolescence: Evidence for social influence from a genetically informative design. *Addiction* 100:430–38.

Timberlake, D. S., S. H. Rhee, B. C. Haberstick, C. Hopfer, M. Ehringer, J. M. Lessem, A. Smolen, and J. K. Hewitt. 2006. The moderating effects of religiosity on the genetic and environmental determinants of smoking initiation. *Nicotine and Tobacco Research* 8:123–33.

Udry, J. R. 2003. *The National Longitudinal Study of Adolescent Health (Add Health), Waves I and II, 1994–1996; Wave III, 2001–2002* [machine-readable data file and documentation]. Chapel Hill: Carolina Population Center, University of North Carolina at Chapel Hill.

6

GENES, GAMES, AND POLITICAL PARTICIPATION

James H. Fowler, Peter J. Loewen, Jaime Settle,
and Christopher T. Dawes

Groups often ask their members to contribute to collective activities. But the benefits of these activities often do not offset the costs of individual participation. Everyone in the group may be better off if everyone cooperates, but each person individually may be better off not cooperating. As a result, we might expect cooperation to fail. Yet modern human society relies on cooperation at a level unseen anywhere else in the animal world (e.g., Stevens and Hauser 2004). We have organized complex systems of government and social assistance, and we regularly join together in smaller acts of cooperation, whether in community groups, sports teams, or explicitly political organizations. We almost constantly engage in commercial activities that require trust in complete strangers (Henrich et al. 2001). All of this adds up to societies that are unrivalled in size and peacefulness (Pinker 2007). But how did we come to cooperate on such a massive scale? Or at all?

It may seem strange to focus on such an abstract question in a book on politics, but the puzzle of cooperation is very closely related to two of our most important questions in political science: (1) How do we organize ourselves to do more than we could on our own? and (2) How do we distribute the fruits of our collective labor? In this chapter we argue that the answers to these questions can be better understood by considering models of early cooperation in premodern times. As we show, the emergence of cooperation relied on a population with different types of people, some of whom were inclined toward taking up costly action for the benefit of others. We also review the use of laboratory experiments from behavioral economics to show that differences between individuals can explain variation in large-scale cooperative acts like voting and other forms of political participation that take place in modern times. And finally, we explore the root of these different types of behavior. Although much of our political behavior is learned and influenced by the environment, we are quickly coming to realize that fundamental differences in participation and political ideology reach deep into our biology, in some cases all the way to our DNA.

The Origins of Cooperation

In his 2006 *Science* review, prominent evolutionary game theorist Martin Nowak declared, "From hunter-gatherer societies to nation-states, cooperation is the decisive organizing principle of human society." However, it remains a mystery how cooperation has evolved given that natural selection generally favors selfish acts because they enhance an individual's ability to survive and reproduce. Cooperation results in the provision of a good that all members of a dyad, group, or society can enjoy regardless of whether they themselves contributed to the good's provision. Those who cooperate pay a cost for doing so, usually denoted by c, and all members of a group enjoy the benefit of the so-called public good that is provided, denoted by b. Those who do not cooperate still receive the good: they get b but do not pay the cost, c. As long as $c > 0$, those that do not cooperate are at an advantage because they have a higher average fitness than cooperators. Eventually, cooperators should be driven out of the population completely, either because they die off or copy the more successful strategy of noncooperation. Even though cooperators will not survive under these conditions, a population of all cooperators produces the highest average fitness while the one with all noncooperators produces the lowest (Nowak 2006; Smirnov and Johnson, chap. 3 in this volume).

Hence the puzzle: if cooperators should be driven to extinction by natural selection, why do we consistently observe cooperation across a wide variety of historical and societal settings? In other words, what explains the evolution of cooperation, especially on a level unmatched in the animal world (Proctor and Brosnan, chap. 2 in this volume)? While this question remains largely unanswered, several mechanisms have been proposed that allow cooperation to evolve, such as kin selection, direct reciprocity, and indirect reciprocity.

Kin selection simply states that natural selection favors cooperation among genetic relatives (Hamilton 1964) because by helping a genetic relative, an individual's genes will be passed along to the next generation indirectly. However, many interactions in which we observe cooperation are between unrelated individuals. Kin selection is accordingly limited in its explanatory power.

Direct reciprocity is based on the assumption that there are repeated interactions between individuals so that the decision to cooperate with an individual in the present period can be conditioned on his or her behavior in past inter-actions (Trivers 1971). In this scenario, the cost of cooperating in the present period is outweighed by the long-run benefits (Axelrod and Hamilton 1981). In public goods games administered in a laboratory setting, individuals play-ing the game repeatedly with the same group members tend to make larger contributions (Gächter and Herrmann 2009). The shortcoming of the theory of direct reciprocity is that many interactions, especially in modern society, are with individuals we have never interacted with before and likely will not interact with in the future. Therefore, it is not possible to condition coopera-tion on directly observed past actions.

Indirect reciprocity overcomes this problem by assuming interactions are observed by a subset of the group that then informs all other members of the group. Like the direct reciprocity scenario, natural selection favors the use of reputation as a tool to decide whether or not to cooperate with others (Nowak and Sigmund 2005). Experimental evidence is also consistent with this theo-retical argument (Gächter and Herrmann 2009).

Cooperation can be achieved under direct and indirect reciprocity because cooperators are able to withdraw cooperation based on direct experience or avoid cooperating with noncooperators by learning their reputation from others. Therefore, noncooperators are no longer at a fitness advantage. With-holding cooperation is straightforward in a dyadic setting; however, in a group where access to a public good cannot be restricted, it is more problematic. An alternative is to directly punish noncooperators who free-ride. The logic is that while noncooperators gain the benefit of the public good without paying the cost, sanctions imposed by other members of the group serve to offset the fit-ness advantage of free-riding. It is important to highlight that this mechanism is not based on reputation or repeated interaction. Laboratory experiments confirm that *some* individuals are willing to use their own money, thus mak-ing themselves worse off, in order to punish noncooperators (Fehr and Gächter 2002; for a detailed review see Gachter and Herrmann 2009) and this result holds in large-scale and small-scale societies around the world (Henrich et al. 2005).

The fact that some people are willing to punish and others are not high-lights an important feature of mathematical models of cooperation. Many evolutionary models help to explain the origin of cooperation and punish-ment, but they predict that *everyone* in the population will eventually engage in the same behavior (e.g., Fowler 2005). Contrast this prediction with the real world: sometimes people cooperate and sometimes they do not. While this might just be a stochastic outcome or could be due to unobserved differences in benefits and costs, recent evidence suggests that cooperative behavior is stable over time and across different experimental contexts (Johnson et al. 2009). In other words, people who cooperate in one context are likely to do so in another, and the same is true for those who do not cooperate. In fact, not only is individual cooperative behavior stable, but recent studies by Wallace et al. (2007) and Cesarini et al. (2008, 2009) suggest that some of the stability in behavior may result from differences in genotypes. Thus, more recent evolutionary models have sought to elaborate equilibria that yield mixed populations, like Hauert et al.'s (2007) recent generalization of the Fowler (2005) model to finite populations. In that model, a mix of cooperators, noncooperators, punishers, and "loners" (people who forgo both the costs and benefits of group activities) survives, and although cooperators and punishers are usually the most prevalent, there is variety in the population and the dominant type tends to cycle from one to another over time.

The Connection to Real Politics

The problem of cooperation, and how it is maintained, is nearly identical to the problem of collective action (Ostrom 1998). In large-scale societies, why do people join political groups, participate in elections, and engage in other kinds of mass behavior when they know their individual effort will not alter the political outcome? An emerging body of work addresses this paradox of participation by exploring whether modern populations are divided into different types of people, some of whom are motivated to cooperate and some of whom are not.

The decision to participate in politics is the most studied behavior in political science. Why do we vote? What makes us attend a rally or protest? How do we decide how much to contribute to a like-minded organization? The main focus of the literature on participation over the last 50 years has been the "paradox of turnout" (Downs 1957; Blais 2000). This paradox has, in the analogy of one author, consumed whole theories of political action, particularly those that rely on a conception of individuals as monolithically self-interested (Grofman 1993). While other classes of explanation exist, the most pertinent assume that individuals are preoccupied by the costs and benefits of voting. These approaches are not the only ones we have on hand (see Blais 2000 for a review), but they are foundational and do act as the starting point for most analyses of political participation.

The decision to vote is very similar to the decision to cooperate discussed in the previous section. The benefits of one party or another winning an election are shared over whole groups of people irrespective of their participation, but the costs of voting are borne by a smaller number of people. What is more, the marginal benefits that one person receives are often outweighed by the costs of voting, especially in the short term. Despite this, we witness large amounts of voting and other forms of political participation. Could it be that this participation paradox is similarly solved by a population endowed with different types of actors, especially some who consistently contribute to cooperative acts (Weber and Murnighan 2008)? A review of recent literature suggests that this might be the case.

Habitual Turnout

Participation in elections is neither universal nor uniform. Some people never vote, while others cast ballots only occasionally. Many voters miss elections only with great exception. Thus, voting can be thought of as *habitual*. This claim has received broad empirical support, both in the United States (Gerber, Green, and Shachar 2003; Green and Shachar 2000; Miller and Shanks 1996; Plutzer 2002; Verba and Nie 1972) and internationally (Franklin 2002; Denny and Doyle 2009). But what is the theoretical reason for such an observed regularity?

Two recent formal theoretical accounts (Bendor, Diermeier, and Ting 2003; Fowler 2006) rely on voters who have different *underlying propensities* to participate in elections. These models assume that voters begin their political lives with different likelihoods of voting in elections, and then update these propensities in response to electoral outcomes. Although Bendor, Diermeier, and Ting's (2003) model generates reasonably high turnout, the people who vote come from a large group of "casual voters" who essentially flip a coin at each election, voting in some and not in others. Fowler (2006) shows evidence from the American National Election Study and the South Bend Election Study that contradicts this result. In fact, most people either habitually vote or habitually abstain.

Fowler's model generates all the properties of the Bendor, Diermeier, and Ting (2003) model, but it also generates an empirically realistic distribution of voting propensities, helping to show how such "always vote" and "always abstain" types could emerge from an adaptive process. Thus, turnout may be driven not by some thoughtful deliberative process, but from the expression of a trait that some people have and others do not. Similarly, Weber and Murnighan (2008) show that "consistent contributors" play an important role in spurring other kinds of collective action, suggesting that variation in behavioral types may be critical for cooperation more broadly conceived.

Patience and Turnout

Election outcomes often matter for a great number of citizens. Depending on which party wins, voters can expect to have their taxes increased or decreased, can expect social programs to change, and can more generally expect to receive benefits if their party wins. But whatever benefits citizens can gain, they cannot reasonably expect them to be delivered quickly. Meanwhile, the costs of voting are immediate. Thus, the decision to vote may depend on a voter's level of patience, which varies substantially from one person to another (Funder and Block 1989; Funder, Block, and Block 1983).

In a laboratory experiment, Fowler and Kam (2006) elicited the degree to which subjects were willing to forgo a payment in one time period for a larger payment in a later time period. Those who were more willing to wait could be understood as being more patient. They then showed that more-patient individuals were more likely to vote, confirming the proposition that more-patient individuals are more likely to participate in elections.

Since patience does not exist uniformly in a population, this connection between patience and turnout is supportive of our general claim that we can explain political behavior by identifying different types of individuals. Individuals vary in their patience, and, these differences in patience emerge at very young ages. As Fowler and Kam note, children as young as four years old have shown variance in willingness to delay immediate gratification, and these differences correlate with their dispositions as measured later in life. What is more, these differences explain a variety of other behaviors, including "drug addiction, educational attainment, savings and investment, and gambling" (2006, 116). By conceiving of a population of types in which some individuals are inclined to be patient and others are not, we can further understand a fundamental act of cooperation such as voting.

Social Preferences and Political Participation

Recent studies also suggest that we can better understand political participation by relaxing a canonical assumption that individuals are self-interested and unconcerned with benefits for others. Theoretical work (Edlin, Gelman, and Kaplan 2007; Jankowski 2007) demonstrates that we can explain high levels of participation by assuming that the utility of some voters is increased when other voters benefit from an election outcome. Recent empirical work has tested these propositions by measuring the "social preferences" of individuals, and showing that those with certain types of social preferences are more likely to participate in politics. Fowler (2006) used a dictator game to reveal pure altruistic social preferences among subjects. He then showed that those who held these preferences and identified with a political party were more likely to vote in elections. Altruism, then, did not have a direct effect on voting, but it did motivate those who believed that one party was better suited to govern than another *and* who revealed concern for others. Moreover, these effects were independent of a standard schedule of control variables, such as political knowledge and interest.

Fowler and Kam (2007) then expanded this work by considering two types of altruism, a general altruism and social identification. The first is a concern for all individuals, while the second is a differentiated concern for some partisans over others. These preferences were measured in a unique dictator game design. They also considered political participation beyond merely voting. Their findings suggested that both altruism and social identification directly explain political participation, again independently of a standard array of control variables.

Loewen (2010) also explored the importance of social preferences in voting. Using a large online sample, he demonstrated that voters with a greater difference in their concern for different partisans groups were more likely to vote in Canadian elections. Moreover, he showed that this effect increased as the size of partisan groups increased. But contrary to Fowler (2006) and Fowler and Kam (2007), he found no role for general altruism. Instead, what was important was the antipathy and affinity individuals felt for different groups.

Finally, Dawes, Loewen, and Fowler (2009) explored the influence of different types of social preferences on political participation. Rather than measuring general altruism or social identities, they used a dictator game designed by Andreoni and Miller (2002) to reveal whether subjects were "Rawlsian" or "Utilitarian" in their social preferences. Rawlsian individuals are concerned with equalizing resources among individuals, while Utilitarians are interested in maximizing the total resources among individuals. Because politics is principally about maximizing total welfare and is rarely about increasing the lot of the worst off, those with Utilitarian preferences should be more likely to participate in politics than Rawlsian individuals, who should be no more likely than selfish subjects. Dawes, Loewen, and Fowler (2009) show that this is exactly the case among their experimental subjects.

Taken together, the preceding four studies suggest that we can better explain participation in politics by taking account of individuals' social preferences and not just their self-interest. Moreover, by conceiving of the population as divided into types, we can understand how different motivations draw individuals into political participation. However, for these arguments to lend support to our claim that politics reflects our more ancient inheritances, we need to demonstrate a heritable origin to these differences.

Origins

What are the origins of social preferences? Is there a deeply set, genetic basis to the types of individuals we have discussed thus far? In short, we argue yes. We have a growing body of literature in political science and economics demonstrating that nature and nurture play a joint role in shaping how people behave in the political realm. Moreover, the evidence is not limited to just participation, but also a broad range of attitudes and dispositions that influence how people engage in politics and decide whether to contribute to group outcomes.

Building on techniques developed by behavioral geneticists during the past 30 years, social scientists have begun to test phenotypes of interest related to political behaviors and attitudes, as well as the underlying values and orientations that support them. Many of the pioneering papers in this subdiscipline use data collected by behavioral geneticists who had the foresight to anticipate that many social behaviors, including explicitly political ones, likely had a heritable component and could be associated with specific genetic variants. The patterns and relationships found thus far are just the beginning of the potential inquiry; the extent of what has already been found indicates significant promise for understanding more about the biological foundations of political behavior.

Evidence from Twin and Extended Family Design Studies

The extension of the twin study approach to political phenotypes is conceptually similar to the use of the methodology in studies that examine phenotypes, such as substance abuse or personality constructs, which are more typically studied using behavioral genetics (BG) techniques (see Eaves et al., chap. 4 in this volume). As with other BG subfields, methodologists suggest that any series of work examining biological influences on political behavior begin with the classical twin design and its variants (Medland and Hatemi 2009). While this approach does not demonstrate the extent to which specific genes or other predictors affect the population mean of a trait, it is useful in demonstrating that individual differences in the trait are genetically influenced before proceeding to a search for specific genes that may be involved.

The underlying foundation of twin studies is rooted in biometric theory and uses structural equation modeling of the observed covariance between monozygotic and dizygotic twins to evaluate the contribution of latent genetic and environmental influences on the trait of interest (Medland and Hatemi 2009). Estimates for the parameters of these latent factors are then assessed for goodness of fit, often using maximum-likelihood criteria, though other approaches can be employed. Extended family designs build on the basic twin study but incorporate knowledge about the genetic relationships with other family members to provide additional leverage in analysis. There are some challenges to the application of these methods to political phenotypes, such as self-report bias and the error induced by measurement, but they are analogous to those faced by scholars who attempt to measure any other complex phenotypes, like personality, attitudes, or addiction.

Twin study analysis has been conducted on a variety of political phenotypes, including participation, partisanship, ideology, and issue opinions. Although many of the large twin and family registries include some data on social and behavior traits, the original focus of these studies was directed toward medical and psychological traits. Consequently, the questions asked on extant surveys are often basic and do not always reflect the most contemporary knowledge of survey response methodology. Yet despite the relative scarcity of data on social behaviors, several important findings have been uncovered.

Using a sample of twins from the Southern California Twin Registry, Fowler, Baker, and Dawes (2008) show that greater than 50% of the variation in turnout behavior can be attributed to additive genetic effects, which we can think of as the sum of the effects of several different genes, rather than the effects of their interactions. This estimate is significantly different than zero in their analysis. In the same article, the finding was replicated in the National Longitudinal Study of Adolescent Health (Add Health). The Add Health sample also includes a battery of questions about other political behaviors, and genetic effects account for 60% of the variance in an index of political participation that includes joining an organization, running for office, donating to a campaign, and attending a rally or march.

Genetic influences on the decision to vote appear to be more direct than influences on other political behavior. For example, there is a modest genetic influence on vote choice in a sample of Australians when the vote was dichotomized between Labor and Conservative, but the genetic influence in vote choice is explained not by a unique genetic contribution to voting preference but rather by shared genetic influences in sociodemographic factors and political attitudes (Hatemi, Morley et al. 2007).

The heritability findings extend to partisanship as well, another frequently studied political behavior. While there is no evidence to suggest that the choice of political party with which one affiliates is heritable, there is evidence that the strength with which one attaches to a political party does have a genetic component. Two independent studies have confirmed that partisanship strength is approximately 60% heritable (Settle, Dawes, and Fowler 2009; Hatemi et al. 2009). This pattern of findings—a genetic basis for the strength of a behavior but not its direction—appears analogous to the findings about religious affiliation and religiosity. The denomination of the church one attends is mostly a product of the environment in which one was raised, but the extent to which a person is religious, as defined by church attendance and prayer, does have a heritable component (Koenig et al. 2005). These are important findings, as they suggest that behaviors with more apparent evolutionary analogues, such as participation, appear more heritable than those with less obvious analogues, such as for whom to vote or with which party to identify.

There is even more evidence suggesting that political attitudes have a heritable component and there is little doubt that the way people think about politics and political issues is influenced by their genes. The first piece published on this topic, and one that initiated much of the interest in this field, is that of Alford, Funk, and Hibbing (2005) who show that ideology is heritable, as measured by a battery of politically related questions from the Wilson-Patterson Attitude Inventory.

In addition to a measure of ideology constructed from several attitude questions, individual political attitudes appear to be heritable. Hatemi and colleagues have taken the lead in showing that political beliefs have a heritable component that can be analyzed using both twin studies and the extended family design (Hatemi, Alford et al. 2007). This team has explored the contribution of genes and the environment at various stages of the life course, finding that while there are no genetic influences on political attitudes prior to adulthood, when political attitudes stabilize in the early twenties, there is a substantial genetic influence (Hatemi, Hibbing et al. 2009). Additionally, there appear to be significant gender differences in whether attitudes toward social and political items have a genetic origin, and different genes may contribute to the difference in attitudes between men and women (Hatemi, Medland, and Eaves 2009).

One set of attitudes has been given particular attention, that of attitudes toward homosexuality and gay rights. Two studies, published in the same edition of *Behavior Genetics*, have confirmed a significant role for a genetic basis of homophobic attitudes, reinforced by the strong assortative mating on characteristics that are associated with attitudes toward homosexuality and gay rights. Both studies evaluate a subsample of the Australian Twin Registry that took a survey on sexual behavior and attitudes. In the twin study, while additive genetic factors account for 36% of the variance, the shared environmental estimate may be subsumed by the extra additive genetic variance arising from assortative mating on homophobic attitudes (Verweij et al. 2008). In other words, much of the apparent effect of parental socialization is actually due to the fact that individuals with similar views on homosexuality are more likely to couple and then pass on their views by way of their genes, rather than their parenting. The second study used a more extended design and found estimates of 50–70% heritability of the individual survey items (Eaves and Hatemi 2008).

The Underpinnings of Political Behavior: Heritability and Economic Games

The collected body of evidence from the twin and extended family designs leaves little doubt that there is a significant role for heritability in explaining political attitudes and behaviors. However, one of the first responses to this literature (Charney 2008) questioned what exactly was heritable about these political outcomes. What specific values and orientations were underlying the propensity to participate or to support liberal social positions? In this vein, scholars turned toward examining whether the preferences that underlie much of our theory about political behavior were also heritable. Significant evidence has been marshaled to support the conjecture that in addition to the political actions themselves, the economics and social preferences and values that guide political action are heritable as well.

In a twist on a classic behavioral economics game, a group of scholars tested members of the Swedish Twin Registry and found that greater than 40% of the variance in behavior of the ultimatum responder in the Ultimatum game could be attributed to heritable factors (Wallace et al. 2007). This is important because responder behavior reveals preferences for punishing other people who have behaved in an unfair way. Using the same sample and moving beyond previous work that simply calculated the intergenerational correspondence between behavior in public goods, risk and giving games, Cesarini and colleagues (2009) determine that 20% of the variance of behavior in two games measuring economic preferences is heritable. The finding on risk-taking was replicated using a small study of Chinese students (Zhong et al. 2009). The dictator game result in particular suggests that genetic variation could play a role in explaining voter turnout via altruism. Finally, these findings extend to the classic trust game, designed to gauge interpersonal trust as measured by one's willingness to invest and reciprocate investment (Cesarini et al. 2008). In both the United States and Sweden, independent twin samples show that cooperative behavior in this game is significantly heritable.

Evidence in support of the idea that there is a genetic basis for cooperation and punishment for unfair behavior greatly bolsters the theoretical case for the underpinnings of more complicated political behaviors. As noted in Zhong et al. (2009), economists can derive and test better models of individual decisionmaking, a fundamental component of the field, with an improved understanding of the genetic, and consequently neurobiological, basis of attitudes toward risk, cooperation, and punishment.

The Evidence from Gene Association Studies

Heritability suggests that there is a genetic basis for many political orientations; genetic association studies take us one step further in identifying the specific gene variants and environmental exposures that help to shape behavior and attitudes. There has been more mixed success in explaining the way that genes and the environment interact to influence behavior. Some scholars in the behavioral genetics community advocate the approach because it is a better approximation of reality. Yet others argue that the approach is akin to "finding a needle in a haystack" given the universe of potential genetic variants and environmental exposures. Despite these challenges, several important relationships, including mediated and moderated relationships, have been found between particular genetic variants and political behaviors. These relationships include those that are direct, where those with the genetic variant in question have a significantly different propensity to exhibit a behavior; mediated, where the effect of some environmental factor is dependent on the presence or absence of the genetic variant; and moderated, where the version of the gene changes the magnitude of the effect of some environmental factor.

While the application of gene association is in its relative infancy, it has already influenced our understanding of political participation. The first study to be published using a genetic association approach demonstrated a role for two genes associated with voter turnout. Using data from the Add Health study, a polymorphism of the MAOA gene was found to increase the likelihood of voting directly, while a variant of the 5HTT gene interacted with the respondent's self-reported religious attendance to increase voter turnout (Fowler and Dawes 2008). Indeed, once the effect of church attendance was conditioned on the gene variant, there was no main (or direct) effect for church attendance, as attendance only predicted greater turnout among those with a particular variant of 5HTT. This finding is of particular note, as it reshapes our understanding of one of the most important predictors of participation. The relationship between religious observance and political participation has been long noted. However, it has been assumed that this represents a wholly environmental or developmental influence on the decision to participate in politics. What this finding suggests is that this environmental influence is also dependent on an individual's genes.

In addition to political participation, other polymorphisms have been found to matter for partisanship, another aspect of politics long attributed to environment. Using the same Add Health data, Dawes and Fowler (2009) found that individuals with the A1 allele of the DRD2 gene are more likely to identify as partisans, and that this relationship mediates an association between the A1 allele and voter turnout.

Gene association studies have also probed political ideology and uncovered an interesting relationship between a genetic factor (the 7R allele of DRD4) and an environmental factor (the number of friendships a respondent names in adolescence). The study finds that the number of friends an individual has in adolescence moderates the effect of the 7R allele of DRD4 on political ideology. For those with the allele, it appears that an increased number of friendships is associated with a more politically liberal ideology as a young adult (Settle et al. 2008). This again reconditions our understanding of something previously understood to be purely environmental.

Other studies probe the microlevel connections between genes and behavior. For example, economists have also examined gene associations. One team finds that the DRD4 7R allele is associated with financial risk-taking in men, consistent with what is known in the behavioral genetics literature about this allele and a propensity toward novelty-seeking and risky behavior in general (Dreber et al. 2009). A second group of scholars has employed association techniques in the experimental dictator game, finding that a vasopressin receptor promoter region is associated with the allocation of funds in the game (Knafo et al. 2008).

Finding further evidence to make the case between specific alleles and environmental exposures will require a significant investment of time and resources. These approaches require large samples, and the strength of the relationship must be able to meet the rigorous statistical standards of the BG community that have been developed to avoid producing false positive results. Replication is a must.

Yet we have reason to believe that we will continue to describe increasingly more variance in behavior as we refine our understanding of the relationship between foundational orientations and preferences and the more complicated political behaviors we seek to explore. Just as we have evidence of heritability, we now have evidence of direct, mediated, and moderated links between genes and political behavior.

Implications and Conclusion

We live in a complex world, and one that does not at first resemble the one in which we evolved. As Kuklinski and Quirk (2000) observe, our mental equipment evolved in a world where our crucial tasks did not resemble those of today. What is more, this older world has been the norm for the vast majority of human existence. The consequence is that "the entire period of agricultural and industrial civilization, about one percent of human history, has been too short to produce further biological adaptation" (162). This was a world with no media, no cities, and no elections. It was one that greatly resembled that of other primates (see chap. 2 in this volume). However, the point of this is not that our politics insufficiently resembles our evolutionary past such that we cannot understand it through this lens. Instead, the implication is that humans are limited by the capacities and constraints we have inherited, whether physiological (see chaps. 7–9 in this volume), cognitive (chap. 10), or genetic (chap. 5). Given these limitations, we should pay particular attention to understanding how modern institutions interact with these limitations to produce the political outcomes we see in today's world.

Voter participation provides a great example of this point. Modern political science has expended great effort in understanding how individual characteristics and institutional arrangements increase or decrease voter turnout. The underlying assumption has been that explaining why some people vote and others do not requires no more information than this. However, even the most sophisticated analyses explain less than a third of the variation in voter turnout (Plutzer 2002). As we have shown, models that take account of fundamental differences between individuals—whether through basic preferences and personality types or through genotypes—can add important information.

As a field, political science is open for the further application of insights from biology, behavioral genetics, neuroscience, and psychology. Indeed, because human action is central to politics, political scientists should feel compelled to pay increasing attention to the factors that constrain human behavior. In the last 50 years, our understanding of politics has been greatly improved by understanding how institutions constrain the choices and actions of actors. It is time that we also recognize how humans are constrained internally. Genes are the institution of the human body. Whether we wish to understand voter participation, public opinion, participation in war, or the behavior of legislators, we should take seriously these other types of constraints.

References

Alford, J., C. Funk, and J. Hibbing. 2005. Are political orientations genetically transmitted? *American Political Science Review* 99 (2): 153–67.

Andreoni, J., and J. Miller. 2002. Giving according to GARP: An experimental test of the consistency of preferences for altruism. *Econometrica* 70 (2): 737–53.

Axelrod, R., and W. D. Hamilton. 1981. The evolution of cooperation. *Science* 211 (4489): 1390–96.

Bendor, J., D. Diermeier, and M. Ting. 2003. A behavioral model of turnout. *American Political Science Review* 92 (2): 261–80.

Blais, A. 2000. *To vote or not to vote? The merits and limits of rational choice theory.* Pittsburgh, Pa.: University of Pittsburgh Press.

Cesarini, D., C. Dawes, J. H. Fowler, M. Johannesson, P. Lichtenstein, and B. Wallace. 2008. Heritability of cooperative behavior in the trust game. *Proceedings of the National Academy of Sciences* 105:3271–76.

Cesarini, D., C. T. Dawes, M. Johannesson, P. Lichtenstein, and B. Wallace. 2009. Genetic variation in preferences for giving and risk taking. *Quarterly Journal of Economics* 124 (2): 809–42.

Charney, E. 2008. Genes and ideology. *Perspectives on Politics* 6:299–319.

Dawes, C. T., and J. H. Fowler. 2009. Partisanship, voting, and the dopamine D2 receptor gene. *Journal of Politics* 71 (3): 1157–71.

Dawes, C. T., P. J. Loewen, and J. H. Fowler. Forthcoming. Social preferences and political participation. *Journal of Politics.*

Denny, K., and O. Doyle. 2009. Does voting history matter? Analyzing persistence in turnout. *American Journal of Political Science* 53:17–35.

Downs, A. 1957. *An economic theory of democracy.* Boston: Addison Wesley.

Dreber, A., C. L. Apicella, D.T.A. Eisenberg, J. R. Garcia, R. S. Zamore, J. K. Lum, and B. Campbell. 2009. The 7R polymorphism in the dopamine receptor D4 gene (DRD4) is associated with financial risk taking in men. *Evolution and Human Behavior* 30:85–92.

Eaves, L. J., and P. K. Hatemi. 2008. Transmission of attitudes toward abortion and gay rights: Effects of genes, social learning and mate selection. *Behavior Genetics* 38 (3): 247–56.

Edlin, A., A. Gelman, and N. Kaplan. 2007. Voting as a rational choice: Why and how people vote to improve the well-being of others. *Rationality and Society* 19 (3): 293–314.

Fehr, E., and S. Gächter. 2002. Altruistic punishment in humans. *Nature* 415:137–40.

Fowler, J. H. 2005. Altruistic punishment and the origin of cooperation. *Proceedings of the National Academy of Sciences* 102 (9): 7047–49.

———. 2006. Altruism and turnout. *Journal of Politics* 68:647–83.

Fowler, J. H., L. A. Baker, and C. T. Dawes. 2008. Genetic variation in political participation. *American Political Science Review* 102 (2): 233–48.

Fowler, J. H., and C. T. Dawes. 2008. Two genes predict voter turnout. *Journal of Politics* 70 (3): 579–94.

Fowler, J. H., and C. Kam. 2006. Patience as a political virtue: Delayed gratification and turnout. *Political Behavior* 28 (2): 335–44.

———. 2007. Beyond the self: Altruism, social identity, and political participation. *Journal of Politics* 69:813–27.

Franklin, M. 2002. The dynamics of electoral participation. In *Comparing democracies 2: Elections and voting in global perspective*, ed. L. Leduc, R. Niemi, and P. Norris, 148–68. Thousand Oaks, Calif.: Sage.

Funder, D. C., and J. Block. 1989. The role of ego-control, ego-resiliency, and IQ in delay of gratification in adolescence. *Journal of Personality and Social Psychology* 57 (6): 1041–50.

Funder, D. C., J. C. Block, and J. Block. 1983. Delay of gratification: Some longitudinal personality correlates. *Journal of Personality and Social Psychology* 44 (6): 1198–1213.

Gächter, S., and B. Herrmann. 2009. Reciprocity, culture and human cooperation: Previous insights and a new cross-cultural experiment. *Articles from Philosophical Transactions of the Royal Society B: Biological Sciences* 364 (1518): 791–806.

Gerber, A. S., D. P. Green, and R. Shachar. 2003. Voting may be habit-forming: Evidence from a randomized field experiment. *American Journal of Political Science* 47 (3): 540–50.

Green, D. P., and R. Shachar. 2000. Habit formation and political behaviour: Evidence of consuetude in voter turnout. *British Journal of Political Science* 30 (4): 561–73.

Grofman, B. 1993. Is turnout the paradox that ate rational choice theory? In *Information, participation and choice: An economic theory of democracy in perspective*, ed. B. Grofman, 93–103. Ann Arbor: University of Michigan Press.

Hamilton, W. D. 1964. The genetical evolution of social behavior, parts I and II. *Journal of Theoretical Biology* 7 (1): 1–52.

Hatemi, P. K., J. Alford, J. Hibbing, N. Martin, and L. Eaves. 2009. Is there a "party" in your genes? *Political Research Quarterly* 62 (3): 584–600.

Hatemi, P. K., J. R. Alford, J. R. Hibbing, S. E. Medland, M. C. Keller, N. G. Martin, and L. J. Eaves. 2007. Not by twins alone: Using the extended family design to investigate genetic influence on political beliefs. *American Journal of Political Science* 54 (3): 798–814.

Hatemi, P., C. Funk, H. Maes, J. Silberg, S. Medland, N. Martin, and L. Eaves. 2009. Genetic influences on political attitudes over the life course. *Journal of Politics* 71 (3): 1141–56.

Hatemi, P. K., S. E. Medland, and L. J. Eaves. 2009. Genetic sources of the gender gap. *Journal of Politics* 71 (1): 262–76.

Hatemi, P. K., K. I. Morley, S. E. Medland, A. C. Heath, and N. G. Martin. 2007. The genetics of voting: An Australian twin study. *Behavior Genetics* 37:435–48.

Hauert, C., A. Traulsen, H. Brandt, M. A. Nowak, and K. Sigmund. 2007. Via freedom to coercion: The emergence of costly punishment. *Science* 316 (5833): 1905.

Henrich, J., R. Boyd, S. Bowles, C. Camerer, E. Fehr, H. Gintis, and R. McElreath. 2001. In search of *Homo economicus*: Behavioral experiments in 15 small-scale societies. *American Economic Review* 91 (2): 73–78.

Henrich, J., R. Boyd, S. Bowles, H. Gintis, E. Fehr, C. Camerer, R. McElreath, et al. 2005. "Economic man" in cross-cultural perspective: Ethnography and experiments from 15 small-scale societies. *Behavioral and Brain Sciences* 28:795–855.

Jankowski, R. 2007. Altruism and the decision to vote: Explaining and testing high voter turnout. *Rationality and Society* 19:5–34.

Johnson, T., C. T. Dawes, J. H. Fowler, R. McElreath, and O. Smirnov. 2009. The role of egalitarian motives in altruistic punishment. *Economics Letters* 102 (3): 192–94.

Knafo, A., S. Israel, A. Darvasi, R. Bachner-Melman, F. Uzefovsky, L. Cohen, E. Feldman, et al. 2008. Individual differences in allocation of funds in the dictator game associated with length of the arginine vasopressin 1a receptor RS3 promoter region and correlation between RS3 length and hippocampal mRNA. *Genes Brain and Behavior* 7 (3): 266–75.

Koenig, L. B., M. McGue, R. F. Krueger, and T. J. Bouchard Jr. 2005. Genetic and environmental influences on religiousness: Findings for retrospective and current religiousness ratings. *Journal of Personality* 73 (2): 471–88.

Kuklinski, J. H., and P. J. Quirk. 2000. Reconsidering the rational public: Cognition, heuristics, and mass opinion. In *Elements of reason*, ed. A. Lupia, M. McCubbins, and S. Popkin, 153–82. New York: Cambridge University Press.

Loewen, P. J. 2010. Affinity, antipathy, and political participation: How our concern for others makes us vote. *Canadian Journal of Political Science* 43:661–67.

Medland, S., and P. K. Hatemi. 2009. Political science, biometric theory, and twin studies: A methodological introduction. *Political Analysis* 17 (2): 191–214.

Miller, W. E., and J. M. Shanks. 1996. *The new American voter*. Cambridge: Harvard University Press.

Nowak, M. A. 2006. Five rules for the evolution of cooperation. *Science* 314 (5805): 1560.

Nowak, M. A., and K. Sigmund. 2005. Evolution of indirect reciprocity. *Nature* 437:1291–98.

Ostrom, E. 1998. A behavioral approach to the rational choice theory of collective action. *American Political Science Review* 92:1–22.

Pinker, S. 2007. A history of violence. *New Republic*, March 17. Accessed online at: http://www .tnr.com/article/history-violence-were-getting-nicer-every-day?page = 0,0.

Plutzer, E. 2002. Becoming a habitual voter: Inertia, resources, and growth in young adulthood. *American Political Science Review* 96 (1): 41–56.

Settle, J., C. T. Dawes, N. A. Christakis, and J. H. Fowler. 2008. Friendships moderate an association between a dopamine gene variant and political ideology. *Journal of Politics* 72 (4): 1189–98.

Settle, J., C. T. Dawes, and J. H. Fowler. 2009. The heritability of partisan attachment. *Political Research Quarterly* 62 (3): 601–13.

Stevens, J. R., and M. D. Hauser. 2004. Why be nice? Psychological constraints on the evolution of cooperation. *Trends in Cognitive Science* 8:60–65.

Trivers, R. L. 1971. The evolution of reciprocal altruism. *Quarterly Review of Biology* 46:35–57.

Verba, S., and N. H. Nie. 1972. *Participation in America: Political democracy and social equality*. New York: Harper and Row.

Verweij, K.J.H., S. Shekar, B. Zietsch, L. J. Eaves, J. M. Bailey, D. I. Boomsma, and N. G. Martin. 2008. Genetic and environmental influences on individual differences in attitudes toward homosexuality: An Australian Twin Study. *Behavior Genetics* 38 (3): 257–65.

Wallace, B., D. Cesarini, P. Lichtenstein, and M. Johannesson. 2007. Heritability of ultimatum game responder behavior. *Proceedings of the National Academy of Sciences* 104:15631–34.

Weber, J. M., and J. K. Murnighan. 2008. Suckers or saviors? Consistent contributors in social dilemmas. *Journal of Personality and Social Psychology* 95 (6): 1340–53.

Zhong, S., S. H. Chew, E. Set, J. Zhang, H. Xue, P. C. Sham, R. P. Ebstein, and S. Israel. 2009. The heritability of attitude toward economic risk. *Twin Research and Human Genetics* 12 (1): 103–7.

7

THE MIND-BODY CONNECTION

Psychophysiology as an Approach to Studying
Political Attitudes and Behaviors

Kevin B. Smith and John R. Hibbing

Musing on the nature of memory, Rosa Coldfield, a character in William
Faulkner's Southern Gothic classic *Absalom, Absalom!*, suggests that what people remember and what people feel is inextricably linked to what they physi-
cally experience. "The brain recalls just what the muscles grope for," says
Rosa. "No more, no less" (Faulkner 1936, 143). The link between psychological
and physiological states is not just the stuff of classic fiction; it is also a scientifically validated phenomenon of great potential use to political science.

Studying the mind-body connection Rosa alludes to can provide at least
two important services. First, psychophysiologists have long known that Rosa
was essentially correct: Psychological states have a physiological basis, and
vice-versa. This is relevant to political scientists because it means physiological measures can index subconscious dispositions and orientations that otherwise might be difficult to assess accurately. For example, the reliability and
validity of self-reported racial attitudes are frequently questioned because
subjects may be tempted to report socially sanctioned views rather than their
true, less socially acceptable opinions. Though responses to survey probes can
be consciously fashioned to fit the prevailing social context, it is much harder
for a subject to control his or her unconscious and involuntary physiological
response to racially charged stimuli. That latter have been shown to be better predictors of attitudes on racial policies than the potentially self-censored
former (Vanman et al. 2004).

Second, the mind-body connection provides a possible route by which
evolution and genetics could plausibly affect social attitudes and behavior.
Several chapters in this volume discuss the genetic basis of political attitudes
and behavior (chaps. 4–6), and still others promote the application of evolu-

tionary theory to explain these same attitudes and behavior (chaps. 1–3). It seems unlikely that there is a gene, say, for supporting the building of a border fence to keep out illegal immigrants, and it seems equally unlikely that millennia of selection pressure has resulted in a psychological "amnesty module." However, genes build physiology and the manner by which physiology reacts to environmental stimuli has been under selection pressure. It is generally accepted that core elements of the autonomic nervous system are rooted in "neural systems [that] are evolutionarily old, shared across mammalian species and have evolved to mediate the behaviors that sustain and protect life" (Bradley and Lang 2007).

The evolutionary process has imbued all humans with an autonomic nervous system, but genetic variation has instilled a remarkable amount of diversity in the specific response levels of individual autonomic nervous systems to standardized stimuli. Physiological response patterns, in turn, appear to correlate with political attitudes, perhaps including those pertaining to illegal immigration. For example, Oxley et al. (2008) provide empirical evidence that variation in autonomic nervous system response to threatening stimuli correlates with opinions on a range of socially protective policies. Physiological findings such as these provide a plausible empirical and conceptual basis for linking genes to attitudes and behavior. Taking full advantage of the potential of the mind-body connection to illuminate the biological basis of attitudes and behaviors requires political scientists to become more broadly acquainted with the concepts and methods of psychophysiology. Our goal in this chapter is to provide our colleagues with an introduction to the basics of psychophysiology.

Psychophysiology is "an old idea but a new science." Its origins trace to a broadly experienced intuition that changes in our bodies are in some way related to changes in our psychological states (Greenfield and Sternbach 1972, v). This link between our bodies and our feelings makes intuitive sense because, consistent with Rosa Coldfield's intuitions, humans experience the world through their physiology (Miller 1978, 14). Physiology registers what the world looks and sounds like, whether it is hot or cold, whether it tastes sweet or bitter, whether it is threatening or welcoming. It does so by increasing or decreasing heart rate and respiration, promoting or retarding digestion, reflexively contracting or relaxing muscles. These physiological changes lead us to feel fearful, elated, attentive, aroused, happy, or disgusted—and because of physiological differences, certain people are more likely than others to register heat, happiness, or threat. It would be surprising if these physiological variations were not relevant to behavior. Those more prone to experiencing heat may take steps that are likely to cool them down—perhaps setting the thermostat to a lower temperature or moving to a locale further from the equator. Similarly, those more prone to feeling threat may take steps to avoid threatening situations or to minimize their vulnerability. They may even advocate policy positions that could diminish the threat felt from out-groups or from in-group norm violators.

The potential payoffs of systematically investigating the connection between psychological and physiological states has not been lost on psychology and for at least half a century a specialized subfield has pursued this task. In contrast, political science, with only a few exceptions, has expressed little interest in gaining insights into the mind by measuring changes in the corporeal body. This lack of attention is unfortunate given that many psychological phenomena of central interest to political science can be reliably indexed physiologically and have known consequences for political predispositions, attitudes, and behavior.[1]

The purpose of this chapter is to provide the following: A basic introduction to the conceptual and analytical frameworks of psychophysiology; an argument for broader employment of these tools in political science; a reasonably detailed primer on various physiological techniques; and an empirical example demonstrating the potential of psychophysiological approaches for political science.

What Is Psychophysiology and Why Should Political Scientists Care?

There is no universal definition of the field of psychophysiology, but it can be broadly thought of as "the scientific study of cognitive, emotional, and behavioral phenomena as related to and revealed through physiological principles and events" (Cacioppo and Tassinary, "Preface" 1990, ix). It is a field that cuts across the biological, behavioral, and social sciences and is based on a core assumption that human thought, emotion, and action are physiologically embodied phenomena; essentially, the mind has a literal physical substrate that can be validly and reliably measured. From this assumption it follows that thought, emotion, and action can be investigated by examining bodily responses to environmental stimuli (Cacioppo and Tassinary, "Psychophysiology" 1990, 5). Physiology and psychology are thus conceptualized as independent but related domains, and the central research task of psychophysiology is to link elements of one domain to the other.

This can be a challenging task because one-to-one relationships between elements of the two domains are rare. For example, there are numerous physiological correlates of fear (e.g., increased heart rate and blood pressure, sweaty palms), but these physiological correlates are also associated with other psychological states (e.g., arousal, anxiety). A further challenge is isolating cause from consequence, as psychology and physiology are often enmeshed in a reciprocal relationship. For example, a feeling of happiness often causes a series of involuntary facial muscle contractions, that is, a smile. Happiness is a psychological state, in other words, that clearly causes a physiological state. Yet a series of laboratory experiments clearly shows this causal chain is reversible; people report feeling happier after simply activating the "smile" muscles by holding a pencil horizontally between their teeth (Bernstein et al. 2000; for a survey of the conceptual framework and research designs addressing the issues of reciprocal psychological-physiological causality, see Cacioppo, Tassinary, and Berntson 2007).

In addition to the conceptual challenges, investigating psychological states through physiology, at least for most political scientists, requires methodological retooling and infrastructure investment. Accurately measuring physiological responses to environmental stimuli demands an appropriately equipped laboratory and the expertise to run it, neither of which is a typical component of most political science departments. These costs, both in the physical and human capital sense, have fallen dramatically with technological advances. Still, the basic ingredients of psychophysiological research— a working knowledge of human central and peripheral nervous systems, a conceptual framework to link these systems to psychological states of interest, and the equipment necessary to collect physiological and psychological data—are far removed from the training and research agendas of most political scientists.

Despite this, political science actually has a relatively long history of recognizing psychophysiology's potential contributions to questions of central importance to the discipline. As long ago as 1910, the president of the American Political Science Association suggested physiology as an appropriate template for the study of politics (Lowell 1910). Since that time physiology has sporadically appeared in the political science research literature, with notable examples being Lodge's work investigating the link between political attitudes and physiology (e.g., Wahlke and Lodge 1972; Lodge et al. 1975), Madsen's investigations of the correlation between whole blood serotonin and power seeking (1985, 1986), Mutz and Reeves's use of physiological measures to assess reaction to political debate (2005), and Oxley et al.'s study correlating political attitudes and physiological response to threat (2008; for an early review of physiology and political attitudes/behaviors, see Peterson, Somit, and Brown 1983). Though several of these studies were published in the discipline's top journals, they stand mostly as exceptions rather than the rule, and it is fair to say that psychophysiology has remained a considerable distance from the political science mainstream. Though the physiologically based research done by political scientists is a relatively small literature, cumulatively it makes a compelling argument for a greater role within the discipline. Enough of a published track record exists to lend credence to the argument that psychophysiology can make important contributions to issues of interest to political scientists.

Psychophysiology is attractive on a variety of fronts. Physiological measures can be used as a supplement or validation tool for the more commonly employed survey self-report measures of psychological states that are thought to be relevant to political orientations. For example, responses to standard, self-report disgust batteries are quite good at predicting some issue attitudes, especially in regards to attitudes on gay marriage (Inbar, Pizarro, and Bloom 2009). Smith et al. (2009) measured physiological response to disgusting stimuli and found this physiological response, in addition to self-reported disgust sensitivity, also predicted certain issue attitudes, particularly attitudes on homosexuality. Interestingly, though independently correlating with the same rough set of issue attitudes, the physiological measures had no correlation with the standardized self-report disgust battery. This suggests that the self-report battery may be picking up socialized attitudes toward disgust (e.g., females tend to score higher on self-report disgust batteries), while the physiological measure may be picking up a more biologically instantiated and involuntary response to disgust (Smith et al. [2009] report no difference between males and females on the physiological disgust measures). In short, disgust sensitivity clearly seems to be the basis for some political attitudes, but disgust sensitivity also seems to have a socialized and a physiological dimension, meaning that using just one approach misses an important means to understand the origins of certain issue attitudes. The potential for psychophysiology to provide these sorts of insights has long been recognized, if rarely employed (see Lodge et al. 1975, 611).

Physiological measures also offer an opportunity to index psychological states that are difficult to access with the techniques typically employed in political science. As an example, consider the difficulty of measuring racial attitudes. Some consider measures constructed from survey self-reports to be unreliable because respondents are likely to report only socially acceptable attitudes. A long-running debate over whether attitudes toward racial policies are a product of racial prejudices or "principled conservatism" has resisted resolution in no small part because of measurement difficulties (see Reyna et al. 2005 for a review). Unlike responses to a survey probe, however, many physiological responses are outside the scope of conscious control or reflective awareness and have been reliably correlated with racial attitudes and behavior (Vanman et al. 2004; Dambrun, Despres, and Guimond 2003).

The primary contribution of a psychophysiological approach, though, is not simply as another measurement technique but as a means to more directly and intuitively connect biology and political attitudes and behaviors. A major theme of this entire volume is that there is a biological, perhaps genetic, basis to political attitudes and behaviors, a claim that has been met with deep skepticism in some quarters (e.g., Charney 2008). To date, the most visible empirical support for the biological instantiation of such attitudes and behaviors has come from heritability studies and, increasingly, genotype-phenotype correlations (Martin et al. 1986; Alford, Funk, and Hibbing 2005; Hatemi et al. 2007; Fowler, Baker, and Dawes 2008; Fowler and Dawes 2008). Since it is highly unlikely that humans carry genetic code directly affecting attitudes toward school prayer or regressive taxation, a chain of intermediate steps must link genes and political attitudes and behavior. Physiology is quite likely a crucial step.

Genes may not build an attitude on a specific issue-of-the-day, but they certainly play a role in constructing the human nervous system. Since physiology is the means by which humans interact with their environment, it makes an obvious target for investigating the biological instantiation of political attitudes and behaviors. It can be thought of as a not-so-missing link between genes (or biology more broadly) and political responses. Genes influence physiology and physiology influences responses to the environment, including political attitudes and behaviors. This is not merely abstract speculation; specific aspects of physiological system performance, such as electrodermal response, are known to be heritable and in turn are particularly relevant to issue attitudes that have also been identified as heritable. Challenging or contradicting these latter attitudes tends to trigger particularly active physiological responses (Creder et al. 2004; Tesser et al. 1998). All this makes physiology an obvious locus of research that seeks a broader, biological, and integrated understanding of political attitudes and behavior.

The Autonomic Nervous System and Its Measurement

Human physiology is a broad and complex area covering all elements of the human nervous system from endocrinology to neuroscience. The nervous system can be broken down into two major divisions: central and peripheral. The central nervous system consists of the brain and the spinal cord and is protected by bone and the blood-brain barrier. The peripheral nervous system connects the central nervous system to the organs and other parts of the body. The peripheral nervous system can be further broken down into two subsystems, the somatic nervous system and the autonomic nervous system (ANS). Roughly speaking, the somatic nervous system and the ANS can be differentiated by the degree of conscious control exercised over them. The somatic system is used to exercise voluntary control of body movement and is not of primary concern here. The ANS, in contrast, operates mostly outside the realm of conscious awareness and involves, among other things, regulation of cardio-respiratory activity, temperature, and digestion.

The central nervous system has attracted considerable attention from researchers seeking to connect physiology to political, social, and economic attitudes and behaviors, especially in the form of brain function studies. Economics has developed an entirely new field—neuroeconomics—focused on studying the brain during human decisionmaking. An increasing number of studies in political science follow a similar path (see Fowler and Schreiber 2008 for a review that discusses implications of neuroscience for the study of political attitudes and behavior). The central nervous system is obviously an incredibly important area of study in psychophysiology, but it is addressed elsewhere in this volume and, with one exception (the startle eyeblink; see below) we will not discuss it here. Our focus instead will be the ANS, a more longstanding target of attention in psychophysiology and, resource-wise, a more practical option for studying biology and politics given that a reasonably well-equipped, ANS-oriented lab can be had for around $20,000 and an fMRI (functional Magnetic Resonance Imagery) costs millions.

The ANS is the "regulator, adjuster and coordinator of vital visceral activities." It is divided into two subsystems: sympathetic and parasympathetic. These can be roughly thought of as the "fight or flight" (sympathetic) and "rest and digest" (parasympathetic) systems. The sympathetic division mobilizes reactions that expend energy in response to threat, stress, or arousal, including increasing heart rate, blood pressure, and directing blood toward voluntary muscles. The parasympathetic division mobilizes reactions associated with restoration and energy conservation, such as decreasing heart rate and increasing digestive activities. These systems are antagonistic, but should not be thought of in "either-or" terms; they act in concert and continuously to adjust bodily functions in response to environmental conditions. For example, the heart is simultaneously under the control of both the sympathetic and parasympathetic systems (Noback and Demarest 1975, 191, 197).

The ANS can be measured via electrochemical changes that occur in nerve cells, muscles, and glands. Obtaining noninvasive measures is possible by placing electrodes on the skin to record the signals produced by the bioelectrical processes of the body. Equipment to measure these changes is readily available across a range of prices. At the low end, a basic heart rate monitor can be had from any sporting goods store for as little as fifty dollars and a simple machine to measure the conductivity of the skin can cost a few hundred dollars. Accurate collection and analysis of physiological data suitable for academic research, however, usually requires more sophisticated equipment that includes a bioamplifier capable of handling inputs from multiple sensors, a system to capture, quantify, and process the signals from the bioamplifier, and some means of presenting a stimulus and correlating the timing of that stimulus with the output from the bioamplifier. Many options exist, ranging from ready-to-use turnkey systems to custom systems designed for specific research purposes.[2]

Three of the commonly collected measures of ANS activity, available in even fairly basic physiological lab systems, are electrodermal activity, electromyography (muscle activity), and various cardiac measures. We first provide basic introductions to these three measures and then demonstrate the manner in which they might be employed to investigate questions of importance to political scientists.

Electrodermal Activity

Electrodermal activity (EDA) is recognized as, "one of the most widely used . . . response systems in the history of psychophysiology" (Dawson, Schell, and Filion 2007, 159). EDA is familiar to most nonexperts as the basis of polygraph testing, that is, the "lie detector" test seen so often in police dramas. Though psychophysiologists in general express considerable skepticism about the validity of the polygraph as a means to scientifically assess the veracity of subject statements (see Office of Technology Assessment 1983), the basic notion that psychological states can be indexed through electrical activity in the skin is widely accepted. The primary approach to measurement involves recording variation in skin conductivity in response to the presentation of stimuli.

Because of the physiological properties of the skin, this variation is widely believed to be a fairly direct means of tapping affective arousal and response

(Dawson, Schell, and Filion 2007). One of the primary functions of skin is to help regulate and maintain a core body temperature, a function accomplished in part by the production of sweat. Eccrine sweat glands are controlled by the sympathetic nervous system and are activated, not just for thermoregulation, but also to prepare the body for action. This activation can be measured because eccrine sweat glands, for all intents and purposes, act like sets of variable resistors; they vary the skin's ability to conduct (or resist) electrical activity as they open/close and as columns of conductive sweat rise/fall.[3]

Eccrine glands are densely concentrated on the palms and fingers and the most common means of recording EDA is to place two electrodes on the palms or fingers.[4] Typically, electrodes in collars configured to standardize the skin area used for recording (1 cm² in our lab) are employed, along with an electrode paste to act as a conductive medium. EDA is measured by passing a small electrical current through these electrodes and collecting data on skin resistance and conductance. Resistance and conductance are related measures, though for a variety of reasons conductance is the preferred approach by psychophysiologists (see Lykken and Venables 1971). Skin conductance level (SCL)—the ability of the skin to conduct an electrical current—is measured in units called microsiemens (µS).[5]

Perhaps the biggest challenge in using electrodermal activity as a research tool, aside from equipment and laboratory protocol considerations (see Stern, Ray, and Quigle 2001), is compiling and scoring the data. Considerable variation occurs across individuals in baseline SCL, with typical scores ranging from 2 to 20 µS and meaningful deviations from this baseline (phasic skin conductance responses that can reliably be attributed to novel stimuli) can be as small as 0.1–1.0 µS. SCL can also show habituation effects during the course of an experimental protocol, especially with repeated exposure to the same or similar stimuli and even these habituation effects vary across individuals. Moreover, SCL data are often highly skewed and can violate distributional assumptions associated with standard parametric statistical techniques. Adding to the challenges of scoring is the continuous nature of the SCL measure. Typically there is a delay on the order of 2–5 seconds after an environmental stimulus before an increase in baseline SCL is evident. This increase continues until it reaches a peak and then gradually returns to baseline levels, leaving room for debate over whether to measure amplitude (the relative strength of the response) or latency (the rapidity with which the response started, stopped, or peaked). Unfortunately, there is no standardized approach to dealing with these issues—but they are tractable. For example, to deal with distributional concerns, it is common to transform the data (logging and square-root transformations are among the most common) and, to deal with individual variations in tonic SCL (i.e., the baseline SCL in the absence of specific stimulus), it is common to compare first differences (changes from a baseline to levels produced by the stimulus in question).

Examples of skin conductance studies relevant to political science include Mutz and Reeves (2005), who used SCL to assess the "emotional, gut-level" responses to incivility in political discourse and its implications for trust in government. They found SCL increased when witnessing uncivil issue debates, which suggests political conflict triggers a sympathetic (fight or flight) nervous system reaction associated with arousal, attention and orientation. Oxley et al. (2008) used SCL to detect physiological differences in response to threatening stimuli between conservatives and liberals, and Smith et al. (2009) found a correlation between SCL changes in response to disgusting stimuli with participants' positions on sex-related issues such as gay marriage. These studies reflect a variety of measurement and research design approaches to dealing with the particular data issues just discussed. For example, Mutz and Reeves used a within-subject experimental design in which participants were exposed to both a high- and a low-civility experimental condition. The within-subject design meant subjects could be compared to themselves (SCL while witnessing civil versus uncivil debate) without elaborate data transformations. In contrast, Oxley et al. and Smith et al. used a between subjects design (comparing mean SCL differences across individuals) and logged the data to normalize distributions before doing a correlational analysis.[6]

Electromyography and the Startle Eyeblink

Electromyography (EMG) is the recording of those electrical signals produced by reflexive and voluntary muscle activity and is commonly used to measure activity in facial muscles. As Darwin noted, facial expressions communicate emotional states, and measuring activation of muscles associated with these emotional states (e.g., frowns or smiles) is widely accepted as means of quantifying affect (Dimberg 1990). The recording process typically consists of placing a pair of electrodes on the desired muscle (along with a ground) and measuring the amplitude of electrical activity in microvolts (μV). The difference in signal between the two electrodes relative to the ground is amplified and used as the basis for analysis (for primers see Tassinary, Cacioppo, and Vanman 2007; Miller and Long 2006).

One important advantage of EMG is that it can directly tap valence, either by measuring facial expressions associated with positive or negative emotions (smiles or frowns) or by modulating EMG response with stimuli of known valence. For example, one of the known properties of the startle eyeblink is that it is modulated by the affective valence of stimuli (Lang, Bradley, and Cuthbert 1990). In simple terms, we blink harder if startled during an aversive stimulus and less so during a pleasant stimuli, which allows researchers to use this technique to investigate valance as well as arousal. Skin conductance, on the other hand, is a good measure of arousal, but it does not capture valance. An individual viewing a video clip of a policy speech being made by a liberal president may exhibit increased SCL, indicating arousal, but what does this mean? Whether the response is negative (perhaps because the experimental participant holds conservative attitudes) or positive (because the participant is liberal) cannot be inferred by an increased SCL.

One of the more common applications of EMG recording is the startle eyeblink, an aversive reflex to a sudden stimulus that involves involuntary contraction of muscles. Technically, the startle eyeblink is considered a noninvasive measure of central nervous system (as opposed to ANS) activity, but it is a fairly simple and valuable recording option for a lab to record.[7] Several methods are available for evoking the startle eyeblink response including acoustic (a loud and unexpected noise), visual (an unexpected flash of light), puffs of air on the face, or even direct electrical stimulation of the muscle (see Blumenthal et al. 2005, 4–7). Measuring the startle eyeblink is typically accomplished by placing electrodes on the orbicularis occuli—the muscle directly below the eye that contracts when a blink occurs. Because the electrical signals from surface EMG recording are fairly weak, it is generally recommended to prepare electrode sites by removing makeup, skin oil, dead skin cells, and anything else that might interfere with conductance from skin surface to electrode (mildly abrasive skin gels are readily available for this task). A conductive electrode gel is also often used to insure good conductivity.

As with SCL, there are a number of data-processing issues with EMG recordings like the startle eyeblink. Raw signals are typically rectified (to make the signal unidirectional), smoothed (e.g., with a moving average), and integrated (cumulatively summed). In most modern systems this sort of processing is done automatically by data acquisition software, and the main decision for the researcher is exactly which measure to extract from the data. Options include latency (e.g., from stimulus onset to peak amplitude), amplitude (e.g., the highest peak in rectified data), or even total area under the curve of a recorded and rectified/smoothed signal. As with SCL, researchers need to account for startle habituation effects since reactions to the same or similar stimuli (e.g., an acoustic startle) tend to diminish over time.

Examples of EMG studies of relevance to political science include Dambrun, Despres, and Guimond's (2003) investigation of the intensity and valence of responses to ethnic-based stimuli among French students (the stimuli were either French or Arab). They placed electrodes on the corrugator supercilii (the "frown muscle") of participants' faces as they viewed the stimuli and counted the number of signal peaks during exposure to the target stimuli. Activation of the corrugator supercilii was higher for the out-group ethnic stimuli and this effect was also correlated ($r = .35$) with negative evaluations of the person depicted in this stimuli. Vanman et al. (2004) calculated mean amplitude recordings of activation in the smile as well as the frown muscles taken as subjects reviewed applications for a scholarship. This review included inspecting photos of 16 applicants (8 black, 8 white). They found EMG recordings to be associated with the race of scholarship recommendations; in essence, white subjects who involuntarily frowned while viewing images of black applicants were more likely to recommend whites for a scholarship. These studies demonstrate the potential for psychophysiological studies to provide insights into decisionmaking and behaviors that would be hard to obtain with standard survey approaches. Oxley et al. (2008) looked at mean amplitude scores for an acoustically induced startle eyeblink as participants were watching a fixation point on a computer screen (i.e., a stimulus with no strong affective intensity or valence). They found that those holding more politically conservative positions on certain issues tended to blink more vigorously and they interpreted this as evidence for ideological differences in response to environmental threat. The latter study is a reasonably direct attempt to use physiology as a basis for identifying the biological instantiation of political orientations since it measures an evolutionarily ancient, involuntary, and unconscious biological processing system (the startle blink is a reflex reaction to environmental threat) that was systematically associated with what amounted to attitudes on issues of the day.

Cardiovascular Measures

There are numerous measures of the human cardiovascular system that can index ANS activity, including heart rate, blood pressure, and respiration. The cardiovascular system allows not only various measures of the sympathetic nervous system, but it also offers one of the few relatively easy and accessible measures of the parasympathetic nervous system.

The primary measures of interest in respiration are breathing rate and amplitude, and there are various means to record such data (see Stern, Ray, and

Quigle 2001, 147–52, for a list). A fairly common (and cheap) approach is to use a strain gauge or bellows, which is simply a device that wraps around the chest and expands and contracts with subject inhalation and expiration, and is capable of recording both respiration rate and depth.

Cardiac measures are more numerous and, at least in some cases, more complicated. The heart can be thought of as a four-chambered, electric pump and there are two basic approaches to measuring the action of this pump. The first is chronotropy (the timing or variability of the pump) and the second ionotropy (contractility, or how hard or how much the heart is pumping). Chronotropy is the most familiar approach and is typically measured using an electrocardiogram (ECG). The ECG is a noninvasive measure of the electrical activity of the heart, recorded through two electrodes typically placed on either side of the chest (they may also be placed on the limbs). An ECG produces the P-Q-R-S-T wave signal familiar to anyone who has watched a television medical drama. This is the basis for measuring interbeat intervals (IBI, which is technically the time elapsed between R-wave peaks), which can easily be transformed into more intuitive metrics such as heart rate expressed in beats per minute (BPM, where BPM = 60000/IBI, if IBI is recorded in milliseconds).

As a general rule, increases in cardiovascular activity (e.g., higher respiration and increased BPM/decreased IBI) are associated with arousal and sympathetic nervous system activity. Care has to be taken in interpreting cardiac measures, however, as the heart is simultaneously under the control of both the sympathetic and the parasympathetic nervous system (for a good primer on this and other issues in cardiovascular psychophysiology, see Berntson, Quigley, and Lozana 2007). This dual control by antagonistic systems, however, has an advantage in that it provides an opportunity to measure parasympathetic nervous system activity. Respiratory sinus arrhythmia (RSA) is a fluctuation in heart rate that is associated with the respiratory cycle (Porges 1986). Most people are intuitively aware of this fluctuation; when we inhale our heart rate increases and when we exhale it decreases. RSA is simply a measure of this variability, and changes in RSA are strongly associated with the activity of the vagus nerve, that is, the nerve controlling parasympathetic nervous system stimulation of the heart (for this reason, RSA is sometimes referred to as "vagal tone"). Increases in RSA are positively associated with parasympathetic system control of the heart.

Essentially, the parasympathetic nervous system acts to slow down the heart, and under most circumstances it is a strong influence on heart rate. This can be concluded since the human heart has an intrinsic heart rate of roughly 100 BPM (cut off the heart from the ANS and it will beat on its own at about 100–105 BPM). Given that average heart rate for most people is something on the order of 70 BPM, it is reasonable to infer that under most conditions likely to exist in a laboratory setting, a subject's heart is going to be under significant parasympathetic nervous system control. The respiratory cycle, in effect, acts as a naturally occurring disruption of this control; it releases the "brake" of the parasympathetic nervous system during inhalation so RSA can be conceptualized as a way to measure the effectiveness of this brake.

Modern equipment makes recording and quantifying RSA straightforward, as long as ECG and respiration inputs are part of the system. RSA is usually collected during a rest or baseline period as opposed to measuring it in response to stimulus exposure. Stimulus exposure such as an acoustic startle would bring significant SNS elements into play that would contaminate readings of the parasympathetic system.

Examples of research relevant to political science that employs cardiovascular physiology include Dambrun, Despres, and Guimond (2003), who during the experiment already described measured respiratory activity during exposure to ethnic stimuli. They simply counted respiration rate (mean inhalation-expiration cycles per 10-second period) and found a significant difference between in-group and out-group stimuli. Blood pressure and heart rate have been used in a number of other studies examining the physiological impacts of racial attitudes and racism (Clark et al. 1999; Utsey and Hook 2007). Increased heart rate is also known to be associated with threat or fear (Dillard 1994), which may have a range of implications for political attitudes and behavior. For example, Oxley et al. (2008) argue that physiological response to threatening stimuli predicts issue attitudes, but their measures were limited to SCL and EMG. Currently, the potential for cardiac response to play a similar role in predicting political attitudes is largely unexplored.

Research Subjects

Psychophysiological research requires investigators to give some thought to subject recruitment and administration. Because human subjects are involved, all research needs to undergo review by institutional review boards (IRBs) and receive appropriate approvals. Fortunately, from the researchers' perspective this should be no more painful than the process associated with survey, experimental, or field investigations that have long been a mainstay of political science research using human subjects. This is because the sorts of physiological measures described above are not invasive (sensors are placed on the skin), pose no particular risks to subjects, and are routinely collected by scholars in other disciplines, particularly psychologists. In our experience, the biggest issue raised by IRBs is not the physiological measurement techniques, but the type of stimuli being presented. In our lab, we have used fairly graphic still and moving images intended to evoke disgust and threat, and in some cases proposing to present them to research participants has (quite correctly) necessitated full board review. In and of itself, however, recording, say, SCL is, at worst, a mild inconvenience for a subject and poses no risk. Psychophysiological research should thus add no IRB-related requirements above and beyond what is typical for engaging in low risk research using human subjects. This is not to say considerations unfamiliar to most political scientists will never come into play. In one of our first groups of subjects, cardiovascular measures revealed that one individual had a decided irregularity. Our protocol had not anticipated such an eventuality so, after consultation with doctors and university attorneys, we broke confidentiality and contacted the participant in question, suggesting that a precautionary medical checkup might be in order. Now, we routinely mention this possibility in the letter of informed consent and we arrange it so a recruiting organization will be in a position to contact subjects in such a situation once we pass along to them the subject ID number. This way no identities will be revealed to the researchers.

IRB issues should be relatively straightforward. However, compared to conducting a survey or running an experiment, subject recruitment and administration in psychophysiological research can be time consuming. There are two reasons for this. First, for most physiological research, surveys or experiments will still have to be conducted. Physiological indicators do not reveal an individual's stance on a particular issue, any more than they reveal socioeconomic status or likelihood of making altruistic allocations in a public goods game. To get that information—that is, variables of central interest to political science research—researchers need to administer a survey instrument or conduct an experiment. In short, psychophysiological research extends traditional research formats rather than replacing them.

Second, administering a lab protocol can create a data-collection bottleneck. Data collection for survey and experimental designs are relatively easy to structure as a parallel process; the survey or experiment can be administered to more than one subject at a time. These designs can also be administered in a way that requires few demands on the subject other than access to a telephone or the Internet. In contrast, the number of participants a psychophysiology lab can process is limited by equipment. One bioamplifier means only one subject at a time. Two bioamplifers doubles that capacity—but it also doubles the resource costs in terms of capital investment. A psychophysiology lab also makes more demands on the subject. For example, assuming an adult, nonundergraduate population, participants will have to make their way to the lab location. Once there, they need to be prepped and have sensors attached, a process that, depending on the measures being obtained, can take 15–20 minutes even with an experienced lab technician. In our lab, it took six weeks to run approximately 350 randomly recruited subjects through a research protocol; this required running the lab 10–12 hours a day, six days a week. Depending on the particular protocol and the physiological readings being taken, we typically allow 60 to 90 minutes of lab time per subject. Taking into account getting to campus, parking, finding the lab, and taking a survey instrument, participating in psychophysiological research can easily demand at least two hours of a participant's time.

These demands can create obvious challenges to subject recruitment but they can be overcome with the proper monetary incentives (we pay subject fees of $25– $100). Even with incentives, though, investigators need to plan for the inevitable no-shows and cancellations. Our fees are relatively generous compared with other human subject labs on our campus and we typically have no show/cancellation rates of approximately 15–20%. The cheapest alternative is to use undergraduate subject pools, though this raises the usual external validity issues. The bottom line is that psychophysiological research can create a particular set of recruitment, logistical, and administrative challenges. None of these are insurmountable, but they require significant advance planning and coordination.

Psychophysiological Research and Political Science: An Illustration

To provide an illustration of the manner in which political scientists might employ the physiological measures described above, we extend previous research suggesting a link between physiology and racial attitudes by testing whether there is a correlation between physiological responses and self-reported attitudes toward race-conscious affirmative action policies. Political science has devoted considerable energy and effort to understanding the source of such attitudes and a broad literature examines whether opposition to affirmative action policies is driven by racial prejudices, by principled opposition to the idea of government treating racial groups unequally, or by some combination of both. The principled approach is most associated with Sniderman and various colleagues who argue affirmative action policies run counter to notions of individualism and equal treatment deeply ingrained in American culture in general and conservative ideology in particular (e.g., Sniderman and Carmines 1997; Sniderman, Crosby, and Howell 2000). Others argue that whites' opposition to affirmative action is rooted in racial prejudice (e.g., Kinder and Mendelberg 2000; Kinder and Sears 1981; Sidanius, Pratto, and Bobo 1996).

A central difficulty in assessing which of these perspectives is correct is the problem of accurately separating racial attitudes from principled ideological positions through the use of standard survey probes (Feldman and Huddy 2005; Neblo 2009). Responses to questions about the biological or social inferiority of particular races (so-called old-fashioned or redneck racism measures) may be proscribed, or at least constrained, by prevailing social expectations. There is deep disagreement over whether instruments purportedly measuring principled ideological objections (so-called racial resentment scales) do any such thing, or whether they are simply proxies for old fashioned racism (Sidanius, Pratto and Bobo 1996). As we have seen, however, physiological responses to racial stimuli have proven to be a reliable means of indexing attitudes (Vanman et al. 2004; Dambrun, Despres, and Guimond 2003). These physiological responses are, for the most part, not under conscious control and as such could constitute deep-seated, gut-level responses rather than conscious and cognitively elaborated self reports. One way to test whether deeply held prejudices or principled ideology is driving policy preferences is thus to empirically assess the correlation between attitudes on race conscious issues and physiological responses to racial stimuli.

We conducted a preliminary test along these lines by bringing approximately 50 adults (all white) into our physiology laboratory in the summer of 2008 (for a description of the sample see Smith et al. 2009). Though the subject of the research was not primarily race, we did ask participants to view a limited number of balanced racial images. These stimuli consisted of blacks and whites in similar dress and surroundings and included, for example, a white gang member and a black gang member; a black businessman and a white businessman. Two images (the gang members) were part of a larger series of images presented to participants for 15 seconds each on a computer screen and separated from each succeeding image by 10-second inter-stimulus intervals (ISIs; a blank screen with a fixation point). We took several physiological recordings, including SCL and IBI, during viewing of these images. During viewing of two other paired racial stimuli—a black businessman and a white businessman—we provoked a startle eyeblink with an acoustic probe (white noise) and recorded blink amplitude.

In order to address the data issues described above, we computed our basic physiological measures, whether the measure was SCL, IBI, or blink ampli-

TABLE 7.1. Physiological reaction to racial stimuli and opposition to race-conscious policies

Attitudinal measure	SCL (Gang member)	IBI (Gang member)	Blink amplitude (Businessmen)
Government should make every effort to improve the social and economic position of blacks	.274[a] (45)	.130 (45)	.252[a] (42)
Because of past discrimination blacks should be given preference in hiring and promotion	.273[a] (47)	.039 (47)	.407[b] (44)
If black people are not getting fair treatment in jobs, the federal government ought to see to it that they do	.273[a] (47)	−.033 (47)	.04 (44)

Note: Pearson's correlations (N) reported

[a] $p < .10$, [b] $p < .05$

Policy questions are on a seven-point scale where higher numbers indicate greater disagreement with policy. Means (N) reported. Physiological measures are proportions where positive numbers indicated greater physiological reaction to black stimuli than white stimuli.

tude (for the startle eyeblink), with the following formula: (black stimulus minus white stimulus)/black stimulus, where we used means for the stimulus period for SCL and IBI and blink amplitude for the startle eyeblink. The resulting score for each individual is a proportion of the SCL during the stimuli, relative to the SCL during preceding ISI, where positive numbers indicate greater physiological reactivity to the black image compared to the white image. Though a fairly blunt approach, these procedures have the advantage of making scores comparable across individuals. In each case, our data were approximately normally distributed, negating the need to engage in any data transformations.

Table 7.1 shows the correlations between these physiological measures and three attitudinal questions on race-conscious policies (policy questions are on a seven-point scale where higher numbers indicate greater disagreement with policy). With IBI, no relationship was evident; coefficient direction was inconsistent and never significant. In some ways this is not surprising since the images are not particularly evocative. What is more surprising, at least in the bivariate analyses, is that the other two physiological measures pick up subtle reactions to fairly innocuous stimuli that in turn are capable of predicting policy attitudes, suggesting that race-conscious policy attitudes can be indexed physiologically—that is, that these sorts of attitudes have, at a minimum, biological markers and perhaps even a biological basis.

Table 7.2 shows that, though it is not true for IBI or SCL, the blink amplitude measure continues to be a robust predictor of attitudes on two race-conscious

TABLE 7.2. Multiple regression analysis of opposition to race-conscious policies

Variable	Government should make every effort to improve the social and economic position of blacks	Because of past discrimination blacks should be given preference in hiring and promotion	If black people are not getting fair treatment in jobs, the federal government ought to see to it that they do
SCL	6.6	5.3	9.8
	(5.4)	(4.7)	(6.4)
IBI	1.62	−.45	2.9
	(2.15)	(1.7)	(2.5)
Blink amplitude	.43[b]	.47[b]	.05
	(.20)	(.16)	(.23)
Ideology	.57[b]	.29[a]	.41[a]
	(.19)	(.15)	(.21)
Age	−.02	.03	−.07[a]
	(.03)	(.02)	(.03)
Gender	.41	−.04	−.62
	(.53)	(.42)	(.59)
Constant	61.1	−58.9	140[b]
	(57.9)	(50)	(67)
Adj-R^2	.20	.19	.16
N	42	44	44

Note: Unstandardized coefficient (standard error) reported

[a] $p < .05$, [b] $p < .10$

policies even in a multiple regression controlling for ideology and some standard demographic variables (gender and age). Ideology, measured on a standard 1 = strongly liberal to 7 = strongly conservative scale, is a consistent predictor of opposition to race-conscious policies, independent of any gut-level orientations picked up by the physiological measures. This provides at least some mild support for the principled conservatism argument, though the hint of an independent effect for physiological reactions to black images means the matter remains far from settled.

Our purposes here, though, are more expository than substantive and we make no claim of any definitive contribution to the ongoing debate about the source of race-related policy attitudes. More images and more participants would be necessary for this. The point we are making with this illustrative analysis is that physiology can be meaningfully incorporated into research on questions of central interest to political scientists.

Conclusion

The potential connection of physiology to political orientations is intriguing in and of itself because it would suggest that orientations—whatever their source—at some point become biologically instantiated. When aligned beside the evidence that genes help to shape political orientations, the role of physiology becomes even more revealing. If the study of political orientations is to be integrated with other aspects of the social sciences, if it is to be grounded in broader life forces and in biology, physiological techniques will play a vital role. Though a certain amount of retooling and equipment acquisition is required, this chapter demonstrates that political scientists can overcome whatever challenges might discourage them from conducting physiological research. They need to do so because unlocking the nature of political orientations is too important a task to leave entirely to those who do not fully understand politics. The belief—so widely held among traditional political scientists—that environmental forces are the sole shaper of political attitudes and behaviors must be subjected to empirical investigation rather than accepted uncritically, and psychophysiological techniques are among the most promising and cost-effective means of providing the requisite evidence.

Notes

1. For example, George Marcus (2002) argues that emotion and rationality are necessary for political thought and action. Though cognition and affect are frequent subjects of psychophysiological research, virtually no work by political scientists seeks to correlate particular physiological states to political decisions.

2. For a list of manufacturers and various options see http://www.psychophys.com/company.html. Good primers on setting up and running a psychophysiology laboratory, including introductions to the collection, processing, and scoring of various ANS measures include Miller and Long 2006; Stern, Ray, and Quigle 2001; and Andreassi 2006. More detailed and technical coverage of these issues can be found in Cacioppo, Tassinary, and Berntson 2007.

3. Good primers on the physiology of EDA as well as its measurement and scoring include Dawson, Schell, and Filion 2007; Stern, Ray, and Quigle 2001, 206–17; and Andreassi 2006, 191–213.

4. A protocol followed by many labs, including our own, is to place the electrodes on the distal phalanges (tips) of the index and middle fingers of the subject's nondominant hand. Other placement possibilities are the medial phalanges and the thenar and hypothenar eminences of the palms. The case for using the distal phalanges is that this practice aids consistent placement of electrodes across subjects—an important consideration since variable placement could have a significant adverse impact on measurement compatibility. The nondominant hand is preferred because it is less likely to have cuts or calluses that may affect skin conductivity.

5. For those familiar with Ohm's law (R = V/I), where resistance is measured in ohms, siemens is simply the inverse of ohms (another term for microsiemens is micromho, i.e., a millionth of an ohm, with ohm spelled backwards).

6. For a more in-depth overview of scoring and design issues see Dawson, Schell, and Filion 2007, 164–67.

7. The primary requirement is a bioamplifer capable of taking inputs from EMG signals. These are not unusual. For example, the bioamplifer used in our lab, manufactured by the James Long Company, includes a fairly standard set of inputs for ECG, SCL, respiration and EMG.

References

Alford, J. R., C. L. Funk, and J. R. Hibbing. 2005. Are political orientations genetically transmitted? *American Political Science Review* 99 (2): 153–68.

Andreassi, J. 2006. *Psychophysiology: Human behavior and psychophysiological response.* Mahwah, N.J.: Lawrence Erlbaum Associates.

Bernstein, D.A., A. Clarke-Stewart, L. A. Penner, E. J. Roy, and C. D. Wickens. 2000. *Psychology.* 5th ed. Boston: Houghton Mifflin.

Berntson, G., K. Quigley, and D. Lozana. 2007. Cardiovascular psychophysiology. In *Handbook of psychophysiology*, ed. J. Cacioppo, L. Tassinary, and G. Berntson, 182–210. New York: Cambridge University Press.

Blumenthal, T., B. Cuthbert, D. Filion, S. Hackley, O. Lipp, and A. Van Boxtel. 2005. Committee report: Guidelines for human startle eyeblink electromyographic studies. *Psychophysiology* 42:1–15.

Bradley, M., and P. J. Lang. 2007. The International Affective Picture System (IAPS) in the study of emotion and attention. In *Handbook of emotion elicitation and assessment*, ed. J. Coan and J. Allen, 29–46. New York: Oxford University Press.

Cacioppo, J. T., and L. G. Tassinary. 1990. Psychophysiology and psychophysiological inference. In *Principles of psychophysiology: Physical, social, and inferential elements*, ed. J. Cacioppo and L. Tassinary. New York: Cambridge University Press.

———, eds. 1990. Preface. In *Principles of psychophysiology: Physical, social, and inferential elements*. New York: Cambridge University Press.

Cacioppo, J. T., L. G. Tassinary, and G. G. Berntson. 2007. Psychophysiological science: Interdisciplinary approaches to classic questions about the mind. In *Handbook of psychophysiology*, ed. J. Cacioppo, L. Tassinary, and G. Berntson, 1–186. New York: Cambridge University Press.

———, eds. 2007. *Handbook of psychophysiology.* 3rd ed. New York: Cambridge University Press.

Charney, E. 2008. Genes and ideologies. *Perspectives on Politics* 6:299–319.

Clark, R., N. Anders, V. Clark, and D. Williams. 1999. Racism as a stressor for African Americans: A biopsychosocial model. *American Psychologist* 54:805–16.

Creder, A., W. Kremen, H. Xian, K. Jacobson, B. Waterman, S. Eisen, M. Tsuang, and M. Lyons. 2004. Stability, consistency, and heritability of electrodermal response lability in middle-aged male twins. *Psychophysiology* 41:501–9.

Dambrun, M., G. Despres, and S. Guimond. 2003. On the multifaceted nature of prejudice: Psychophysiological responses to ingroup and outgroup ethnic stimuli. *Current Research in Social Psychology* 8:187–206.

Dawson, M., A. Schell, and D. Filion. 2007. The electrodermal system. In *Handbook of psychophysiology*, ed. J. Cacioppo, L. Tassinary, and G. Berntson, 159–81. New York: Cambridge University Press.

Dillard, J. 1994. Rethinking the study of fear appeals: An emotional perspective. *Communication Theory* 4:295–323.

Dimberg, U. 1990. Facial electromyography and emotional reactions. *Psychophysiology* 27:481–94.

Faulkner, W. 1936. *Absalom, Absalom!* New York: Random House.

Feldman, S., and L. Huddy. 2005. Racial resentment and white opposition to race-conscious programs: Principles or prejudice? *American Journal of Political Science* 49:168–83.

Fowler, J. H., L. A. Baker, and C. Dawes. 2008. Genetic variation in political participation. *American Political Science Review* 102 (2): 233–48.

Fowler, J. H., and C. T. Dawes. 2008. Two genes predict voter turnout. *Journal of Politics* 70 (3): 579–94.

Fowler, J. H., and D. Schreiber. 2008. Biology, politics, and the emerging science of human nature. *Science* 322 (5903): 912–14.

Greenfield, N. S., and R. A. Sternbach. 1972. *Handbook of psychophysiology*. New York: Holt, Rinehart, and Winston.

Hatemi, P. K., K. I. Morley, S. E. Medland, A. C. Heath, and N. G. Martin. 2007. The genetics of voting: An Australian twin study. *Behavior Genetics* 37:435–48.

Inbar, Y., D. A. Pizarro, and P. Bloom. 2009. Conservatives are more easily disgusted than liberals. *Cognition and Emotion* 23 (4): 714–28.

Kinder, D., and T. Mendelberg. 2000. Individualism reconsidered. In *Racialized politics: The debate about racism in America*, ed. D. Sears, J. Sidanius, and L. Bobo, 44–74. Chicago: University of Chicago Press.

Kinder, D., and D. Sears. 1981. Prejudice and politics: Symbolic racism versus racial threats to the good life. *Journal of Personality and Social Psychology* 72:275–87.

Lang, P., M. Bradley, and B. Cuthbert. 1990. Emotion, attention, and the startle reflex. *Psychological Review* 97:377–95.

Lodge, M., D. V. Cross, B. Tursky, and J. Tanenhaus. 1975. The psychophysical scaling and validation of a political support scale. *American Journal of Political Science* 19:611–49.

Lowell, A. L. 1910. The physiology of politics. *American Political Science Review* 4:1–15.

Lykken, D., and P. H. Venables. 1971. Direct measurements of skin conductance: A proposal for standardization. *Psychophysiology* 8:656–72.

Madsen, D. 1985. A biochemical property relating to power seeking in humans. *American Political Science Review* 79 (2): 448–57.

———. 1986. Power seekers are different: Further biochemical evidence. *American Political Science Review* 80:261–69.

Marcus, G. 2002. *The sentimental citizen: Emotion in Democratic politics*. University Park: Pennsylvania State University Press.

Martin, N. G., L. J. Eaves, A. C. Heath, R. Jardine, L. M. Feingold, and H. J. Eysenck. 1986. Transmission of social attitudes. *Proceedings of the National Academy of Sciences* 83:4364–68.

Miller, A., and J. Long. 2006. Psychophysiology principles, pointers and pitfalls. In *Developmental psychophysiology: Theory, systems, method*, ed. L. A. Schmidt and S. J. Segalowitz, 367–423. New York: Cambridge University Press.

Miller, J. 1978. *The body in question*. New York: Random House.

Mutz, D. C., and B. Reeves. 2005. The new videomalaise: Effects of televised incivility on political trust. *American Political Science Review* 99:1–15.

Neblo, M. 2009. Three-fifths a racist: A typology for analyzing public opinion about race. *Political Behavior* 31:31–51.

Noback, C., and R. Demarest. 1975. *The human nervous system: Basic principles of neurobiology.* New York: McGraw-Hill.

Office of Technology Assessment. 1983. *Scientific validity of polygraph testing.* Washington, D.C.: U.S. Congress.

Oxley, D. R., K. B. Smith, J. R. Alford, M. V. Hibbing, J. L. Miller, M. Scalora, P. K. Hatemi, and J. R. Hibbing. 2008. Political attitudes vary with physiological traits. *Science* 321 (5896): 1667–70.

Peterson, S., A. Somit, and B. Brown. 1983. Biopolitics in 1982. *Politics and the Life Sciences* 2:76–80.

Porges, S. W. 1986. Respiratory sinus arrhythmia: Physiological basis, quantitative methods, and clinical implications. In *Cardiorespiratory and cardiosomatic psychophysiology*, ed. P. Grossman, K. Jansen, and D. Vaitl, 101–15. New York: Plenus.

Reyna, C., P. J. Henry, W. Korfmacher, and A. Tucker. 2005. Examining the principles in principled conservatism: The role of responsibility stereotypes as cues for deservingness in racial policy decisions. *Journal of Personality and Social Psychology* 90:109–28.

Sidanius, J., F. Pratto, and L. Bobo. 1996. Racism, conservatism, affirmative action, and intellectual sophistication: A matter of principled conservatism or group dominance? *Journal of Personality and Social Psychology* 70:476–90.

Smith, K., D. Oxley, M. Hibbing, J. Alford, and J. Hibbing. 2009. The ick factor: Physiological sensitivity to disgust as a predictor of political attitudes. Paper presented at the annual meeting of the Midwest Political Science Association, Chicago, March 31–April 3.

Sniderman, P., and E. Carmines. 1997. *Reaching beyond race.* Cambridge: Harvard University Press.

Sniderman, P., G. Crosby, and W. Howell. 2000. The politics of race. In *Racialized politics: The debate about racism in America*, ed. D. Sears, J. Sidanius, and L. Bobo, 236–39. Chicago: University of Chicago Press.

Stern, R., W. Ray, and K. Quigle. 2001. *Psychophysiological recording.* New York: Oxford University Press.

Tassinary, L., J. Cacioppo, and E. Vanman. 2007. The skelemotor system: Surface electromyography, In *Handbook of psychophysiology*, ed. J. Cacioppo, L. Tassinary, and G. Berntson, 267–99. New York: Cambridge University Press.

Tesser, A., D. Whitaker, L. Martin, and D. Ward. 1998. Attitude heritability, attitude change and physiological responsivity. *Personality and Individual Differences* 24:89–96.

Utsey, S., and J. Hook. 2007. Heart rate variability as a physiological moderator of the relationship between race-related stress and psychological distress in African Americans. *Cultural Diversity and Ethnic Minority Psychology* 13:250–53.

Vanman, E. J., J. Saltz, L. Nathan, and J. Warren. 2004. Racial discrimination by low-prejudiced whites: Facial movements as implicit measures of attitudes related to behavior. *Psychological Science* 15:711–14.

Wahlke, J. C., and M. G. Lodge. 1972. Psychophysiological measures of political attitudes and behavior. *Midwest Journal of Political Science* 16:505–37.

8

HORMONES AND POLITICS

Rose McDermott

Why do some people confronted with a threat choose to fight, while others confronted with the same threat choose to retreat? When challenges differ, the level of provocation can help explain differences in behavior. But when people confront the same situation, individual differences also enter into explaining why some people behave in a more aggressive manner, while others choose to placate or retreat in the face of attack. Hormones provide a critical link in examining individual variance in such responses, and these reactions can take place in political as well as sexual contexts.

In my research involving simulated war games, the level of testosterone obviously differed between men and women by the typical factor of about 10 times. While testosterone levels could predict the difference in aggression between men and women, variance among women was not sufficient to predict variance in aggression within each sex. As a result, it was impossible to determine if testosterone alone was responsible for the increased aggression we witnessed among male subjects, or whether such behavior resulted from some other ineluctable aspect of being male. We did find that individuals tended to be overconfident about their prospects for success in our simulated war games. Those who were overconfident proved more likely to attack, and such tendency proved more evident in males than females. In addition, testosterone did relate to individual expectations of success, such that those with higher levels of testosterone reported higher estimated likelihood of victory (Johnson et al. 2006). Thus, testosterone, while important (as explained more in detail below), is not the only hormone, and hormones operate in exquisitely subtle environmental contexts that trigger their release or their inhibition. Examining the interaction between hormones and political context can provide a wealth of information in seeking to explain the individual differences than can help observers understand the variance that represents the nature of human aggression.

Early research into the effect of hormones on humans focused more exclusively on neuroendocrine physiology and how particular hormones affected particular acts or behavior, particularly those related to mating and repro- duction. Several recent developments have allowed for more sophisticated investigation into the functioning of the endocrine system within a broader context of dynamic social behaviors and relationships (Adkins-Regan 2009). The first shift resulted simply from more researchers becoming interested in social relationships instead of single social acts or behaviors. Adkins-Regan provides the best example of the difference provided by this subtle change in perception. If a researcher wants to explain differences in monogamous ver- sus profligate mating propensities, focusing on the act of mating will not pro- vide informative cues. Rather, the social aspects that define whether a person has one or multiple sexual partners provides opportunities for more relevant discoveries. Second, the increasingly availability and lowered cost of noninva- sive techniques for measuring hormones from saliva samples has opened the door for many studies to take place in the midst of social interactions. Last, another turn in focus moved the research in human behavioral endocrinology away from a focus on pathological outcomes to a more theoretically driven investigation into the normal adaptive purpose and functioning of hormones from within an evolutionary perspective. This work formed a convergence among biological anthropologists, evolutionary psychologists, and behav- ioral endocrinologists.

The recent work in human behavioral endocrinology has begun to examine the ways in which hormones and social behaviors manifest reciprocal causal interactions and help establish and maintain enduring social bonds among humans. As it has become increasingly evident that hormones play just as important a role in human social as sexual behavior, we would expect such influence to manifest in the political realm as well, since political relations remain inherently social in nature. This chapter begins with a theoretical overview of the study of human behavioral endocrinology, and then proceeds with an overview of some of the politically relevant findings related to specific hormones.

Human Behavioral Endocrinology

In discussing the influence of hormones on behavior, it appears all too easy to characterize such operation in simplistic terms that posit a direct relation- ship between, say, testosterone and aggression or dominance. And yet such an easy association does not describe these subtle relationships and interactions any more accurately than claiming that a particular gene "causes" a certain behavior. Such simple and direct causal pathways, which fail to recognize the critical influence of environment on all aspects of development and behavior, almost never accurately characterize the operation of such pervasive and influential biological variables.

Several key insights provide the theoretical foundation for a behavioral edifice designed to promote effective and efficient social relationships among humans, which appear essential to survival. First, as Ellison and Gray (2009) brilliantly document, basic hormonal physiology precipitates as well as follows particular patterns of social interaction. This means that hormones must be understood, and should be explored, within a two-layer context that examines both their ultimate cause and purpose, resulting from a combination of evolutionary processes and local ecological environmental pressures on particular population structures, as well as their proximate cause in the immediate phenotypic physiology and development of the individual. In each of these areas, the critical significance of environmental cues and triggers to both potentiate and diminish the operation of particular hormonal responses must be continually recognized.

In examining the ultimate causes of human behavioral endocrinology in evolution and ecology, at least two lines of research emerge as relevant. First, studies of animals allow researchers to examine the structure and operation of such systems. In this regard, it is important to note that the basic endocrine system exists in all mammals and most other vertebrates in remarkably similar fashion, suggesting the widespread effectiveness and efficiency of the overall system. While the nature of many of the social relationships that such systems support may vary across species, the same basic mechanisms exist and may have been exapted for diverse purposes over the course of human evolution to entrain ever more complex social and political relationships.

Second, an evolutionary perspective encourages a functional analysis of hormones within the context of the psychological mechanisms they potentiate, sustain, and ameliorate. This approach recognizes that hormones mediate particular outcomes through their influence on diverse aspects of social behavior rather than cause them directly. For example, oxytocin does not cause a woman to love her baby; rather, oxytocin shifts particular emotional states, or feelings of happiness or trust or bondedness, alters attention toward the child, and literally affects the experience of certain stimuli (making infant odors less objectionable, for example) in order to increase the likelihood that the mother will love her baby *depending* on her particular previous developmental history. Here, developmental history, reflecting more proximate causes of endocrine response, comes to the fore in eliciting specific behavior. If the mother was abused by her own mother, she would find touch more aversive than another mother who was nurtured by her parent. If a mother hated the father of her baby, she might find aspects of the child's appearance or temperament reminiscent of the father more aversive than a mother who cherished her baby's father. In other words, the hormones do not directly cause a particular behavior but rather affect the probabilistic odds of a specific adaptive outcome (i.e., loving your child) through their effect on affect, memory, sensory experience, attention, and other aspects of social behavior. Note here the widespread infiltration of psychological processes by which hormones exert their effects on outcomes of interest.

In appreciating the subtle and diverse manifestation of hormonal influence on social relationships and outcomes of interest, it remains critically important to recognize the essential role played by environment, socialization, and individual developmental history in creating, maintaining, and extinguishing the preferences and behaviors we seek to explicate. Hormonal responses are not determined solely by biology but rather emerge as the result of a hugely complex interplay of environmental and endogenous factors. The social environment inhabited by any given individual plays a key role in understanding the multifaceted links between hormones and behavior. Moreover, these effects remain interactive and reciprocal in nature. Any sophisticated understanding of the operation of human behavioral endocrinology within the context of complex social and political behaviors must incorporate an integration of reproductive ecology, and the motivational forces that drive these exigencies, with a nuanced appreciation of the impact of individual life history in mediating the effect of such processes in any given person or situation.

With this caution in mind, it remains useful to examine some of what is known about the operation of particular hormones within the context of the complex social systems in which they interact to the extent that these effects might also exert political consequences. The rest of the chapter undertakes that task. This becomes particularly important in light of the environmental hormonal exposure to which all humans are increasingly exposed, knowingly or unknowingly, especially in food such as meat, chicken, and milk. As particular hormones become targeted for strategic use in pharmaceutical and cosmetics, the effect of this manipulation on social relationships remains unclear.

Myriad hormones operate to orchestrate many aspects of human behavior and social interaction. These include serotonin, dopamine, progesterone, estrogen, and melatonin. However, a more limited set have been explored extensively for their potential effect on political behavior thus far, and the following discussion concentrates on those hormones. Thus, the overview provided below concentrates on testosterone, cortisol, vasopressin, oxytocin, and monoamine oxidase A, exploring the extent to which these hormones may affect human political behavior in systematic and meaningful ways.

Testosterone

Androgens represent a class of steroid hormones that regulate the development of male sexual characteristics, among other activities. Androgens are produced primarily in the male testes, female ovaries, and the adrenal cortex of both sexes. Testosterone is the most prevalent and significant of these hormones, but the adrenals produce five additional types of androgens. Androgens accomplish a remarkable group of tasks, including the development of both primary and secondary male sexual characteristics. In addition, androgens are involved in the development of muscle mass and fat accumulation. Negative side effects can occur in those who have excess androgens, including those who take supplemental androgens to enhance sports performance. Such effects include male pattern baldness, liver disease, acne, infertility, and impotence.

Testosterone in particular has studied for its influence on the regulation of sexual desire in both males and females, and has been implicated in the manifestation of aggression. Its chemical structure was first characterized by Leopold Ruzicka in 1935, and he is the one responsible for its name. It has been examined extensively in relation to social structure (Kemper 1990), human pair bonding and mating (Lukaszewski and Roney 2009), fatherhood (Gray and Campbell 2009), and aggression (Mazur and Booth 1998). In vertebrate animal studies, testosterone "accounts for most, and perhaps all, of the sex differences in neural structure and behavior" (Morris, Jordan, and Breedlove 2004, 1034). In particular, testosterone molds the masculine development of the adult nervous system, enhances prototypically male behaviors, and diminishes typically female ones. Good evidence for the role of testosterone in the permanent masculinization of the brain exists in rats and other animals. Although primarily produced by the testes, which creates the primary hormonal signal, once inside the brain, testosterone is metabolized into two other substances: dihydrotestosterone by 5-reductase or estradiol by aromatase, the first of which appears to be responsible for masculinization and the second of which controls defeminization (Auger et al. 2000). Most often, testosterone is measured by what is referred to as basal T, which reports on the level of testosterone in the blood at a particular moment in time. In many studies, levels of basal T can predict variance in such behavioral outcomes as dominance and antisocial tendencies.

The potential social and political influence of testosterone appears most relevant through its mediation on several important social behaviors, including recognition and response to changes in social status, influence on aggression and antisocial behaviors, and impact on peer and family relationships. With regard to status hierarchies, there appears to exist a reciprocal relationship between testosterone and dominance displays. Keep in mind that dominance displays can be nonaggressive in nature. In particular, testosterone seems to mediate the reaction to challenge, especially in the face of competitive social contexts. For example, testosterone typically increases in males in the face of challenge; after competition, losers' testosterone tends to fall, while winners' testosterone levels rise (Mazur and Booth 1998). Interestingly, this characteristic can be mediated by coalitional status, such that men who engage in inter-village competition display higher levels of testosterone and cortisol than those same men when engaged in intravillage competition. Moreover, men in these groups show lower testosterone activation in the presence of attractive potential mates who are pair-bonded to men in their coalitional group than to women attached to men outside their group. As Wagner, Flynn, and England (2002) argue, "The lower levels of C and T during within-village matches, compared to between-coalition matches, suggest that activation of endocrine mechanisms might be contingent upon the context of competition."

Testosterone also seems to play a role in demonstrations of antisocial behavior, including rebellion against authority and financial risk-taking. In particular, men with high testosterone and judged to embody highly masculinized facial features were much more likely to take financial risks in an investment game using real money than men with lower levels of the hormone (Apicella et al. 2008).

Not surprisingly, one of the areas where the influence of testosterone has been investigated in detail concerns mating and parenting behavior. One of the most robust findings in this literature documents how men in committed romantic relationships have an average of 21% lower testosterone than men who remain unattached (Burnham et al. 2003). Most of the theoretical arguments developed to explicate this disparity argue that such hormonal regulation modules in response to the differential allocation of energy to mating versus parenting. While seeking a mate, higher levels of testosterone can prove beneficial, but once mated, progeny benefit most from the differential investment of the father in the welfare of the child, as opposed to his continuing efforts to seek additional mating opportunities. Evidence in further support of this argument comes from research showing that men who maintain romantic interests outside their primary relationship demonstrate higher levels of testosterone, meaning men with one sexual partner have lower testosterone than those with either multiple or no partners, suggesting that testosterone facilitates mating efforts by increasing mate-seeking behavior, and promoting same-sex competition (McIntyre et al. 2006).

Indeed, married men have lower testosterone than unmarried men, but married men without children display higher levels of testosterone. Again, here, however, social factors appear to modulate the expression of hormonal signatures. Married men without children who show higher levels of spousal investment and spend more time with their wives have lower testosterone than men who are less committed (Gray et al. 2002). Moreover, unpaired men without prior relationship history have lower testosterone than single men who possess such experience. Men in the first six months of a relationship tend to have higher testosterone than men in later stages of an established relationship, also indicating differential behavioral allocations of energy to mating based on duration of romantic attachment (Gray et al. 2004). Men with higher testosterone are less likely to marry, more likely to divorce if they do marry, and more likely to leave a marriage because of difficult relationships with their wives. They are also more likely to cheat on, hit, or throw things at their spouse, and show decreased quality of marital interactions than their lower-testosterone brethren (Booth and Dabbs 1993). Again, some of these relational difficulties are likely modulated through subtler influences on other aspects of social behavior. For example, administered testosterone diminishes the likelihood of facial mimicry, whereby one person mirrors the emotional facial expression of the other; this failure to display emotional resonance may reduce the likelihood of partners to feel bonded or understood by their mate (Ellison and Gray 2009).

Cortisol

Cortisol is the hormone primarily involved in responding to both internal and external sources of stress. Cortisol appears to influence memory and learning, and also preferentially affects the parts of the brain that are actively involved in fear conditioning, although all these effects appear modulated by sex (Stark 2006). Prolonged or extreme exposure to glutocosteroids such as cortisol, in reaction to stress, appear to cause atrophy in the hippocampus in primates, leading to what appear to be permanent impairments in learning and memory, among other cognitive functions, at least in some individuals (Sapolsky 1996).

In nonhuman primates, chronically elevated levels appear to be associated with a status of social subordination. For example, cortisol rises in response to stress after losing fights. It appears that part of the function of this dynamic, at least reproductively, is that chronic elevation of cortisol can suppress reproduction. In this way, the secretion of cortisol operates to decrease rates of reproduction among social subordinates (Creel 2001). However, this view is complicated by the fact that cortisol often remains elevated among dominant individuals and can represent a cost associated with high social status, at least among chimpanzees (Muller and Wrangham 2004).

The reconciliation of this seeming contradiction can be found in the research Robert Sapolsky has conducted over the last several decades among baboons in the Serengeti in East Africa. He has documented a quite nuanced interaction between social stimuli and endocrine responses among these primates. In particular, in the context of stable social hierarchies, high-status males have lower cortisol levels than lower-ranking ones (Sapolsky 1983). However, this effect disappears in the context of an unstable social hierarchy, where higher-ranking males often display increased levels of testosterone. In careful observations, Sapolsky showed that cortisol levels are neither predicted nor disrupted by the overall social stability of the hierarchy, but rather are affected by shifts and instability in the social ranking of the individual. In particular, baboons who were challenging higher-ranking males up to three steps above them displayed no increased cortisol level; however, males being challenged by others three ranks below them or less manifested much higher levels of cortisol (Sapolsky 1992).

Moreover, the extent to which the individual's hormonal system reacted to stress appeared modulated by additional social factors as well. In particular, social subordinates showed higher stress, as measured by amount of cortisol, when they were submitted to an increased number of stressors, but also when they had decreased opportunities to garner social support, especially from close kin (Abbott et al. 2003).

Some similar findings have been reported among human males as well. Specifically, rates of cortisol appear higher in men with reputations for illicit social behavior. Men with higher cortisol levels report more depressed moods and are rated as less trustworthy, agreeable, influential, and helpful by peers than their lower-cortisol peers. In an interesting environmental interaction, men with higher rates of cortisol were more likely to have had their fathers absent as caregivers when they were children (Decker 2000).

Vasopressin

Vasopressin is a neuropeptide that is secreted by the pituitary gland. Vasopressin is synthesized and regulated by testosterone and remains exquisitely sensitive to developmental hormonal experiences, offering one mechanism by which the link between biology and culture might be explored. Like oxytocin, vasopressin appears involved in critical social behaviors such as social recognition, communication, parental care, and social bonding. In particular, again like oxytocin, vasopressin plays a role in the communication of socially relevant information, especially signals triggered by smell. In earlier work, it seemed that vasopressin improved all kinds of behavioral regulation, including memory and learning, while oxytocin impaired these functions. However, in stressful socially relevant situations triggered by a sense of smell, both vasopressin and oxytocin affected coping (Engelmann et al. 1996).

This hormone is increasingly recognized as particularly vital to partner preference and copulation, particularly in men. Specifically, vasopressin is released during male sexual arousal, increasing male sex drive, but impairs female sexual interest in sexual contact, possibly due to the connection between release of vasopressin and feelings of aggression (Hiller 2005). As a result, vasopressin may account for some observed sex differences, including the impact of puberty on sexual expression, the instigation and display of aggressive and protective feelings toward partners, and the constancy of sexual interest within the context of committed romantic relationships. Based on work originally conducted in voles, vasopressin promotes male- affiliative bonding in nonmonogamous species. Evidence suggests that male-affiliative bonding depends on the release of both vasopressin and dopamine, each of which enhances the rewards associated with smells that signal particular identity in a partner. In particular, recent evidence suggests that variance on a particular polymorphism, the AVPR1A R3 allele, can predict partner bonding, marital problems, and marital status and quality as judged by one's partner (Keverne and Curley 2004). Vasopressin may also be implicated in the quality of sibling relationships.

Oxytocin

Like vasopressin, oxytocin is a neuropeptide secreted by the pituitary gland which remains critical to partner preference and copulation. While vasopressin is synthesized by testosterone, oxytocin is regulated by estrogen and remains quite sensitive to development hormonal experiences. Oxytocin has been implicated in prosocial affiliation and soothing responses to stress. Certainly oxytocin plays a role in social attachment, social recognition, and aggression (Kirsch et al. 2005) by reducing anxiety and influencing the conditioning and extinction of fear.

Oxytocin appears necessary for subjective pleasure, arousal, and orgasm in both sexes, and is secreted at orgasm by both men and women, ostensibly encouraging both pleasure and bonding (Hiller 2005). Oxytocin is also released in women during lactation, an observation made more socially significant by the finding that in hunter-gatherer societies, most female mate choice happens while women are nursing, something less evident in societies where birth control is more common (Ellison and Gray 2009).

Recent studies into the function of oxytocin have focused on its role in the development and expression of social trust. Kosfeld et al. (2005) and others argue that the experience of such trust proves crucial to successful economic and political exchanges, affecting the operation of markets as well as the experience of political legitimacy. Oxytocin appears to increase trust by increasing the willingness of individuals to bear heightened social risks specifically involving interpersonal interactions (Kosfeld et al. 2005). In particular, oxytocin appears to diminish the experience of fear and anxiety, and reduces activation in the amygdala (Kirsch 2005). Indeed, Baumgartner et al. (2008) report that oxytocin seems to operate by diminishing the processing of fear as well as inhibiting the experience of feedback, especially in the face of social betrayal. Heinrichs and Domes (2008) find supporting evidence for way in which oxytocin counteracts social anxiety by showing how oxytocin helps overcome the avoidance of physical proximity, reduces defensiveness, and facilitates approach. This triadic ballet of social behavior obviously potentiates the likelihood of successful mating activity as well. Moreover, oxytocin appears to aid in so-called mind-reading, operationalized as the ability to detect and infer mental states in others from subtle social cues in eye gaze (Domes et al. 2007).

Monoamine Oxidase A

Monoamine oxidase A (MAOA) represents a genetic polymorphism on the gene that encodes monoamine oxidase; this x-linked genetic variant with the low-activity form (MAOA-L) occurs among approximately 35% of most North American and European populations, but emerges among up to 65% of Maori populations. Its manifestation in this population led to MAOA being dubbed "the warrior gene." The gene for MAOA codes for the enzyme that plays a key role in the catabolism of several other neurotransmitters, including serotonin and dopamine.

MAOA-L has been implicated in increased incidence of behavioral, particularly physical aggression, and appears to operate through enhanced impulsivity and propensity for violence. A clear social interaction appears to render individuals with the low-activity form of MAO particularly vulnerable to adult displays of aggression. In particular, there seems to be an interaction between those with MAOA-L and the occurrence of traumatic early life events, particularly those that take place between the ages of 11 and 15, around puberty, which predisposes these individuals to greater likelihood of engaging in aggression as an adult (Caspi and Moffitt 2006; Frazzetto et al. 2007).

The environmental mechanism that modulates the genetic risk appears to operate through its influence on social evaluation and emotional regulation. Specifically, neuroimaging research has suggested that the reason for the propensity for MAOA-L individuals to react impulsively lies in the hyperresponsive nature of the amygdala during emotional arousal, along with concomitant diminished reactivity in the regulatory regions of the prefrontal cortex (Eisenberger et al. 2007). Indeed, the amygdala and hippocampus appear hyperreactive during aversive recall among those at genetic risk for impulsivity and violence (Meyer-Lindenberg et al. 2006).

In my own research, we found that MAOA predicted behavioral aggression following provocation (McDermott et al. 2009). In a power-to-take game, subjects who had a minimal amount of money taken from them (20%) did not differ in their tendency to aggress against their opponent. However, when more significant amounts of money were taken from subjects (80%), those with MAOA-L displayed a significantly greater likelihood of using their own earnings to pay to punish their opponent by making them eat hot sauce, knowing that this action would diminish their own earnings. This study demonstrated a clear gene by environment (level of provocation) effect, exploring the emergence of behavioral aggression in a social context.

Conclusions

The influence of hormones on human behavior remains subtle, profound, and pervasive. A biosocial model that incorporates the influence of both ultimate evolutionary and ecological factors in combination with proximate phenotypical neurophysiological and development variables provides the most appropriate and comprehensive approach to examining human behavioral endocrinology. This perspective allows enlightening insights into the intertwined causal connections between biology and environment. Moreover, such an approach extends a hand to those who wish to investigate the interaction between hormones and political preferences and outcomes of interest.

Hormones modulate important features of human social interaction, such as feelings, attention, memory, learning, recognition, and communication, which pose endemic political consequences. Understanding the complex nature of these interactions does not constitute an easy task; however, failure to incorporate their import into models of political preferences risks neglecting an influential factor in sculpting such critical political variables as trust, status, and aggression.

This chapter has focused a great deal of discussion around the role of testosterone, particularly in potentiating aggression. Yet, while violent interactions are important, they are far less commonplace in modern Western societies than perhaps in previous times, or in other cultures. However, testosterone, like any hormone's influence, remains context specific. Once we change the nature of competition, say from violence to political control of resources, as occurs in an election perhaps, then the effects may appear the same. The following chapter details just such an examination of the influence of testosterone in the face of a direct political competition.

This brief overview of the influence of hormones in political contexts has presented only a cursory outline of the myriad hormonal forces that help shape and infuse our daily lives. Humans, individually and collectively, would not have survived without the social relationships we have been able to cultivate, maintain, and, in some important cases, dissolve. Equally important, feelings of attachment can offer comfort, sustenance, and even protection against negative health outcomes. Many of the physiological mechanisms that undergird and support these processes derive from human endocrinology, as designed by evolution and shaped by individual human development. By providing a biological backbone to the experiential reinforcement and incentives that drive humans to live, work, love, and kill one another, hormones support a flexible and adaptive structure designed to respond effectively and contingently to the challenges and opportunities continually posed by the ecological environments we inhabit.

References

Abbott, D., B. Keverne, F. Bercovitch, C. Shively, S. Mendoza, W. Saltzman, C. Snowdon, et al. 2003. Are subordinates always stressed? A comparative analysis of rank differences in cortisol levels among primates. *Hormones and Behavior* 43910:67–82.

Adkins-Regan, E. 2009. Under the influence of hormones. *Science* 324 (5931): 1145–46.

Apicella, C. L., A. Dreber, B. Campbell, P. B. Gray, M. Hoffman, and A. C. Little. 2008. Testosterone and financial risk preferences. *Evolution and Human Behavior* 29:384–90.

Auger, A. P., M. J. Tetel, and M. M. McCarthy. 2000. Steroid receptor coactivator-1 (SRC-1) mediates the development of sex-specific brain morphology and behavior. *Proceedings of the National Academy of Sciences USA* 97:7551–55.

Baumgartner, T., M. Heinrichs, A. Vonlanthen, U. Fischbacher, and E. Fehr. 2008. Oxytocin shapes the neural circuitry of trust and trust adaptation in humans. *Neuron* 58 (4): 639–50.

Booth, J., and J. Dabbs. 1993. Testosterone and men's marriages. *Social Forces* 72 (2): 463–77.

Burnham, T., J. Chapman, M. McIntyre, S. Lipson, and P. Ellison. 2003. Men in committed relationships have lower testosterone. *Hormones and Behavior* 44 (2): 119–22.

Caspi, A., and T. Moffitt. 2006. Gene-environment interactions in psychiatry: Joining forces with neuroscience. *Nature Review Neuroscience* 7:583–90.

Creel, S. 2001. Social dominance and stress hormones. *Trends in Ecology and Evolution* 16910:491–97.

Decker, S. 2000. Salivary cortisol and social status among Dominican men. *Hormones and Behavior* 38 (1): 29–38.

Domes, G., M. Henrichs, A. Michel, C. Berger, and S. Herpertz. 2007. Oxytocin improves "mind reading" in humans. *Biological Psychiatry* 61 (6): 731–33.

Eisenberger, N. I., B. M. Way, S. E. Taylor, W. T. Welch, and M. D. Lieberman. 2007. Understanding genetic risk for aggression: Clues from the brain's response to social exclusion. *Biological Psychiatry* 61:1100–1108.

Ellison, P., and P. Gray. 2009. *Endocrinology of social relationships*. Cambridge: Harvard University Press.

Engelmann, M., C. Wotjak, I. Neumann, M. Ludwig, and R. Landgraf. 1996. Behavioral consequences of intracerebral vasopressin and oxytocin: Focus on learning and memory. *Neuroscience and Biobehavioral Reviews* 20 (3): 341–58.

Frazzetto, G., et al. 2007. An early trauma and increased risk for physical aggression during adulthood: The moderating role of MAOA genotype. *PLoS One* 2:e486.

Gray, P., and B. Campbell. 2009. Human male testosterone, pair bonding and fatherhood. In *Endocrinology of social relations*, ed. P. Ellison and P. Gray, 272–93. Cambridge: Harvard University Press.

Gray, P., J. Chapman, T. Burnham, M. McIntyre, S. Lipson, and P. Ellison. 2004. Human pair bonding and testosterone. *Human Nature* 15 (2): 119–31.

Gray, P., S. Kahlenberg, E. Barrett, S. Lipson, and P. Ellison. 2002. Marriage and fatherhood associated with lower testosterone in males. *Evolution and Human Behavior* 23 (2): 193–201.

Heinrichs, M., and G. Domes. 2008. Neuropeptides and social behavior: Effects of vasopressin and oxytocin in human. *Progress in Brain Research* 170:337–50.

Hiller, J. 2005. Gender differences in sexual motivation. *Journal of Men's Health and Gender* 2 (3): 339–45.

Johnson, D.D.P., R. McDermott, E. Barrett, J. Cowden, R. Wrangham, M. McIntyre, and S. Rosen. 2006. Overconfidence in wargames: Experimental evidence on expectations, aggression, gender and testosterone. *Proceedings of the Royal Society of London B-Biological Sciences* 273 (1600): 2513–20.

Kemper, T. 1990. *Social structure and testosterone*. Rutgers, N.J.: Rutgers University Press.

Keverne, E., and J. Curley. 2004. Vasopressin, oxytocin and social behavior. *Current Opinion in Neurobiology* 14 (6): 777–83.

Kirsch, P., C. Esslinger, Q. Chen, D. Mier, S. Lis, S. Siddhanti, H. Gruppe, V. Mattay, B. Gall-hofer, and A. Meyer-Lindenberg. 2005. Oxytocin modulates neural circuitry for social cognition and fear in humans. *Journal of Neuroscience* 25 (49): 11489–93.

Kosfeld, M., M. Heinrichs, P. Zak, U. Fischbacher, and E. Fehr. 2005. Oxytocin increases trust in humans. *Nature* 435:673–76.

Lukaszewski, A. W., and J. Roney. 2009. Estimated hormones predict female's mate prefer-ences for dominant personality traits. *Personality and Individual Differences* 47 (3): 191–96.

Mazur, A., and J. Booth. 1998. Testosterone and dominance in men. *Behavior and Brain Sciences* 21:353–63.

McDermott, R., D. Tingley, J. Cowden, G. Frazzetto, and D. Johnson. 2009. Monoamine oxi-dase A gene (MAOA) predicts behavioral aggression following provocation. *Proceedings of the National Academy of Sciences* 106 (7): 2118–23

McIntyre, M., S. Gangestad, J. Chapman, T. Burnham, M. O'Rourke, and R. Thornhill. 2006. Romantic involvement often reduces male testosterone but not always—moderating ef-fect of extrapair sexual interest. *Journal of Personality and Social Psychology* 91 (4): 42–51.

Meyer-Lindenberg, A., et al. 2006. Neural mechanisms of genetic risk for impulsivity and violence in humans. *Proceedings of the National Academy of Sciences USA* 103:6269–64.

Morris, J., C. Jordan, and M. Breedlove. 2004. Sexual differentiation of the vertebrate nervous system. *Nature Neuroscience* 7:1034–39.

Muller, M., and R. Wrangham. 2004. Dominance, cortisol and stress in wild chimpanzees (*Pan troglodytes schweinfurthii*). *Behavioral Ecology and Sociobiology* 55 (4): 332–40.

Ruzicka, L. 1937. The male sex hormones. *Chemical Reviews* 20 (1): 69–79.

Sapolsky, R. 1983. Individual differences in cortisol secretory patterns in the wild baboons: Role of negative feedback sensitivity. *Endocrinology* 113 (6): 2263–67.

———. 1992. Cortisol concentrations and the social significance of rank instability among wild baboons. *Psychoneuroendocrinology* 17 (6): 701–9.

———. 1996. Why stress is bad for your brain. *Science* 273 (5276): 749–50.

Stark, R., O. Wolf, K. Tabbert, S. Kagerer, M. Zimmerman, P. Kirsch, A. Schienle, and D. Vaitl. 2006. Influence of the stress hormone cortisol on fear conditioning in humans: Evidence for sex differences in the response of the prefrontal cortex. *Neuoroimage* 32 (3): 1290–98.

Wagner, J., M. Flynn, and B. England. 2002. Hormonal responses to competition among male coalitions. *Evolution and Human Behavior* 23 (6): 437–42.

9

TESTOSTERONE AND THE BIOLOGY OF POLITICS

Experimental Evidence from the 2008
Presidential Election

Coren L. Apicella and David A. Cesarini

Although scholars have long recognized the central role politics plays in our lives they have only recently begun to study the biology underlying political behavior. Hormones have been implicated in a number of social behaviors, and behavioral endocrinology, a relatively new subfield of biology, seeks to understand the reciprocal relationship between hormones and behavior. In this chapter, we focus on testosterone (T), a 19-carbon steroid hormone best known for its role in the development and maintenance of masculine features. The intent of this chapter is to provide a basic framework for understanding testosterone action and its influence on behavior in the political domain.

We will also include an illustration of how the field of endocrinology can be used to inform political science by describing a study we conducted during the 2008 U.S. presidential election where we examine changes in testosterone levels of male participants with varying levels of partisan identification as they watched the election unfold. This chapter is meant to go beyond describing the mechanisms and channels by which T affects behavior by also addressing the reciprocal nature between testosterone and behavior. We also attempt to ground our understanding of this relationship within an evolutionary framework. Toward this end, we can ask: Does testosterone affect political behavior? Does political behavior affect testosterone? And if there is a relationship between testosterone and political behavior, what, if any, is the adaptive significance of such a relationship?

A Primer on Testosterone

As we learned in the previous chapter, the endocrine system is a system of cellular communication where information about an individual's physical and social world is transduced in an integrative fashion with the genome, through its regulation of gene expression, and the nervous system. Given the highly integrative and reciprocal manner by which the endocrine system operates, the scientific study of the interrelationships between hormones and behaviors is a complex one.

Testosterone is a steroid hormone in the family of androgens because it has 19 carbons. All steroids begin as a progestin with 21 carbons. Progestins are precursors for androgens, which in turn, are precursors for estrogens, which only have 18 carbons. The significance of this is that women first make androgens that are aromatized into estrogens. Similarly, men aromatize androgens into estrogens but in relatively smaller quantities. Thus it is the relative amounts of hormones synthesized by each sex that vary. The largest amounts of testosterone are produced by the leydig cells of the testes in men and to a lesser extent by the adrenal gland. Women synthesize about one-eighth of the amount of testosterone as men and this is done so in roughly equal quantities in both the ovaries and the adrenal gland. Finally, T displays a diurnal rhythm in both sexes where the highest and most variable amounts are in the morning.

Due to the development of radioimmunoassay, behavioral endocrinological research has flourished in the past 50 years. Before this, measurement of endogenous T was difficult because it circulates in the bloodstream in very minute quantities. Often testosterone will be measured in nanograms (ng, 10^{-9} g) and will be reported as a percentage relative to 100 ml of blood plasma. Typical levels for men are around 10ng/ml. Today it is also possible to measure free T (e.g., the biologically active or "unbound" testosterone) in saliva. This sampling method is often more practical for behavioral researchers than blood plasma measurement as it is less invasive and samples often do not require immediate refrigeration or freezing. While T is secreted into the bloodstream in spurts, so that levels change considerably within minutes, salivary measurement is able to pick up moment to moment changes.

Many behavioral endocrinologists rely on observational (i.e., nonexperimental) studies as an initial approach for documenting relationships between T and behavior. Though such observational studies are a useful first step, interpreting correlations derived from observational data is complicated. One complication arises because of reciprocal causality; T might be causing behavior and behavior might be affecting T levels. Without carefully controlled experiments, in which hormones or social/behavioral contexts are manipulated, it is difficult to establish causality.

Adding to the complexity is the fact that T also has two different processes by which it exerts its influence. That is, it has both organizational and activational effects. In mammals, T exerts organizational effects on the brain early in ontogeny during sexual differentiation and again during puberty. These organizational effects are more permanent and affect male behavior in the long term by programming how individuals respond to current levels of T or what we call the activational or nonpermanent effects of T. Teasing apart organizational from activational effects is difficult because the organizational effect of T may not be related to current levels (Wallen and Hassett 2009). Thus, consideration of exposure during these critical periods of development, as well as current circulating levels of T, is essential to fully understand the role T has in influencing behavior (Apicella et al. 2008).

The last 20 years has witnessed a surge in studies that attempt to identify relationships between circulating T and social behavior. Testosterone has been associated with increased aggression (Archer 2006), sensation seeking (see, e.g., Roberti 2004 for a review), hostility (Hartgens and Kuipers 2004), mate-seeking (Roney, Mahler, and Maestripieri 2003), food acquisition (Worthman and Konner 1987), dominance (Mazur and Booth 1998), and, more recently, financial risk-taking (Apicella et al. 2008).

Testosterone is found to rise in men in response to challenges and winners of competitive interactions often experience a relative increase in T compared to losers (Wingfield et al. 1990; Mazur and Booth 1998). This differential T response has been found for physical competitions, for example, wrestling (Elias 1981) and tennis (Booth et al. 1989) and even noncognitive chance-based competitions such as coin tosses (McCaul, Gladue, and Joppa 1992). Interestingly, fans of sports teams also experience a similar pattern of response though they themselves are not participants in the competition (Kemper 1990). Since political elections are also a form of competition we decided to examine whether this differential response in T also holds in the political domain. The study described below uses the 2008 presidential election as a natural experiment to examine T responses in men to the election outcome.

A Natural Experiment: Testosterone Response Following the 2008 U.S. Presidential Election

Rationale

Males of many primate species devote considerable effort to gaining status and dominance since it often confers a reproductive advantage (Wrangham, "Evolution" 1999). Competitions are important not only in determining status hierarchies within groups but also for establishing dominance over other groups. Hierarchies are often established through direct physical fighting, but in humans status contests are also resolved through complex social and political arrangements, for example, large-scale elections.

It has been suggested that political participation, which at the individual level can be costly, occurs not only out of self-interest but also out of concern for members of one's in-group (Fowler and Kam 2007). Individuals tend to organize their world into cultural groups formed on the basis of kin, shared values, and norms, and at times subtle and even arbitrary symbolic differences (Tajfel et al. 1971; Efferson, Lalive, and Fehr 2008). In-group favoritism, where reward allocation is biased toward members of one's own group, has been demonstrated in a number of domains (Yamagishi, Jin, and Kiyonari 1999), including politics. Not surprisingly, both Republicans and Democrats are more charitable to members of their own party than to members of the opposing party (Fowler and Kam 2007). Despite the potential importance of group membership, little work has been conducted on hormonal responses to group competitions, with the literature on sport teams being an important exception (Bernhardt et al. 1998), which finds that spectator T responses parallel those of participants in sports event, though not always as strongly.

As mentioned earlier, T levels respond differently to winning and losing, with members of losing teams experiencing a relative decline. Here we wanted to examine whether this finding also holds for political competitions. To do this, we examined T responses in men with varying levels of partisan identification by election outcome. We hypothesized that strength of partisan identification would be associated with the T response so that a stronger attachment to the losing party will be correlated with a stronger relative decline in T.

This T response may have an adaptive function. Elevated T levels in winners of competitions may serve to reinforce the successful behavior and encourage further dominance-seeking behaviors (Wingfield et al. 1987; Mazur 1985). Overconfidence, believed to be mediated in part by T, has been postulated as a source of intergroup conflict and war (Johnson et al. 2006). Conversely, the decline in T exhibited after losses may serve to inhibit behaviors that escalate conflict. Therefore, we were also interested in examining whether political wins and losses, along with their associated T responses, affect individuals' levels of investment and commitment to their political group. To do this, we measured generosity toward an individual's political party using a standard dictator game (Forsythe et al. 1994), both before and after the election. Participants were given five dollars (USD), of which any amount could be anonymously donated to their political party. Thus supporting one's political ingroup requires individuals to incur a small pecuniary cost and can be thought of as a measure of both support and affirming commitment (Fowler and Kam 2007). We hypothesized that loss should be associated with a relative decline in group support.

Methods

Twenty-four male participants were recruited via e-mail lists of political organizations or clubs at colleges in the greater Boston area. The sample included men between the ages of 18 and 32 (mean 22.70, S.D. 4.00) who were not taking psychotropic or hormonal medication. Based on self-report, the sample was 50% White, 25% Asian, 21% Hispanic, and 4% Other. Of the nine Republicans who participated, four were strong Republicans, two were moderate Republicans, and three were weak Republicans. Of the thirteen Democrats, five self-identified as strong Democrats, seven as moderate, and one as weak. Two subjects reported being politically Independent. The study was approved by the Harvard University's Committee on the Use of Human Subjects in Research. Participation was anonymous and all subjects gave informed consent to participate.

Subjects were instructed to arrive at 6:45 p.m. to a cinema on the Harvard campus rented solely for the purpose of the study. Subjects were provided with a t-shirt for their candidate and other political paraphernalia. The cinema was decorated with American flags, red and blue balloons, and streamers. On the cinema screen, we projected the election coverage of CNN. Subjects remained at the study site throughout the evening. Three subjects, however, were recruited from a nearby campus common area that was also broadcasting CNN's election coverage. These subjects were also given political paraphernalia in support of their candidate, were in the presence of a research assistant, and did not differ systematically from the primary sample in their T levels and pattern of change.

Three unstimulated saliva samples via passive drool were provided throughout the course of the evening for salivary T measurement. Upon arrival, the first sample was collected from participants. Participants were asked to spit through a straw into a small polystyrene tube. Subjects also filled out a short questionnaire to gauge political preferences. Basic demographic information was also collected. Finally, subjects were given an envelope containing five one-dollar bills, of which they could anonymously donate any share to the party of their preferred candidate. Subjects were required to submit an envelope to the experimenters even if they decided not to make a donation.

A second saliva sample was provided at 8:40 p.m., just as CNN projected an Obama win in Pennsylvania. Several crucial swing states, including Colorado, Indiana, Florida, Missouri, North Carolina, Ohio, and Virginia, had not yet been called. A third saliva sample was collected at 11:15 p.m., approximately fifteen minutes after CNN, and all other major networks, called the election to Obama. At this point, a second envelope with five one-dollar bills was distributed and subjects could make an anonymous donation to their party of up to five dollars.

Results

Each subject reported the strength of their partisan identification on a seven-point scale with categories Strong Democrat (assigned the value –3) Moderate Democrat (–2), Weak Democrat (–1), Independents (0) and so on up to Strong Republicans (3). Summary statistics are reported in table 9.1, disaggregated by party affiliation.

TABLE 9.1. Summary statistics. Testosterone is measured in pg/ml from saliva samples obtained at approximately 7.00 pm (Testosterone 1), 8.30 (Testosterone 2) and 11.00 (Testosterone 3). Donations were solicited at approximately 7pm (Donation Amount 1) and 11 pm (Donation Amount 2). The "Total" column includes two subjects who reported being politically independent.

	Democrats (n=13)		Republicans (n=9)		Total (n=24)	
	Mean	S.D.	Mean	S.D.	Mean	S.D.
Testosterone 1	42.15	16.79	53.28	20.81	49.33	21.62
Testosterone 2	33.28	10.28	37.07	20.69	36.38	20.20
Testosterone 3	39.16	14.43	35.02	11.28	36.21	13.39
Donation 1 (USD)	1.92	2.18	2.89	2.52	2.32	2.32
Donation 2 (USD)	1.46	2.30	.56	1.67	1.09	2.07
Age (in years)	23.07	3.75	21.69	3.37	22.78	4.00
Race (1 if white)	.46	.52	.56	.53	0.50	0.51

Since the data were collected over a period of 4 hours, there was an average decline of T of 13.12 pg/mL over the course of the evening (paired t-test; two-sided, t = 2.62, p = 0.015, two-sided, n = 24). This decline is consistent with the natural diurnal pattern of T (Dai et al. 1981). There was also a decline in the average donation amount, from $2.13 on average before the election to $1.00 after the election result. This decline was statistically significant (paired t-test; t = 2.45, p = 0.022, two-sided, n = 24) and discernible in both Democrats and Republicans. The differences between Republicans and Democrats in donations and testosterone levels at arrival were not significant at the 5% level and we are hence reluctant to attach too much significance to them.

Our primary hypothesis was that the T response to the electoral outcome would be a function of the strength of partisan identification. We defined the T response as the difference between T measured at the beginning of the evening, before any results had been announced, and the end of the evening, shortly after Wolf Blitzer announced on CNN that Barack Obama had won the election.

Regressing the T response on partisan identification, the coefficient on partisan identification is quantitatively large and statistically significant (linear regression; β = -4.53, p = 0.045, two-sided, n = 24). This coefficient suggests that moving one integer up the partisan scale, for example going from being a Weak Democrat to a Moderate Democrat, is associated with experiencing a 4.53 pg/mL smaller T decline, on average, during the course of the evening. The relationship retains significance if the two Independent observations are not included (linear regression; β = -4.17, p = 0.027, two-sided, n = 22). The correlation between the T response and partisan identification is illustrated graphically in the first panel of figure 9.1.

A second hypothesis concerned the effect of the electoral outcome on the willingness to donate to one's in-group. We find some evidence in support of the proposition that defeat depresses the willingness to donate to one's in-group. Regressing the difference in donation on partisan identification, the coefficient on partisan identification is just shy of significant (linear regression; β = −.41, p = 0.055, two-sided, n = 22). This result excludes the two Independents, who were both offered the opportunity to donate money to the party of either candidate but declined to do so. Including the Independents does not appreciably change the result (linear regression; β = -0.40, p = 0.054, two-sided, n = 24). Finally, exploratory analyses reveal that the change in testosterone is associated with the change in donations within partisans (linear regression; β = 4.71, p = 0.012, two-sided, n = 22), but the statistical

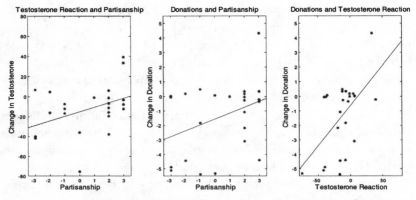

FIGURE 9.1. The left panel is a scatterplot of the change in testosterone pg/mL (third sample minus first sample) against the partisan identification, where −3 is Strong Democrat, −2 is Moderate Democrat, −1 is Weak Democrat, 0 is Independent, and so on up to 3 for Strong Republicans. The middle panel is a scatterplot of the change in donation (donation after the Democratic win minus the donation before the Democratic victory) against partisan identification. The unit is $USD. For expositional clarity (several points in the original dataset were overlapping) the donation change has been jittered. The right-hand panel plots the testosterone change against the donation change. A blue star denotes a Democratic individual, a red star denotes a Republican individual, and a black star denotes an Independent individual.

significance vanishes when the Independents are included (linear regression; $\beta = 3.70$, $p = 0.105$, two-sided, $n = 24$).

Conclusions

Recent research in political science has sought to uncover specific biological substrates that underlie variation in political traits including ideology and behavior. Studies of twins have shown that much individual variation in both political attitudes and behaviors can ultimately be traced to genes (Fowler, Baker, and Dawes 2008; Martin et al. 1986; Alford, Funk, and Hibbing 2005). Scholars have also taken tentative steps toward understanding how specific genes, often interacting with the environment, influence complex traits such as voting (Fowler and Dawes 2008) and strength of partisanship (Hatemi et al. 2008). Other lines of work ask how neuroscience can inform political science (McDermott 2004) and how individual differences in physiological reactions to fearful stimuli can predict political views (Oxley et al. 2008). This study was meant to be used as an example of how the field of behavioral endocrinology can be used to understand political behavior.

The results reported here provide a demonstration of a differential hormonal reaction in partisan supporters of an election. The stronger a subject was attached to the party of the losing candidate, the greater his relative testosterone decline. The relative decline in testosterone in losers may serve to appropriately calibrate, or adjust, confidence to realistic levels and promote withdrawal behavior from contests that are likely to result in further harm, while an increase in testosterone in winners may prime the winner for subsequent competition and further status elevation, possibly through its effects on confidence (Wrangham, "Is military incompetence" 1999; Johnson 2004). In this way, testosterone serves as a biological reinforcer of behavior (Wingfield et al. 1987; Mazur 1985). Consistent with this hypothesis, Mehta and Josephs (2006) reported that following defeat, losers who experienced an increase in testosterone were more likely to enter anew into competition compared to losers who did not experience such an increase.

In line with the hypothesis that decreased testosterone may result in the withdrawal of investment we found that partisan identification was associated with a decline in generosity, as measured by anonymous donations made before and after the electoral outcome was announced. In addition, within partisan subjects, the decline in generosity was predicted by the decline in testosterone. These results are not inconsistent with conventional wisdom that higher testosterone overall should be associated with less prosociality and decreased investment (Harris et al. 1996), as there is some evidence of the testosterone response being correlated with change in donations. Here we did not, however, find a relationship between overall testosterone levels and donation amount.

Although wide-scale elections are evolutionarily novel, coalition building and dominance seeking likely played a crucial role in human evolution. Men are concerned with gaining dominance as the spoils of increased status often include increased resources and access to mates (Wrangham, "Is military incompetence" 1999; Chagnon 1968). While most animals compete in dyads, humans frequently compete in groups. In addition, dominance contests in animals are mostly physical, while human contests are often socially determined (Boehm 1999).

In light of the small sample size, it is important to be modest about these findings. Yet many studies that have examined changes in testosterone by competition outcome have used comparable samples sizes (van Anders 2007). We also emphasize that these results were obtained under far from ideal conditions. It is likely that the testosterone response is muted when a defeat or victory is expected. The implied probability of an Obama win, as inferred from the prices on the online betting markets, was approximately 90% the day before the election. This figure probably masks much heterogeneity in beliefs, but suggests that an Obama victory was widely anticipated though not certain. The fact that we still find a large, but imprecisely estimated, differential testosterone response suggests the election was deemed to be of sufficient significance to generate a hormonal reaction.

We suggest that future work examine hormonal changes in the context of political competitions using larger and more diverse samples. In summary, we report novel data suggesting that the "winner-loser effect" also holds true in the political arena. We suggest that findings such as these, if successfully incorporated into models of political behavior, might ultimately lead to a more comprehensive political science.

Note

Samples were frozen by midnight and stored at $-20°C$. Samples were packed in dry ice and shipped via FedEx overnight delivery to Salimetrics of State College, Pennsylvania. Samples were assayed for salivary T in duplicate using a highly sensitive enzyme immunoassay (Cat. No. 1-2402, Salimetrics LLC, State College). The test used 25 μl of saliva per determination, has a lower limit of sensitivity of 1.0 pg/mL, standard curve range from 6.1 pg/mL to 600 pg/mL, an average intra-assay coefficient of variation of 4.6% and an average inter-assay coefficient of variation of 8.25%. Method accuracy determined by spike recovery averaged 104.4% and linearity determined by serial dilution averaged 99.9%.

References

Alford, J. R., C. L. Funk, and J. R. Hibbing. 2005. Are political orientations genetically transmitted? *American Political Science Review* 99 (2): 153–67.

Apicella, C. L., A. Dreber, B. Campbell, P. B. Gray, M. Hoffman, and A. C. Little. 2008. Testosterone and financial risk preferences. *Evolution and Human Behavior* 29:384–90.

Archer, J. 2006. Testosterone and human aggression: An evaluation of the challenge hypothesis. *Neuroscience and Biobehavioral Review* 30:319–45.

Bernhardt, P. C., J. M. Dabbs Jr., J. A. Fielden, and C. D. Lutter. 1998. Testosterone changes during vicarious experiences of winning and losing among fans at sporting events. *Physiological Behavior* 65:59–62.

Boehm, C. 1999. *Hierarchy in the forest: The evolution of egalitarian behavior.* Cambridge: Harvard University Press.

Booth, A., G. Shelley, A. Mazur, G. Tharp, and R. Kittock. 1989. Testosterone and winning and losing in human competition. *Hormones and Behavior* 23:556–71.

Chagnon, N. A. 1968. *Yanomamo, the fierce people.* New York: Rinehart and Winston.

Dai, W., L. Kuller, R. LaPorte, J. Gutai, L. Falma, and A. Gagguela. 1981. Epidemiology of plasma T levels in middle-age men. *American Journal of Epidemiology* 114:804–16.

Efferson, C., R. Lalive, and E. Fehr. 2008. The coevolution of cultural groups and in-group favoritism. *Science* 321:1844–49.

Elias, M. 1981. Serum cortisol, testosterone, and testosterone-binding globulin responses to competitive fighting in human males. *Aggressive Behavior* 7:215–24.

Forsythe, R., J. L. Horowitz, N. E. Savin, and M. Sefton. 1994. Fairness in simple bargaining experiments. *Games and Economic Behavior* 6:347–69.

Fowler, J. H., L. A. Baker, and C. T. Dawes. 2008. Genetic variation in political participation. *American Political Science Review* 102:233–48.

Fowler, J. H., and C. T. Dawes. 2008. Two genes predict voter turnout. *Journal of Politics* 70 (3): 579–94.

Fowler, J. H., and C. D. Kam. 2007. Beyond the self: Altruism, social identity, and political participation. *Journal of Politics* 69:811–25.

Harris, J. A., J. P. Rushton, E. Hampson, and D. N. Jackson. 1996. Salivary testosterone and self-report aggressive and pro-social personality characteristics in men and women. *Aggressive Behavior* 22:321–31.

Hartgens, F., and H. Kuipers. 2004. Effects of androgenic-anabolic steroids in athletes. *Sports Medicine* 34: 513–54.

Hatemi, P. K., J. R. Alford, J. R. Hibbing, N. G. Martin, and L. Eaves. 2008. Is there a "party" in your genes? *Political Research Quarterly*: doi:10.1177/1065912908327606.

Johnson, D. 2004. *Overconfidence and war*. Cambridge: Harvard University Press.

Johnson, D.D.P., R. McDermott, E. S. Barrett, J. Cowden, R. Wrangham, M. H. McIntyre, and S. P. Rosen. 2006. Overconfidence in wargames: Experimental evidence on expectations, aggression, gender and testosterone. *Proceedings of the Royal Society of London B-Biological Sciences* 273 (1600): 2513–20.

Kemper, T. D. 1990. *Social structure and testosterone*. New Brunswick, N.J.: Rutgers University Press.

Martin, N. G., L. J. Eaves, A. C. Heath, R. Jardine, L. M. Feingold, and H. J. Eysenck. 1986. Transmission of social attitudes. *Proceedings of the National Academy of Sciences* 83:4364–68.

Mazur, A. 1985. A biosocial model of status in face-to-face primate groups. *Social Forces* 64:377–402.

Mazur, A., and A. Booth. 1998. Testosterone and dominance in men. *Behavior and Brain Sciences* 21:353–63.

McCaul, K. D., B. A. Gladue, and M. Joppa. 1992. Winning, losing, mood, and testosterone. *Hormones and Behavior* 26:486–504.

McDermott, R. 2004. The feeling of rationality: The meaning of neuroscientific advances for political science. *Perspectives on Politics* 2:691–706.

Mehta, P. H., and R. A. Josephs. 2006. Testosterone change after losing predicts the decision to compete again. *Hormones and Behavior* 50:684–92.

Oxley, D. R., K. B. Smith, M. W. Hibbing, J. L. Miller, J. R. Alford, P. K. Hatemi, and J. R. Hibbing. 2008. Political attitudes vary with physiological traits. *Science* 321 (5896): 1667–70.

Roberti, J. W. 2004. A review of behavioral and biological correlates of sensation seeking. *Journal of Research in Personality* 38:256–79.

Roney, J. R., S. V. Mahler, and D. Maestripieri. 2003. Behavioral and hormonal responses of men to brief interactions with women. *Evolution and Human Behavior* 24:365–75.

Tajfel, H., M. G. Billig, R. P. Bundy, and C. Flament. 1971. Social categorization and intergroup behavior. *European Journal of Social Psychology* 1:149–78.

Wallen, K., and J. Hassett. 2009. Neuroendocrine mechanisms underlying social relationships. In *Endocrinology of social relationships*, ed. P. T. Ellison and P. B. Gray, 32–54. Cambridge: Harvard University Press.

Wingfield, J. C., G. F. Ball, A. M. Dufty Jr., R. E. Hegner, and M. Ramenofsky. 1987. Testosterone and aggression in birds. *American Scientist* 75:602–8.

Wingfield, J. C., R. E. Hegner. A. M. Dufty Jr., and G. F. Ball. 1990. The "Challenge Hypothesis": Theoretical implications for patterns of testosterone secretion, mating systems, and breeding strategies. *American Nature* 136:829–46.

Worthman, C. M., and M. J. Konner. 1987. Testosterone levels change with subsistence hunting effort in !Kung San men. *Psychoneuroendocrinology* 12:449–58.

Wrangham, R. 1999. Is military incompetence adaptive? *Evolution and Human Behavior* 20:3–17.

———. 1999. Evolution of coalitionary killing. *Yearbook of Physical Anthropology* 42:1–30.

Yamagishi, T., N. Jin, and T. Kiyonari. 1999. Bounded generalized reciprocity: In-group boasting and in-group favoritism. *Advances in Group Processes* 16:161–97.

10

FROM SCAN TO NEUROPOLITICS

Darren Schreiber

All political behavior is reflected in the brain, yet the brain has been treated largely as a black box by political science because of the previous limitations on our ability to make useful inferences about it. Despite being a very young field, social cognitive and affective neuroscience (SCAN) has already converged on a set of consistent results that have been verified though a variety of methods. Neuropolitics can advance the agenda of political science by founding our theories in modern notions of human nature that are in harmony with our sibling disciplines and advance the agenda of neuroscience by providing the context that drove the evolution of the human brain.

A common misconception about research into the neural correlates of social phenomena is that it entails the presumption of a form of biological determinism. This seems to stem from a fear that neuroimaging might either reveal the soul to be an illusion or firmly resolve a nature/nurture debate in favor of nature (Wolfe 1996). Unless one assumes a rather unusual version of dualism, the presumption is that all mental activity is at least reflected in the brain. Thus, one can give a central role to individual agency or to the influence of culture and context, while still considering how those would alter and be altered by the structure and function of the brain.

A study a few years ago asked people who were experts in either classical ballet or the Brazilian martial art of capoeira and nonexperts to view video clips of people performing similar moves from either style (Calvo-Merino et al. 2005). People who had developed expertise in a style of movement had higher levels of activity in brain regions associated with movement when they viewed clips of their own style than when viewing the other style. The most logical inference from this experiment is not that some people are born to be ballet dancers and some are born to be capoeira dancers because their brains differ; rather it is that learning these movement styles alters the function of the brain.

This inference is further supported by a study where a group of students was taught to juggle and then asked to practice each day for three months, then asked not to juggle for another three months (Draganski et al. 2004). Structural brain images were generated for the students before training, after the practice period, and after the interval with no practice. The neocortex in portions of the mid-temporal area increased in size as subjects learned to juggle and then atrophied slightly as they ceased practice. As these two examples show, engaging in the world alters the function and structure of the brain. Our biology (as reflected in our brains) responds to our environment.

Demonstrating the effect of individual agency on the brain is far more complex experimentally (see, e.g., Maye et al. 2007), but again, if one believes that brain activity is correlated with mental life, then neuroimaging may reflect the consequences or even components of individual agency. Data showing brain activity in regions known to be involved in auditory perception do not tell us whether the person is intentionally imagining a voice, actually hearing a voice, or having an hallucination of a voice (see Sommer et al. 2008). In this manner, neuroimaging data are like all other data and can constrain our explanations, but we should neither fear nor hope that neuroimaging data will resolve metaphysical debates.

We should also be careful about the kind of inferences we expect imaging data to support. Merely showing that a part of the brain has heightened activity during a task does not demonstrate that this brain region is a "module" for that task or that the task is "localized" in that region (van Eijsden et al. 2009). Having a brain region respond to the sound of a piano does not tell us that this is the "piano" region of the brain. While the brain may exhibit specialization or task localization under some circumstances, it is also highly integrated and able to adapt to utilize other resources when important functions are disrupted. A sighted subject who is blindfolded for five days will learn to read Braille using canonically visual regions of the brain, but when the blindfold is removed, it takes less than 24 hours for the Braille reading to be diverted to another part of the brain (Merabet et al. 2008). Attempts to describe the contribution of a brain region to mental function must be understood in this context and must not be misconstrued as neophrenology.

Neuroimaging may provide us evidence that the same region of the brain that enables us to feel pleasure from the spiritual ecstasy of silent prayer (Schjodt et al. 2008) is involved when we punish people who violate social norms (de Quervain et al. 2004) or when we desire a sports car (Erk et al. 2002). While this data may allow us to make a number of interesting inferences about the pleasurable nature of each of these activities, it does not tell us about the existence of God, the value of a particular social norm, or true quality of the car. Taking the results of neuroscience seriously does not require us to reject free will (Mele 2009) and may even necessitate the rejection of a merely reductionist project (Mitchell 2009). The hard questions of political science will remain the hard questions as neuropolitics develops. However, our field of potential answers will likely be narrowed a bit by the data that this approach generates.

Why Neuropolitics?

With an explosive amount of research taking place in SCAN, what can political science gain that will help to refine our theories? Political science has long been built on theories about the nature of social cognition and affect, but the disconnect between our theories and the results obtained by SCAN is problematic. Political science is built on founding assumptions about how individuals process their world and make choices in it.

Debates are currently raging about the relevance of neurophilosophy (Churchland 2007), neuroeconomics (Clithero, Tankersley, and Huettel 2008), and neurolaw (Rosen 2007) to each of their nonneuro counterparts. Each of these fields, like political science, has longstanding traditions about the appropriate modes of inquiry, but also has assumptions and provisional answers that the fields hold sacrosanct. Regardless of whether data from neuroimaging confirm, refute, or are ambiguous about these prior beliefs, that data constrain the set of explanations we are able to give.

While it might still be reasonable to treat the mind as a black box, it is certainly no longer reasonable to treat the brain that way. The many metaanalyses cited in this chapter demonstrate that even in the very early years of SCAN we have sets of results that appear to be at least somewhat robust, if not precise or conclusive. Traditions that dichotomized affect and cognition have been consistently undermined, whereas traditions that claimed a distinctly social character for interpersonal interactions (as opposed to interactions with objects) have been consistently supported.

When I attended the very first meeting of the SCAN movement at the start of the millennium, I noted the predominance of gray hair and the domain specificity of the knowledge of the participants. These older luminaries in their disciplines were like the scattered people after Babel. The economists needed to have the neuroscience explained. And the primatologists did not know what an ultimatum game was.

As the decade closed and I attended later incarnations of the SCAN meetings, I was struck by the fact that most of the attendees were well under 30 and cross-trained in a variety of disciplines, often under the tutelage of the same luminaries I had met at the first meeting. The neuroeconomists knew their neuroanatomy, were collaborating on primate experiments, and could easily converse with other neuro-scholars trained in a mash of psychology, molecular biology, neuroscience, ethology, philosophy, and law. *New York Times* columnist David Brooks (2009) shared my impression of this community and noted that a search for "social cognitive neuroscience" on Google in 2001 yielded 53 hits, whereas a search now yields 1.5 million more.

The common set of questions discussed by this agglomeration of scholars sits at the heart of political science. Is there a human nature and what is it? How do we value our choices and why do we decide the way we do? How do our biology and our experience interact? And how do our experiences shape our biology?

Dominant paradigms in political science such as rational-choice theory and behaviorism do a poor job at integrating with the insights being developed at the nexus where SCAN resides. A series of experiments has consistently shown that people will choose to route a train away from a track where it would have killed six people and thus sacrifice the one person sitting on the track the train is switched to. However, subjects are typically unwilling to push a person off a bridge if that would stop an out-of-control trolley and save the six people down the track (Greene et al. 2001). Rational-choice theory does not do good job at accounting for this discrepancy, or for the facts that lesions to the medial prefrontal cortex increase (Koenigs et al. 2007) and that cognitive task load decreases (Greene et al. 2008) the likelihood of the utilitarian judgment in the trolley/train dilemma. Similarly behaviorism is at a loss when identical gambling patterns arise from the neurologically distinct mental processes of Republicans and Democrats (Schreiber et al. 2009).

There are a variety of approaches to neuropolitics (Lieberman, Schreiber, and Ochsner 2003), ranging from bringing political science into the scanner (e.g., replicating political tasks like attitudinal response or economic games), bringing results from the scanner to political science methods (e.g., testing implications using survey experiments), or re-evaluating scanning work in light of political science theories (e.g., using classic psychological tasks and their neurocorrelates to distinguish party members). I also contend that many SCAN researchers are running experiments that could easily become relevant to central questions of political science with the addition of only a few variables that would likely clarify the experimental results.

Neuropolitics is an opportunity for political science to connect with a broader conversation that is taking place across a wide range of disciplines about human nature. The amazing variety of methods reflected in SCAN are already bearing fruit and yielding results that parallel very old lines of argument (e.g., moral iniquity, utilitarianism vs. deontology, theory of moral sentiments) that have swayed political discourse. There are low-cost routes for political scientists to engage in this conversation and generate theories that are more commensurable with work beyond our own field. But first, it is important to have a basic understanding of how SCAN makes its claims.

SCAN's Methods

One of the challenges that neuropolitics faces as a subfield is that many of the tools employed by SCAN are unfamiliar to political scientists. This unfamiliarity leads us to then be poor consumers of the results, overreacting to methodological controversies (e.g., Vul et al. 2009) or believing spurious results merely because there is a pretty brain picture attached (McCabe and Castel 2008). This section provides a brief overview of the variety of methods that SCAN researchers have been employing, providing relevant examples for each of the methods. I also provide a more detailed discussion of the most commonly used method, functional magnetic resonance imaging (fMRI).

The study of the alterations to the structure of the brain that accompany learning juggling was done with structural magnetic resonance imaging (MRI). In MRI a subject is placed in the center of a large superconducting magnetic field and pulsed with a sequence of radio waves that alter the alignment of the subatomic particles that comprise the subject's brain and body. The resonance of this signal varies widely depending on the composition of the matter, thus allowing the differentiation of skull from soft tissue, but also allowing for more fine-grained distinctions among the grey matter (neural cell bodies and other structures) and white matter (sheathed nerve fibers). The technique to image the structure of the brain with MRI is essentially the same as imaging a person's knee (although pulse sequences will vary). The insight in the juggling study, however, relied upon the use of a statistical technique known as voxel-based morphometry (VBM), which detects subtle changes in the composition and thickness of brain regions (Draganski et al. 2004).

Another technique for investigating the structural differences among people's brains is diffusion tensor imaging (DTI). DTI is another creative use of the MRI signal, this time to investigate the diffusion of water molecules in the brain. Because water will more easily diffuse within a neuron rather than across the cellular membrane, we can use DTI to generate maps of neural connections within a living, healthy person. One recent DTI study demonstrated that lower levels of neural connectivity within Broca's area (a brain region involved in language processing) in healthy subjects corresponded to poorer abilities at learning a new grammar (Floel et al. 2009). Another DTI study recently showed that learning to juggle also alters the white matter in the brain that facilitates neural connections (Scholz et al. 2009).

I will discuss functional MRI (fMRI) in more depth at the end of this section, but it relies on roughly the same technology that underpins structural MRI. When an fMRI study is conducted, a high-resolution structural MRI image is first acquired of the subject so that the functional data may be overlaid upon it. The essential difference with fMRI is that a sequence of images is acquired over a period of time (a typical scanning sequence lasts 5–10 minutes), which allows inferences about the change in the flow of blood through the brain.

Positron emission tomography (PET) scanning also investigates the flow of blood in the brain to make inferences about mental processes. In PET imaging, the subject is injected with radioactive sugar water,[1] which is metabolized by neural tissue. Since the radioactive molecule has a short half-life, it will quickly decay and emit an antimatter particle (a positron). When the positron collides with an electron (its matter counterpart), they annihilate each other and produce photons that are picked up by the detector surrounding the person's head. PET scanning is useful because the data it generates enable far more direct inferences about metabolic processes in the brain and provide an absolute metric (whereas the value of the MRI signal has no absolute baseline and is only meaningful in relative changes). While fMRI has exploded in use, PET (despite the radiation risks) has been particularly valuable in the investigation of phenomena like the resting state networks that will be discussed later in this chapter (e.g., Raichle et al. 2001).

Another pair of imaging techniques that provide far greater temporal resolution, but sacrifice on spatial resolution, is electroencephalography (EEG) and magnetoencephalography (MEG). In EEG a web of electrodes is placed on the participant's scalp and millisecond scale readings are taken of the electrical activity at each node. With a larger number of nodes, one can make increasingly accurate inferences about the spatial location of the origin of the electrical activity in neural tissue. MEG uses a series of superconducting quantum interference devices (SQUIDs) to similarly measure the changes in electrical signals in the brain, but provide a much better spatial resolution, while preserving the millisecond temporal resolution of EEG. A study of conflict processing in liberals and conservatives relied upon EEG to make inferences about how potential differences in basic cognitive processing might be associated with political ideology (Amodio et al. 2007).

One of the oldest and yet most important tools for studying brain function has been the study of people with unhealthy brains, typically known as lesion studies. The most famous lesion patient is Phineas Gage who had a metal rod shoot through the frontal lobe of his brain in 1848 as the result of an explosion while he was tamping down gunpowder (Sanfey, Hastie et al. 2003). Gage miraculously survived the accident, but many of the social aspects of his personality were drastically altered. Antonio Damasio and Hanna Damasio pioneered the more systematic study of lesions with a database mapping out lesions in a large number of patients who could then be included in experiments to see what cognitive deficits pertained to particular focal brain lesions (see Glascher et al. 2009; Damasio and Damasio 1989). The study of autism patients in particular has been illuminating in understanding the social nature of the brain because some people with autism are so high functioning in other forms of intelligence but have tremendous difficulty navigating the social world (Frith and Frith 1999). The blindfolded Braille readers study described above used the transcranial magnetic stimulation (TMS) technique of electromagnetic pulses that briefly disrupt neural function in order to verify when the visual areas of the brain were being recruited for reading Braille (Merabet et al. 2008). TMS is a relatively noninvasive way of conducting lesion studies in healthy subjects.

The final approach involves the study of animals to develop insight into political intelligence (e.g., chapter 2 in this volume). For instance, by designing experiments that provide parallel tasks to both human infants and chimpanzees, researchers have looked at the contrasts between social and technical intelligence (Herrmann et al. 2007), the tendency toward altruistic acts (Warneken and Tomasello 2009), and a wide range of other cognitive tasks (Premack 2007). By comparing the neuroanatomical differences and the cognitive differences between humans and chimpanzees we can also make inferences about the linkages between structure and function (Premack 2007).

While each of the methods briefly described above are important for the particular kinds of insights they can facilitate about social and political mental processes, the real explosion in SCAN has been propelled by fMRI (Friston 2009). The reason for fMRI's transformation of neuroscientific research is that it filled a gap in their toolkit.[2] Functional MRI allows for studies with a temporal resolution between fractions of a second and hours, a spatial resolution between millimeters and the full size of the brain, and a very small level of invasiveness. The technique takes advantage of the fact that oxygenated and deoxygenated hemoglobin have different magnetic properties and generates a blood oxygen level dependent (BOLD) MRI signal that is believed to correspond to changes in neural activity.[3]

While the brain is constantly active, an increase in cognitive effort requiring specific mental processes increases neural activity in the regions important for those mental processes. Since the metabolic rate of the neurons supporting that increased activity goes up, additional oxygenated blood flows into the region to support the additional workload. That shift in the ratio of oxygenated to deoxygenated hemoglobin alters the BOLD MRI signal slightly (typically on the order of a fraction of a percent) and those slight changes are then used to make inferences about the change in neural activity. While there are an incredible number of interactions and variables between the neural activity and the measurement of the BOLD signal, the relationship between the two is essentially linear, which is what allows fMRI to function as well as it has.

While experimenters have crafted far more ingenious paradigms for exploiting the properties of the BOLD signal, the two basic designs are the block and event-related methods. In the block design, a stimulus (e.g., a photo) is provided for an extended period of time (e.g., 20 seconds) with the hope that this will provoke a more easily detectable sustained response to the stimulus. If a tone is played for a period and then ceases, we might expect to observe that brain areas involved in the perception of the one will be very active during the tone and then cease activity when the tone stops. Two central limitations of the block design are the limited number of repeated stimuli one can fit into a scanning session and the tendency of the brain to habituate quickly to a stimulus. In the event-related design, the analysis of the BOLD is timed to an event such as the subject pressing a button in response to a task. Initially, block designs were more common, but as statistical methods and experimental results have accumulated, the event-related design has become the more prevalent. An example of a more interesting experimental design involved having subjects merely watch a video clip; the experiments then looked for common patterns of brain activity as subjects received the same stimulus (Hasson et al. 2004).

During a typical fMRI scanning session, data is repeatedly acquired at intervals that typically range from a second to four seconds (constrained by a number of tradeoffs between temporal and spatial resolution) with about 50,000 voxels (cubic millimeter measurements) collected during each acquisition. This generates gigabytes of data per participant that is subjected to noise from head movement, breathing, signal drift over time, and a wide range of other artifacts. Further complicating the analysis of this 4D data is that each of the 50,000 time series is not independent, but probably correlates with each other in complicated ways.

Preprocessing fMRI data entails registering the data to the structural image collected for that participant and then warping that participant's brain onto a common reference brain so that data from a number of participants can be compared. Algorithms are used to identify portions of the data that are not brain so that they can be removed from the statistical analysis. And one must compensate for standard problems like the flow of air into the sinus cavities that causes artifacts in the magnetic signal. Data is typically smoothed, filtered, and normalized to compensate for known issues with the fMRI signal, such as its lack of a natural baseline.

After the preprocessing stages, the data is often analyzed with general linear model applied, treating each voxel of the brain as an independent time series. The pattern of experimental stimuli is used as the basis for the model and each voxel is analyzed for how well its time series fits a prediction based upon the timing of the onset of each instance of the stimulus and knowledge of the typical hemodynamic response function that is reflected in the BOLD fMRI signal. If an individual participant is scanned multiple times, the data analysis from each of the runs is statistically aggregated into a 3D image summarizing the level of fit of the model at each voxel in the brain. Typically, a group-level result is generated by using the analyses of the individual participants and fitting a hierarchical model that either identifies the common patterns of brain activity in the group or identifies contrasts between groups.

There are a wide variety of ways of analyzing fMRI data and presenting the results, so the consumer of such results must take care to actually note what the exact data display is representing. Often, the result is a map of the fit of the model at each voxel in the brain in terms of z-scores. Positive z-scores (typically indicating higher neural activity during the task condition) are conventionally marked with colors in the hotter range of the color spectrum (e.g., yellow, orange, red) while negative z-scores (often either neural activity below a resting baseline or below a control condition) are colored with cooler colors. In order to focus attention on only the brain regions that are most likely to be actually responding to the task, a variety of approaches are taken to thresholding the data. Since a whole brain scan typically involves tens of thousands of active voxels, researchers will often set a number of contiguous voxels that must have z-scores above a certain value in order for a cluster of activations to be considered significant, or they will use assumptions from Gaussian random field theory to identify clusters that are most likely to be truly responding to the task based upon the spatial extent and the intensity of response to the stimulus, or they will set a false discovery rate (the expected proportion of false positives among voxels above a threshold).

It is important to emphasize that images typically displayed in articles using fMRI are not of a single subject; rather, they represent the responsiveness of the brains of a group of subjects warped into a common space. The images also do not represent the intensity of the BOLD fMRI signal, since that signal has an arbitrary value. Rather, the activity level indicated in the images is usually a thresholded map of the z-score for the model at each particular voxel, with only statistically significant voxels colored in.

Often the z-scores are represented on a slice through the brain. Axial slices view the brain as if looking down on a person's head; sagittal slices view the brain from the side of a person's head; and coronal slices render the image as if looking face to face. Because neuroimaging developed as an interdisciplinary field merging varying intuitions, it is important to note that occasionally the images are flipped so that left is on the right and right is on the left. The uneven use of this radiological convention combined with the fact that the "Analyze" data format did not specify the orientation of the image caused frequent problems in the past, but these have been resolved with the adoption of the Neuroimaging Informatics Technology Initiative (NIfTI) format.

In addition to representing data on slices, occasionally volume rendering or surface rendering is used. To help with visualization of the location of the activation, sometimes an entire head is represented with wedges removed and the data displayed on the remaining interior spaces. Surface rendering is used when the relevant activity is in the neocortex. The wrinkles of the neocortex allow the skull to enclose a much larger surface area of grey matter than it otherwise would be able to contain. The compression of this large surface yields a series of gyri (hills) and sulci (valleys) that can be flattened out in order to visualize activity patterns that might be difficult to notice when looking only at a volumetric rendering. In these images, the gyri are typically colored lighter and the sulci are colored darker.

Another common approach to analyzing fMRI data is the use of a set of regions of interest (ROIs) from which the fMRI data is extracted and analyzed. If one has theoretic reasons to believe that a particular brain region is involved in a task then it often makes sense to simply analyze that specific region rather than testing the hypothesis against the whole brain. This avoids many of the multiple comparison problems faced with whole brain analysis. ROIs are usually defined either anatomically (e.g., expecting the amygdala is responding to a threatening stimulus) or functionally (e.g., expecting that the portion of the fusiform gyrus that responds to faces will respond more strongly to familiar faces than unfamiliar faces). While identifying the anatomical ROIs poses some difficulty due to natural variability in the structure of the brain, many of the fMRI data analysis software packages now have built-in tools for identifying the anatomy based on standardized atlases. The functional ROIs, however, require a localizer task to identify the region (Saxe, Brett, and Kanwisher 2006). The fusiform face area (FFA) is a classic example of a functional ROI since its location in the fusiform guys varies person by person. The FFA is not an anatomically defined region and it can only be identified by the intensity and specificity of the voxels' responsiveness to human faces.

The use of functional ROIs has gained some sensational and negative publicity recently and led to claims of "voodoo correlations" in neuroimaging (Vul et al. 2009). The problem that these authors pointed to in this meta-analysis was that the same data used by researchers to identify the area responding to the task were then used to identify the relationship between neural activity and the behavior. This issue is familiar to political scientists as selecting on the dependent variable. However, in neuroimaging the problem can be even subtler. Selecting voxels based on their responsiveness to task A and then comparing the responsiveness to task B can simultaneously overestimate the effect from task A and underestimate the effect from task B. Another issue is that the ROI analyses were often done using only a single peak voxel (rather than an average of a cluster of voxels), effectively choosing the most responsive case out of 50,000. Despite the hype that this critique of data analysis methods in neuroimaging received in the press, there are numerous correctives that are easily applied, as the authors note.

Basic Results

Although SCAN is a very new field, researchers have already converged on a set of consistent results that demonstrate the role of a relatively small set of brain regions in a wide variety of social behavior. In this section, I review a few brain regions and their role in important social cognition functions. I then detail the mental functions that have been frequently studied with fairly consistent results.

As mentioned above, the fusiform face area (FFA) is a region of the fusiform gyrus in the temporal lobe that responds specifically to faces. Other regions known to be heavily involved in the processing of faces include the amygdala, the occipital face area (OFA), superior temporal sulcus (STS), and the premotor face area. If the human brain has evolved for social cognition (Schreiber 2007) and given that faces convey a tremendous amount of information about affect and intention (Capella and Schreiber 2006), then having brain regions with functional specialization for processing faces would be a valuable way of aiding efficient social cognition. Deficits in the FFA and other face-processing regions appear to correlate with the impaired social cognition attendant to autism (Kleinhans et al. 2008).

The FFA appears to be involved in perceiving gender characteristics, although the subjective ascription of gender appears to rely more on the prefrontal cortex (Freeman et al. 2009). Similarly, the FFA is involved in processing cues about racial identity, and higher levels of activity there appear to be correlated with increased ability to recognize people of the same race (Golby et al. 2001). In fact, it may be that the FFA has greater specialization for facial identity and that other areas like the superior temporal sulcus (Winston et al. 2004) and the amygdala are reacting to the affective status of the face (Vuilleumier et al. 2003).

The amygdala is a small, almond-shaped region and is often discussed as being involved in the processing of fear (LeDoux 2000, 2007). However, the story is far more complex. Claims have been made for the involvement of the amygdala in positive emotions (Holland and Gallagher 2004) and social cognition (Adolphs 2003). Research showing the amygdala as connected to implicit racial attitudes has been particularly prominent (Phelps et al. 2000; Lieberman et al. 2005)

A meta-analysis of 385 functional brain imaging studies with a total of 5,307 individual subjects confirms that the role of the amygdala in fear processing appears to be robust (Costafreda et al. 2008), but also shows that disgust seems just as likely to activate the amygdala. While fear and disgust consistently activated the amygdala, so did other negative emotions like sadness and anger and some positive emotions surrounding humor and sexuality, although negative emotions seemed to provoke stronger reactions than positive emotions and happiness provoked the lowest responses. A second meta-analysis concluded that positive emotions were able to elicit as strong of responses from the amygdala (Sergerie, Chochol, and Armony 2008). Meta-analysis (Costafreda et al. 2008) also demonstrates that explicit attention to stimuli was significantly less likely to activate the amygdala than was passive experience, a result consistent with the theory that the amygdala is related to automatic processing (Lieberman, Schreiber, and Ochsner 2003). Of particular interest is the strong result showing that amygdala responses can be attenuated by intentional repression of emotion.

The down-regulation of the amygdala as a result of conscious processing has been shown in the context of racial (Lieberman et al. 2005) and emotional processing (Taylor et al. 2008). This interaction between more automatic amygdala processes and more controlled frontal lobe processes is important for clarifying the nature of implicit attitudes, especially in the context of race.

Some have treated such automatic attitudes as if they reveal 'true' attitudes (e.g., Kristof 2008), rather than recognizing the individuals have both automatic and controlled attitudes that have distinct cognitive, affective, behavioral, and neural components (Dovidio et al. 1997; Lieberman, Schreiber, and Ochsner 2003).

While the role of the amygdala in racial processing has been robustly demonstrated, its role is nuanced. Because other race faces morphed with the face of the participant deactivate the amygdala, some have argued that the amygdala is computing an interaction of personally and socially relevant characteristics (Platek and Krill 2009). Consistent with this theory, as individuals become more familiar with foreigners, amygdala activity diminishes (Derntl et al. 2009). It is also worth noting that dark skin tones are more likely to activate the amygdala, regardless of race (Ronquillo et al. 2007).

Another brain region important to social and affective processing is the insula, a thumb-sized region that runs laterally along the sides of the brain and is located a few centimeters above the ear and a few centimeters into the interior of the brain. Because the insula has been implicated in such a wide variety of interesting social phenomena, its function is being intensely researched (Blakeslee 2007). The human insula is particularly interesting because it appears to have a very different structure than in many of our primate cousins and even has a particular type of neuron (the von Economo or spindle cell neuron) which appears to occur only in animals with complex sociality. The evolutionarily older part of the insula is closer to the back of the brain and responds to physiological stimuli like pain or temperature. The anterior insula, which is closer to the front of the brain, in contrast, appears to integrate the objective stimulus with our perceptions of it. Thus, while activity in the posterior insula increases with objective increases in a burning temperature, the activity in the anterior insula increases with the painful perception of temperature increase (Craig 2009). Others have argued that the insula is integrating representations of current and future perceptual states into a general subjective feeling state (Singer, Critchley, and Preuschoff 2009).

The notion that the insula plays a primary role in interoception, the perception of internal physiological states, is supported by its activity during pain, temperature, and itch perception (Craig 2002). While the posterior portion of the insula responds to the sensation of pain in ourselves, it has been observed that the anterior insula responds to the experience of pain in ourselves and in others (Singer et al. 2004). The engagement of the anterior insula in empathic responses has been supported by a number of studies (Singer and Lamm 2009; Craig 2009). Intriguingly, activity in and thickness of the gray matter in the anterior insula corresponded with heightened interoceptive awareness (Critchley et al. 2004) and interoceptive awareness has been shown to be related to empathic ability (Singer, Critchley, and Preuschoff 2009). However, a proposed simulation role for the insula is undermined by recent findings that the anterior insula appears to be engaged even when a patient who is congenitally unable to experience pain is observing pain in others (Danziger, Faillenot, and Peyron 2009).

Some evidence suggests that the insula not only is active during our own physical pain or observation of physical pain in others, but also in the pain from social exclusion (Eisenberger, Lieberman, and Williams 2003) and the perception of social suffering in others (Immordino-Yang et al. 2009). The insula is often ascribed a role in the processing of disgust, whether experienced in the individual or perceived in others (Wicker, Keysers et al. 2003); however, more recent work suggests that only a certain type of disgust activates the insula (Borg, Lieberman, and Kiehl 2008). Other studies show a role for the anterior insula when a person rejects unfair offers in the ultimatum game (Sanfey, Rilling et al. 2003). It is unclear whether the responsiveness of the insula in such cases is due to violations of social norms or to expectations of risk (Knutson and Bossaerts 2007). The complex pattern of activity in the insula strongly suggests that the insula plays a role in integrating our own feelings and experiencing the states of others, but the details of its role in social cognition have yet to be fully articulated.

Most of the work on empathy has studied connections for negative emotions like pain or disgust, but a greater affinity for a person also increases our experience of personal reward when we see that person benefiting and is related to greater activity in the ventral striatum (Mobbs et al. 2009). The striatum is the largest component of the basal ganglia, which also includes the globus pallidus and substantia nigra. The striatum itself is comprised of the caudate, putamen, and nucleus accumbens. The most interesting function of the basal ganglia for social science is its role in reward, and thus decisionmaking and learning.

The basal ganglia have been well established as being involved in reward processing (Delgado 2007). Activity in these regions has been shown for both basic physical pleasures like food and more socially complex pleasures like giving either as charity or taxation (Harbaugh, Mayr, and Burghart 2007) or witnessing the suffering of an envied person (Takahashi et al. 2009). Neuroscientists have described hedonic "liking" processes that appear to be distinct from motivational "wanting" processes, but both appear to involve subcomponents of the basal ganglia (Walter et al. 2005; Smith et al. 2009). The basal ganglia are thus implicated in decisionmaking (Balleine, Delgado, and Hiko-saka 2007), but their role does not require conscious awareness. When subjects are subliminally flashed a symbol of a higher monetary value, their behavior can subconsciously respond as their striatum react (Pessiglione et al. 2007). In fact, direct neural recording shows that specific neurons will respond prefer-entially to the expected value of a choice (Samejima et al. 2005). Of particular interest, however, is that social phenomena like cooperating with a person appear to cause higher levels of activity than merely cooperating with a com-puter (Rilling et al. 2002, 2004).

Because of their roles in valuation, reward, and decisionmaking, the basal ganglia are often implicated in neuro-economic studies. When individuals make decisions in the face of uncertainty (Platt and Huettel 2008; Rushworth and Behrens 2008), express socially relevant preferences (Fehr and Camerer 2007), encode value (Seymour and McClure 2008), play economic games (San-fey 2007; Krueger, Grafman, and McCabe 2008), build a reputation (Izuma, Saito, and Sadato 2008), and compute the value of present versus future re-wards (Rangel, Camerer, and Montague 2008; Doya 2008; Kalenscher and Pen-nartz 2008) the basal ganglia are typically involved. However, complicating matters is the clear evidence that distinct neural systems underpin particu-lar types of decisionmaking, be they automatic or deliberative, conscious or unconscious, fast or slow, associative or rule-based, or affective or cognitive (Sanfey and Chang 2008). There are multiple reward pathways through the basal ganglia connecting to a variety of regions such as the amygdala, insula, prefrontal cortex, and anterior cingulate. There is not a single place in the brain representing value and multiple circuits may be involved in decision-making that are even outside of the traditional reward pathways (Rushworth, Mars, and Summerfield 2009).

Another brain region with important implications for decisionmaking is the anterior cingulate cortex (ACC). The cingulate gyrus is a part of the limbic system and runs along the midline of the brain below the neocortex. The por-tion closer to the forehead is known as the anterior cingulate and has been shown to have an important role in both decisionmaking and the detection of mental conflict. It has been described as an alarm system in the brain, notify-ing the executive functions of the frontal lobe that a problem is worth con-scious attention (van Veen and Carter 2002; Carter and van Veen 2007). The ACC then is processing the decisions and potential conflicts regardless of conscious attention. In fact, it appears to function with the insula when ap-proaching an effortless coordination game, in contrast to the effortful domi-nance exhibited in solvable games (Kuo et al. 2009).

By attending to conflicts in mental states, decisions, and outcomes, the ACC plays a key role in decisionmaking (Botvinick 2007) as well as generating potential choices (Rushworth et al. 2007). Single-neuron recording studies demonstrate the role of neurons in the ACC integrating choices and rewards (Williams et al. 2004). And lesions in the ACC do not appear to impair error detection, but do impair the integration of choices and consequences (Walton et al. 2007). In a related vein, the ACC also appears involved in cognitive dissonance and the dissonance reduction attendant to attitude change (van Veen et al. 2009).

The ACC also activates in a number of social contexts (Dichter et al. 2009; Rudebeck, Bannerman, and Rushworth 2008), as when we detect errors in the actions of others. The intensity of the ACC activity when we detect others' errors appears to be modulated by whether we feel affiliation with them (Newman-Norlund et al. 2009). The ACC also seems to be active when we feel threatened by political candidates and do not vote for them (Spezio et al. 2008). Similarly, while the pain of social exclusion activates the ACC (Eisenberger, Lieberman, and Williams 2003), that activity is heightened when we are excluded by someone of the same race (Krill and Platek 2009).

The change in ACC function by social salience is consistent with its role in a "salience network" along with the fronto-insular cortex. This salience network is suggested as modulating brain function between an attentional "central executive network" and the "default mode network" (Sridharan, Levitin, and Menon 2008). Others have suggested that the rostral portion of the ACC is particularly synchronized with the default mode network (Margulies et al. 2007).

This default mode network (DMN) was identified by Marcus Raichle after the insight of looking for task independent deactivations (Gusnard and Raichle 2001; Raichle et al. 2001). Rather than only looking to see what areas increased in activity when the brain went from being at rest to focusing on a particular cognitive task, Raichle's innovation was to look for parts of the brain that were very active during rest and then did little regardless of which task the brain was engaged in. The discovery of the network, its robustness, and the intensity of its metabolic activity led to a well over a hundred subsequent investigations (Raichle and Snyder 2007).

Of particular interest was that the parts of the DMN actually did function as a network. Activity in the posterior cingulate (Fransson and Marrelec 2008) and the medial prefrontal appeared to be functionally connected and later investigation would show this corresponded with structural connectivity as well (Damoiseaux and Greicius 2009; Greicius et al. 2009). While the network can be consistently identified in subjects even after long periods of time

(Meindl et al. 2009; Shehzad et al. 2009), it is subject to disruption. Deep sleep, for instance, decouples the DMN (Horovitz et al. 2009), even though it still maintained coherence under anesthesia (Martuzzi et al. 2010). More important, its function appeared to suffer under a variety of different mental disorders (Broyd et al. 2009), for instance autism (Iacoboni 2006; Kennedy, Redcay, and Courchesne 2006) and even in the induced stress from a catastrophic earthquake (Lui et al. 2009).

The dysfunction during autism and the fact that the DMN appeared only to truly activate during social tasks (Iacoboni et al. 2004; Rilling et al. 2008) has led to suggestions that the network is centrally important in social cognition (Schreiber 2007; Schilbach et al. 2008). Other suggestions have been that the DMN is important for sense of self (Gusnard et al. 2001; Wicker, Ruby et al. 2003), mind wandering (Mason et al. 2007), free will (Goldberg, Ullman, and Malach 2008), and moral judgment (Greene et al. 2001; Moll et al. 2007). One particularly nice experiment demonstrated the DMN activating (the social moral judgment task), at rest, and deactivating (the cognitively demanding Stroop task) (Harrison et al. 2008). Other work has shown that the DMN is engaged during sophisticated political judgment (Westen et al. 2006), but deactivated when political novices try to do the same task (Schreiber 2005; Fowler and Schreiber 2008).

While the posterior cingulate is now best known for its role in the DMN (Immordino-Yang et al. 2009), the medial prefrontal cortex (mPFC) has been known to be important for social cognition for quite a while. The disruption of Phineas Gage's social behavior (Macmillan 2000) when his medial prefrontal lobe was damaged (Ratiu et al. 2004) was an early clue. But early imaging work suggested a particularly important role for contemplating the mental states of others (Frith and Frith 1999. 2006) and showed that people strategized about the choices of other people using the mPFC (McCabe et al. 2001). Other work showed the role of the mPFC in a variety of moral and ethical judgments (Greene et al. 2001; Cunningham et al. 2003; Heekeren et al. 2003). In particular, interpersonal connection appeared to discount purely utilitarian judgment (Greene et al. 2001) unless there was damage to the mPFC (Ciaramelli et al. 2007). Dehumanizing others diminishes the function of the region (Harris and Fiske 2006, 2007) and considering one's place in an unstable social hierarchy activates it (Zink et al. 2008). It has been suggested that it is the anterior rostral portion of the mPFC that is particularly focused on both attending to our own mental states and those of others, while the posterior portion monitors our actions and the orbital portion monitors the outcomes of choices (Amodio and Frith 2006). Others contend that the role of the mPFC in valuation can be contrasted with the role of the dorsolateral prefrontal cortex (DLPFC) in self-control (Hare, Camerer, and Rangel 2009).

More generally, the DLPFC is known for its role in executive function and making choices in the midst of conflicting considerations (Mansouri, Tanaka, and Buckley 2009; Wittfoth et al. 2009), for example, in mixed strategy games (Barraclough, Conroy, and Lee 2004). The region is involved in deciding to punish others for their violations of social norms (Sanfey, Rilling et al. 2003) and holding them responsible for those violations (Buckholtz et al. 2008). In a potentially related function, the DLPFC activates during self-criticism, in contrast to the ventrolateral prefrontal cortex's (VLPFC) activation during self-assurance (Longe et al. 2009).

This emotional-regulation function of the VLPFC has been demonstrated in the context of tamping down amygdala activity in response to racial stimuli (Lieberman et al. 2005). The down regulation of the amygdala by the VLPFC is related to the degree of psychosocial resources a person has (Taylor et al. 2008). The interplay between the VLPFC and amygdala appears in a variety of different contexts (Lee and Siegle 2009).

It is important to keep in mind that contrary to a naïve modularity hypothesis, the brain regions described above are all involved in a series of sometimes overlapping networks. In addition to the DMN, at least eight other coherent networks are functionally connected during rest, most of which have established structural connections as well (van den Heuvel et al. 2009). Much of our previous knowledge about this connectedness depended on dissection and animal models, but with techniques like DTI it is now possible to model structural connections in the same healthy subjects that are participating in the functional studies. And, although prior analysis of the functional data was biased by statistical models that had localization implicit in the design, more statistical approaches that model functional connectivity are being utilized. So while it is useful to attempt to discern the patterns in types of mental functions that recruit particular brain regions, it is also important to keep in mind that the brain is networked on both the micro and macro scales (van den Heuvel et al. 2008; Modha and Singh 2010).

The Nature of the Human Animal

Aristotle contended that we are, by nature, political animals. This assessment continues to be borne out as SCAN develops our understanding of the human brain. We observe politics, however, in a wide variety of animals (see chapter 2 in this volume) and the deeper question of precisely what kind of political animal we are remains. Neuropolitics has the potential to aide in our answering that question. Exploring the function of the brain will reveal more about the mind and illuminate the political context it operates in.

Notes

1. Having volunteered for a PET study, I can attest that it is odd to feel the warmth of the radiation as it follows up one's veins.

2. Viewing the 1988 version of the famous mapping of neuroscientific tools on a log/log plot of temporal and spatial resolution one can easily see the deficit in methods that the next coming decade's development of fMRI was to fill (Churchland and Sejnowski 1988).

3. Spezio and Adolphs (2007) note many of the challenges involved in properly interpreting the results from the BOLD signal analysis

References

Adolphs, R. 2003. Is the human amygdala specialized for processing social information? *Annals of the New York Academy of Sciences* 985:326–40.

Amodio, D. M., and C. D. Frith. 2006. Meeting of minds: The medial frontal cortex and social cognition. *Nature Review Neuroscience* 7 (4): 268–77.

Amodio, D. M., J. T. Jost, S. L. Master, and C. M. Yee. 2007. Neurocognitive correlates of liberalism and conservatism. *Nature Neuroscience* 10 (10): 1246–47.

Balleine, B. W., M. R. Delgado, and O. Hikosaka. 2007. The role of the dorsal striatum in reward and decision-making. *Journal of Neuroscience* 27 (31): 8161–65.

Barraclough, D. J., M. L. Conroy, and D. Lee. 2004. Prefrontal cortex and decision making in a mixed-strategy game. *Nature Neuroscience* 7 (4): 404–10.

Blakeslee, S. 2007. A small part of the brain, and its profound effects. *New York Times*, February 6.

Borg, J. S., D. Lieberman, and K. A. Kiehl. 2008. Infection, incest, and iniquity: Investigating the neural correlates of disgust and morality. *Journal of Cognitive Neuroscience* 20 (9): 1529–46.

Botvinick, M. M. 2007. Conflict monitoring and decision making: Reconciling two perspectives on anterior cingulate function. *Cognitive Affective and Behavioral Neuroscience* 7 (4): 356–66.

Brooks, D. 2009. The young and the neuro. *New York Times*, October 12.

Broyd, S. J., C. Demanuele, S. Debener, S. K. Helps, C. J. James, and E. J. Sonuga-Barke. 2009. Default-mode brain dysfunction in mental disorders: A systematic review. *Neuroscience and Biobehavioral Review* 33 (3): 279–96.

Buckholtz, J. W., C. L. Asplund, P. E. Dux, D. H. Zald, J. C. Gore, O. D. Jones, and R. Marois. 2008. The neural correlates of third-party punishment. *Neuron* 60 (5): 930–40.

Calvo-Merino, B., D. E. Glaser, J. Grezes, R. E. Passingham, and P. Haggard. 2005. Action observation and acquired motor skills: An fMRI study with expert dancers. *Cerebral Cortex* 15 (8): 1243–49.

Capella, J. N., and D. Schreiber. 2006. The interaction management function of nonverbal cues: Theory and research about mutual behavioral influence in face-to-face settings.

In *The SAGE handbook of nonverbal communication*, ed. V. Manusov and M. L. Patterson, 361–77. Thousand Oaks, Calif.: Sage Publications.

Carter, C. S., and V. van Veen. 2007. Anterior cingulate cortex and conflict detection: An update of theory and data. *Cognitive Affective and Behavior Neuroscience* 7 (4): 367–79.

Churchland, P. S. 2007. Neurophilosophy: The early years and new directions. *Functional Neurology* 22 (4): 185–95.

Churchland, P. S., and T. J. Sejnowski. 1988. Perspectives on cognitive neuroscience. *Science* 242 (4879): 741–45.

Ciaramelli, E., M. Muccioli, E. Ladavas, and G. di Pellegrino. 2007. Selective deficit in personal moral judgment following damage to ventromedial prefrontal cortex. *Social Cognitive Affective Neuroscience* 2 (2): 84–92.

Clithero, J. A., D. Tankersley, and S. A. Huettel. 2008. Foundations of neuroeconomics: From philosophy to practice. *PLoS Biology* 6 (11): e298.

Costafreda, S. G., M. J. Brammer, A. S. David, and C. H. Fu. 2008. Predictors of amygdala activation during the processing of emotional stimuli: A meta-analysis of 385 PET and fMRI studies. *Brain Research Review* 58 (1): 57–70.

Craig, A. D. 2002. How do you feel? Interoception: The sense of the physiological condition of the body. *Nature Review Neuroscience* 3 (8): 655–66.

———. 2009. How do you feel—now? The anterior insula and human awareness. *Nature Review Neuroscience* 10 (1): 59–70.

Critchley, H. D., S. Wiens, P. Rotshtein, A. Ohman, and R. J. Dolan. 2004. Neural systems supporting interoceptive awareness. *Nature Neuroscience* 7 (2): 189–95.

Cunningham, W. A., M. K. Johnson, J. C. Gatenby, J. C. Gore, and M. R. Banaji. 2003. Neural components of social evaluation. *Journal of Personality and Social Psychology* 85 (4): 639–49.

Damasio, H., and A. R. Damasio. 1989. *Lesion analysis in neuropsychology.* New York: Oxford University Press.

Damoiseaux, J. S., and M. D. Greicius. 2009. Greater than the sum of its parts: A review of studies combining structural connectivity and resting-state functional connectivity. *Brain Structure and Function* 213 (6): 525–33.

Danziger, N., I. Faillenot, and R. Peyron. 2009. Can we share a pain we never felt? Neural correlates of empathy in patients with congenital insensitivity to pain. *Neuron* 61 (2): 203–12.

de Quervain, D. J., U. Fischbacher, V. Treyer, M. Schellhammer, U. Schnyder, A. Buck, and E. Fehr. 2004. The neural basis of altruistic punishment. *Science* 305 (5688): 1254–58.

Delgado, M. R. 2007. Reward-related responses in the human striatum. *Annals of the New York Academy of Sciences* 1104:70–88.

Derntl, B., U. Habel, S. Robinson, C. Windischberger, I. Kryspin-Exner, R. C. Gur, and E. Moser. 2009. Amygdala activation during recognition of emotions in a foreign ethnic group is associated with duration of stay. *Social Neuroscience* 4 (4): 294–307.

Dichter, G. S., J. N. Felder, J. W. Bodfish, L. Sikich, and A. Belger. 2009. Mapping social target detection with functional magnetic resonance imaging. *Social Cognitive Affective Neuroscience* 4 (1): 59–69.

Dovidio, J. F., K. Kawakami, C. Johnson, B. Johnson, and A. Howard. 1997. On the nature of prejudice: Automatic and controlled processes. *Journal of Experimental Social Psychology* 33 (5): 510–40.

Doya, K. 2008. Modulators of decision making. *Nature Neuroscience* 11 (4): 410–16.

Draganski, B., C. Gaser, V. Busch, G. Schuierer, U. Bogdahn, and A. May. 2004. Neuroplasticity: Changes in grey matter induced by training. *Nature* 427 (6972): 311–12.

Eisenberger, N. I., M. D. Lieberman, and K. D. Williams. 2003. Does rejection hurt? An fMRI study of social exclusion. *Science* 302 (5643): 290–92.

Erk, S., M. Spitzer, A. P. Wunderlich, L. Galley, and H. Walter. 2002. Cultural objects modulate reward circuitry. *Neuroreport* 13 (18): 2499–2503.

Fehr, E., and C. F. Camerer. 2007. Social neuroeconomics: The neural circuitry of social preferences. *Trends Cognitive Science* 11 (10): 419–27.

Floel, A., M. H. de Vries, J. Scholz, C. Breitenstein, and H. Johansen-Berg. 2009. White matter integrity in the vicinity of Broca's area predicts grammar learning success. *Neuroimage* 47 (4): 1974–81.

Fowler, J. H., and D. Schreiber. 2008. Biology, politics, and the emerging science of human nature. *Science* 322 (5903): 912–14.

Fransson, P., and G. Marrelec. 2008. The precuneus/posterior cingulate cortex plays a pivotal role in the default mode network: Evidence from a partial correlation network analysis. *Neuroimage* 42 (3): 1178–84.

Freeman, J. B., N. O. Rule, R. B. Adams, Jr., and N. Ambady. 2009. The neural basis of categorical face perception: Graded representations of face gender in fusiform and orbitofrontal cortices. *Cerebral Cortex* 20 (6): 1314–22.

Friston, K. J. 2009. Modalities, modes, and models in functional neuroimaging. *Science* 326 (5951): 399–403.

Frith, C. D., and U. Frith. 1999. Interacting minds—a biological basis. *Science* 286:1692–95.

———. 2006. The neural basis of mentalizing. *Neuron* 50 (4): 531–34.

Glascher, J., D. Tranel, L. K. Paul, D. Rudrauf, C. Rorden, A. Hornaday, T. Grabowski, H. Damasio, and R. Adolphs. 2009. Lesion mapping of cognitive abilities linked to intelligence. *Neuron* 61 (5): 681–91.

Golby, A. J., J.D.E. Gabrieli, J. Y. Chiao, and J. L. Eberhardt. 2001. Differential responses in the fusiform region to same-race and other-race faces. *Nature* 4 (8): 845–50.

Goldberg, I., S. Ullman, and R. Malach. 2008. Neuronal correlates of "free will" are associated with regional specialization in the human intrinsic/default network. *Conscious Cognition* 17 (3): 587–601.

Greene, J. D., S. A. Morelli, K. Lowenberg, L. E. Nystrom, and J. D. Cohen. 2008. Cognitive load selectively interferes with utilitarian moral judgment. *Cognition* 107 (3): 1144–54.

Greene, J. D., R. B. Sommerville, L. E. Nystrom, J. M. Darley, and J. D. Cohen. 2001. An fMRI investigation of emotional engagement in moral judgment. *Science* 293 (5537): 2105–8.

Greicius, M. D., K. Supekar, V. Menon, and R. F. Dougherty. 2009. Resting-state functional connectivity reflects structural connectivity in the default mode network. *Cerebral Cortex* 19 (1): 72–78.

Gusnard, D. A., E. Akbudak, G. L. Shulman, and M. E. Raichle. 2001. Medial prefrontal cortex and self-referential mental activity: Relation to a default mode of brain function. *Proceedings of the National Academy of Sciences* 98 (7): 4259–64.

Gusnard, D. A., and M. E. Raichle. 2001. Searching for a baseline: Functional imaging and the resting human brain. *Nature Review Neuroscience* 2 (10): 685–94.

Harbaugh, W. T., U. Mayr, and D. R. Burghart. 2007. Neural responses to taxation and voluntary giving reveal motives for charitable donations. *Science* 316 (5831): 1622–25.

Hare, T. A., C. F. Camerer, and A. Rangel. 2009. Self-control in decision-making involves modulation of the vmPFC valuation system. *Science* 324 (5927): 646–48.

Harris, L. T., and S. T. Fiske. 2006. Dehumanizing the lowest of the low: Neuroimaging responses to extreme out-groups. *Psychological Science* 17 (10): 847–53.

———. 2007. Social groups that elicit disgust are differentially processed in mPFC. *Social Cognitive Affective Neuroscience* 2 (1): 45–51.

Harrison, B. J., J. Pujol, M. Lopez-Sola, R. Hernandez-Ribas, J. Deus, H. Ortiz, C. Soriano-Mas, M. Yucel, C. Pantelis, and N. Cardoner. 2008. Consistency and functional specialization in the default mode brain network. *Proceedings of the National Academy of Sciences* 105 (28): 9781–86.

Hasson, U., Y. Nir, I. Levy, G. Fuhrmann, and R. Malach. 2004. Intersubject synchronization of cortical activity during natural vision. *Science* 303 (5664): 1634–40.

Heekeren, H. R., I. Wartenburger, H. Schmidt, H. P. Schwintowski, and A. Villringer. 2003. An fMRI study of simple ethical decision-making. *Neuroreport* 14 (9): 1215–19.

Herrmann, E., J. Call, M. V. Hernandez-Lloreda, B. Hare, and M. Tomasello. 2007. Humans have evolved specialized skills of social cognition: The cultural intelligence hypothesis. *Science* 317 (5843): 1360–66.

Holland, P. C., and M. Gallagher. 2004. Amygdala-frontal interactions and reward expectancy. *Current Opinions in Neurobiology* 14 (2): 148–55.

Horovitz, S. G., A. R. Braun, W. S. Carr, D. Picchioni, T. J. Balkin, M. Fukunaga, and J. H. Duyn. 2009. Decoupling of the brain's default mode network during deep sleep. *Proceedings of the National Academy of Sciences* 106 (27): 11376–81.

Iacoboni, M. 2006. Failure to deactivate in autism: The co-constitution of self and other. *Trends in Cognitive Science* 10 (10): 431–33.

Iacoboni, M., M. D. Lieberman, B. J. Knowlton, I. Molnar-Szakacs, M. Moritz, C. J. Throop, and A. P. Fiske. 2004. Watching social interactions produces dorsomedial prefrontal and medial parietal BOLD fMRI signal increases compared to a resting baseline. *Neuroimage* 21 (3): 1167–73.

Immordino-Yang, M. H., A. McColl, H. Damasio, and A. Damasio. 2009. Neural correlates of admiration and compassion. *Proceedings of the National Academy of Sciences* 106 (19): 8021–26.

Izuma, K., D. N. Saito, and N. Sadato. 2008. Processing of social and monetary rewards in the human striatum. *Neuron* 58 (2): 284–94.

Kalenscher, T., and C. M. Pennartz. 2008. Is a bird in the hand worth two in the future? The neuroeconomics of intertemporal decision-making. *Progressive Neurobiology* 84 (3): 284–315.

Kennedy, D. P., E. Redcay, and E. Courchesne. 2006. Failing to deactivate: Resting functional abnormalities in autism. *Proceedings of the National Academy of Sciences* 103 (21): 8275–80.

Kleinhans, N. M., T. Richards, L. Sterling, K. C. Stegbauer, R. Mahurin, L. C. Johnson, J. Greenson, G. Dawson, and E. Aylward. 2008. Abnormal functional connectivity in autism spectrum disorders during face processing. *Brain* 131 (Pt 4): 1000–1012.

Knutson, B., and P. Bossaerts. 2007. Neural antecedents of financial decisions. *Journal of Neuroscience* 27 (31): 8174–77.

Koenigs, M., L. Young, R. Adolphs, D. Tranel, F. Cushman, M. Hauser, and A. Damasio. 2007. Damage to the prefrontal cortex increases utilitarian moral judgements. *Nature* 446 (7138): 908–11.

Krill, A., and S. M. Platek. 2009. In-group and out-group membership mediates anterior cingulate activation to social exclusion. *Frontiers in Evolutionary Neuroscience* 1:1.

Kristof, N. D. 2008. Our racist, sexist selves. *New York Times*, April 6.

Krueger, F., J. Grafman, and K. McCabe. 2008. Neural correlates of economic game playing. *Philosophical Transactions of the Royal Society of London B: Biological Sciences* 363 (1511): 3859–74.

Kuo, W. J., T. Sjostrom, Y. P. Chen, Y. H. Wang, and C. Y. Huang. 2009. Intuition and deliberation: Two systems for strategizing in the brain. *Science* 324 (5926): 519–22.

LeDoux, J. 2007. The amygdala. *Current Biology* 17 (20): R868–74.

LeDoux, J. E. 2000. Emotion circuits in the brain. *Annual Review Neuroscience* 23:155–84.

Lee, K. H., and G. J. Siegle. 2009. Common and distinct brain networks underlying explicit emotional evaluation: A meta-analytic study. *Social Cognitive Affective Neuroscience* Accessed from Social Cognitive and Affective Neuroscience Advance Access, published March 6, 2009.

Lieberman, M. D., A. Hariri, J. M. Jarcho, N. I. Eisenberger, and S. Y. Bookheimer. 2005. An fMRI investigation of race-related amygdala activity in African-American and Caucasian-American individuals. *Nature Neuroscience* 8 (6): 720–22.

Lieberman, M., D. Schreiber, and K. Ochsner. 2003. Is political sophistication like learning to ride a bicycle? How cognitive neuroscience can inform research on political thinking. *Political Psychology* 24 (4): 681–704.

Longe, O., F. A. Maratos, P. Gilbert, G. Evans, F. Volker, H. Rockliff, and G. Rippon. 2009. Having a word with yourself: Neural correlates of self-criticism and self-reassurance. *Neuroimage* 49 (2): 1849–56.

Lui, S., X. Huang, L. Chen, H. Tang, T. Zhang, X. Li, D. Li, et al. 2009. High-field MRI reveals an acute impact on brain function in survivors of the magnitude 8.0 earthquake in China. *Proceedings of the National Academy of Sciences* 106 (36): 15412–17.

Macmillan, M. 2000. Restoring Phineas Gage: A 150th retrospective. *Journal of the History of Neuroscience* 9 (1): 46–66.

Mansouri, F. A., K. Tanaka, and M. J. Buckley. 2009. Conflict-induced behavioural adjustment: A clue to the executive functions of the prefrontal cortex. *Nature Review Neuroscience* 10 (2): 141–52.

Margulies, D. S., A. M. Kelly, L. Q. Uddin, B. B. Biswal, F. X. Castellanos, and M. P. Milham. 2007. Mapping the functional connectivity of anterior cingulate cortex. *Neuroimage* 37 (2): 579–88.

Martuzzi, R., R. Ramani, M. Qiu, N. Rajeevan, and R. T. Constable. 2010. Functional connectivity and alterations in baseline brain state in humans. *Neuroimage* 49 (1): 823–34.

Mason, M. F., M. I. Norton, J. D. Van Horn, D. M. Wegner, S. T. Grafton, and C. N. Macrae. 2007. Wandering minds: The default network and stimulus-independent thought. *Science* 315 (5810): 393–95.

Maye, A., C. H. Hsieh, G. Sugihara, and B. Brembs. 2007. Order in spontaneous behavior. *PLoS One* 2 (5): e443.

McCabe, D. P., and A. D. Castel. 2008. Seeing is believing: The effect of brain images on judgments of scientific reasoning. *Cognition* 107 (1): 343–52.

McCabe, K., D. Houser, L. Ryan, V. Smith, and T. Trouard. 2001. A functional imaging study of cooperation in two-person reciprocal exchange. *Proceedings of the National Academy of Sciences* 98 (20): 11832–35.

Meindl, T., S. Teipel, R. Elmouden, S. Mueller, W. Koch, O. Dietrich, U. Coates, M. Reiser, and C. Glaser. 2009. Test-retest reproducibility of the default-mode network in healthy individuals. *Human Brain Mapping* 31 (2): 237–46.

Mele, A. R. 2009. *Effective intentions: The power of conscious will.* New York: Oxford University Press.

Merabet, L. B., R. Hamilton, G. Schlaug, J. D. Swisher, E. T. Kiriakopoulos, N. B. Pitskel, T. Kauffman, and A. Pascual-Leone. 2008. Rapid and reversible recruitment of early visual cortex for touch. *PLoS One* 3 (8): e3046.

Mitchell, M. 2009. *Complexity: A guided tour.* New York: Oxford University Press.

Mobbs, D., R. Yu, M. Meyer, L. Passamonti, B. Seymour, A. J. Calder, S. Schweizer, C. D. Frith, and T. Dalgleish. 2009. A key role for similarity in vicarious reward. *Science* 324 (5929): 900.

Modha, D. S., and R. Singh. 2010. Network architecture of the long-distance pathways in the macaque brain. *Proceedings of the National Academy of Sciences* 107 (30): 13485–90.

Moll, J., R. de Oliveira-Souza, G. J. Garrido, I. E. Bramati, E. M. Caparelli-Daquer, M. L. Paiva, R. Zahn, and J. Grafman. 2007. The self as a moral agent: Linking the neural bases of social agency and moral sensitivity. *Social Neuroscience* 2 (3–4): 336–52.

Newman-Norlund, R. D., S. Ganesh, H. T. van Schie, E. R. De Bruijn, and H. Bekkering. 2009. Self-identification and empathy modulate error-related brain activity during the observation of penalty shots between friend and foe. *Social Cognitive Affective Neuroscience* 4 (1): 10–22.

Pessiglione, M., L. Schmidt, B. Draganski, R. Kalisch, H. Lau, R. J. Dolan, and C. D. Frith. 2007. How the brain translates money into force: A neuroimaging study of subliminal motivation. *Science* 316 (5826): 904–6.

Phelps, E. A., K. J. O'Connor, W. Cunningham, E. S. Funayama, J. C. Gatenby, J. C. Gore, and R. B. Mahzarin. 2000. Performance on indirect measures of race evaluation predicts amygdala activation. *Journal of Cognitive Neuroscience* 12 (5): 729–38.

Platek, S. M., and A. L. Krill. 2009. Self-face resemblance attenuates other-race face effect in the amygdala. *Brain Research* 1284:156–60.

Platt, M. L., and S. A. Huettel. 2008. Risky business: The neuroeconomics of decision making under uncertainty. *Nature Neuroscience* 11 (4): 398–403.

Premack, D. 2007. Human and animal cognition: Continuity and discontinuity. *Proceedings of the National Academy of Sciences* 104 (35): 13861–67.

Raichle, M. E., A. M. MacLeod, A. Z. Snyder, W. J. Powers, D. A. Gusnard, and G. L. Shulman. 2001. A default mode of brain function. *Proceedings of the National Academy of Sciences* 98 (2): 676–82.

Raichle, M. E., and A. Z. Snyder. 2007. A default mode of brain function: A brief history of an evolving idea. *Neuroimage* 37 (4): 1083–90; discussion 1097–99.

Rangel, A., C. Camerer, and P. R. Montague. 2008. A framework for studying the neurobiology of value-based decision making. *Nature Review Neuroscience* 9 (7): 545–56.

Ratiu, P., I. F. Talos, S. Haker, D. Lieberman, and P. Everett. 2004. The tale of Phineas Gage, digitally remastered. *Journal of Neurotrauma* 21 (5): 637–43.

Rilling, J., D. Gutman, T. Zeh, G. Pagnoni, G. Berns, and C. Kilts. 2002. A neural basis for social cooperation. *Neuron* 35 (2): 395–405.

Rilling, J. K., J. E. Dagenais, D. R. Goldsmith, A. L. Glenn, and G. Pagnoni. 2008. Social cognitive neural networks during in-group and out-group interactions. *Neuroimage* 41 (4): 1447–61.

Rilling, J. K., A. G. Sanfey, J. A. Aronson, L. E. Nystrom, and J. D. Cohen. 2004. Opposing BOLD responses to reciprocated and unreciprocated altruism in putative reward pathways. *Neuroreport* 15 (16): 2539–43.

Ronquillo, J., T. F. Denson, B. Lickel, Z. L. Lu, A. Nandy, and K. B. Maddox. 2007. The effects of skin tone on race-related amygdala activity: An fMRI investigation. *Social Cognitive Affective Neuroscience* 2 (1): 39–44.

Rosen, J. 2007. The brain on the stand. *New York Times Magazine*, March 11.

Rudebeck, P. H., D. M. Bannerman, and M. F. Rushworth. 2008. The contribution of distinct subregions of the ventromedial frontal cortex to emotion, social behavior, and decision making. *Cognitive Affective and Behavioral Neuroscience* 8 (4): 485–97.

Rushworth, M. F., and T. E. Behrens. 2008. Choice, uncertainty and value in prefrontal and cingulate cortex. *Nature Neuroscience* 11 (4): 389–97.

Rushworth, M. F., T. E. Behrens, P. H. Rudebeck, and M. E. Walton. 2007. Contrasting roles for cingulate and orbitofrontal cortex in decisions and social behaviour. *Trends in Cognitive Science* 11 (4): 168–76.

Rushworth, M. F., R. B. Mars, and C. Summerfield. 2009. General mechanisms for making decisions? *Current Opinion in Neurobiology* 19 (1): 75–83.

Samejima, K., Y. Ueda, K. Doya, and M. Kimura. 2005. Representation of action-specific reward values in the striatum. *Science* 310 (5752): 1337–40.

Sanfey, A. G. 2007. Social decision-making: Insights from game theory and neuroscience. *Science* 318 (5850): 598–602.

Sanfey, A. G., and L. J. Chang. 2008. Multiple systems in decision making. *Annals of the New York Academy of Sciences* 1128:53–62.

Sanfey, A. G., R. Hastie, M. K. Colvin, and J. Grafman. 2003. Phineas gauged: Decision-making and the human prefrontal cortex. *Neuropsychologia* 41 (9): 1218–29.

Sanfey, A. G., J. K. Rilling, J. A. Aronson, L. E. Nystrom, and J. D. Cohen. 2003. The neural basis of economic decision-making in the Ultimatum Game. *Science* 300 (5626): 1755–58.

Saxe, R., M. Brett, and N. Kanwisher. 2006. Divide and conquer: A defense of functional localizers. *Neuroimage* 30 (4): 1088–96; discussion 1097–99.

Schilbach, L., S. B. Eickhoff, A. Rotarska-Jagiela, G. R. Fink, and K. Vogeley. 2008. Minds at rest? Social cognition as the default mode of cognizing and its putative relationship to the "default system" of the brain. *Conscious Cognition* 17 (2): 457–67.

Schjodt, U., H. Stodkilde-Jorgensen, A. W. Geertz, and A. Roepstorff. 2008. Rewarding prayers. *Neuroscience Letters* 443 (3): 165–68.

Scholz, J., M. C. Klein, T. E. Behrens, and H. Johansen-Berg. 2009. Training induces changes in white-matter architecture. *Nature Neuroscience* 12:1370–71.

Schreiber, D. 2005. Evaluating politics: A search for the neural substrates of political thought. Ph.D. diss., University of California–Los Angeles.

———. 2007. Political cognition as social cognition: Are we all political sophisticates? In *The affect effect: Dynamics of emotion in political thinking and behavior*, ed. A. Crigler, M. MacKuen, G. E. Marcus and W. R. Neuman, 48–70. Chicago: University of Chicago Press.

Schreiber, D., A. N. Simmons, C. T. Dawes, T. Flagan, J. H. Fowler, and M. P. Paulus. 2009. Red brain, blue brain: Evaluative processes differ in Democrats and Republicans. Paper given at American Political Science Association meeting, Toronto, September.

Sergerie, K., C. Chochol, and J. L. Armony. 2008. The role of the amygdala in emotional processing: A quantitative meta-analysis of functional neuroimaging studies. *Neuroscience and Biobehavioral Review* 32 (4): 811–30.

Seymour, B., and S. M. McClure. 2008. Anchors, scales and the relative coding of value in the brain. *Current Opinion in Neurobiology* 18 (2): 173–78.

Shehzad, Z., A. M. Kelly, P. T. Reiss, D. G. Gee, K. Gotimer, L. Q. Uddin, S. H. Lee, et al. 2009. The resting brain: Unconstrained yet reliable. *Cerebral Cortex* 19 (10): 2209–29.

Singer, T., H. D. Critchley, and K. Preuschoff. 2009. A common role of insula in feelings, empathy and uncertainty. *Trends in Cognitive Science* 13 (8): 334–40.

Singer, T., and C. Lamm. 2009. The social neuroscience of empathy. *Annals of the New York Academy of Sciences* 1156:81–96.

Singer, T., B. Seymour, J. O'Doherty, H. Kaube, R. J. Dolan, and C. D. Frith. 2004. Empathy for pain involves the affective but not sensory components of pain. *Science* 303 (5661): 1157–62.

Smith, K. S., A. J. Tindell, J. W. Aldridge, and K. C. Berridge. 2009. Ventral pallidum roles in reward and motivation. *Behavioral Brain Research* 196 (2): 155–67.

Sommer, I. E., K. M. Diederen, J. D. Blom, A. Willems, L. Kushan, K. Slotema, M. P. Boks, et al. 2008. Auditory verbal hallucinations predominantly activate the right inferior frontal area. *Brain* 131 (Pt 12): 3169–77.

Spezio, M., and R. Adolphs. 2007. Politics and the evolving neuroscience literature. In *The affect effect: Dynamics of emotion in political thinking and behavior*, ed. A. Crigler, M. MacKuen, G. E. Marcus and W. R. Neuman, 71–95. Chicago: University of Chicago Press.

Spezio, M. L., A. Rangel, R. M. Alvarez, J. P. O'Doherty, K. Mattes, A. Todorov, H. Kim, and R. Adolphs. 2008. A neural basis for the effect of candidate appearance on election outcomes. *Social Cognitive and Affective Neuroscience* 3 (4): 344–52.

Sridharan, D., D. J. Levitin, and V. Menon. 2008. A critical role for the right fronto-insular cortex in switching between central-executive and default-mode networks. *Proceedings of the National Academy of Sciences* 105 (34): 12569–74.

Takahashi, H., M. Kato, M. Matsuura, D. Mobbs, T. Suhara, and Y. Okubo. 2009. When your gain is my pain and your pain is my gain: Neural correlates of envy and schadenfreude. *Science* 323 (5916): 937–39.

Taylor, S. E., L. J. Burklund, N. I. Eisenberger, B. J. Lehman, C. J. Hilmert, and M. D. Lieberman. 2008. Neural bases of moderation of cortisol stress responses by psychosocial resources. *Journal of Personality and Social Psychology* 95 (1): 197–211.

van den Heuvel, M. P., R. C. Mandl, R. S. Kahn, and H. E. Hulshoff Pol. 2009. Functionally linked resting-state networks reflect the underlying structural connectivity architecture of the human brain. *Human Brain Mapping* 30 (10): 3127–41.

van den Heuvel, M. P., C. J. Stam, M. Boersma, and H. E. Hulshoff Pol. 2008. Small-world and scale-free organization of voxel-based resting-state functional connectivity in the human brain. *Neuroimage* 43 (3): 528–39.

van Eijsden, P., F. Hyder, D. L. Rothman, and R. G. Shulman. 2009. Neurophysiology of functional imaging. *Neuroimage* 45 (4): 1047–54.

van Veen, V., and C. S. Carter. 2002. The anterior cingulate as a conflict monitor: fMRI and ERP studies. *Physiological Behavior* 77 (4–5): 477–82.

van Veen, V., M. K. Krug, J. W. Schooler, and C. S. Carter. 2009. Neural activity predicts attitude change in cognitive dissonance. *Nature Neuroscience* 12 (11):1469–74.

Vuilleumier, P., J. L. Armony, J. Driver, and R. J. Dolan. 2003. Distinct spatial frequency sensitivities for processing faces and emotional expressions. *Nature Neuroscience* 6 (6): 624–31.

Vul, E., C. Harris, P. Winkielman, and H. Pashler. 2009. Puzzlingly high correlations in fMRI studies of emotion, personality, and social cognition. *Perspectives on Psychological Science* 4 (3): 274–90.

Walter, H., B. Abler, A. Ciaramidaro, and S. Erk. 2005. Motivating forces of human actions: Neuroimaging reward and social interaction. *Brain Research Bulletin* 67 (5): 368–81.

Walton, M. E., P. L. Croxson, T. E. Behrens, S. W. Kennerley, and M. F. Rushworth. 2007. Adaptive decision making and value in the anterior cingulate cortex. *Neuroimage* 36 (Suppl. 2): T142–54.

Warneken, F., and M. Tomasello. 2009. Varieties of altruism in children and chimpanzees. *Trends in Cognitive Science* 13 (9): 397–402.

Westen, D., P. Blagov, K. Harenski, C. Kilts, and S. Hamann. 2006. Neural bases of motivated reasoning: An fMRI study of emotional constraints on partisan political judgment in the 2004 U.S. presidential election. *Journal of Cognitive Neuroscience* 18 (11): 1947–58.

Wicker, B., C. Keysers, J. Plailly, J. P. Royet, V. Gallese, and G. Rizzolatti. 2003. Both of us disgusted in my insula: The common neural basis of seeing and feeling disgust. *Neuron* 40 (3): 655–64.

Wicker, B., P. Ruby, J. P. Royet, and P. Fonlupt. 2003. A relation between rest and the self in the brain? *Brain Research Review* 43 (2): 224–30.

Williams, Z. M., G. Bush, S. L. Rauch, G. R. Cosgrove, and E. N. Eskandar. 2004. Human anterior cingulate neurons and the integration of monetary reward with motor responses. *Nature Neuroscience* 7 (12): 1370–75.

Winston, J. S., R. N. Henson, M. R. Fine-Goulden, and R. J. Dolan. 2004. fMRI-adaptation reveals dissociable neural representations of identity and expression in face perception. *Journal of Neurophysiology* 92 (3): 1830–39.

Wittfoth, M., D. M. Schardt, M. Fahle, and M. Herrmann. 2009. How the brain resolves high conflict situations: Double conflict involvement of dorsolateral prefrontal cortex. *Neuroimage* 44 (3): 1201–9.

Wolfe, T. 2000. Sorry, but your soul just died. In *Hooking Up*, 89–109. New York: Picador.

Zink, C. F., Y. Tong, Q. Chen, D. S. Bassett, J. L. Stein, and A. Meyer-Lindenberg. 2008. Know your place: Neural processing of social hierarchy in humans. *Neuron* 58 (2): 273–83.

11

CONCLUSION

Peter K. Hatemi and Rose McDermott

In compiling this volume, we sought to provide a foundation for neurobiological approaches to political behavior. In so doing, we do not pretend that we have been able to do justice to the depth and breadth of the growing body of literature, within political science as well as in outside disciplines, exploring the myriad ways in which heritable, biological, and physiological factors influence, shape, and direct political and social choices and preferences. Rather than attempt to provide a comprehensive overview, we instead offer incisive exemplars of the way in which nuanced and subtle work in this emerging field might progress. Our hope is that these models will inspire and direct others to pursue similar work to address the many untapped areas of inquiry at the intersection of biological and political sciences in a rigorous, conscientious, and sensitive manner.

The study of politics from a biological perspective does not exclude or otherwise diminish the import of environmental and social factors. Indeed, we hope to solicit interest from scholars in the field whose work encompasses these more traditional approaches to the study and understanding of political attitudes, preferences, and behavior. We hope that the illustration these chapters provide documents the new and exciting theoretical and empirical work that can be done in this area.

We nonetheless recognize that many people retain reservations regarding the utility and practicality of approaching politics from a neurobiological perspective. We believe that the demonstrations in this volume go some way toward explaining what these biological approaches do, and how they can be used within the discipline to address critical questions of interest and why it matters to incorporate these approaches into existing models of political behavior. We do not support a simplistic approach to these issues, nor do we suggest that merely including these factors without a guiding theoretical framework will prove valuable. Rather, we encourage interested scholars to learn the basic theories, models, and methods that would allow them to address their political questions of interest in a careful way, as well as collaborate with investigators in other fields to work on problems of common concern. In this way, as in any regular pattern of progress in normal science, aggregation of knowledge can occur. Studies that attack a given puzzle from a variety of different perspectives, using a variety of methods, can develop a more refined and contextualized understanding of the variables under investigation. Adding additional factors of consideration can serve to broaden and clarify the sources, operation, and consequences of political preferences; if such forces prove irrelevant or insignificant, this can be discovered in the course of analysis, just as any other variable might be falsified.

At the outset of this volume, we argued that the utility of a biological approach could be discerned by its ability to pose novel questions, to address previously unresolved and important conundrums using new methods and techniques, or point to previously unexplored areas of inquiry. We believe that the various chapters contained in this volume have proven persuasive in this regard to readers. Below we provide our brief assessment of the comparative value and added advantage offered by a biological approach to politics.

We well recognize that the important and interesting political questions that can be addressed from a biological perspective do not differ from those that can be asked using any other theoretical or methodological approach. Biological approaches may add new factors for consideration, or new variables to consider, but does not restrict or otherwise constrain the nature of the political variables and puzzles under consideration. As with any other model, sophisticated biological work should proceed by first theorizing the purported causal mechanism and then collecting the relevant data, and running the appropriate analysis to see if the hypothesized relationships hold true. In some cases, this may entail adding a biological element to a model that previously neglected its impact. In other cases, it may involve exploring the way in which biological factors mediate environmental factors; such an approach may help to reorient theories that have previously produced inconsistent or contradictory results to illuminate the way in which genetic factors interact with environmental ones to more accurately predict political preferences based on particular biological typologies.

Often biological models display environments and nature as competing forces. This is more often due to statistical limitations. However, no modern or accurate exploration of behavior, including those in this volume, sees these forces as competing. Rather, when considering biological influences, it is essential to incorporate explicitly environmental political context into any study of political behaviors. The majority of work thus far has examined the origins and sources of both social and political variables. But such initial explorations remain incomplete without a full recognition of the operation of individual variance upon these environmental and institutional political factors. By the time this volume comes to press, additional work will already be in progress that will refine the specific political conditions and contexts that activate heritable and biological mechanisms and those that flow from them. As with theories that only focus on environmental variables, paradigms that only incorporate biological factors remain similarly limited in scope. It is only by creating models with an explicit recognition of the influence of *both* biology and environment that we can begin to develop more comprehensive models of political choice and decisionmaking.

We hope that this volume has helped readers understand the complex and sophisticated nature of the relationship between biology and environment in influencing the political and social attitudes and behaviors we have sought to explicate. We believe that the previous chapters have proved persuasive in demonstrating the empirical basis for clarifying the underlying mechanisms and relationships involved in the dynamic interplay between genetics and socialization. We believe, at the very least, that we have shown how we can explain much more by incorporating elements of biology into our models than we can by excluding it.

What does it mean if something is influenced by biology? Can we still influence it through social policy? What if we can't? We take such concerns very seriously. At least two critical aspects of this problem exist. The first relates to how this work might be used and perceived by others. The best possible response to this is to conduct empirical work with care, thoughtfulness, and sensitivity. Scholars exploring this area need to remain self-conscious of this aspect of their work and take care not to overstate or overgeneralize the implications of their research; this attention to broader influence is not so different from those who conduct research in other controversial areas such as stem cell regeneration. Just because such work might be condemned by those who oppose some aspect of its political implications does not mean that such research should cease to progress, but rather it adds an additional responsibility on the part of those who conduct biological research to carefully convey the meaning and limitations of their findings. This added impetus should only serve to spur researchers to conduct the best and more careful work possible.

In addition, knowing more about the nature of biological and genetic influences actually provides a great deal of additional information about environmental factors as well. For instance, genetically informative samples can offer information about which factors are heavily influenced by common environment and which ones appear more impervious to external influences. This information may allow informed policymakers to make wiser choices about where to invest money so that efforts are concentrated where they can and will make a difference, rather than being thrown at factors that remain relatively less susceptible to environmental influence and control.

Finally, the amount of care, attention, detail, oversight, and requirements for replication adhered to in the world of genetics research really has no parallel in the experience of the vast majority of social and political scientists. Social scientists may not be aware of these procedures, but the level of ethical oversight remains at the highest level. Demands for replication remain paramount in the scientific community in a way that is simply unknown to most social scientists; in addition, often thousands of people work in consortia on the same problem, such as unlocking the genome, or discovering some of the genetic factors involved in breast cancer (BRCA1 and BRCA 2), and each group must prove accountable and transparent in procedures and data to other team members. These processes add a high degree of credibility and oversight, which remains very important both for purposes of replicability but also for ensuring the ethical treatment of subjects.

Transparency remains a critical value in interpreting findings and assessing the utility of the methods we advocate. Transparency also aids in our ability to pay attention to central debates in other relevant disciplines because it opens up the possibility for substantive conversations on topics of mutual interest. These various scientific disciplines nonetheless agree on fundamental methodological aspects of scientific inquiry. However, this call toward including biological perspectives raises a significant challenge to many scholars who may never have taken a biology course through their entire lives, those who do not know what DNA is, and those not trained in techniques common in other fields. The great many political scientists might find the argot of other fields impenetrable or experience the demands of keeping up in one's own field sufficiently overwhelming without having to tackle the demands of learning another. Indeed, the limitations of a certain study or approach in one field may be well known, but such knowledge would not be intuitive in others. For example, in political science, partisanship, ideology, and vote choice are seen as distinct elements that cannot be used interchangeably. In neuroscience they have been labeled as politics. One of the most efficient strategies for overcoming such challenges is to seek out collaborations with scientists skilled in the methods of interest, perhaps from outside the discipline, who nonetheless share substantive interests that can be examined in concert. Such scholars are often eager to team with others who offer interesting and challenging substantive questions and problems. Various opportunities exist to establish such collaboration through attending conferences or contacting scholars directly whose work offers promising possibilities for mutual over-lapping research. Such an approach is useful not only for empirical research but for evaluation, such that reviewers might also include those from other fields, to simply comment on the methods or discussion when needed.

We suggest that political scientists have a moral and ethical obligation to undertake research into the biological and genetic bases of political choice because such work is already being undertaken by governmental, corporate, and private interests. Only when scholars who do not remain beholden to pri-vate or financial interests engage in such research can the findings be widely disseminated, evaluated, and publically discussed. Only when such factors become part of the public debate can such knowledge become transparent, and potentially be used for the public good, as opposed for the public ill or private political or financial gain without the knowledge of those who might be exploited. Burying our heads in the sand will not stop interested others from exploring and utilizing such knowledge as might be useful to them. Only by conducting our research in an ethical and transparent way, disseminating the data and results widely and openly, and encouraging public discussion of our findings and their proper interpretation and meaning can we mitigate the forces we fear and prevent abuses that permeated the past from repeating.

In conclusion, work that examines political questions and problems, such as cooperation, aggression, ideology, discrimination, and identity, using bio-logical variables is progressing rapidly outside the field of political science. Schreiber's review speaks to this explosion in relevant research quite elo-quently. The field will continue to develop with or without the contribution of those best trained and positioned to add value and sophistication to the biological exploration of political phenomena. We hope that this volume will go some distance toward demonstrating, through training and example, the myriad opportunities that exist for novel techniques to deepen our under-standing of how political forces influence humans, and how they, in turn, shape the larger political body.

Index

Page numbers in italics indicate figures and tables.

abortion: genetic influence on opinions on, 35; quantitative variance components for political and social attitudes toward, 192, *193*, 196

adaptations: in evolutionary psychology, 28, 29; human adaptability, 25; not all maintain their usefulness over time, 29–30; two levels of analysis of, 50

adaptive learning, models of, 78–79, *80*

Add Health (Study of Adolescent Health), 189, 192, 196–97, 215, 218, 219

additive genetic effects: in analysis of family resemblance, 111, 114, 116, 125, 126, 127, 129, 135, 139, 141, 153; in attitude toward homosexuality, 217; as component of variance, 105; and gene-environment interaction variance, 204; in voter turnout behavior, 215

Adkins-Regan, E., 248

affirmative action, physiological reactions and attitudes toward, 239–42

age: development of social and political attitudes in childhood, 141–49; genetic and environmental effects not dependent on, 117; life-course perspective, 37, 141–42, 188, 202, 203–4, 216

agent-based models, 79

agents in evolutionary game theory, 82

aggression: MAOA-L associated with, 257; oxytocin associated with, 256; in primates, 62–63; testosterone associated with, 247, 251, 252, 258; vasopressin associated with, 255

Alford, J., 35, 216

alliances. *See* coalitions and alliances

altruism: general, and social identification, 213; rational actor models and, 15; reciprocal, 52; and voting, 213

American Journal of Sociology, 201

American National Election Study, 211

Amodio, D. M., 35

amygdala, 256, 257, 283, 284–85, 287, 290

Andreoni, J., 213

androgens, 251, 262

anterior cingulate cortex (ACC), 287–88

anterior insula, 285–86

antisocial behavior, testosterone and, 252

anxiety, oxytocin and experience of, 256

Apicella, C. A., 196, 252

assortative mating: correlation between relatives increased by, 158; fitting models for spousal resemblance, 170, 171, 172–74, 175–76; in genetic model of inheritance of family resemblance, 116–17, 132; genetic variance increased by, 158; genotypic, 117; and joint analysis of twin and nuclear family data, 133, 135, 139; as mechanism of mate selection, 103; in nongenetic model of inheritance of family resemblance, 115; phenotypic, 103, 111, 115, 116, 125, 133, 135, 153, 158, 159–65, 169–70, 172–74, 175–76; potential significance of, 103; shared environment versus genetic consequences of, 153–54; in spousal correlation, 111; and twin studies, 125, 126, 127, 131, 132

astrology, quantitative variance components for political and social attitudes toward, *195*

attitudes: development of social and political attitudes in childhood, 141–49; evolutionary models provide foundation for empirical research on, 22; gene-environment correlation and political attitudes, 202–3; heritability of political, 216; interaction between endogenous and environmental factors in, 26; mind-body connection illuminates biological basis of, 225; small genetic differences affect, 27; universality and variance interact to produce, 21

Australian (OZ20K) study, 107, *107*, 151

Australian Twin Registry, 217

autism, 279, 289

autonomic nervous system, 229–37; functions of, 230–31; measurement of, 231–37; neural systems at root of, 225; as outside conscious awareness, 230; in peripheral nervous system, 230; political attitudes correlate with variations in, 225; subsystems of, 230–31

AVPR1A R3 allele, 255

Axelrod, R., 83

baboons: group punishment in, 56; threats in, 62, 62

Baker, L. A., 35, 197, 215

basal ganglia, 286–87

basal T, 251–52

Baumgartner, T., 256

behavioral endocrinology, 248–51. *See also* hormones

behavioral phylogeny, 48–51

behaviorism: limits of, 13, 276; as partial explanation of political behavior, 9, 35; past environments neglected in, 27

Bendor, J., 211

biology: biological approach to political behavior, 1–8, 35–38, 300–304; interaction of environment and, 1, 3–4, 7, 17, 26–27, 33, 38–39, 102, 249, 301–3; mind-body connection illuminates biological basis of attitudes, 225; modeling cultural and biological inheritance of social and political behavior, 101–84; overlapping agendas with social science, 6; social policy and results from, 302–3. *See also* evolution; genetics; nature-nurture juxtaposition

Boardman, J. D., 189–90

Boehm, C., 56

BOLD (blood oxygen level dependent) MRI, 279–80

bonobos, 50, 63

Booth, J., 252

Bradley, M., 225

brain: amygdala, 256, 257, 283, 284–85, 287, 290; anterior cingulate cortex (ACC), 287–88; basal ganglia, 286–87; black-box approach to, 273, 275; default mode network (DMN), 288–89; different brain activity in those on political left and right, 35; functional magnetic resonance imaging (fMRI) studies, 277, 278, 279–83; fusiform face area (FFA), 283–84; individual agency's effect on, 274; insula, 285–86, 287; lesion studies, 279; medial prefrontal cortex (mPFC), 289–90; neocortex, 274, 282, 287; neuroimaging studies of, 273–74; regions of interest (ROIs), 282–83; specialization and localization in, 274; structural MRI studies, 277; variance within broad patterns in, 21

Brooks, David, 276

Brosnan, S. F., 15

Burden, B. C., 198

busing, quantitative variance components for political and social attitudes toward, 192, 193

Button, T. M., 191

Cacioppo, J. T., 226

Campbell, A., 158

capitalism, quantitative variance components for political and social attitudes toward, 192, 193, 196

capuchin monkeys, 52–53

cardiovascular measures, 235–37

Caspi, Avshalom, 36, 185, 203

Cattell, R. B., 104, 105

causation, 7

censorship, quantitative variance components for political and social attitudes toward, 192, 194

central executive network, 288

central nervous system, 230

Cesarini, D. A., 196, 210, 217

Chen, K., 16

childhood, development of social and political attitudes in, 141–49

chimpanzees: in barpull task, 54, 55; coalitions and alliances among, 64; comparing human neuroanatomy with that of, 279; cortisol and dominance in, 254; endowment effect in, 58–59; grooming among, 63; group hunting by, 54; group punishment among, 56; primates to which humans are most closely related, 50; ritualized greetings in, 62; social learning in, 60; symbols used by, 58; trade among, 57–58

chronotropy, 236

church attendance: correlations between married relative pairs, 160, 161–63; correlations between relatives in United States and Australia, 110, 111, 113; fitting models for spousal resemblance, 172, 175; genetic and environmental effects vary with age, 142; as index of phenotypic assortment, 164–65; and joint analysis of twin and nuclear family data, 136, 137, 138, 140, 141; as measurement for studying family resemblance, 102, 109; model-fitting results of genetic model of inheritance in nuclear families, 123–24; model-fitting results of nongenetic model of inheritance in nuclear families, 119–21; models for twin resemblance, 127, 128, 129, 130; relative contributions of genetic familial influences on outcome measures, 124; relative contributions of genetic transmission on outcome measures, twin data without spouse pairs, 129; relative contributions of genetic transmission on outcome measures, twin data with spouse pairs, 131; relative contributions of phenotypic familial influences on outcome measures, 121; and social homogamy, 166; spousal correlation and, 153; and voter turnout, 218–19

cingulate gyrus, 287

civility, 233

civil society, evolutionary game theoretic model of, 80, 82, 85–93

cleaner fish, 55–56

Clutton-Brock, T. H., 55

coalitions and alliances: in human dominance contests, 269; among primates, 63–64; testosterone levels and, 252

cognition, social. *See* social cognition

cognitive energy, conservation of, 16

Cohen, M. D., 83

collective action, 80

common environment. *See* shared environment

complex adaptive behavior, 21

computational evolutionary models, 79; creating and studying, 93–95; programming, 94–95, 96–98

conflict: and cooperation seen as opposition forces, 14, 24; evolutionary models and, 22

convergent evolution, 49–50

cooperation: basal ganglia in, 287; behavior genetics on choice of, 36; breaks down if not all partners benefit, 55; and conflict seen as opposition forces, 14, 24; costs and benefits of, 208; evolutionary models and, 22; explanations of, 51–52; heritability of, 218; in human evolution, 14–15; human levels as unique, 9, 51, 64, 207; mechanisms in evolution of, 208–9; methodology for studying, 52–53; origins of, 208–10; political participation compared with, 210; among primates, 51–55; punishment for cheating, 55–56, 209, 218; stability over time, 209–10

cortisol, 253–54

Cosmides, Leda, 29, 31

courage, 23

Coventry, W. L., 202

cross-species alliance, 64

Damasio, Antonio, 279

Damasio, Hanna, 279

Dambrun, M., 235, 237

Darwin, Charles, 23, 49

Dawes, C. T., 35, 197, 213, 215, 216, 218, 219

Dawson, M., 231

death penalty: genetic influence on opinions on, 35; quantitative variance components for political and social attitudes toward, *194*

decisionmaking: accounting for endogenous and environmental factors, 20; anterior cingulate cortex in, 287–88; basal ganglia in, 286, 287; brain activity in, 16; under conditions of inequity, 59–60; as creative, not merely revelatory, 15; levels of analysis problem in theories of, 20; multiple circuits involved in, 287; among primates, 57–60; about property and possessions, 57–59; scientific advancements in study of, 1; seemingly irrational, 15–16

default mode network (DMN), 288–89

DeFries, J. C., 187

DeFries-Fulker model, 197, 199

delayed gratification, 212

depression, 203

Despres, G., 235, 237

determinism, neuroimaging seen as presuming, 273. *See also* genetic determinism

de Waal, F. B. M., 15

dictator games, 213, 217, 219, 265

Diermeier, D., 211

diffusion tensor imaging (DTI), 277–78, 290

dihydrotestosterone, 251

direct reciprocity, 208–9

disgust: amygdala activated by, 284; self-report disgust batteries on attitudes toward homosexuality, 228

divorce, quantitative variance components for political and social attitudes toward, 192, *193*, 196

dizygotic (DZ) twins: and development of social and political attitudes in shared environment, 142–49; and equal environments assumption, 151–52; expected correlations between relatives, 134; genetic correlation between, 125, 197; and joint analysis of twin and nuclear family data, 133, 135, 137; models for twin resemblance, 124–31; offspring of, 106–7; spouses of, 106; twin types, 105, 124

dolphins, 64

Domes, G., 256

dominance (genetic), 177n5; as component of variance, 105; in family resemblance in nuclear families, 111–12; and joint analysis of twin and nuclear family data, 135, 137, 139

dominance (social): cortisol levels and, 254; human contests for, 264, 269; in nonhuman primates, 61–63; testosterone associated with, 252, 263

dopamine, 255, 257

dorsolateral prefrontal cortex (DLPFC), 290

"double advantage" phenomena, 104–5

Downs, A., 80, 158

Down's syndrome, 27

draft (military), quantitative variance components for political and social attitudes toward, *194*

DRD2-A1 allele, 219

DRD4-7R allele, 192, 219

Durkheim, Emile, 39, 101

Dynamo package (Mathematica 5), 91

Eaves, Lindon, 35, 142, 189, 197

eccrine sweat glands, 232

economics: behavioral, 207, 217; evolutionary principles applied to, 80; gene association studies in, 219; neuroeconomics, 230, 275, 276, 287 educational attainment: correlation between married relative pairs, 161–63; correlations between relatives in United States and Australia, 110, 111, 113; delayed gratification and, 212; fitting models for spousal resemblance, 172; genetic effects for women versus men, 191; genetic influence on, 35; and joint analysis of twin and nuclear family data, 136, 137, 138, 140, 141; as measurement for studying family resemblance, 102, 109; model-fitting results of genetic model of inheritance in nuclear families, 123–24; model-fitting results of nongenetic model of inheritance in nuclear families, 119–21; models for twin resemblance, 127, 128, 130, 131; relative contributions of genetic familial influences on outcome measures, 124; relative contributions of genetic transmission on outcome measures, twin data without spouse pairs, 129; relative contributions of genetic transmission on outcome measures, twin data with spouse pairs, 131; relative contributions of phenotypic familial influences on outcome measures, 121; spousal correlation and, 153

electrocardiogram (ECG), 236

electrodermal activity, 231–33

electroencephalography (EEG), 278

electromyography, 233–35

Ellison, P., 249, 253

empathy, 286

endocrinology, human behavioral, 248–51. See also hormones

endowment effect, 58–59

England, B., 252

environment: biological approach illuminates nature of effects, 4–5; in Darwin's theory, 49; different sources of environmental variation, 19; in gene-environment interplay perspective, 187; humans adapt to and alter, 24; individual traits in interpretation of, 25–26; interaction of biology and, 1, 3–4, 7, 17, 26–27, 33, 38–39, 102, 249, 301–3; local, 20; modeling cultural and biological inheritance of social and political behavior, 101–84; as multidimensional, 197, 202; as not everything, 35; and origins of preferences, 18; past and present environments as mediators of genetic expression, 26–27; social-scientific definition of, 187, 196; in traditional approaches to political behavior, 13; in traditional approaches to political science, 1. See also gene-environment interplay perspective; nature-nurture juxtaposition; shared environment; socialization; unique environment

equal environments assumption, 132, 135, 151–52

equilibria: equilibrium strategies, 20; in evolutionary game theory, 85–86; out-of-equilibrium dynamics, 74, 78, 86, 96; rational-choice models assume, 81–82

errors, anterior cingulate cortex in detection of, 288

estradiol, 251

estrogens, 262

ethnicity: electromyographic studies on responses to, 235; respiratory activity and response to, 237. See also race

evolution, 75–77; comprehensive illumination offered by, 5, 20, 37; cooperation and trust in human, 14–15; earlier approach to incorporating as theory of preferences, 28–32; empirical link between political behavior and, 33–34; evidence for, 22; features of, 72, 75; human understanding in changing of, 8; human universals in, 20–21; increasing acceptance of evolutionary models, 38–40; as intrinsically rational, 26; "just so" stories, 96; literal and figurative meanings of, 74; as model for human political behavior, 19–27; negative reaction to evolutionary models, 38; as not restricted to biology, 22; overview, 23–27; populations as unit of evolutionary analysis, 75–76; previous theoretical models compared with, 9; rapidity of change, 31–32; as substrate-independent, 75; as theory for political behavior, 13–46; what other primates can tell us about evolutionary roots of our own political behavior, 47–71. See also evolutionary modeling; fitness (biological); natural selection

evolutionary game theory, 77–78; agents, 82; asymmetric games, 90; components of, 82; creating and studying a computational evolutionary model, 93–95, 96–98; payoffs, 83–84; rules of interaction, 83; rules of replication, 84; specifying a model, 82–84; strategies, 77–78, 82–83; studying a model, 85–93; types of strategy, 82

evolutionary imitation, 79

evolutionary modeling, 72–100; in economics, 80; evolutionary models help bridge gap between social and hard sciences, 26; evolutionary models provide insight where rational choice and socialization models fail, 14, 37; formal evolutionary models, 77–80; generality of, 77; nonrational behavior modeled by, 74; out-of-equilibrium dynamics captured by, 74, 78, 86, 96; in political science, 72, 77, 80–93; rational-choice models compared with, 73, 81–82, 96; renaissance of, 80. See also evolutionary game theory evolutionary psychology (EP), 28–32; applicability to political science of, 31–32; central problem of, 33; empirical and theoretical challenges to, 30–31; HG hypotheses in, 29; human universals as focus of, 29, 31; modern revisions and extensions of, 32

evolutionary stable strategies (ESS), 78, 86–89

extended family design studies, 215, 217

extended twin (ET) kinships: defined, 105–6, 106; richness of, 106–7

faces: brain regions for processing, 283–84; electromyographic study of facial expressions, 233–35

Falconer, Douglas, 105

families: between-family differences, 104; family clusters and individual differences, 104–8; measurements for studying family resemblance, 108–9; as primary group, 104; within-family differences, 104

fear: amygdala in processing of, 284; oxytocin and experience of, 256

federal housing, quantitative variance components for political and social attitudes toward, 195

Filion, D., 231

financial risk-taking, 219, 252, 263

Fisher, R. A., 105, 111, 116, 117, 151, 155, 177n5

fitness (biological): behavioral phylogeny and understanding, 49; cooperation and increase in, 51; of cooperators and noncooperators, 208, 209; in evolutionary game theory, 84, 86, 87, 89–90; hunter-gatherer adaptations and, 30; kin selection and increase in, 52; political preference and mate selection and, 34; reproductive versus common notion of, 23; "survival of the fittest," 24–25

5HTT gene, 218

Flynn, M., 252

foreign aid, quantitative variance components for political and social attitudes toward, 193

Fowler, J. H., 6, 35, 185, 197, 210, 211, 212, 213, 215, 216, 218, 219

fraternal twins. See dizygotic (DZ) twins

Frazzetto, G., 40n4

free will, 275, 289

friendships, among chimpanzees, 63

Fulker, D. W., 105

functional magnetic resonance imaging (fMRI), 277, 278, 279–83

Funk, C., 35, 117, 154, 216

fusiform face area (FFA), 283–84

Gage, Phineas, 279, 289

Galton, Francis, 122, 124

game theory: heritability of political behavior and, 217–18. See also evolutionary game theory

gay marriage: self-report disgust batteries on attitudes toward, 228; skin-conductance levels and reactions to, 233

gay rights: genetic influences on attitudes toward, 216–17; quantitative variance components for political and social attitudes toward, 192, 195

gender: fusiform face area perceives characteristics of, 284; gene-environment interplay perspective on genetic influences in gender gap, 192; and heritability of political attitudes, 216; versus sex, 18–19; testosterone and masculinization, 251, 261

gene association studies, 218–20

gene-environment correlation (rGE), 187–88; active correlation, 188; evocative correlation, 187; gene-environment interaction interpretation affected by, 202; in gene-environment interplay perspective, 185; life-course perspective on, 203; as not necessarily causation, 186; passive correlation, 187–88; and political attitudes, 202–3

gene-environment interaction (GxE), 188–91; empirical example of, 196–201; and gene association studies, 218; gene-environment correlation affects interpretation of, 202; in gene-environment interplay perspective, 185; social control model, 190–91; social distinction model, 191; social push model, 191; social triggering model, 188–89

gene-environment interplay perspective, 185–206; case for, 201–2; life-course perspective on, 203–4; overview of, 186–201; in political science, 191–96, 204. See also gene-environment correlation (rGE); gene-environment interaction (GxE)

genetic algorithms, 79

genetic determinism, 154–55; genetic variance as not implying that individual genes have large effects or correspond to specific behavioral outcomes, 157

genetic differences: attitudes and preferences affected by, 27; differential expression as function of secular upbringing, 150–51; eradicated by cumulative effects of postnatal environment, 142; individual differences as in part function of, 154–55; number and genomic location of heritable differences, 155; personality traits affected by, 23; political science assumes genetic identity, 156; proportion that translates into manifest phenotype differences, 156–57 genetic model of inheritance in nuclear families, 116, 116–17; expected correlations between family members under nongenetic model and, 117; fitting the model, 118; model-fitting results, 122–24

genetics: behavior, 5, 20, 33, 36, 104–5, 214, 218, 219; humans have greatest within-species variation, 24, 27; incorporating into political science, 155–58; past and present environments as mediators of, 26–27; psychiatric, 4, 36; social policy and results from, 302–3; variation in hunter-gatherer groups, 29. See also additive genetic effects; gene-environment interplay perspective; genetic determinism; genetic differences; genetic transmission

genetic transmission: evolutionary psychology on, 28; human culture shapes, 24; as mechanism of retention in biological evolution, 77; of political preferences, 23, 34, 35, 38–39. See also genetic model of inheritance in nuclear families

Gilbert, C. P., 198
Gintis, H., 15, 17, 90
Glimcher, P., 16
glucocorticoids, 253–54
Goodall, Jane, 63
Graham, Jesse, 35
Gray, P., 249, 253
greetings, ritualized, 61–62
grooming, 63
group hunting, 53–54
Guimond, S., 235, 237
Guo, G., 188–89

habitual turnout, 211
Haidt, Jonathan, 35
Hamilton, W. D., 52
happiness, 227, 250
Hatemi, Peter K., 34, 36, 117, 148, 154, 157, 192, 215, 216
Hauert, C., 210
heart, measures of autonomic nervous system activity, 236–37
Heath, A. C., 167, 190
Heinrichs, M., 256
Hibbing, J., 35, 216
Hobbes, Thomas, 19
homologies, 49–50
homosexuality: genetic influences on attitudes toward, 216–17; self-report disgust batteries on attitudes toward, 228. See also gay rights
hormones, 247–60; environmental cues and triggers for, 249–50; human behavioral endocrinology, 248–51; noninvasive techniques for

measuring, 248; two-layer context of, 249. See also testosterone

human behavior: biological advancements in study of, 1; individual differences in context of, 20–22, 39–40. See also political behavior

human universals: evolutionary psychology focuses on, 29, 31; evolutionary theory rests on, 20–21; merging with study of individual differences, 32–34; moving to individual differences from, 27–34

hunter-gatherer (HG) societies, 28–29, 30, 31

identical twins. See monozygotic (MZ) twins

ideology: electromyographic studies on differential responses, 235; gene association studies on, 219; gene-environment interplay perspective on genetic influences on, 192; heritability of, 216; parental influence on, 142; personality's effects on, 157; as predictor of opposition to race-conscious affirmative action, 242

ignorance, "rational," 92

immigration: genetic influence on opinions on, 35; quantitative variance components for political and social attitudes toward, 195

indirect reciprocity, 209

individual differences: automotive analogy for, 21–22; in context of human universals, 20–22, 39–40; empirical testing of, 32–34; family clusters and, 104–8; in interpretation of environment, 25–26; merging human universals with study of, 32–34; moving from human universals to, 27–34; in nature-nurture binary, 186; not all subject to evolutionary pressures, 39; as a function of inherited genetic differences, 154–55; provide insight about ontogeny of human differences, 102, 104; shared environment as contributor to differences in, 129; variance within broad patterns in the brain, 21

individualism, methodological, 96

inequity: capuchin monkeys accept short-term, 53; decisionmaking under conditions of, 59–60

in-groups, 264, 267

inheritance: heritability of political attitudes, 216; heritability of political views, 199–200; heritability of voter turnout, 185, 215; models for cultural and biological in nuclear families, 114–41; of social and political behavior, 101–84. See also genetic transmission

institutional review boards (IRBs), 237–38

insula, 285–86, 287

interaction, rules of, 83

interbeat intervals (IBIs), 236, 240–42
interoception, 285–86
is/ought fallacy, 8

Jaffee, S. R., 202
Jencks, C., 104–5
Jinks, J. L., 105, 150
Joreskog, Karl, 167
Josephs, R. A., 269

Kam, C., 212, 213
Kamin, L. J., 155
Keller, M. C., 202
Kendler, K. S., 190, 203
kin selection, 52, 208
Kosfeld, M., 256
Kuklinski, J. H., 220
!Kung, 29, 56

Lacy, D., 198
Lakoff, George, 35
Lang, P. J., 225
language, 64–65
Lasswell, H. D., 48, 65
latent traits: environment moderates effects of ge-
    netic, 192; phenotypic assortment for, 164–65;
    in twin studies, 215
Lee, A., 111, 122
lesion studies, 279
levels of analysis problem, 20
Lewontin, R. C., 155
liberalism/conservatism: correlations between
    married relative pairs, 161–63; correlations be-
    tween relatives in United States and Australia,
    110, 111, 113; development of social and politi-
    cal attitudes in shared environment, 142–49;
    electromyographic studies on differential
    responses, 235; fitting models for spousal
    resemblance, 172, 175; gene-environment in-
    terplay perspective on genetic influences in,
    192; genetic effects emerge in early adulthood,
    154; genetic-environment covariance for, 203;
    ideology as predictor of opposition to race-
    conscious affirmative action, 242; and joint
    analysis of twin and nuclear family data, 136,
    137, 138, 140, 141; as measurement for studying
    family resemblance, 102, 109; model-fitting
    results of genetic model of inheritance in
    nuclear families, 122–24; model-fitting results
    of nongenetic model of inheritance in nuclear
    families, 119–21; models for twin resemblance,
    127, 128, 130; principled conservatism, 228,
    239–40, 242; relative contributions of genetic
    familial influences on outcome measures, 124;
    relative contributions of genetic transmission
    on outcome measures, twin data without
    spouse pairs, 129; relative contributions of
    genetic transmission on outcome measures,
    twin data with spouse pairs, 131; relative con-
    tributions of phenotypic familial influences
    on outcome measures, 121; spousal correlation
    and, 153
life-course perspective, 37, 141–42, 188, 202, 203–4,
    216
linear structural relationship (LISREL) models,
    167
Link, B. G., 189
Lodge, M., 227
Loehlin, J. C., 187
Loewen, P. J., 213
Lumsden, C. J., 101
Lustick, I., 38

Madsen, D., 227
magnetic resonance imaging (MRI): functional,
    277, 278, 279–83; structural, 277
magnetoencephalography (MEG), 278
MAOA (monoamine oxidase A), 36–37, 218, 256–57
Marcus, George, 243n1
Martin, Nick G., 35, 157
Maslow, Abraham, 19
mate selection: extended twin relationships for
    studying, 106; genetic markers of political
    preference compared with those for, 34;
    mechanisms, 103; oxytocin and female mate
    choice, 256; testing assumptions about,
    158–76; in transmission of information, 9. See
    also assortative mating; random mating
Mather, K., 150
maximum likelihood (ML) method, 118, 177n6
Mayhew, David, 72, 73
Mazur, A., 252
McDermott, R., 6, 196, 257
medial prefrontal cortex (mPFC), 289–90
Mehta, P. H., 269
Melis, A. P., 54
Mendelian inheritance, 105, 116, 132, 144
migration, 25
military drill, quantitative variance components
    for political and social attitudes toward, 195
Miller, J., 213
mixed-strategy Nash Equilibrium, 88–90, 94
models, evolutionary. See evolutionary modeling
modern art, quantitative variance components for
    political and social attitudes toward, 194
modularity hypothesis, 290
Moffitt, T. E., 185, 203
monoamine oxidase A (MAOA), 36–37, 218, 256–57

monozygotic (MZ) twins: and development of social and political attitudes in shared environment, 142–49; and equal environments assumption, 151–52; expected correlations between relatives, 134; genetic correlation between, 125, 197; and joint analysis of twin and nuclear family data, 133, 135, 137; models for twin resemblance, 124–31; offspring of, 106–7; "special environment" of, 152; spouses of, 106; twin types, 105, 124

moral judgment, 289

moral majority, quantitative variance components for political and social attitudes toward, 194

Morley, K. I., 215

multipopulation models, 82

Murnighan, J. K., 211

mutations, 8, 20, 21, 31

mutualism, 52

Mutz, D. C., 227, 233

Nash equilibria, 85–86, 87, 88–90, 94

natural selection, 22–23; as applicable to behavior, 49; based on adaptive traits at early period in human development, 14; complex adaptive behaviors evolve as function of, 21; and cooperation, 51, 208; as matter of reproductive success, 23, 24; "survival of the fittest," 24–25

nature-nurture juxtaposition, 17–19; costs versus benefits of, 186; drives animosity toward evolution, 38; evolutionary models and, 22; joint role in shaping political behavior, 214; neuroimaging seen as resolving, 273; political science and debates of 1970s to 1990s, 6; scientific approach refutes, 3–4

neocortex, 274, 282, 287

nervous system: central, 230; sympathetic, 230–31, 232, 233. See also autonomic nervous system; brain

neuroeconomics, 230, 275, 276, 287

neuroimaging: diffusion tensor imaging (DTI), 277–78, 290; electroencephalography (EEG), 278; and individual agency, 274; limitations on inferences from, 274–75; magnetoencephalography (MEG), 278; negative publicity regarding, 283; as not resolving metaphysical debates, 273, 274; positron emission tomography (PET) scanning, 278; radiological conventions unevenly applied in, 282. See also magnetic resonance imaging (MRI)

Neuroimaging Informatics Technology Initiative (NIfTI), 282

neurolaw, 275

neurophilosophy, 275

neuropolitics, 273–99; approaches to, 276–77; reasons for adopting approach, 275–77; variety of approaches to, 276–77. See also social cognitive and affective neuroscience (SCAN)

neuroticism: correlations between married relative pairs, 161–63; correlations between relatives in United States and Australia, 109, 110, 112–13; environmental influences on, 112; fitting models for spousal resemblance, 171, 172; and joint analysis of twin and nuclear family data, 136, 137, 138, 139, 140; as measurement for studying family resemblance, 102, 108, 109; model-fitting results of genetic model of inheritance in nuclear families, 123–24; model-fitting results of nongenetic model of inheritance in nuclear families, 119–21; models for twin resemblance, 127, 128, 130; relative contributions of genetic familial influences on outcome measures, 124; relative contributions of genetic transmission on outcome measures, twin data without spouse pairs, 129; relative contributions of genetic transmission on outcome measures, twin data with spouse pairs, 131; relative contributions of phenotypic familial influences on outcome measures, 121

nongenetic model of inheritance in nuclear families, 114–16, 115; expected correlations between family members under genetic model and, 117; fitting the model, 117–18; model-fitting results, 118–21

nonshared environment. See unique environment

Nowak, Martin, 208

nuclear families: data on family resemblance in non-twin, 109–14; expected correlations between, 117, 134; integrating twin and nuclear family data, 132–41; models for cultural and biological inheritance of resemblance, 114–41

nuclear power, quantitative variance components for political and social attitudes toward, 195

nurture. See nature-nurture juxtaposition

occipital face area (OFA), 283

overconfidence, 247, 264–65

Oxley, D. R., 6, 225, 227, 233, 235, 237

oxytocin, 250, 255–56

pacifism, quantitative variance components for political and social attitudes toward, 192, 194

pain, insula in response to, 285, 286

paradox of turnout, 210

parasympathetic nervous system, 230–31, 236–37

Parker, G. A., 55

partisan intensity: gene association studies on, 219; genetic influence on, 35, 185; testosterone levels and, 266–68, 269

party affiliation. See political affiliation

patience, and turnout, 212
payoffs in evolutionary game theory, 83–84
Pearson, K., 111, 122
Pedersen, N. L., 190
peripheral nervous system, 230
Perot, Ross, 198–201
Peterson, D. A. M., 198
personality traits: genetic differences play role in explaining differences in, 23; genetic influences change across developmental period, 203; genetic influences modulating impact of social background and individual situation on political choice, 157
Peterson, D. A. M., 198
Phelan, J., 189
"phenotypic assortative mating with error" model, 164, 165, 170
physiology: connection between physiological and psychological states, 225–27; genetic influence on, 225; measuring responses, 227; psychophysiology, 224–46. See also nervous system
Platt, M. L., 16
political affiliation: correlations between married relative pairs, 161–63; correlations between relatives in United States and Australia, 110, 111, 113; fitting models for spousal resemblance, 172, 175; heritability of strength of, 216; and joint analysis of twin and nuclear family data, 136, 137, 138, 139, 140, 141; as measurement for studying family resemblance, 102, 108, 109; model-fitting results of genetic model of inheritance in nuclear families, 122–24; model-fitting results of nongenetic model of inheritance in nuclear families, 119–21; models for twin resemblance, 127, 128, 129, 130, 131; quantitative variance components for political and social attitudes, 192, 195; relative contributions of genetic familial influences on outcome measures, 124; relative contributions of genetic transmission on outcome measures, twin data without spouse pairs, 129; relative contributions of genetic transmission on outcome measures, twin data with spouse pairs, 131; relative contributions of phenotypic familial influences on outcome measures, 121; social and unique environmental influences in, 153; spousal correlation and, 153. See also partisan intensity
political behavior: biological approach to, 1–8, 35–38, 300–304; defining, 48; development of social and political attitudes in childhood, 141–49; empirical link between evolutionary theory and, 33–34; evolutionary models provide foundation for empirical research on, 22; evolution as model for human, 19–27;

experimental studies of primates, 51–60; gene-environment interplay perspective and, 191–96, 204; heritability of, 217–20; hormones and, 247–60; inheritance of social behavior and, 101–84; interaction between endogenous and environmental factors in, 26; limited predictability of current models, 18; multivariate models for explaining how latent effects of genes and environment translate into observed differences in, 157; observational studies of primates, 61–64; origins of social preferences, 214–20; predictable patterns of, 37; small genetic differences affect, 27; social comparison in, 60; testosterone and biology of politics, 261–72; traditional approaches to, 13; universality and variance interact to produce, 21; what other primates can tell us about evolutionary roots of our own, 47–71; work published outside the discipline, 6. See also political affiliation; political participation
political participation, 210–14; gene association studies on, 218–19; gene-environment interplay perspective on genetic influences on, 191, 197–201; genetic influence on, 185; in-groups in, 264; social preferences and, 212–14. See also voter turnout
political science: collaborations with scientists from other fields, 303–4; evolutionary modeling in, 72, 77, 80–93; evolutionary models and four classic concerns of, 22; evolution as theory for, 13–46; genetic identity assumed by, 156; incorporating genetic and biological mechanisms into, 155–58; increasing acceptance of evolutionary models in, 38–40, 101–2; necessity of paying increasing attention to human internal constraints, 220–21; psychophysiology in, 227–29; standard social science model in, 17–18; traditional approaches to, 1, 2, 3; typical models in, 157. See also neuropolitics; political behavior
polygraph (lie detector) testing, 231
positron emission tomography (PET) scanning, 278
Posner, S. F., 152
possessions, primate decisionmaking about, 57–59
posterior insula, 285
power: among primates, 61–63; through coalitions and alliances, 63–64
preferences: accounting for endogenous and environmental factors in, 20; biological approaches provide endogenous sources of, 4, 5, 37; earlier approach to incorporating evolution as theory of, 28–32; evolutionary models provide foundation for empirical research on,

preferences (*continued*)
22; evolutionary psychology on, 28; formation of, 22; as genetic noise or mutation, 31; genetic sources as side effects, 33–34; genetic transmission of political, 23, 34, 35, 38–39; inherent elements in, 25; interaction of biology and environment in, 26–27; not all adaptations maintain their usefulness over time, 29–30; only within particular environments can certain ones be expressed, 26; origins of, 15–17, 18, 22, 37; as philosophical question, 19; in rational actor models, 13, 14, 15; revealed, 15; scientific advancements in study of, 1; shared environment and individual differences in, 129; small genetic differences affect, 27; structures, 19, 20, 27, 30, 34; tautological recourse to, 18; universality and variance interact to produce, 21. *See also* social preferences

premotor surface area, 283

presidential election of 2008, testosterone response following, 264–70

Price, T. S., 202

primates, 47–71; coalitions and alliances among, 63–64; cooperation among, 51–55; cortisol and subordination in, 254; decisionmaking among, 57–60; decisions about property and possessions, 57–59; decisions under conditions of inequity, 59–60; dominance and power among, 61–63; experimental studies of political behavior in, 51–60; group size limits, 64; observational studies of political behavior in, 61–64; punishment among, 55–56; social learning in, 60; taxa of, 50–51. *See also* chimpanzees

principal-agent problem, 80

progestins, 262

"Promethean genotype" theory, 101, 108, 154

property, primate decisionmaking about, 57–59

property taxes, quantitative variance components for political and social attitudes toward, 195

proximate level of analysis, 50

psychology: connection between physiological and psychological states, 225–27; psychophysiology, 224–46. *See also* evolutionary psychology (EP)

psychophysiology, 224–46; application to racial attitudes, 239–42; defined, 226–27; origins of, 225; in political science, 227–29; subject recruitment and administration, 237–39; surveys and experiments in addition to, 238; usefulness of, 228–29

punishment: heritability of, 218; human institutional forms of, 64; of noncooperators, 209; among primates, 55–56

Quirk, P. J., 220

race: amygdala in racial attitudes, 284–85, 290; electromyographic studies on differential responses to, 235; fusiform face area processes cues about, 284; measuring racial attitudes, 224, 228–29; physiological reactions and race-conscious affirmative action, 239–42; quantitative variance components for political and social attitudes on segregation, 194; respiratory activity and response to, 237

racial resentment scales, 240

Raichle, Marcus, 288

Raine, A., 191

random matching, 83, 95

random mating: fitting models for spousal resemblance, 171, 172–74; and genetic model of inheritance in nuclear families, 122; and nongenetic model of inheritance in nuclear families, 120; and spousal sorting on political preference, 39; and twin studies, 125, 126, 127

rational actor models: biological approaches provide endogenous sources of preferences for, 4; evolutionary modeling versus, 73, 81–82, 96; evolutionary models as superior to, 14, 34; limited explanatory capacity of, 13–14; limits of, 13–17, 276; origins of preferences not addressed in, 15, 37; as partial explanation of political behavior, 9, 35; past environments neglected in, 27; phenomena not accounted for by, 15; preferences in, 13, 14, 15; versus social constructionism, 6; as tautological, 15; in traditional approaches to political behavior, 13

rationality: in adaptive learning models, 78–79; assumed in rational-choice models, 81; as biological and not merely cognitive, 16–17; self-interest not necessarily implied by, 17. *See also* rational actor models

Rawlsian individuals, 213

reductionism, 7, 275

Reeves, B., 227, 233

regions of interest (ROIs), 282–83

religiosity: heritable component of, 35, 216; quantitative variance components for political and social attitudes toward, 193. *See also* church attendance

replication (experimental), 303

replication, rules of (game theory), 78, 84

replicator dynamics models, 84, 90–91, 92, 94–95

reputation, 209, 287

respiratory (breathing) rate and amplitude, 235–36, 237

respiratory sinus arrhythmia (RSA), 236–37

retention: as feature of evolution, 75, 76; in Mayhew's analysis of Congress, 72; in Sabato's analysis of attack journalism, 73

Riolo, R. L., 83

risk-taking, financial, 219, 252, 263

Robinson, Gene, 35–36

Rose, S., 155

Rousseau, Jean-Jacques, 19

Rustichini, A., 16

Rutter, M., 185, 203

Ruzicka, Leopold, 251

Sabato, Larry, 72–73, 93

salience network, 288

Sapolsky, R. M., 56, 254

Schell, A., 231

school prayer: chain of intermediate steps between genes and behavior, 229; quantitative variance components for political and social attitudes toward, 192, 193, 196

Schreiber, Darren, 6, 304

segregation, quantitative variance components for political and social attitudes toward, 194

selection: as feature of evolution, 75, 76; in Mayhew's analysis of Congress, 72; in Sabato's analysis of attack journalism, 73. See also natural selection

self, default mode network in sense of, 289

self-interest: narrow conceptions of, 14; political participation and, 213, 264; rationality does not necessarily imply, 17

self-report disgust batteries, 228

serotonin, 257

Settle, J. E., 192, 216

sex: family resemblance applies to both sexes, 114; versus gender, 18–19; oxytocin and, 256; testosterone and, 247, 251, 262; and twin studies, 125, 127; vasopressin and, 255

Share, L. J., 56

shared environment: age differences in effects of, 142; and attitude toward homosexuality, 217; in both genetic and nongenetic models, 116; as component of variance, 105; effects as persistent and cumulative, 154; versus genetic consequences of assortative mating, 153–54; in heritability of political views, 199–200; and joint analysis of twin and nuclear family data, 134, 135, 137–38, 141; in nongenetic model of inheritance in nuclear families, 117, 120, 121; in twin studies, 125–31, 132; and variation in conservatism, 144–48

single-population models, 82

skin, electrodermal activity, 231–33

skin conductance level (SCL), 232–33, 234, 238, 240–42

Smith, K., 233

Sniderman, P., 239–40

SNP GABRA2, 202

social cognition: amygdala in, 284; default mode network in, 289; face-processing in, 283–84; insula in, 286; medial prefrontal cortex in, 289; political science and theories of, 275

social cognitive and affective neuroscience (SCAN), 273–99; basic results of, 283–90; methods of, 277–83. See also neuroimaging

social constructionism, versus rational actor models, 6, 40n1

social-control model, 190–91, 202

social-distinction model, 191, 202

social homogamy: fitting models for spousal resemblance, 171, 172–74, 175; as mechanism of mate selection, 103; versus phenotype selection, 154; in spousal correlation, 111; testing assumptions about mate selection, 165–66

socialism, quantitative variance components for political and social attitudes toward, 195

socialization: in attitudes toward homosexuality, 217; development of social and political attitudes in childhood, 141–49; evolutionary models provide insight where it fails, 14; gender, 196; and gene-environment correlation, 186; limits of, 13–17; not everyone is socialized in same manner, 13, 14; one cannot socialize height, 112; self-report disgust batteries pick up on socialized attitudes, 228

social learning in primates, 60

social maneuvering, 63

social preferences: origins of, 214–20; and political participation, 212–14

social psychology, 37

social-push model, 191, 202

social science: boundary with natural sciences, 17, 38; Durkheim on independence of, 39, 101; evolutionary models help bridge gap between hard sciences and, 26; evolutionary theories as consistent with, 26; evolutionary theory's potential in, 80; overlapping agendas with biology, 6; replication required in, 303; on sex and gender, 18–19; standard model of, 18

social-triggering model, 188–89, 192, 196, 198, 199, 202

somatic nervous system, 230

South Bend Election Study, 211

Southern California Twin Registry, 215

specific environment. See unique environment

Spencer, Herbert, 24

spousal interaction: distinguishing assortative mating from, 153–54, 158, 169–70; fitting models for spousal resemblance, 170–71, 172–74, 175; as mechanism of mate selection, 103; in

spousal interaction (*continued*)
  spousal correlation, 111; testing assumptions
    about mate selection, 166–70
spousal resemblance: distinguishing assortative
    mating from spousal interaction, 153–54, 158;
    fitting models for, 170–76; testing assump-
    tions about mate selection, 158–59
stability, evolutionary, 78
startle eyeblink, 234, 235, 241–42
stature: correlations between relatives in United
    States and Australia, 110, 111–12; fitting models
    for spousal resemblance, 171, 172; as influ-
    enced substantially by genetic factors, 112;
    and joint analysis of twin and nuclear family
    data, 136, 137, 138, 140, 141; as measurement
    for studying family resemblance, 102, 108,
    109; model-fitting results of genetic model
    of inheritance in nuclear families, 123–24;
    model-fitting results of nongenetic model
    of inheritance in nuclear families, 119–21;
    models for twin resemblance, 126–27, 128, 129,
    130; relative contributions of genetic familial
    influences on outcome measures, 124; relative
    contributions of genetic transmission on
    outcome measures, twin data without spouse
    pairs, 129; relative contributions of genetic
    transmission on outcome measures, twin
    data with spouse pairs, 131; relative contribu-
    tions of phenotypic familial influences on
    outcome measures, 121
Stearns, E., 188–89
strategies, in evolutionary game theory, 77–78,
    82–83
stress: cortisol and, 253–54; oxytocin and, 256
striatum, 286
structural magnetic resonance imaging (MRI), 277
suicide, 15
superior temporal sulcus (STS), 283, 284
surface rendering, 282
"survival of the fittest," 24–25
sweat glands, eccrine, 232
Swedish Twin Registry, 217
sympathetic nervous system, 230–31, 232, 233

Tassinary, L. G., 226
testosterone, 251–53; aggression associated with,
    247, 251, 252, 258, 263; as biological reinforcer
    of behavior, 269; and biology of politics, 261–
    72; diurnal rhythm in, 262, 267; dominance as-
    sociated with, 252, 263; and masculinization,
    251, 261; measurement of, 262; organizational
    and activational effects of, 263; primer on,
    262–63; reciprocal relationship with behavior,
    261; response following presidential election
    of 2008, 264–70; in response to competition,

252, 263, 264–65; vasopressin synthesized and
    regulated by, 255
thermoregulation, 232
third-party candidates, 198–99
third-party punishment, 55–56
Thornton, L. M., 190
threats: anterior cingulate cortex in perception
    of, 288; physiological responses to, 237; in
    primates, 62–63
Timberlake, D. S., 190
Ting, M., 211
Tooby, John, 29, 31
trade, 57–58
transcranial magnetic stimulation (TMS), 279
transmission of information, mate selection in, 9
transparency, 303, 304
traumatic early life events, 40n4
Trivers, R. L., 52
trolley problem, 276
trust: in human evolution, 14–15; in modern hu-
    man society, 207; oxytocin and, 250, 256; trust
    game, 218
turnout. *See* voter turnout
twins: in Add Health (Study of Adolescent
    Health), 189, 196–97; and development of so-
    cial and political attitudes in shared environ-
    ment, 142–49; expected correlations between,
    126, 134; integrating twin and nuclear family
    data, 132–41; models for twin resemblance,
    124–31; and phenotypic assortative mating,
    159–65; and social homogamy, 165–66; and
    spousal interaction, 166–70; in study of
    political phenotypes, 214–17; twin kinship
    design yields 80 distinct correlations between
    relatives, 151–52; types of, 105; underlying
    foundation of twin studies, 215

ultimate level of analysis, 50
ultimatum game, 217, 275, 286
uncivil debates, 233
unions, quantitative variance components for
    political and social attitudes toward, 195
unique environment: in both genetic and non-
    genetic models, 116; as component of vari-
    ance, 105; in genetic model of inheritance in
    nuclear families, 122, 124, 132; in heritability
    of political views, 199–200; and joint analysis
    of twin and nuclear family data, 139; models
    for twin resemblance, 129, 131; in party af-
    filiation, 153; and variation in conservatism,
    144–48
unmarried couples living together, quantitative
    variance components for political and social
    attitudes toward, 192, 193
utilitarianism, 213, 276, 277

Vanman, E. J., 235
variation: components of variance, 105, 176n2; as feature of evolution, 75, 76; in Mayhew's analysis of Congress, 72; in Sabato's analysis of attack journalism, 72–73
vasopressin, 255
Veblen, Thorstein, 80
ventrolateral prefrontal cortex (VLPFC), 290
Ventura, Jesse, 198
Verhulst, B., 157
Vigil, Jacob, 35
Virginia (VA30K) study, 107, 107, 142, 151
voter turnout: gene association studies on, 218–19; habitual, 211; heritability of, 35, 185, 215; paradox of, 210; patience and, 212; standard analyses explain only one third of variation in, 220
voting behavior: evolutionary psychology and, 31; genetic influence in vote choice, 36, 113, 215; specific genes and, 268; traditional models of, 18; work lacking on genetic and social influences on, 203. See also voter turnout
voxel-based morphometry (VBM), 277

Wagner, J., 252
Wallace, B., 210
"warrior gene," 256
weak triggering, 188, 190, 204
Weber, J. M., 211
weighted least squares (WLS) method, 118, 135, 170, 177n6
Westen, Drew, 35
Wilson, E. O., 17, 38, 101
Wilson-Patterson Attitude Inventory, 216
"winner-loser effect," 252, 263, 270
women's lib, quantitative variance components for political and social attitudes toward, 193
Wrangham, R., 264
Wright, S., 126

X-rated material, quantitative variance components for political and social attitudes toward, 194

Zamboni, G., 35
Zhong, S., 218
z-scores, 281, 282